HOUSE PRICE INDICES

A Special Issue of the Journal of
Real Estate Finance and Economics

edited by
Thomas G. Thibodeau
Southern Methodist University

Reprinted from the
Journal of Real Estate Finance and Economics
Vol. 14: 1/2 (1997)

KLUWER ACADEMIC PUBLISHERS
Boston/Dordrecht/London

The Journal of Real Estate Finance and Economics

Volume 14, Numbers 1/2, January/March 1997

Special Issue on House Price Indices, Guest Editor: Thomas G. Thibodeau

Distributors for North America:
Kluwer Academic Publishers
101 Philip Drive
Assinippi Park
Norwell, Massachusetts 02061 USA

Distributors for all other countries:
Kluwer Academic Publishers Group
Distribution Centre
Post Office Box 322
3300 AH Dordrecht, THE NETHERLANDS

Library of Congress Cataloging-in-Publication Data

A C.I.P. Catalogue record for this book is available from the Library of Congress.

Printed on acid-free paper.

Printed in the United States of America

Journal of Real Estate Finance and Economics, 14: 5–9 (1997)
© 1997 Kluwer Academic Publishers

Introduction

THOMAS G. THIBODEAU

This issue of *The Journal of Real Estate Finance and Economics* contains 13 articles on house price measurement. It is an outlet for current research on the various procedures being used to compute cross-sectional or temporal house price indices. Topics of interest include research that: (1) evaluates hedonic, repeat-sales, or hybrid approaches to constructing house price indices; (2) evaluates alternative sources of data on house prices and corresponding housing characteristics; (3) identifies the most influential land, structural, neighborhood, and proximity determinants of house prices (and associated changes in house prices); (4) provides a methodology for identifying housing market segments; (5) incorporates spatial autocorrelation in house price indices; and (6) provides more accurate estimates of the variance in house prices.

Temporal variation in house prices is frequently measured using the repeat sales methodology. A repeat sales house price index is computed by averaging rates of appreciation for properties that sell more than once. The technique was originally developed by Bailey, Muth, and Nourse (1963) and was recently popularized by Case and Shiller (1987, 1989). The procedure is currently being used by the Federal National Mortgage Association and the Federal Home Loan Mortgage Corporation to compute national and regional house price indices (Abraham and Schauman (1991) and Stephens et al. (1995)) and to estimate property values for underwriting residential mortgages.

Housing is a composite commodity that consists of a bundle of various categories of characteristics (e.g., land, structural, neighborhood, and proximity characteristics). The change in the price of a composite commodity is measured as the rate of change in market values for a fixed bundle of characteristics. The standard repeat-sales house price index controls for property-specific changes by eliminating properties that change structural characteristics between sales. However, since repeat sales house price indices do not screen all important structural and neighborhood characteristics, the resulting price index may mix house price changes with housing quantity/quality changes.

A repeat-sales house price index measures the rate of appreciation in the price of homes that sell at least twice. Homes that sell once, or not at all, are excluded from repeat sales house price indices. If appreciation rates for excluded properties differ from appreciation rates for properties that sell repeatedly, then a repeat-sales house price index will yield biased estimators of appreciation rates for either the stock of housing or for the subpopulation of transactions. For example, new homes are excluded from repeat-sales house price indices. Depending on market conditions, the appreciation rate for new residential contruction may differ substantially from appreciation rates for older properties. In addition, homes that lack desirable features and properties that have undesirable characteristics are unlikely to sell repeatedly. These properties will also be underrepresented in a repeat sales sample.

Just as the price index for an individual property should keep the property's bundle of characteristics fixed between pricing periods, an aggregate house price index should price the same aggregate bundle of characteristics over time. If the mix of properties that sells over time varies, and if the housing market is segmented by property type (or dwelling size, age, or any other important characteristic) so that appreciation rates vary across housing submarkets, then a price index constructed from repeat transactions will yield inaccurate estimates of appreciation.

Housing markets are also segmented by location. That is, price levels and appreciation rates can vary substantially by neighborhood within metropolitan areas. To obtain accurate estimates of appreciation, house price indices should be constructed for individual neighborhoods. However, a property must sell twice to be included in a repeat-sales index, and few neighborhoods have sufficient repeat transactions to develop statistically reliable house price indices at the neighborhood level.

Most of the following articles provide additional insight into the statistical properties of repeat-sales house price indices. Some provide suggestions for correcting the biases associated with these indices. Goetzmann and Spiegel develop a distance-weighted repeat-sales house price index. They expand the usual geographic proximity concept of distance to include property characteristics and neighborhood socioeconomic variables and estimate the parameters of a generalized least-squares model at the zip code level using data for the San Francisco Bay area. They report that: (1) zip code level appreciation rates vary substantially within metropolitan San Francisco; and (2) median household incomes significantly influence the covariance of neighborhood housing returns. The distance-weighted repeat-sales technique can be used to circumvent small sample problems and to yield neighborhood-level house price indices.

In order for a property to be observed as a repeat sale, the property's offer price must exceed its reservation price on (at least) two occasions. Gatzlaff and Haurin employ a sequential censored sample estimation procedure to evaluate repeat-sales house price indices. They report that repeat-sales house price indices are biased estimates of the change in the price of housing and that the bias is correlated with the annual percentage change in nonagricultural employment.

Meese and Wallace examine median, hedonic, repeat-sales, and hybrid house price indices using data for Oakland and Fremont, CA. They evaluate alternative house price indices using a nonparametric statistical procedure and conclude that: (1) repeat sales are not representative of all transactions in a housing market; (2) characteristic prices do not remain constant over time; and (3) an index constructed from median sales is not statistically different from a Fisher's Ideal house price index, which is computed from a hedonic specification estimated using a locally weighted regression procedure.

The standard repeat-sales price index provides some control for temporal variation in the bundle of housing characteristics that is priced by eliminating properties that report changes in (some) structural characteristics between sales. Dombrow, Knight, and Sirmans illustrate that this procedure fails to control for changes in some important housing characteristics that are not employed in the filter (e.g., vacancy status and below-market financing) and does not adequately control for changes in the implicit prices of screened housing characteristics. They estimate a modified repeat sales specification that explicitly incorporates housing characteristics and test for omitted variable bias and for parameter stability. They find some evidence of aggregation bias in repeat sales house price indices and identify both included and excluded housing characteristics as potential sources for bias.

Chinloy, Cho, and Megbolugbe compare the statistical properties of the first and second moments of the purchase price distribution to the distribution of appraisals for the 3.7 million repeat transactions on mortgages purchased by Fannie Mae and Freddie Mac between January 1975 and December 1993. They conclude that: (1) single-family appraisals systematically exceed purchase prices by about 2%; and (2) appraisal smoothing does not occur universally. Since the Freddie Mac–Fannie Mae repeat transactions database is dominated by purchase-appraisal pairs, the Freddie–Fannie house price index systematically overestimates house price appreciation over time. Finally, Chinloy, Cho, and Megbolugbe develop an optimal updating rule for revising appraisals.

Kuo develops a general Bayesian framework for repeat sales house price indices. Alternative price indices, including indices developed by Bailey, Muth, and Nourse (1963), Case and Shiller (1987, 1989), Webb (1988), Hill, Knight, and Sirmans (1995), and Goetzmann and Spiegel (1995), are special cases of the general Bayesian model. Kuo evaluates the alternatives with repeat-sales data for the four cities examined by Case and Shiller using posterior odds ratios. He concludes that, in general, two-error models statistically dominate one-error models. More specifically, the Goetzmann and Spiegel repeat-sales price index dominates the alternatives for three of the four cities examined.

Steele and Goy examine the potential for bias in repeat-sales price indices attributable to quick repeat sales using 1988–1990 data from Kitchener–Waterloo. They report that: (1) the first transaction prices for properties that sell again within a two-year period are biased downward estimates of market value; and (2) the second transaction prices for quick repeat sales are unbiased. Consequently, the rate of appreciation for quick repeats overestimates changes in the market price of housing. Steele and Goy provide a statistic that can be used to correct for the bias in quick repeats and caution against using generalized least-squares procedures that assign more weight to transactions with short holding periods.

Geltner uses simulation analysis to examine the accuracy of estimates of annual return volatility, beta (the normalized contemporaneous covariance with an exogenous innovation), and first-order autocorrelation coefficients generated by three repeat-sales house price indices. Assuming either efficient or sluggish housing markets, and for observation-rich or observation-poor scenarios, he compares the statistical properties of the estimated return series to the true market return series. He concludes that no repeat-sales index dominates the alternatives and that it is possible to construct reliable repeat sales price indices for housing submarkets under a variety of conditions.

Case, Pollakowski, and Wachter examine housing characteristics and appreciation rates for properties that transact frequently in four counties during the 1977–1989 period. They report higher appreciation rates for properties that trade frequently and argue that econometric procedures used to construct unbiased house price indices should incorporate the relationship between transaction frequencies and appreciation rates.

Kiel and Zabel use American Housing Survey (AHS) data for three metropolitan areas surveyed in a three- or four-year cycle during the 1975–1991 period to evaluate hedonic, repeat-sales, and hybrid house price indices. Using confidential U.S. Bureau of the Census data, they supplement publicly available AHS data with census-tract-level neighborhood information. They also examine the statistical consequences of top-coding the house value distribution and of reporting the owner's house value estimate in a range (rather than the point estimate). They conclude that house price indices computed from specifications that omit neighborhood characteristics confound increases in neighborhood quality with increases in the price index (for a constant quality neighborhood). They also report that significant differences exist between house price indices computed from data that are representative of the entire housing stock in a metropolitan area and indices that are computed using only transactions data.

Can and Megbolugbe develop a hedonic house price index incorporating the spatial autocorrelation that is prevalent in neighborhood house prices. Using data on 944 single-family property transactions in Dade County, Florida in 1990, they compare price indices obtained from a traditional hedonic equation with two hedonic house price specifications that explicitly incorporate the effects of house price spatial autocorrelation. They conclude that spatial hedonic house price specifications can compensate for the lack of information on important neighborhood characteristics and, when incorporated, significantly increase the precision of house price indices.

Goodman and Goodman compare condominium and cooperative prices using the 1987 National AHS. They summarize the important differences between these two forms of ownership and estimate hedonic house price equations using the Box–Cox procedure. They report that, on average, condominium prices were 12% higher than cooperative prices. They also note that the condominium premium varied with the bundle of housing characteristics that were priced.

Finally, Follain and Calhoun combine owners' estimates of market value with the original purchase prices reported in the *1991 Survey of Residential Finance* to construct "quasi repeat sales" multifamily property price indices. They construct a national index and separate indices for four states (California, Florida, New York, and Texas) for the 1983–1991 period and report substantial regional variation in multifamily property prices. For example, for the 1983–1991 period, Texas apartment property values declined by 22% in nominal terms, while multifamily prices in New York rose by over 30%.

I want to thank the individuals who refereed papers submitted to *The Journal of Real Estate Finance and Economics* special issue on house price indices. They are acknowledged below.

References

Abraham, J. M., and W. S. Schauman. "New Evidence on Home Prices from Freddie Mac Repeat Sales," *Journal of the American Real Estate and Urban Association* 19(3) (1991), 333–352.

Bailey, M. J., R. F. Muth, and H. O. Nourse. "A Regression Method for Real Estate Price Index Construction," *Journal of the American Statistical Association* 58 (December 1963), 933–942.

Case, K. E., and R. J. Shiller. "Prices of Single-Family Homes Since 1970: New Indexes for Four Cities," *New England Economic Review* (September/October 1987), 45–56.

Case, K. E., and R. J. Shiller. "The Efficiency of the Market for Single-Family Homes," *American Economic Review* 79 (1989), 125–137.

Goetzmann, W., and M. Spiegel. "Non-Temporal Components of Residential Real Estate Appreciation," *Review of Economics and Statistics* 77(1) (1995), 199–206.

Hill, R. C., J. R. Knight, and C. F. Sirmans. "Estimating Capital Asset Price Indexes," *Review of Economics and Statistics* (forthcoming, May 1997).

Stephens, W., Y. Li, V. Lekkas, J. Abraham, C. Calhoun, and T. Kimner. "Conventional Mortgage Home Price Index," *Journal of Housing Research* 6(3) (1995), 389–418.

Webb, Cary. "A Probabilistic Model for Price Levels in Discontinuous Markets," In W. Eichhorn (ed.), *Measurement in Econometrics*. Heidelberg: Physica-Verlag, 1988.

Referees

Journal of Real Estate Finance and Economics, 14: 11–31 (1997)
© 1997 Kluwer Academic Publishers

A Spatial Model of Housing Returns and Neighborhood Substitutability

WILLIAM N. GOETZMANN
Yale School of Management, Box 208200, New Haven, CT 06520-8200

MATTHEW SPIEGEL
University of California at Berkeley, Haas School of Business

Abstract

This article provides a method for estimating housing indices at the local level. It develops a "distance-weighted repeat-sales" procedure to exploit the factor structure of the error-covariance matrix in the repeat-sales model. A distance function defined in characteristic and geographical space provides weights for the generalized least-squares model, and allows the use of *all* of the repeated sales in a metropolitan area to measure returns for the specific neighborhood of interest. We use distance-weighted repeat sales to estimate return indices for all zip codes in the San Francisco Bay area over the period 1980–1994.

When distance is defined in terms of socioeconomic characteristics, we find that median household income is the salient variable explaining covariance of neighborhood housing returns. Racial composition and educational attainment, while significant, are much less influential. Zip-code level indices often deviate dramatically from the citywide index, depending upon income levels. This has implications for investors and lenders. Our results indicate that rates of return may vary considerably within a metropolitan area. Thus, simply using broad metropolitan area indices as a proxy for capital appreciation within a specific neighborhood may not be justified.

Key Words: housing returns, distance-weighted repeat-sales method, neighborhood substitutability

Repeat-sales data within small geographic areas are typically sparse, and this naturally impedes efforts to construct accurate local housing indices. The smaller the definition of the geographical unit, the fewer repeat sales can be used to construct an index, and the less accurate the index becomes. This article provides a method for estimating housing indices for arbitrarily small neighborhoods. Our solution exploits the intuition that the returns to investment in nearby homes should be highly correlated. We model the covariance matrix of repeat-sales errors, using a distance function defined in characteristic and geographical space. This model provides weights for a GLS repeated-sale estimator, and allows us to use *all* of the repeated sales in the citywide sample to measure returns for the specific neighborhood of interest. We apply our "Distance-Weighted Repeat-Sales" (DWRS) procedure to estimate return indices for all zip codes in the San Francisco Bay area over the period 1980–1994.

The DWRS procedure allows one to estimate the influence of particular geographic and socioeconomic factors as determinants of the return covariance across homes. Further, one can interpret the estimated parameters as indicating the salient factors that make different neighborhoods good or poor substitutes for each other. To see why, consider two neighborhoods, A and B, which are identical in all ways except for factor X, and further suppose that home buyers do not care about X's value. In a competitive market, A and B must have highly correlated capital appreciation returns. If, for example, A appreciates relative to B, then potential buyers will flock to B (the relatively cheap area) and avoid A (the relatively over priced area). Conversely, if buyers regard X as crucial to their choice, there is no reason to believe that the prices in neighborhoods A and B will move together.

The model estimated in this article defines distance in terms of geographical proximity, median household income, average educational attainment, and racial composition. We find that median household income is the salient variable explaining the covariance among neighborhood housing returns. Racial composition and educational attainment, while significant, are much less influential. Geographical proximity is nearly meaningless as a determinant of the covariance among returns.

Our results have immediate implications for lenders, equity holders, and tax authorities. We find that rates of return may vary considerably within a metropolitan area. Consequently, there are opportunities for within-city diversification. In addition, our results suggest that simply using broad metropolitan area indices as a proxy for capital appreciation within a specific neighborhood may not be justified. Finally, the "Distance-Weighted Repeat-Sale" procedure allows accurate estimates of the covariance of housing returns within metropolitan areas, and suggests that low covariances imply gains to diversification for lenders, equity holders, and tax authorities.

The DWRS methodology also has applications to a range of assets, including bonds, commercial real estate, and collectibles, or any other asset whose heterogeneity can be described within an econometrically meaningful characteristic space.[1] While we apply it here to housing, it has natural application to any market that is characterized by infrequent trading. This includes the intra-day stock market, in which minute-by-minute prices are unobserved.

1. Background

Two techniques are commonly used to construct housing price indices. The first, repeat-sales, was first described by Bailey, Muth, and Nourse (1963) and subsequently extended by Case and Shiller (1987), who developed a three-stage estimator called weighted-repeat-sales (WRS). This methodology uses matched purchase and sale price–date pairs for homes within a defined geographical area. The total capital appreciation return from each repeated sale is the dependent variable in a weighted least-squares regression that "explains" these returns by the time periods over which the asset was held.

The second method estimates the value of a "representative" house in the market for each period via a set of priced characteristics. This uses individual home prices rather than matched sale pairs, and in addition makes use of attribute information such as the number of bedrooms, baths and other amenities. Research on the relative merits of the "hedonic" and repeat-sales methods includes Halvorsen and Pollakowski (1981), and Meese and Wallace (1991, 1995), Case, Pollakowski, and Wachter (1991), and Clapp and Giaccotto (1992). While no method clearly emerges the winner, the literature thus far makes the trade-offs between the two methods clear. The repeat-sales approach throws away potentially useful information from unique sales, while hedonic indices are not invariate to the choice of variables. When ample data exist, repeat-sales does a good job at estimation. When data are sparse, hedonic procedures are superior.

The primary methodological advantage of the WRS lies in its ability to estimate housing returns without an explicit specification of how characteristics map into prices. Shiller (1991) shows that the matched prices used in the WRS offer a perfect hedonic control, as long as characteristics of the assets do not change between purchase and sale dates. One limitation is that the approach ignores housing's spatial nature. A WRS index assumes that, in any one period, all homes in the sample appreciate at the same rate times a white-noise error term. Since data sets often cover fairly large cities, the appreciation assumptions must hold over potentially distant and dissimilar neighborhoods. Further problems arise if the appreciation assumptions fail and the concentration of housing sales varies from neighborhood to neighborhood over time.[2] Hedonic indices cure some of the problems associated with a WRS index by estimating the value of individual housing characteristics. Thus, dissimilar areas can appreciate at different rates. However, hedonic models also make some fairly strong assumptions, in particular, the assumption that all relevant determinants of value are included in the model specification. To help alleviate the omitted variables problem, Meese and Wallace (1991) employ a non-parametric estimation technique. Their procedure estimates a separate index at each location by using a weighted average of the local observations.

2. Empirical Methodology

2.1. A Spatial Model of Housing Returns

The standard-weighted repeat-sales (WRS) technique provides a useful introduction to the distance-weighted methodology developed here. A WRS analysis examines a data set that contains paired observations on various homes over time. An observation pair consists of a date b, and a price P_b when a family buys the house; and a date s, and a price P_s when the family sells it. Let r_t equal one plus the return to housing in period t, and ε_t an error term. The WRS model then assumes that the price process can be written as

$$P_s = P_b \prod_{t=b+1}^{s} r_t \varepsilon_t. \tag{1}$$

Taking logs produces the familiar linear system

$$\ln(P_s) - \ln(P_b) = \sum_{t=b+1}^{s} \ln(r_t) + \ln(\varepsilon_t). \tag{2}$$

Typically, the WRS model imposes the assumption that the $\ln(\varepsilon_t)$ are independently identically distributed normal random variables with mean zero, and variance σ_ε^2. This allows the researcher to use standard generalized least-squares techniques to produce efficient estimates for the log returns.

Goetzmann and Spiegel (1995) argue that the WRS equation (2) should be modified to allow for a return component associated with housing transactions. Their analysis indicates that this component tends to be positive, and they find evidence that it may be due to home improvements that occur around the time of a sale. Whatever the cause, a transaction-specific return can be added to (2) by introducing a return h that occurs whenever a home changes hands, and an error term η on the sale date. This leads to the following variant of (2)

$$\ln(P_s) - \ln(P_b) = \ln(h) + \ln(\eta) + \sum_{t=b+1}^{s} \left[\ln(r_t) + \ln(\varepsilon_t)\right]. \tag{3}$$

For the purposes of estimation, (3) differs from the WRS model in that the dummy matrix contains a column of ones which identifies the $\ln(h)$ term.

While the WRS model provides an easily estimated model, it ignores housing's spatial nature. As the famous real estate cliché says, the three most important elements of real estate value are "location, location, and location." Yet, (2) and (3) implicitly assume a uniform return structure across the entire sample area. To rectify this problem, the DWRS model treats the r_t terms as spatially correlated random variables.

First, assume that the return on a house at location ℓ, in period t, consists of three components. The first component $\bar{r}$ represents one plus the per period expected return on housing. One can generalize this return in a manner similar to the APT by assuming the $\bar{r}$ depends upon a set of factors. If these factors vary over time and by location, then one can instead write expected housing returns as $\bar{r}_t(\ell)$.

Second, assume that there exists a location-specific return $r_t(\ell)$ equal to one plus the local return at time t. Suppose that a home at location ℓ increases by 10% over some period of time. We expect nearby homes to increase by approximately 10% as well, depending upon the degree to which these locations are economic substitutes for each other. We model this location-specific factor in the following manner. Assume that $\ln(r_t(\ell))$ follows a normal distribution, with mean zero, and variance σ_r^2. Then the *covariance* between $\ln(r_t(\ell))$ and $\ln(r_t(m))$ declines monotonically as the distance between ℓ and m increases. Note that distance does not have to mean physical distance. Distance can include any number of characteristics such as school quality, town services, and other factors. To allow for general characteristic spaces, let $d_t(\ell, m)$ represent some measure of the distance between the two locations at time t. The model estimated in this article makes the assumption that $\text{cov}(\ln(r_t(\ell)), \ln(r_t(m))) = \sigma_r^2 \exp(-d_t(\ell, m))$. In general, one can use any functional form such that the covariance declines monotonically in d.

While housing returns in a neighborhood may be highly correlated, obviously there still remain individual differences among homes. To account for changes peculiar to a house, the model introduces a final random variable $\varepsilon_t(\ell)$. This variable represents one plus a house-specific return in period t. The model assumes that $\ln(\varepsilon_t(\ell))$ is normally distributed with mean zero, and variance σ_ε^2. Because ε represents events unique to a particular house, we assume that the $\ln(\varepsilon_t(\ell))$ are uncorrelated across both time and space. Note that ε acts as a house-specific idiosyncratic error term in both the WRS and DWRS models.

Based upon the assumptions given above, the model in (3) can now be rewritten as

$$
\ln(P_s(\ell)) - \ln(P_b(\ell)) = \ln(h) + \ln(\eta(\ell))
$$
$$
+ \sum_{t=b(\ell)+1}^{s(\ell)} \left[\ln(\bar{r}_t(\ell)) + \ln(r_t(\ell)) + \ln(\varepsilon_t(\ell))\right], \tag{4}
$$

where $b(\ell)$ and $s(\ell)$ represent the purchase and sale dates for the house a location ℓ. For simplicity, the model assumes that the $\ln(h)$ terms do not depend upon location (and thus a location parameter has not been included) and that the $\ln(\eta(\ell))$ error terms are independently and identically distributed across homes.

While (4) provides a description of housing returns, it cannot be estimated directly. In order to produce estimates of the locational returns, the empirical procedure must make use of the covariance relationships.[3]

The DWRS model assumes that the $\ln(\eta(\ell))$, $\ln(r_t(\ell)$, and $\ln(\varepsilon_t(\ell))$ terms in (4) are all normally distributed with zero means and variances of σ_η^2, σ_r^2, and σ_ε^2, respectively. Define

$$
e(\ell) \equiv \ln(P_s(\ell)) - \ln(P_b(\ell)) - \ln(h) - \sum_{t=b(\ell)+1}^{s(\ell)} \ln(\bar{r}_t). \tag{5}
$$

Then, treating $\ln(\eta(\ell))$, $\ln(r_t(\ell))$, and $\ln(\varepsilon_t(\ell))$ as error terms, we may express the location-specific deviations from the market index as:

$$
E[(e(\ell) - e(m))^2] = 2\sigma_\eta^2 + (n(\ell) + n(m))(\sigma_r^2 + \sigma_\varepsilon^2) - 2\sigma(\ell, m)\sigma_r^2 e^{-d(\ell,m)}. \tag{6}
$$

Here, $n(\ell) = s(\ell) - b(\ell)$ represents the number of periods between sales for the house at location ℓ, and $\sigma(\ell, m) = \max\{0, \min[s(\ell, s(m)] - \max[b(\ell), b(m)]\}$, which equals the number of periods in which both homes overlap in the data set. Equation 6 provides a means for estimating the model's variance and distance parameters and distinguishes the DWRS methodology from both WRS and hedonic models.

The specification in (6) also provides some interesting economic intuition. When potential homeowners enter the market, they must choose among imperfect substitutes. However, while public services and other housing attributes do vary, there exists a limit to the magnitude by which housing prices can differ among neighborhoods. The distance function (d) in (6) provides an estimate of that limit. If an attribute has a large coefficient in d, that means that it is a salient characteristic in housing choice. Thus, if two homes differ in exposure to this factor, they are poor substitutes, and potential buyers will not care if the relative prices change. If buyers do not care about the relative prices across the two neighborhoods, then the return innovations will display low correlation levels. Conversely, homes can differ widely on an attribute with a small coefficient, and buyers will still consider substituting one house for the other, leading to a high correlation among the returns.

Using (4) and (6), one can employ maximum likelihood techniques to estimate the model parameters. However, alternative approaches, such as generalized method of moments, are also potentially applicable. In this article, we use a two-step procedure that first estimates (4) and then uses the residuals to estimate (6). As we show below, the model estimates themselves contain useful information about housing substitutability, irrespective of their value as determinates of weights in the weighted repeat-sales procedure.

2.2. Creating Local Housing Indices

Once estimated, the distance-weighted model allows for the construction of local area indices, $r_t(\ell)$. To do this, we use the projection theorem to write

$$\ln(r_t(\ell)) = \ln(r_t(m)) \exp(-d_t(\ell, m)) - \delta_t(\ell, m), \tag{7}$$

where δ_t equals a normally distributed error term with mean zero. To calculate the variance of $\delta_t(\ell, m)$, we square both sides of (7) to get,

$$\sigma_r^2 = \sigma_r^2 \exp(-2d_t(\ell, m)) + \sigma_\delta^2, \tag{8}$$

which rearranges to

$$\sigma_\delta^2 = \sigma_r^2[1 - \exp(-2d_t(\ell, m))]. \tag{9}$$

Notice that when two houses occupy the same location $d_t(\ell, m) = 0$, and thus the two homes have the same return index. As the distance between the homes increases, σ_δ^2 increases, which implies that the correlation between the housing return indices declines.

We now utilize (9) to replace the location ℓ in (4) with location m. Some manipulation and substitution for $\ln(r_t(m)) \exp(-d_t(\ell, m))$ by using (7) gives:

$$\ln(P_s(m)) - \ln(P_b(m)) = \ln(h) + \ln(\eta) + \sum_{t=b+1}^{s} \ln(\bar{r}_t(m)) \tag{10}$$

$$+ \frac{\ln(r_t(\ell)) + \delta_t(\ell, m)}{\exp(-d_t(\ell, m))} + \ln(\varepsilon_t(\ell)).$$

By treating the $\ln(\bar{r}_t(\ell))$ and $\ln(h)$ terms as known, one can use ordinary least squares to estimate the model. In fact, this specification is now a modified version of the well-known weighted-repeat-sales (WRS) model adapted to produce consistent estimates of the local area returns. Notice that (10) allows one to construct neighborhood indices. Thus, the model can produce accurate indices, even if returns vary from one local to the next, or if regional sales densities change over time.

3. San Francisco Bay Area Housing Returns

3.1. Date and Hedonic Controls

The database which we use contains 131,603 repeat sales in the San Francisco Bay Area covering the period 1980–1994. Each observation consists of the zip code, the date, and transaction price of each sale. For estimation purposes, we assume that all homes within a zip code are located at the population centroid for the zip code. For socioeconomic information, we use census tract data from 1980 and 1990 mapped into zip codes.

One important justification for using socioeconomic measures as the basis for estimating the local indices is that they act as controls for variation in housing types and quality. Selection bias is a major concern in the construction of housing indices. Gatzlaff and Haurin (1993) point out that repeat-sales indices may be upward biased due to observations being conditioned upon sale.[4] The use of hedonic controls has the potential for reducing or eliminating certain types of selection bias, if the selection is conditional upon socioeconomic or geographical variables. To illustrate this point, suppose that homes in lower income neighborhoods have lower capital appreciation and turn over infrequently when compared to their higher income counterparts. Low-income areas will thus be underrepresented in a repeat-sales data set, and as a consequence the estimated citywide index will be biased, because it is based solely upon homes that sold, i.e., homes in high-income neighborhoods.

An analysis of the San Francisco Bay repeat-sales data finds that there does exist a sample selection problem. Table 1 reports the percentage of transactions, by quintiles of socioeconomic characteristics in the database. It shows that less than 6% of the observations in the database comes from zip codes representing the lowest quintile of median household

Table 1. Percentage of all observations by characteristic quintile.

This table reports the socioeconomic composition of the sample used in the distance-weighted repeat-sales estimates for the San Francisco Bay area. For example, the table indicated that 15.28% of the observations used in the estimation procedure come from zip codes in the second income quintile. Census tracts were mapped into the appropriate zip codes. "Income" refers to the Median Household Income of residents in the zip code. "Education 4+ Years in College" refers to the fraction of adult residents surveyed who attained an education level of at least a four-year college program. "WHITE," "BLACK," "ASIAN," "HISPANIC," and "OTHER" refer to the fraction of residents in the zip code who reported themselves as belonging to the respective ethnic group.

	Income	Education 4+ Years College	White	Black	Asian	Hispanic	Other
Quintile 1 (low)	0.0588	0.1691	0.2043	0.0912	0.0659	0.1469	0.1344
Quintile 2	0.1528	0.2179	0.2012	0.2652	0.2368	0.2093	0.2141
Quintile 3	0.1917	0.2800	0.2245	0.2353	0.2550	0.2088	0.2095
Quintile 4	0.2694	0.1674	0.2422	0.2137	0.2224	0.2310	0.2582
Quintile 5 (high)	0.3274	0.1657	0.1277	0.1946	0.2200	0.2039	0.1838

income, while more than 30% of the sales data comes from the highest quintile. We do not know whether this discrepancy is due to the differential rates of home ownership across median family income levels or to the low turnover rates for homes in lower income neighborhoods. The table also shows that zip codes with the highest proportion of white residents are underrepresented, and that the zip codes with the lowest proportions of black and Hispanic residences are likewise underrepresented. In fact, the table indicates that an index for the San Francisco Bay area that equally weights all repeat-sales observations will mostly capture the behavior of middle-income neighborhoods of average racial composition and educational attainment.

Another way to look at the fluctuating composition of a citywide index that does not employ hedonic controls is to consider the variation in the number of transactions which come from any given neighborhood. Figure 1 shows the fluctuations which one might expect. The graph takes three sample zip codes and plots the variation through time of the fraction of repeat-sales data that it contributes to the estimation procedure. The contribution is normalized to the zip code's average contribution. Thus, a value of two at a specific point in time indicates that, for that particular quarter, the zip code is represented by twice as many observations as is typical for that zip code. The zip codes were chosen as the two largest in terms of sample size (94550 and 94583 with 7,312 and 5,976 observations, respectively)

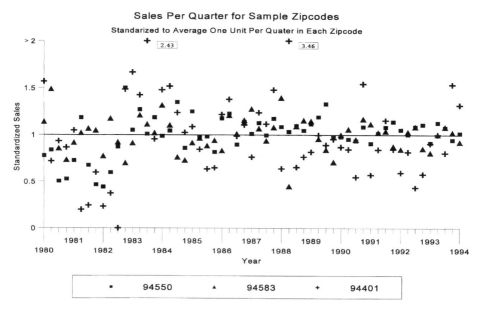

Figure 1. This figure takes three sample zip codes and plots the variation through time of the fraction of repeat-sales data that it contributes to the estimation procedure. The contribution is normalized to the zip code's average contribution. Thus, a value of two at a specific point in time indicates that, for that particular quarter, the zip code is represented by twice as many observations as is typical. The zip codes were chosen as the two largest in terms of sample size (94550 and 94583) and the median zip code in terms of sample size (94401).

and the median zip code in terms of sample size (94401 with 1,044 observations). Notice that proportions vary dramatically through time, as sales are concentrated first in one area and then another. If the rate of sales is conditional upon the capital appreciation, as conjectured in Gatzlaff and Haurin (1993) and Goetzmann (1995), then this variation will almost certainly induce a positive bias in the resulting index. The distance-weighting procedure implicitly controls for this geographic variation in the transactions used in the index by creating an index for one specific location. Once the individual location indices are estimated, the researcher is free to choose any weighting scheme, tilted towards any set of hedonic characteristics or sales processes which he or she chooses. In the description that follows, we apply the methodology for the distance-weighted repeat-sales measure to estimate the Bay Area zip code indices and the relative importance of socioeconomic and geographical factors as determinants of return and covariance.

3.2. Empirical Model and Results

The actual model uses the following functional specification for the expected log return for housing in each zip code per quarter:

$$\ln(\bar{r}_t(\ell)) = a_0 + a_1 * \text{MEDINC} + a_2 * \text{EDUC16P} + a_3 * \text{BLACK}$$
$$+ a_4 * \text{ASIAN} + a_5 * \text{HISPANIC} + a_6 * \text{OTHER}. \tag{11}$$

The a_j's represent parameters for estimation, and the variables in the above equation represent the following information for the zip code in which a given home is located:

MEDINC: Median income in thousands of dollars
EDUC16P: Percentage of the population with a college or graduate degree
BLACK: Percentage of the population identifying themselves as black
ASIAN: Percentage of the population identifying themselves as Asian
HISPANIC: Percentage of the population identifying themselves as Hispanic
OTHER: Percentage of the population identifying themselves as neither white
            nor in any of the above categories.

To obtain the covariance among housing returns, we estimate two Euclidean distance specifications. The first uses several census variables in addition to physical distance:

$$de(\ell, m) = \left(b_0 * \Delta\text{MILES}^2 + b_1 * \Delta\text{MEDINC}^2 + b_2 * \Delta\text{EDUC15L}^2 \right.$$
$$+ b_3 * \Delta\text{EDUC16P}^2 + b_4 * \Delta\text{WHITE}^2 + b_5 * \Delta\text{BLACK}^2$$
$$\left. + b_6 * \Delta\text{ASIAN}^2 + b_7 * \Delta\text{HISPANIC}^2 + b_8 * \Delta\text{OTHER}^2 \right)^{1/2}. \tag{12}$$

The variable ΔMILES^2 equals the squared distance, in miles, between the homes located at ℓ and at m. The term ΔWHITE^2 equals the squared difference in the percentage of the population identifying themselves as white. Finally, $\Delta\text{EDUC15L}^2$ equals the squared difference in the percentage of the population with less than four years of college. All of the other variables have meanings analogous to those in (11), except that the Δ symbol represents the difference in the attribute between the zip codes for house ℓ and m, and the superscript 2 indicates that the analysis uses the squared difference.

To form a base case, we estimate a second specification that uses only the mileage variable:

$$dp(\ell, m) = b_0 * abs(\Delta MILES). \tag{13}$$

Estimation of the model's parameters and standard errors occurs in several stages. The estimation process begins with the standard WRS methodology by running (11) with an OLS procedure. As is well-known, this produces consistent estimates of the parameters in question. Next, for each observation I, the prediction error from the first stage (e_i) is paired with the prediction error from observation $I + 1$, except for the last observation, which is paired with observation 1.[5] These errors are then used in (6) to produce a system of N equations. The parameters for either (12) or (14) are then estimated via nonlinear least squares (NLLS).

Because of the spatial correlation structure, the variance-covariance matrix has an entry at every location, which impacts the calculation of the standard errors. The variance of the e_i's can be found in (6),

$$E[e(\ell)^2] = \sigma_\eta^2 + n(\ell)(\sigma_r^2 + \sigma_\varepsilon^2), \tag{14}$$

and from the same equation the covariances equal

$$E[e(\ell)e(m)] = o(\ell, m)\sigma_r^2 e^{-d(\ell,m)}. \tag{15}$$

Let V equal the variance–covariance matrix formed from (14) and (15). Then the formula for the covariance of the OLS parameter estimates can be written as $(x'x)^{-1}x'Vx(x'x)^{-1}$.[6] Unfortunately, given the large sample size used in this study, calculating the standard errors via $(x'x)^{-1}x'Vx(x'x)^{-1}$ does not appear technically feasible. The problem lies with the matrix V, which in this case is over $100,000 \times 100,000$. Thus, the study only reports the standard errors calculated by an OLS package. Because of the covariances that exist across locations, these standard errors are underestimated. Nevertheless, under the null hypothesis that there does not exist any spatial correlation (so that either σ_r^2 equals zero, or all of the homes are "infinitely" far from each other), they should be approximately correct, since V becomes a diagonal matrix.[7]

As an alternative to the OLS standard errors, the article also presents standard errors generated from a bootstrap procedure. Under the null hypothesis that the homes have uncorrelated return innovations, a bootstrap procedure can be used to calculate confidence intervals for the parameters in (6). The bootstrap procedure draws repeat-sales observations from the data with replacement, and then reestimates the model. This is then repeated until a specified number of runs have been conducted.

3.3. Empirical Results: Factors Affecting Covariance

The San Francisco Bay area has a diverse population and a diverse set of neighborhoods. Table 2 displays the distribution of the data by zip code. For example, the median column lists the median value among all zip codes in the data set. As one can see, while most neighborhoods are predominantly white, quite a few have high minority concentrations. The white population varies from as low as 7.8% to 100% of the residents in particular zip codes. Among the minority populations, blacks show the most neighborhood heterogeneity, ranging from 0% to 84% of the population. While Asians and Hispanics represent somewhat smaller population groups, some zip codes have concentrations of over 33%.

Since only 1980 and 1990 census data are available, we obviously measure several of the independent variables with error. To get some idea as to how serious this problem may be, Table 3 lists the correlation between the 1980 and 1990 census population figures. Except for the OTHER race, the figures along the diagonal are quite high.[8] This implies that neighborhoods tend to be quite stable in demographic terms, thus mitigating the errors in variables problem. Among the cross-correlations, the Asian–Black, and Asian–Hispanic results seem quite surprising. In general, one expects the racial variables to display negative correlations, since the percentages are constrained to add up to 100. Nevertheless, these two cross-correlations are positive. This implies that high 1980 levels in the black or Hispanic populations tend to be associated with above average 1990 levels in the Asian population.

Estimates of (11) can be found in Table 4. Contrary to the finding in Goetzmann and Spiegel (1995), the $\ln(h)$ estimate comes out negative. This implies that, on average, sales

Table 2. Distribution summary of socioeconomic characteristics.

This table reports five quantiles of socioeconomic variables for the zip codes in the San Francisco Bay area used in the article. The variables are taken from the 1980 census, and census tracts were mapped into the appropriate zip codes. "MEDINC" refers to the Median Household Income of residents in the zip code. "EDUC15L" refers to the fraction of adult residents surveyed who attained an education level of at least a three years of college. "EDUC16P" refers to the fraction of adult residents surveyed who attained an education level of at least a four-year college program. "WHITE," "BLACK," "ASIAN," "HISPANIC," and "OTHER" refer to the fraction of residents in the zip code who reported themselves as belonging to the respective ethnic group. Thus, for instance, the median percentage of white residents across all zip codes in the area in 1980 was 87.30%.

Variable	Min	25%	Median	75%	Max
MEDINC	4.32	17.64	21.53	25.35	42.08
EDUC15L	28.00	69.40	81.30	86.60	96.70
EDUC16P	3.30	13.40	18.70	30.60	72.00
WHITE	7.80	76.00	87.30	93.10	100.00
BLACK	0.00	0.07	2.10	6.00	84.20
ASIAN	0.00	2.50	4.50	8.20	36.40
HISPANIC	0.00	1.30	2.90	6.40	37.10
OTHER	0.00	0.30	0.60	1.00	8.50

Table 3. Correlation between 1980 and 1990 census variables.

This table reports the correlation between the values of each variable reported in the 1980 and 1990 census surveys. Census tracts were mapped into the appropriate zip codes. "MEDINC" refers to the Median Household Income of residents in the zip code. "EDU15L" refers to the fraction of adult residents surveyed who attained an education level of at least three years of college. "EDUC16P" refers to the fraction of adult residents surveyed who attained an education level of at least a four-year college program. "WHITE," "BLACK," "ASIAN," "HISPANIC," and "OTHER" refer to the fraction of residents in the zip code who reported themselves as belonging to the respective ethnic group.

	MEDINC	EDUC15L	EDUC16P	WHITE	BLACK	ASIAN	HISPANIC	OTHER
MEDINC	0.83							
EDUC15L	−0.51	0.68						
EDUC16P	0.51	−0.68	0.89					
WHITE	0.41	0.07	0.32	0.93				
BLACK	−0.38	−0.08	−0.20	−0.73	0.98			
ASIAN	−0.05	−0.10	0.01	−0.57	0.18	0.85		
HISPANIC	−0.23	0.06	−0.45	−0.55	0.01	0.50	0.86	
OTHER	−0.35	0.20	−0.32	−0.07	−0.03	0.02	0.18	0.21

"reduce" the value of a house. A more reasonable interpretation is that once a house has been sold, an immediate resale must go to the next highest bidder, resulting in a negative intercept.[9]

The median income parameter has a negative coefficient, which implies that homes in wealthy areas appreciated at a lower rate than homes in poorer neighborhoods. This may be an artifact of survivorship, since abandonment in the sample is not recorded. In contrast to the median income variable, the education variable has a positive sign. All else being equal, better educated neighborhoods had higher returns than less educated neighborhoods.

The omitted racial variable is white. Thus, increasing the fraction of the neighborhood population that is either black or other and reducing the white population reduces returns. In contrast, increasing either the Asian or Hispanic populations while decreasing the white population increases returns. However, one must keep in mind that the estimated coefficients are very small. To provide some feeling for the magnitudes, replacing 1% of the black residents in a neighborhood with Hispanic residents (to induce the greatest possible impact) will increase expected returns by only .000091 per quarter.

Since the spatial model allows us to estimate what factors affect neighborhood substitutability, we now turn to the estimates of (6) for further evidence. The estimates from the two specifications used to estimate the distance between houses can be found in Tables 5 and 6. A priori we know that the parameters on each variable cannot be negative. Thus, it seems sensible to restrict the estimation process to the non-negative values. One way to do this is by estimating $\exp(\text{parameter}_j)/100$, which also ensures that confidence intervals will remain within feasible parameter values.[10] Thus, our estimate of b_0 (the mileage parameter) in (12) equals $\exp(-14.515398) = 0.0000000049664$. Similar calculations for (14) yield an estimate of 0.000031894168. Notice that even when the characteristic space only includes physical distance, the mileage parameter plays only a minor role. Consider two homes, one located 30 miles north of San Francisco, the other 30 miles south. The model (14) estimates indicate that their local component returns will have a covariance about 99.8% as large as

Table 4. Parameter estimates for the OLS regression model.

This table reports the ordinary least-squares parameter estimates for a model explaining deviations from the area-wide housing index via a set of socioeconomic variables taken from the 1980 census data. OLS and Bootstrap standard errors for the coefficients are reported. The model estimated is:

$$\ln(r_s(l)) = a_0 + a_1 * \text{MEDINC} + a_2 * \text{EDUC16P} + a_3 * \text{BLACK} + a_4 * \text{ASIAN} + a_6 * \text{OTHER}$$

Parameter	$\ln(h)$	$\ln(\bar{r})$	MEDINC	EDUC16P	BLACK	ASIAN	HISPANIC	OTHER
Estimate	-0.011550	0.020195	-0.000078	0.000017	-0.000046	0.000024	0.000045	-0.001581
OLS SE	0.001301	0.000236	0.000007	0.000004	0.000003	0.000006	0.000007	0.000101
Bootstrap SE	0.001170	0.000276	0.000010	0.000006	0.000004	0.000007	0.000008	0.000125

Table 5. Parameter estimates and bootstrapped confidence ranges: Socioeconomic variables and physical distance.

The bootstrap values are coefficient estimates generated under the null hypothesis that the observations are independent from each other. This conforms to a null that the exponentiated values of the distance parameters are zero. This is generated by randomizing over the repeat-sales observations with replacement. The fractile value is the empirical fractile of the actual value, based upon 250 bootstrap iterations. Extreme fractile values indicate that the actual estimated values do not conform well to the bootstrap under the null. Zero values in the .05 quantile column indicate that, under the null hypothesis, a coefficient value of zero cannot be rejected at traditional confidence levels. The coefficients are generated by the model:

$$de(\ell, m) = \{(e^{b_0} * \Delta MILES^2 + e^{b_1} * \Delta MEDINC^2 + e^{b_2} * \Delta EDUC15L^2 + e^{b_3} * \Delta EDUC16P^2 + e^{b_4} * \Delta WHITE^2$$
$$+ e^{b_5} * \Delta BLACK^2 + e^{b_6} * \Delta ASIAN^2 + e^{b_7} * \Delta HISPANIC^2 + e^{b_8} * \Delta OTHER^2)/100\}^{1/2}$$

$$(17)$$

Variable	Actual	Min	0.05	0.25	0.50	0.75	0.95	Max	Fractile
σ_η^2	0.066521	0.038294	0.047579	0.059060	0.065883	0.073597	0.081530	0.091020	0.531381
σ_ι^2	0.014243	0.011815	0.013904	0.015215	0.016097	0.017001	0.018576	0.019880	0.083682
σ_ε^2	0.017786	0.012869	0.013973	0.015372	0.016232	0.017252	0.018547	0.019922	0.845188
Miles	0.000000	0.000000	0.000000	0.000000	0.000000	0.000003	0.000010	0.000020	0.188285
Med. Income	0.002997	0.000000	0.000446	0.001016	0.001403	0.002013	0.003147	0.005932	0.920502
Educ. 15	0.000312	0.000016	0.000104	0.000332	0.000464	0.000606	0.000886	0.001418	0.221757
Educ. 16	0.000254	0.000085	0.000211	0.000326	0.000439	0.000568	0.000793	0.001433	0.108787
White	0.000002	0.000000	0.000000	0.000000	0.000000	0.000002	0.000002	0.000113	0.849372
Black	0.000088	0.000000	0.000000	0.000000	0.000017	0.000091	0.000256	0.000551	0.744770
Asian	0.000102	0.000000	0.000000	0.000003	0.000068	0.000271	0.000915	0.001801	0.560669
Hispanic	0.000138	0.000000	0.000000	0.000000	0.000001	0.000015	0.000283	0.001054	0.866109
Other	0.000494	0.000009	0.000255	0.000391	0.000463	0.000547	0.001717	0.083597	0.589958

Notes: The coefficients reported are the exponentiated values. The bootstrapped quantiles are based upon 250 iterations.

Table 6. Parameter estimates and bootstrapped confidence ranges: Physical distance model only.

The bootstrap values are coefficient estimates generated under the null hypothesis that the observations are independent from each other. This conforms to a null that the exponentiated values of the distance parameters are zero. This is generated by randomizing over the repeat-sales observations with replacement. The fractile values is the empirical fractile of the actual value, based upon 250 bootstrap iterations. Extreme fractile values indicate that the actual estimated values do not conform well to the bootstrap under the null. Zero values in the .05 quantile column indicate that, under the null hypothesis, a coefficient value of zero cannot be rejected at traditional confidence levels. The coefficients are generated by the model:

$$de(l,m) = \left[\frac{e^{b_0} * \Delta\text{MILES}^2}{100} \right]^{1/2}$$

Variable	Actual	Min	0.05	0.25	0.50	0.75	0.95	Max	Fractile
σ_η^2	0.066378	0.035896	0.048648	0.059942	0.065475	0.071970	0.080638	0.088859	0.529680
σ_l^2	0.008882	0.008290	0.008995	0.009790	0.010295	0.010883	0.012102	0.012613	0.050228
σ_ϵ^2	0.023156	0.020146	0.020669	0.021466	0.021976	0.022542	0.023297	0.023731	0.917808
Miles	0.000032	0.000000	0.000000	0.000000	0.000000	0.000001	0.000006	0.000017	1.000000

Notes: The coefficients reported are the exponentiated values. The bootstrapped quantiles are based upon 250 iterations.

the return covariance for two homes in the same neighborhood. One might have expected this result a priori. Imagine there are three neighborhoods A, B, and C, with B between A and C. Then the returns in A and C will be closely linked through B. If prices in A go up, that will force up prices in B, which in turn will force up prices in C. If people moving into the area are sufficiently flexible among adjoining areas, the return correlation among A and C will be very high.

The inability of a pure physical distance model (14) to fit the data can be seen in the estimate of σ_r^2. The combination of the small parameter estimates for mileage and σ_r^2 cause the model to treat all homes as if they exist in the same neighborhood, with substantial degrees of house-specific risk. In contrast, the full model allows for a much greater degree of correlation in the return to homes at similar locations, and less house-specific risk. The peculiar structure of the San Francisco Bay Area housing market may explain why physical distance plays such a small role. The Bay Area has numerous hills and valleys. As a result, the value of a home often depends upon its altitude above sea level. Homes high up on a hill are worth more. Thus, knowing the distance between two homes may tell a buyer much less than knowing their relative altitudes. Since most other cities do not share this geological feature, physical distance may play a larger role in their estimated housing returns.

While physical distance plays a minor role in the correlation estimates when it appears alone, it becomes completely negligible when other neighborhood characteristics enter the model. Rather, median household income dominates the estimates. From Table 2, the difference between two neighborhoods in the top and bottom quartile equals 7.7 thousand dollars. For model (12), if all the other differences equal zero, this difference in median income will reduce the return covariance between the neighborhoods by 34%. While the race and education variables also play a strong role, they are much less important. Nevertheless, changing the racial composition of a neighborhood seems to change the covariance of returns with respect to other neighborhoods. Based upon the estimates from model (12), the return covariance between homes in an all white neighborhood and an otherwise identical all black, Asian, or Hispanic neighborhood will exhibit 20%, 19%, and 17% of the covariance of homes in the same neighborhood. If whites are replaced in the above comparison with any other group, the return covariance percentages will fall even further. However, one should be very careful about drawing conclusions from these numbers. No neighborhood's black population composes more than 85% of the zip code, and the maximal numbers for Hispanic and Asians is about 38%. Thus, within the sample, racial factors never loom as large as neighborhood income when determining the correlation among housing return innovations.

Estimating the conditional covariances between neighborhoods is useful for a number of reasons. Low covariances among areas separated in terms of median household income imply that there are potentially large reductions in risk to portfolios that are diversified across neighborhoods. For mortgage lenders, the dynamics of the housing pricing indices within a metropolitan area reflect changing loan-to-value ratios. Our analysis indicates that lending in only high median family income neighborhoods, while potentially attractive in terms of qualifying a borrower, may have adverse portfolio effects. Conversely, a policy of lending across income-diversified neighborhoods has potential for reducing the volatility of the portfolio. The same guidelines hold true for equity investors in housing, as well as for municipalities. Property tax flows are conditioned, over the long term, upon capital appreciation. Analysis of how rates differ across neighborhoods may provide useful information about the uncertainty of future cash flows and guidelines for targeted urban development. While the evidence for mortgage lender redlining is mixed (see Holmes and Horvitz (1994), and Schill and Wachter (1993) for example), it would appear to have been a poor strategy from a risk and return perspective in the San Francisco Bay area over the period of our study. Diversification across neighborhoods with varying income and educational compositions would have reduced portfolio volatility, measured in loan-to-value ratios.

An important caveat in the interpretation of the estimated coefficients is that the variables are not independent. Median household income in the 1990 census is positively correlated with the proportion of white residents, and negatively correlated with the proportion of black residents. This colinearity is likely to affect the magnitude of the coefficient estimates, and indeed may even affect the sign of a less detailed model. For instance, suppose one omits median household income from the specification. Then racial composition will appear to be a fair instrument. The specification may thus produce a *positive* relative return for nonwhite neighborhoods. The same potentially holds true for geographical distance. In cities where a home's view plays less of a role, the household income will vary geographically. In this case, the omission of median household income may make physical distance appear to be a key variable defining the covariance of errors. While economists are willing to make the assumption of ceteris paribus for purposes of analysis, home buyers, lenders, and policy makers may not have that luxury, and any "comparative statics" applied should be based upon reasonable expectations about covariation in variables.

3.4. Empirical Results: Indices

The indices that result from the distance-weighted repeat-sales procedure demonstrate how widely the dynamics of capital appreciation may vary, even within a single metropolitan area. Figure 2 plots five zip code indices chosen from the sample of 188. Notice that the cumulative returns over 14 years vary from a low of 25% to a high of 275%. The figure also shows two distinct "groups." Zip codes 94554, 94586, and 95450 have all had nearly flat returns since 1990, while 94544 and 94621 have shown increases in the 1990s. Our study is confined to the San Francisco Bay area, and thus differences in the capital appreciation dynamics across zip codes may not be as dramatic for different metropolitan areas. In Goetzmann and Spiegel (1995), we found the average correlation in housing returns within the San Francisco Bay area to be small relative to three other areas, namely, Dallas, Chicago, and Atlanta. Map 1 illustrates the differences in the five-year capital appreciation returns by quartile. It is a patchwork of different rates of return, with areas of high return interspersed with areas of low return. A closer look at the map shows, however, that there is some aggregation at the local level. Contiguous zip codes typically "lump" together in the same capital appreciation quartile, due to continuities in socioeconomic variables within the region. For instance, in the lowest quartile, a dollar invested at the end of 1988 returned between $.97 and $1.16 in nominal terms. Typical areas with this low capital appreciation are cities in the Northeast Bay such as Martinez, Pinole, and Benizia, as well as towns in the South Bay such as Hayward City and Union City. Zip codes with the high capital

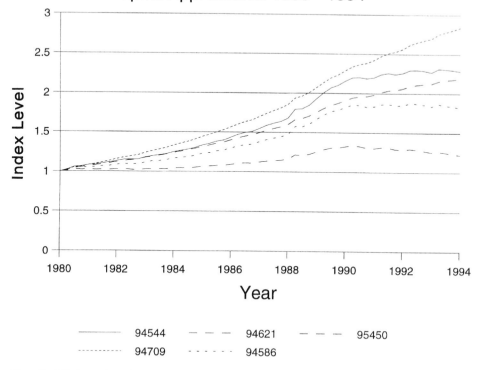

Figure 2. This figure shows the capital appreciation index over the 1980–1994 period for five representative zip codes in the San Francisco Bay area, estimated by the distance-weighted repeat-sales method. The index is scaled to show the changing value of $1 invested in housing in December 1979.

appreciation, ranging from 23% to 36% over the past five years are a bit more concentrated in Marin County, Berkeley, and the environs west of Palo Alto. The range of rates of return in the Bay area suggests that one citywide index is likely to do a poor job at estimating the dynamics of housing appreciation within any single neighborhood. This is bad news for practitioners using indices constructed on a citywide level to calculate loan-to-value ratios. The magnitude of the deviation from a single index can be important. For example, the five-year returns for the zip codes in our sample range from −3% to +36%.

4. Conclusion

Previous methods of estimating the returns to illiquid assets have fallen into either the repeat-sales of hedonic-modeling classes. The spatial model presented here can be interpreted as an extension of both of these approaches. In particular, it overcomes some of the selection bias problems associated with the estimation of a citywide index when socio-economic characteristics are associated with resale frequency.

An examination of housing returns in the San Francisco Bay area using the distance-weighted repeat-sales model reveals patterns of interest to homeowners, mortgage lenders, and civic authorities. First, it appears clear that zip codes in the Bay area had widely differing rates of return over the past 14 years. This is certainly of interest to lenders wishing to recalculate loan-to-value ratios of a housing loan portfolio. It is also of interest to homeowners wishing to gauge how far their neighborhood's return might deviate from the return of homes in a typical neighborhood. It is also useful to both lenders and home investors to know that low income and better educated neighborhoods had higher returns than high income or low education neighborhoods, at least in the metropolitan area examined in this study. A cautionary note to "redliners" in mortgage lending is that, while race had some impact on returns, it was minor at best.

The motivation for decomposing a regional housing return index into its neighborhood-level constituents is that the price dynamics contain information about intra-regional substitutability. What we found was that people seem to be much less concerned with physical distance than with social distance. The most important empirical result of this study is the finding that socioeconomic variables strongly influence the covariance of neighborhood housing returns. The return correlation between high and low income neighborhoods is surprisingly small, and no other factor seems to have as much influence. Apparently, the

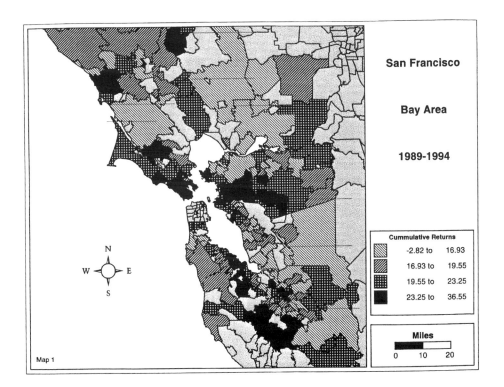

difference between the "haves" and the "have-nots" extends to the pattern of capital appreciation of their homes. To the extent that the home is the major asset in the lower income
homeowner's portfolio, the differential appreciation rate over the 1980–1994 period was
effectively a trend towards parity. Whether this trend was due to endogenous or exogenous
factors is an open question.

While this article only applies the DWRS methodology to housing, it can be used to
address a number of issues. For example, suppose a researcher needs a corporate bond index
for issues with an "BB" rating. Since these bonds are both scarce and thinly traded, it will
be difficult to construct a reliable index that uses only BB-rated corporate bonds. However,
one expects that similarly rated bonds will have similar returns. Thus, one can construct a
hedonic space, and DWRS will then use all available bond data to help construct the BB
index. Other applications may include intra-day stock indices. For any asset, if one divides
time into fine enough intervals, that asset will not trade during most of the time periods
under study. By employing a DWRS procedure, this problem can be overcome.

Acknowledgments

The authors thank three anonymous referees and editor Tom Thibodeau for helpful comments. We also thank participants in the workshops at University of British Columbia, U. C.
Berkeley, Boston College, Duke University, MIT, and Rutgers University for useful suggestions. We thank Xongshin Zhang for research assistance. We also thank the Yale Finance
Institute and the University of California for research support.

Notes

1. While financial models have not taken advantage of the spatial correlations among assets, other fields have.
   Cressie (1993), for instance, discusses the problem from the viewpoint of geostatistics.
2. For example, suppose neighborhood A appreciates at 10%, and neighborhood B at 6%. Now consider a data
   set containing one home in A that sells in periods 0 and 2, and another home in B that sells in periods 1 and 2.
   The WRS index will report appreciation rates of 14.1% in period 1, and 6% in period 2. In reality, if the two
   neighborhoods have equal housing densities, then the "true" citywide index should appreciate at a steady 8%
   per period.
3. As an aside, note that the return structure in (4) can depend upon individual housing characteristics. This implies
   that, with the proper data set, any hedonic model can be modified for use as a distance-weighted estimator.
4. Taylor(1992, 1983) shows that, in a market with heterogeneous assets, a spurious negative autocorrelation may
   be induced through quality-selection filtering. Goetzmann (1995) simulates this filter for various seller reserve
   rules and shows how the index may be biased.
5. Prior to estimation, the observations are randomly ordered, to prevent spatial or temporal clustering in this stage
   of the estimation process.
6. In principle, one can obtain a more efficient estimate of the parameters in (11) by using GLS to estimate the
   model's parameters.
7. Only approximately, since the time between sales still induces some heterogeneity in the variance of the error
   terms.
8. The other category tends to be very small and thus may be volatile on a percentage basis. Further, we suspect
   that from 1980 to 1990 many individuals who may have previously identified themselves as "OTHER" may
   have moved into one of the larger categories.

9. This result may be due to the fact that the distance-weighted repeat-sales approach implicitly provides hedonic controls, whereas the citywide index estimated in Goetzmann and Spiegel (1995) is biased towards neighborhoods which transact.

10. The division by 100 helps to scale the numbers and to speed up convergence.

References

Bailey, M. J., R. F. Muth, and H. O. Nourse. "A Regression Method for Real Estate Price Index Construction," *Journal of the American Statistical Association* 58 (1963), 933–942.

Case, B., H. Pollakowski, and S. Wachter. "On Choosing Among Price Index Methodologies," *Journal of the American Real Estate and Urban Economics Association* 19 (1991), 286–307.

Case, B., and J. Quigley. "The Dynamics of Real Estate Prices," *Review of Economics and Statistics* 73 (1991), 50–58.

Case, K., and R. Shiller. "Prices of Single Family Homes Since 1970: New Indexes for Four Cities," *New England Economic Review* (1987), 45–56.

Clapp, J., and C. Giaccotto. "Estimating Price Trends for Residential Property: A Comparison of Repeat Sales and Assessed Value Methods," *Journal of Real Estate and Finance and Economics* 5 (1992), 357–374.

Cressie, N. A. *Statistics for Spatial Data.* New York: John Wiley & Sons, Inc., 1993.

Gatzlaff, D., and R. Haurin. "Selection Bias and Real Estate Index Construction." Working paper, Florida State University, Tallahassee, 1993.

Goetzmann, W. "The Effect of Seller Reserves on Market Index Estimation." Working paper, Yale School of Management, 1995.

Goetzmann, W., and M. Spiegel. "Non-Temporal Components of Residential Real Estate Appreciation," *Review of Economics and Statistics* (September 1995), 199–206.

Halvorsen, R. and H. Pollakowski. "Choice of Functional Form for Hedonic Price Equations," *Journal of Urban Economics* 10 (1981), 37–49.

Holmes, A., and P. Horvitz. "Mortgage Redlining: Race, Risk and Demand," *Journal of Finance* 49(1) (1994), 81–99.

Meese, R., and N. Wallace. "Nonparametric Estimation of Dynamic Hedonic Price Models and the Construction of Residential Housing Price Indices," *American Real Estate and Urban Economics Association Journal* 19 (1991), 308–332.

Meese, R., and N. Wallace. "Construction of Residential Housing Prices Indexes: A Comparison of Repeat Sales, Hedonic Regression, and Hybrid Approaches," *Journal of Real Estate Finance and Economics* (this issue).

Schill, M. H., and S. M. Wachter. "A Tale of Two Cities: Racial and Ethnic Geographic Disparities in Home Mortgage Lending in Boston and Philadelphia," *Journal of Housing Research* 4(2) (1993), 245–275.

Shilles, Robert. "Arithmetic Repeat Sales Price Estimators," *Journal of Housing Economics* 1 (1991), 110–126.

Taylor, W. "The Estimation of Quality-Adjusted Auction Returns With Varying Transaction Intervals," *Journal of Financial and Quantitative Analysis* 27 (1) (1992), 131–142.

Taylor, W. "The Estimation of Quality-Adjusted Rates of Returns in Stamp Auctions," *Journal of Finance* 38 (1983), 1095–1110.

Journal of Real Estate Finance and Economics, 14: 33–50 (1997)
©1997 Kluwer Academic Publishers

Sample Selection Bias and Repeat-Sales Index Estimates

DEAN H. GATZLAFF
Department of Insurance, Real Estate, and Business Law, The Florida State University, Tallahassee, FL 32306

DONALD R. HAURIN
Departments of Economics and Finance, The Ohio State University, 1945 N. High Street, Columbus, OH 43210

Abstract

Analysis of variations in house values among localities requires reliable house value indices. Gatzlaff and Haurin (1994) indicate that traditional hedonic house value index estimates, using only information from a sample of sold homes to estimate value movements for the entire housing stock, may be subject to substantial bias. This article extends previous work by adapting the censored sample procedure to the repeat-sales index estimation model. Using data from Dade County, Florida, a house value index constructed from a sample of homes selling more than once, rather than all houses in a locality, is found to be biased. The bias is shown to be highly correlated with changes in economic conditions.

Key Words: house price index, sample selection, housing markets

Measuring and examining price movements is central to understanding market behavior. Because the value of housing represents a significant portion of the nation's wealth, the construction and accuracy of house price indices has received considerable attention.[1] Recent interest in measuring house prices has escalated due to studies that suggest house price changes are predictable (Case and Shiller, 1989; Hosios and Pesando, 1991) and to those that forecast dramatic real house value declines over the next 15 years (Mankiw and Weil, 1989).[2]

Gatzlaff and Haurin (1994) indicate that empirical methods frequently used to derive house values may be subject to substantial bias. They argue that if variations in economic conditions affect offer and reservation prices, then a sample composed only of sold houses may change in a nonrandom manner.[3] Correction requires joint estimation of the probability that a house will sell and the sale price. Gatzlaff and Haurin estimate house value indices using a censored regression procedure and find that a value index based on standard hedonic price estimates using only sold homes is biased and tends to affect the cyclical movements of the value of the housing stock most during periods of economic growth.

This study extends previous work by applying the censored sample procedure to the widely applied repeat-sales model (Bailey, Muth, and Nourse, 1963; Case and Shiller, 1989). It is argued that a sample of sold houses (especially a sample of only repeat sales) is not a random sample of the stock of housing; thus, house value indices derived from the repeat-sales estimation procedure are possibly subject to substantial bias. Gatzlaff and Haurin (1994) suggest that the possible outcomes of sample selection include either dampening or magnifying the reported house value cycles. Our current study estimates the changes in house values for a single locality and compares estimates from the standard repeat-sales index with those from a selection corrected model. The study concludes by correlating deviations between the two index estimates with factors such as population growth, construction activity, employment rates, and changes in per capital income.

1. The Hedonic and Repeat-Sales Index Estimation Methods

House value changes are typically estimated using either the hedonic-price method or the repeat-sales method. Because housing assets are heterogeneous, these methods are applied to control for the differences in the characteristics that exist between properties. Using samples of sold homes, both methods attempt to hold constant the quantity and quality of the housing attributes to establish a "constant-quality" value series.

The hedonic method hypothesizes that property value is viewed as a function of a bundle of property characteristics (Rosen, 1974):

$$V_{it} = f(X_{it}),\tag{1}$$

where V_{it} denotes the value of property i at time t, $i = 1, \ldots, n$, and $t = 1, \ldots, T$. Value is a function of X_{it}, a set of structural and locational characteristics for property i at time t. The underlying rationale for this method is that the property-specific characteristics are assumed to be identifiable and measurable. Use of the hedonic method to create a house value index requires measuring and "pricing" these characteristics for each locality and for each point in time. There are two traditional hedonic models: a strictly cross-sectional model and an explicitly intertemporal model.

In the cross-sectional model, implicit prices of the property characteristics are estimated separately in each period. The resulting series of estimates is applied to a standardized bundle of house characteristics. The resultant series of constant-quality house values can then be transformed to estimate a time-series house value index.[4] The explicit intertemporal hedonic model measures house value variations by including in the estimation process a dummy variable for each index period in addition to the full vector of property characteristics. A common specification of the explicit intertemporal model is

$$P_{it} = \sum_{j=1}^{J} \beta_j X_{jit} + \sum_{t=1}^{T} c_t D_t + e_{it},\tag{2}$$

where P_{it} denotes the log of the transaction price of property i at time $t(i = 1, \ldots, n; t = 1, \ldots, T)$, β_j denotes the vector of estimated coefficients for the log of each of the j property characteristics, $(j = 1, \ldots, J)$, and c_t denotes a vector of estimated coefficients for each of the time dummies, D_t. The time dummies are set equal to 1 if the ith house is sold in period t, otherwise 0. In this specification, the coefficients of the time dummy variables represent the log of the cumulative price index.

The repeat-sales method is estimated using a sample of homes that have been sold more than once. Introduced initially by Bailey, Muth, and Nourse (1963), and revived more recently by Case and Shiller (1989), it can be viewed as an extension of the explicit intertemporal model. Taking the difference between the log of the second sale price and the log of the initial sale price, as specified in (2), yields

$$P_i^2 - P_i^1 = \left(\sum_{j=1}^{J} \beta_j X_{ji}^2 + \sum_{t=1}^{T} c_t D_t^2 \right) - \left(\sum_{j=1}^{J} \beta_j X_{ji}^1 + \sum_{t=1}^{T} c_t D_t^1 \right) + e_i^{21}, \qquad (3)$$

where the second and the initial sale periods are represented by superscripts, and X_{ji}^2 and X_{ji}^1 denote the vectors of physical and locational characteristics at the two sale dates. If the physical and locational characteristics and their coefficients do not change over time, the change in the transaction prices between the two dates is found to be a function of the time between sales. In this case, (3) simplifies to:

$$P_i^2 - P_i^1 = \sum_{t=1}^{T} c_t (D_i^2 - D_i^1) + e_i^{21}. \qquad (4)$$

To estimate (4), the dependent variable is set as the log of the price relative, $\ln(P_{it}/P_{it})$, and the time dummies are set at -1 for the initial sale date, $+1$ for the second sale date, and 0 otherwise.[5] The estimated coefficients c_t represent the log of the cumulative price index for period t. To normalize the index at 1.0, the time dummy for the initial period is set equal to zero. The primary advantage of the repeat-sales model is that it requires only sale price information and does not require direct measurement of the time-invariant property characteristics, observed or unobserved.

Potential problems with applying the repeat-sales method have been identified by Haurin and Hendershott (1991). Concerns include the randomness of the sample, reductions in sample size, non-applicability to single cross-sectional comparisons, lack of consideration of changes in neighborhood or structural quality (e.g., aging), lack of consideration of changes in the house and neighborhood implicit prices, and ex post revision of earlier house price index numbers with the addition of subsequent repeat sales. Some of these problems have been addressed in a hybrid hedonic/repeat-sales method developed by Case and Quigley (1991) and tested by Case, Pollakowski, and Wachter (1991). However, the hybrid method does not directly address the problem created by restricting the sample to sold properties.[6]

2. A Joint Model for House Sales and Values

2.1. Single-Period Model: A Review

In the following discussion, the natural log of the seller's reservation price of house i in period t is denoted P_{it}^R, and the offer price P_{it}^O. Specifically,

$$P_{it}^O = \sum_{j=1}^J \beta_j^O X_{jit} + \sum_{t=1}^T c_t D_t + \epsilon_{it}^O, \tag{5}$$

and

$$P_{it}^R = \sum_{j=1}^J \beta_j^R X_{jit} + \sum_{t=1}^T c_t D_t + \epsilon_{it}^R, \tag{6}$$

In (5) and (6), $\epsilon_i = (\epsilon_{it}^R, \epsilon_i^O)$ is N(0, $\sum$), where

$$\sum = \begin{pmatrix} \sigma_{RR} & \sigma_{RO} \\ \sigma_{RO} & \sigma_{OO} \end{pmatrix}. \tag{7}$$

The log transaction price, P_{it}, is observed only if the offer equals or exceeds the reservation price.

$$
\begin{aligned}
P_{it} &= P_{it}^O && \text{if } P_{it}^O - P_{it}^R \geq 0 \\
&\text{unobserved} && \text{if } P_{it}^O - P_{it}^R < 0.
\end{aligned} \tag{8}
$$

The expected sale price that results from this process is:

$$E(P_{it}) = \sum_{j=1}^J \beta_j X_{jit} + \sum_{t=1}^T c_t D_t + E(\epsilon_{it}^O \mid P_{it}^O - P_{it}^R \geq 0). \tag{9}$$

The observability of P_{it} depends on the probability structure of the process that generates the reservation and offer prices. Gatzlaff and Haurin (1994) show that estimating values using only a sample of sold properties is selective and that biased estimates may result.

A sample selectivity correction model was introduced by Heckman (1974, 1979) and further discussed by Dhrymes (1986). Heckman outlined a procedure that allows consistent estimates of β to be obtained even though not all houses transact.[7] His approach requires specifying the model that determines the observability conditions, creating a correction variable, and then estimating the equation of interest.

Consistent with Gatzlaff and Haurin (1994), the threshold value of the ith house selling (S_{it}) in period t is specified as:

$$S_{it}^* = \sum_{k=1}^K \delta_k X_{ikt}^H + \sum_{m=1}^M \theta_m X_{imt}^P + \sum_{n=1}^N \kappa_n Z_{nt} + \nu_{it}, \tag{10}$$

where any of k house attributes, X^H; any of m personal attributes, X^P; or any of n local or national macroeconomic factors, Z, affect the probability of a sale. We assume that the error term, v_{it}, is normally distributed. S_{it}^* is not observable—only the outcome is observed. Thus,

$$S_{it} = \begin{array}{ll} 1 & if\ (P_{it}^O - P_{it}^R) \geq 0, \\ 0 & otherwise. \end{array} \tag{11}$$

The first step in the correction procedure is to estimate (11) as a probit model. In the second step of the procedure, the inverse Mills ratio (λ_{it}), created from the probit results, is included as an independent variable in the standard intertemporal hedonic price equation (9) such that:

$$P_{it} = \sum_{j=1}^{J} \beta_j X_{jit} + \sum_{t=1}^{T} c_t D_{it} + \gamma \lambda_{it} + \eta_{it}. \tag{12}$$

Heckman shows that the problem encountered when estimating an equation with a selected sample is similar to an omitted variable problem; however, the inclusion of λ_{it} corrects for the potential bias of β_j and c_t. Greene (1981) indicates that if OLS is applied to (12), the standard errors of the coefficients are biased, and thus a further correction is needed.

2.2. Repeat-Sales Model

Variations of the problem of selective sequential observation are considered by Poirier (1980), Fishe, Trost, and Lurie (1981), Tunali (1983), and Lee and Maddala (1985). In these cases the interest often lies in deriving unbiased estimates of a behavior where the sample has been affected by sequential selection. However, the repeat-sales model differs because sales in both periods are relevant for the analysis. In the *compete* sample, an observed first sale (S_i^1) occurs at time t following (11). A second sale is observed only if a first sale occurs:

$$S_i^2 = \begin{array}{ll} 1 & if\ (P_i^{1O} - P_i^{1R}) \geq 0 \quad and\ if \quad (P_i^{2O} - P_1^{2R}) \geq 0 \\ 0 & if\ (P_i^{1O} - P_i^{1R}) \geq 0 \quad and\ if \quad (P_i^{2O} - P_1^{2R}) < 0 \\ unobserved & if\ (P_i^{1O} - P_i^{1R}) < 0. \end{array} \tag{13}$$

Equation (13) simply indicates that a house is at risk of a second sale only if there has been a first sale. In a *repeat-sales* sample, both sales must occur for there to be an observation. The condition for joint observation of both first and second sale is:

$$(S_i^1, S_i^2) = \begin{array}{l} observed\ if\ (P_i^{1O} - P_i^{1R}) \geq 0\ and\ if\ (P_i^{2O} - P_i^{2R}) \geq 0, \\ unobserved\ otherwise. \end{array} \tag{14}$$

The condition in (14) differs from that in (11); that is, there are "unused" first-sale observations.[8] The restriction in (14) helps to explain the problem of ex post index revision that occurs when new second sales bring previously omitted first-sale data into the sample.

Including these prior sales affects the value of the house price index estimated for earlier periods, perhaps many years prior. If the first sales continued in the initial repeat-sales sample are a nonrandom sample of homes, selection bias may be present in the first estimate of the house price index, and the amount of ex post revision of the house price index could be substantial.[9]

The correction method for double selectivity requires a modification of the two-step procedure described above. First, we assume that the threshold value S_i^{2*} for the second sale is similar in form to that for the first sale (10), updating the year of sale, and thus X^P and Z. We denote the stochastic error as v_i^2.

The random errors in the two sale price equations are ϵ_i^1 and ϵ_i^2. The covariance matrix of the four error terms ($v_i^1, v_i^2, \epsilon_i^1, and \epsilon_i^2$) is:

$$\sum = \begin{pmatrix} 1 & \sigma_{12} & \sigma_{13} & \sigma_{14} \\ \sigma_{12} & 1 & \sigma_{23} & \sigma_{24} \\ \sigma_{13} & \sigma_{23} & \sigma_{33} & \sigma_{34} \\ \sigma_{14} & \sigma_{24} & \sigma_{34} & \sigma_{44} \end{pmatrix} \tag{15}$$

The repeat-sales method differences the log values of sale price in the two periods where sales are observed. The expectation of the log sales price in each period, conditional on sales being observed in *both* periods (denoted 1 and 2), is: [10]

$$E(P_i^1 \mid S_i^1 = 1 \text{ and } S_i^2 = 1) = \sum_{j=1}^{J} \beta_j X_{ji}^1 + \sum_{t=1}^{T} c_t D_t^1 + E(\epsilon_i^1 \mid S_i^1 = 1 \text{ and } S_i^2 = 1)$$

$$= \sum_{j=1}^{J} \beta_j X_{ji}^1 + \sum_{t=1}^{T} c_t D_t^1 + \sigma_{13}\lambda_1 + \sigma_{23}\lambda_2. \tag{16}$$

$$E(P_i^2 \mid S_i^1 = 1 \text{ and } S_i^2 = 1) = \sum_{j=1}^{J} \beta_j X_{ji}^2 + \sum_{t=1}^{T} c_t D_t^2 + E(\epsilon_i^2 \mid S_i^1 = 1 \text{ and } S_i^2 = 1)$$

$$= \sum_{j=1}^{J} \beta_j X_{ji}^2 + \sum_{t=1}^{T} c_t D_t^2 + \sigma_{14}\lambda_1 + \sigma_{24}\lambda_2. \tag{17}$$

The expressions for the lambdas are defined in Tunali (1983, p. 12) and Tallis (1961, p. 226).[11] The coefficients of the lambdas differ between (16) and (17) because of the different correlations of the error terms. Assuming that the characteristics of the property do not change over time, the difference between (17) and (16) is:

$$(E(P_i^2 \mid S_i^1 = 1 \text{ and } S_i^2 = 1) - E(P_i^1 \mid S_i^1 = 1 \text{ and } S_i^2 = 1)$$

$$= \sum_{t=1}^{T} c_t(D_t^2 - D_t^1) + (\sigma_{14} - \sigma_{13})\lambda_1 + (\sigma_{24} - \sigma_{23})\lambda_2. \tag{18}$$

Our repeat-sales estimation equation is:

$$P_i^2 - P_i^1 = \sum_{t=1}^{T} c_t(D_t^2 - D_t^1) + (\sigma_{14} - \sigma_{13})\lambda_1 + (\sigma_{24} - \sigma_{23})\lambda_2 + \eta_i. \qquad (19)$$

Recalling that the sale prices are in natural logs, the left-hand side is a log price relative. Equation (19) shows that estimating unbiased coefficients of the house price index in a repeat-sales sample requires considering possible sample selection at the time of both sales. Comparing (4) and (19), we note that two selection correction terms must be included in the repeat-sales estimation to derive unbiased measures of the time period dummy variables' coefficients.

3. The Data

Annual repeat-sales house value indices for the Miami MSA (Dade County) are estimated from 1971 to 1995 using data from the Florida Department of Revenue's (DOR) 1995 property tax records. These data are maintained as part of a larger database that includes information on the two most recent selling prices and dates (month and year), as well as a limited set of property characteristics and owner characteristics (i.e., owner's name, address, and property exemption claims) for every parcel in the State of Florida.

The data used here were drawn from a dataset consisting of solely single-family detached residences (land use code 01) located in the Miami MSA. A series of steps, consistent with Gatzlaff and Ling (1994), were first conducted to delete incomplete and incompatible observations (e.g., homes selling for $1) or apparent data errors. All single-family detached properties were included that had a total living area of more than 600 square feet and less than 6,000 square feet. In addition, all properties included in the data set have a lot size of more than 1,500 square feet and less than 5 acres.

The full dataset is too large to apply the truncated bivariate technique. A procedure which randomly selects a small sample of repeat-sale, once-sold, and never-sold observations for each year was adopted to demonstrate the method of correcting bias in a repeat-sales sample. Three percent of all repeat-sale, once-sold, and never-sold observations were initially selected. The repeat-sale observations were assigned a year of first sale and second sale. The once-sold observations were assigned a year of first sale and randomly assigned a year of no second sale. Finally, the never-sold observations were randomly assigned a year of no first sale. This procedure yielded a set of 6,223 observations of single-family homes of which 1,674 sold twice, 1,899 sold once, and 2,650 never sold during the 25-year estimation period. Summary statistics of the homes that sold are reported in Table 1.

Inspection of Table 1 reveals no substantial differences between the characteristics of the data having a first sale versus the characteristics of the data having sold twice. However, some change in the characteristics of the properties that sold during different times of the study period is evident. For example, the mean living area and the mean lot size of the homes that sold increased by approximately 7.5% from 1971 to 1995. Finally, the mean age of the homes that sold increased from approximately 15 years old to about 30 years old.

Table 1. Summary statistics of sale observations.
(By year of sale)
Miami MSA, 1971–1995

Year of Sale	Panel A: Observations With Initial Sale					Panel B: Observations With Second Sale				
	Obs.	Mean Sale Price	Mean Liv. Area	Mean Lot Size	Mean Year Built	Obs.	Mean Sale Price	Mean Liv. Area	Mean Lot Size	Mean Year Built
1971	133	26.0	1.56	7.03	1955	N.A.	N.A.	N.A.	N.A.	N.A.
1972	133	29.0	1.64	6.75	1955	N.A.	N.A.	N.A.	N.A.	N.A.
1973	194	33.3	1.56	6.94	1958	17	35.7	1.81	7.77	1955
1974	165	40.0	1.62	7.13	1958	18	34.4	1.55	6.71	1957
1975	128	40.0	1.63	7.23	1959	16	44.3	1.62	7.95	1962
1976	168	39.7	1.63	7.14	1958	25	38.6	1.65	6.83	1958
1977	189	43.3	1.67	7.14	1958	34	43.1	1.62	7.37	1959
1978	208	48.8	1.69	7.47	1959	50	44.5	1.61	7.11	1959
1979	153	55.6	1.69	7.35	1959	62	51.1	1.54	7.28	1958
1980	153	67.3	1.71	7.30	1958	37	66.4	1.56	7.83	1957
1981	118	82.0	1.71	7.44	1960	30	82.7	1.73	7.00	1958
1982	101	75.6	1.62	7.76	1960	47	79.6	1.78	7.57	1961
1983	129	78.4	1.64	7.24	1959	42	75.6	1.68	7.52	1957
1984	114	87.6	1.84	7.25	1959	59	85.1	1.67	7.13	1958
1985	126	83.3	1.81	7.23	1962	62	85.6	1.73	8.24	1962
1986	158	90.7	1.80	8.38	1961	86	83.1	1.72	6.95	1961
1987	163	93.4	1.77	8.01	1962	113	95.1	1.84	7.44	1959
1988	168	97.4	1.79	7.71	1962	122	98.3	1.76	8.18	1959
1989	149	102.1	1.80	8.01	1964	112	101.8	1.78	7.60	1961
1990	139	110.1	1.84	7.74	1965	112	114.1	1.91	7.72	1959
1991	124	97.5	1.73	7.33	1962	92	123.8	1.95	8.01	1963
1992	152	105.4	1.73	7.82	1961	119	118.5	1.82	8.03	1962
1993	154	113.9	1.78	7.54	1964	178	133.3	1.85	8.01	1964
1994	154	111.9	1.68	7.14	1962	187	127.2	1.76	7.80	1962
1995	N.A.	N.A.	N.A.	N.A.	N.A.	54	153.2	1.93	8.09	1962

Notes:
Summary values stated in 000s, except for the number of observations and the mean year built.
Repeat-sales data were not retained if the year of sale was identical for both the initial and second sale.
Data for 1995 include only the first two quarters.

4. Estimation Procedures and Results

Estimation of (19) requires deriving the values of the two sample selection correction variables, λ_1 and λ_2. We approach the problem using a truncated bivariate probit model for derivation of the lambdas, and use Greene's (1981) method for estimation of the correct standard errors in the OLS repeat-sales estimation. The two components of the bivariate probit are univariate probits on whether a property ever sold once and a truncated probit on whether a once-sold property sold twice. The bivariate probit accounts for possible correlation between these two outcomes.[12]

Aside from the sample size considerations discussed in the previous section, observations used in the first probit consist of all properties listed in the property tax record—those that sold as well as those that did not sell in a particular year. Each year we record whether the property sold for the first time or remained unsold. The sample for the second probit consists of properties that had sold once previously, and we observe whether they have sold a second time during subsequent years. From the bivariate probit estimation, we calculate values of the lambdas for each property and year of observation. These values are then included in the repeat-sales estimation suggested by (19). Statistically significant coefficients of the lambdas indicate sample selection, and we compare estimates of the coefficients of the vector of time dummy variables derived from (19) and (4) to measure the degree of bias.

Empirical estimates of the bivariate counterpart to (10) and (11) are reported in Table 2. Panel A reports model estimates on the probability of whether a house initially sold in a particular year (dependent var. = 1 if the first sale occurs; else 0).[13] Panel B reports the sequential model estimate of whether a house sold in a particular year, given that it had previously sold (if first sale = 1, then, dependent var. = 1 if second sale occurs; else 0).

Two sets of explanatory variables are included: property characteristics and macroeconomic variables. Unfortunately, owner attributes, which may yield additional explanatory power to the model are unobservable for the first sale of properties which sell twice. The property characteristics include total living area (LIV), total lot area (LOT), and year built (YRB). Macroeconomic variables include indicators related to the level of economic activity: the local unemployment rate (UER), and movements in mortgage interest rates, a mortgage "lock-in" variable (LOCKIN). LOCKIN is the difference between the current annual effective interest rate on 30-year fixed-rate mortgages and the average effective rate over the previous 20 quarters. Higher unemployment rates and greater lock-in effect should both serve to reduce house sales; thus, negative coefficients on both variables are expected.

House sales in the Miami area were cyclical with significant downturns occurring from 1974 to 1976 and from 1981 to 1983. The bivariate probit estimation results indicate that the probability of a first sale increases with LIV and decreases with YRB and LOCKIN. In addition, the probability of a second sale for properties that have sold once also increases with LIV and decreases with LOCKIN. Alternative model specifications indicate that UER is also highly correlated (negatively) with the probability of sales; however, collinearity with LOCKIN reduces its explanatory power in the reported model specification.[14]

The selection corrected repeat-sales index, SEL, is constructed directly from the estimation of (19) and includes in the estimation λ_1 and λ_2. The bivariate probit model estimate of the first and second sale events yields values for λ_1, and λ_2.[15] Estimates of the selection corrected repeat-sales model are reported in Table 3. The coefficients on λ_1 and λ_2 are estimated to be 0.405 and −0.682, respectively. Both estimates are found to be significant at a 1% level (t-stats equal 4.02 and −3.69).[16]

Two alternative annual repeat-sales index estimates are reported in Table 3: a standard repeat-sales index (STD), and a selection corrected repeat-sales index (SEL). The standard repeat-sales index is constructed from the estimation of (4), the traditional Bailey, Muth, and Nourse model. This model uses information from only the sold properties (1,674 observations) and does not attempt to control for changes in the sample selection correction variable, λ_{it}. The STD index movements are generally consistent with those previously reported for the Miami MSA by Gatzlaff and Ling (1994).

Table 2. Bivariate estimation of the probability of a sale.

	Panel A: Probability of First-sale Estimates			Panel B: Probability of Second-sale Estimates		
	OLS	Probit	Bivar. Probit	OLS	Probit	Bivar. Probit
Independent Variable	β (t-stat)	β (t-stat)	β (t-stat)	β (t-stat)	β (t-stat)	β (t-stat)
INTERCEPT	2.566 (2.66)	5.292 (2.14)	5.292 (1.87)	−3.346 (−2.45)	−9.797 (−2.81)	−2.793 (−0.85)
LIV*	0.714 (6.45)	1.855 (6.42)	1.855 (5.01)	0.637 (4.39)	1.164 (4.37)	2.203 (5.57)
LOT*	0.024 (1.38)	0.061 (1.36)	0.061 (1.16)	0.040 (1.81)	0.103 (1.79)	0.103 (1.87)
YRB*	−0.011 (−2.17)	−0.028 (−2.17)	−0.027 (−190)	0.020 (2.82)	0.050 (2.80)	0.009 (0.54)
UER*	−0.012 (−0.42)	−0.031 (−0.43)	−0.031 (−040)	−0.273 (−4.92)	−0.695 (−4.88)	0.029 (0.27)
LOCKIN*	−0.062 (−1.64)	−0.160 (−1.65)	−0.160 (−159)	0.262 (4.48)	0.066 (4.44)	−0.636 (−5.64)
Observations	6223	6223	6223	3573 (Obs.)	3573	6223
Adjusted-R^2	0.01			0.02		
Log-Likelihood	−4419	−4216		−2544	−2428	−7782
Restr. Log-Likelihood, (slope = 0)	−4447>	−4245		−2586	−2470	
Chi-squared		57 (p < 0.01)			84 (p < 0.01)	

Notes:
Probability of first-sale estimate: Dependent var. = 1 if house initially sold in a particular year; otherwise 0.
Probability of second-sale estimate: If house sold once, then dependent var. = 1 if house has second sale in a particular year; otherwise 0.
LIV: Total living area of the house (000s of sq. ft); LOT: Lot size (000s of sq. ft); YRB: Year built; UER: Average annual unemployment rate in the Miami MSA; and
LOCKIN: Difference between the current effective interest of the 30-year fixed-rate mortgage and the average rate over the previous 20 quarters.
* Coefficient estimates for variables are $\times 10^{-1}$.

Table 3. Annual index and appreciation estimates
Miami MSA, 1971–1995.

YEAR	SEL Model Estimates		Index Estimates		Annual Appreciation Estimates		
	β	Std. Err.	STD	SEL	Δ STD	Δ SEL	DEV
1971	N.A.	N.A.	1.000	1.000	0.075	0.073	0.002
1972	0.071	0.037	1.075	1.073	0.122	0.117	0.005
1973	0.181	0.034	1.206	1.198	0.109	0.093	0.016
1974	0.270	0.035	1.338	1.310	0.042	0.029	0.013
1975	0.299	0.036	1.394	1.348	−0.031	−0.032	0.001
1976	0.266	0.035	1.350	1.304	0.089	0.090	−0.001
1977	0.351	0.034	1.471	1.421	0.059	0.054	0.005
1978	0.404	0.033	1.558	1.498	0.174	0.153	0.021
1979	0.546	0.034	1.830	1.726	0.229	0.205	0.024
1980	0.733	0.036	2.249	2.081	0.116	0.097	0.019
1981	0.825	0.039	2.509	2.282	−0.019	−0.025	0.006
1982	0.799	0.042	2.460	2.223	0.013	0.036	−0.023
1983	0.835	0.037	2.493	2.304	0.041	0.061	−0.020
1984	0.894	0.036	2.595	2.444	−0.015	−0.007	−0.008
1985	0.887	0.032	2.555	2.428	0.001	−0.005	0.006
1986	0.882	0.035	2.557	2.416	0.068	0.068	0.000
1987	0.945	0.034	2.732	2.572	0.034	0.028	0.006
1988	0.973	0.035	2.824	2.645	0.055	0.057	−0.002
1989	1.028	0.036	2.980	2.795	0.038	0.031	0.007
1990	1.058	0.037	3.094	2.881	−0.000	−0.000	−0.000
1991	1.058	0.038	3.093	2.880	0.033	0.035	−0.002
1992	1.092	0.038	3.197	2.981	0.042	0.038	0.004
1993	1.129	0.038	3.331	3.093	0.087	0.085	0.002
1994	1.211	0.038	3.622	3.355	0.052	0.048	0.004
1995	1.258	0.046	3.809	3.517	N.A.	N.A.	N.A.
LAMBDA(1)	0.405	0.101					
LAMBDA(2)	−0.682	−0.185					
1971–1980:	Mean annual appreciation				0.098	0.088	0.011
	standard deviation				0.068	0.062	0.009
1981–1990:	Mean annual appreciation				0.022	0.024	−0.002
	standard deviation				0.029	0.030	0.011
1971–1994:	Mean annual appreciation				0.059	0.055	0.004
	standard deviation				0.060	0.054	0.011

Notes:
STD: Repeat-sales house value index estimated using standard procedures.
SEL: Repeat-sales house value index estimated using the bivariate sample selection correction procedure.
LAMBDA(1): Lambda from probit estimation of probability of a first sale.
LAMBDA(2): Lambda from probit estimation of probability of a second sale.
DEV: Denotes difference in the estimated annual percentage rate of change in STD and SEL, (DEV = ΔSTD − ΔSEL).

Substantial deviation between STD and SEL can be observed by casual inspection of the index values listed. STD and SEL are graphed in Figure 1, and a pattern of differences in the index movements between STD and SEL is evident. Inspection of Figure 1 suggests that the differences in the index levels may be cyclical. The spread between the indices increases during the mid to late 1970s and then converges in the early 1980s. Again, the index levels appear to diverge during the late 1980s until the end of the study period.

The annual percentage changes (annual appreciation rates) constructed from STD and SEL are also reported in Table 3. Case and Shiller (1989) suggest that the ratio of the standard deviation of the changes in the index level to the average standard error of the estimates is a useful indicator of the precision of index (or changes in the index) estimates. For the annual appreciation rates of STD and SEL, the ratio is 1.81 and 1.54, respectively. This indicates that the annual changes are measured with a reasonable degree of precision. Consistent with other studies, Table 3 indicates that appreciation during the 1970s was dramatically different than that of the 1980s. The average annual appreciation rate from 1971 to 1980 is estimated to be 9.8% and 8.8% by STD and SEL, respectively. In contrast, average annual appreciation during the period 1981 to 1990 was estimated to be only 2.2% and 2.4% by the two respective index methods. While the standard deviation of ΔSTD is similar to that of ΔSEL during the 1981–1990 period, it is almost 10% higher for ΔSTD during the more volatile 1971–1980 period.

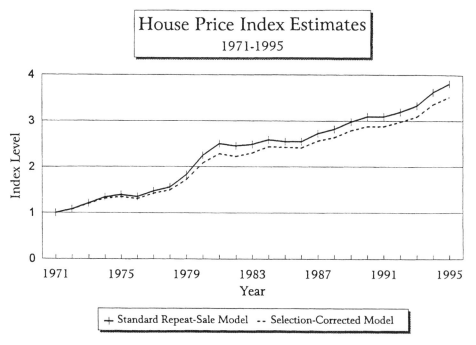

Figure 1.

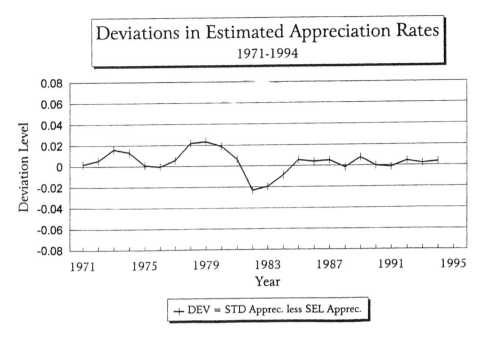

Figure 2.

The last column in Table 3 indicates the differences in the annual percentage changes in STD and SEL (DEV = ΔSTD $-$ ΔSEL). These differences are graphed in Figure 2. Two observations are apparent from inspection of the differences. First, they follow a serially correlated pattern. Second, the differences appear to be related to economic cycles. During periods of economic growth in the mid-1970s and 1980s, differences in the appreciation rates are positive; while during periods of economic slowdowns the differences are negative. This result suggests that biases in the standard repeat-sales index may be related to economic conditions affecting the offer and reservation prices.

To determine whether the deviations between the percentage changes in the indices are correlated with general economic variables, summary statistics of the economic indicators are first provided. Data are collected on five demographic and economic variables for the Miami MSA: (1) the annual percentage change in population, ΔPOP; (2) the annual percentage change in the number of nonagricultural jobs, ΔJOB; (3) the average annual unemployment rate, UER; (4) the annual number of house starts, stated as a percentage of the total housing stock, HSE; and (5) the annual percentage change in the real per capita income ΔINC.[17] The means, standard deviations, and minimum and maximum values of each of these variables are reported in Panel A of Table 4.

Simple correlation statistics between the variables and the annual percentage changes in STD and SEL are reported in Panel B of Table 4. The correlation between changes in the variables are, for the most part, consistent with expectations. Annual rates of appreciation as estimated by STD and SEL are found to be very highly correlated is estimated by STD

Table 4. Comparison statistics.
Miami MSA, 1971–1995

	Panel A: Summary Statistics of Annual Rates						
	ΔSTD	ΔSEL	ΔPOP	ΔJOB	UER	HSE	ΔINC
Mean	5.89	5.52	1.81	2.54	7.70	2.51	1.06
Std. Dev.	6.09	5.49	1.27	3.00	1.99	1.47	2.65
Minimum	−3.13	−3.23	0.01	−4.93	4.10	0.88	−5.61
Maximum	22.88	20.55	4.49	8.42	12.60	7.26	6.35

	Panel B: Correlations of Annual Rates						
ΔSTD	1.00						
ΔSEL	0.98	1.00					
ΔPOP	0.44	0.39	1.00				
ΔJOB	0.67	0.64	0.37	1.00			
UER	−0.40	−0.36	−0.37	−0.63	1.00		
HSE	0.44	0.41	0.64	0.70	−0.58	1.00	
ΔINC	0.33	0.25	0.44	0.41	−0.76	0.42	1.00

Notes:
Statistics in Panel A stated as percentages.
ΔSTD: Annual house price appreciation estimated using the standard repeat-sales model.
ΔSEL: Annual house price appreciation estimated including a selection correction variable in the repeat-sales model.
ΔPOP: Annual percentage change in the population (Miami MSA).
ΔJOB: Annual percentage change in the nonagricultural jobs (Miami MSA).
UER: Annual unemployment rate (Miami MSA).
HSE: Annual housing starts, stated as a percentage of the total housing stock (Miami MSA).
ΔINC: Annual percentage change in the per capita income ($1987) (Miami MSA).

and SEL are found to be very highly correlated (correlation coefficient = 0.98). Moderate to strong positive correlations are found between the percentage changes in both indices and ΔPOP, ΔJOB, HSE, and ΔINC. Consistent with this, UER is found to be negatively correlated with the annual house appreciation rates.

To examine whether the differences between the two indices are correlated with economic cycles, DEV is regressed on the economic factors. Table 5 reports the results of six OLS estimates. The first model, 1.1, regresses DEV on ΔPOP, ΔJOB, UER, HSE, and ΔINC. Because of the high degree of multicollinearity, only ΔJOB is found to be statistically significant at a 5% confidence level. However, these variables explain nearly 53% of the variation in DEV, as indicated by the R^2 statistic. The F-statistic of 4.01 is statistically significant at a 5% level.

Regression estimates are also reported for each of the variables regressed independently. DEV is significantly positively correlated with ΔPOP, ΔJOB, and ΔINC; and significantly negatively correlated with UER. These results suggest that the standard repeat-sales model overestimates increases in the value of the housing stock during periods of growth, as well

Table 5. Regression of deviation in appreciation on selected economic variables. Miami MSA, 1971–1995

$$(\text{DEV}_t = \beta_0 + \Sigma \beta_N \text{ VARB}_{Nt} + e_t)$$

VAR	1.1 β (t-stat)	2.1 β (t-stat)	2.2 β (t-stat)	2.3 β (t-stat)	2.4 β (t-stat)	2.5 β (t-stat)
β_0	−0.015 (−0.982)	−0.004 (−1.041)	−0.001 (−0.512)	0.022 (2.579)	−0.003 (−0.796)	0.001 (0.686)
ΔPOP	0.293 (1.505)	0.414 (2.575)				
ΔJOB	0.221 (2.436)		0.200 (3.077)			
UER	0.151 (0.901)			−0.234 (−2.196)		
HSE	−0.222 (−1.047)				0.286 (1.956)	
ΔINC	0.199 (1.816)					0.225 (3.045)
Obs.	24	24	24	24	24	24
R^2	0.53	0.23	0.30	0.18	0.15	0.30
Adj-R^2	0.40	0.20	0.27	0.14	0.11	0.26
F-stat.	4.01	6.63	9.47	4.82	3.83	9.27

Notes:

DEV: Denotes Δ STD − Δ SEL.

VARB: Denotes a vector of independent variables.

ΔPOP: Annual percentage change in the population (Miami MSA).

ΔJOB: Annual percentage change in the nonagricultural jobs (Miami MSA).

UER: Annual unemployment rate (Miami MSA).

HSE: Annual housing starts, stated as a percentage of the total housing stock (Miami MSA).

ΔINC: Annual percentage change in the per capita income ($1987) (Miami MSA).

as underestimates the movements during periods of economic weakness. Hence, deviations between STD, the standard observed index, and SEL, the "true" index, are found to be related to economic cycles.

Finally, there exists weak evidence that the standard repeat-sales index magnifies the actual movements of the value of the overall housing stock. This is illustrated by the relatively small increase in the coefficient of variation of the appreciation rates estimated using STD versus SEL for the 1971–1994 period in Table 3 and by regression analysis. Regressing annual changes in SEL on DEV yields a positive and significant beta coefficient (2.42; *t*-stat = 2.58). This suggests that estimates of STD magnify the "true" changes in the value of the housing stock. However, there is only a small increase in the coefficient of variation of the appreciation rates of the STD versus that of SEL (1.017 versus 0.982) for the entire 1971–1994 period, and this increase is not found in all subperiods. Thus, evidence that the standard repeat-sales index magnifies the "true" index due to sample selection bias is weak.

5. Conclusion

Reliable estimates of changes in the value of housing require careful consideration of the sample used in the analysis. Because only a small percentage of houses typically sell each year (or some other measured interval), the sample of houses that sell may have nonrandom statistical properties which can bias the index estimate.

This study reports evidence that changing economic conditions affect the statistical composition of the sample of sold homes. Sales only occur if the property is marketed and the offer price exceeds the seller's reservation price. When variations in economic conditions affect offer and reservation prices, then a sample composed only of the sold houses changes in a nonrandom manner. Regression estimates using this sample result in estimated house value variations that differ from the true variation in values of the stock.

To correct for this type of sample selection bias requires application of the Heckman selection correction model. This study extends previous work by adapting the truncated bivariate procedure to the repeat-sales model. While the repeat-sales method holds constant house quality (subject to the limitations noted), the sales may have occurred during different economic conditions. For example, a particular house may first sell in a downturn and later sell during an upturn. Nonrandomness of samples in any years of the series may bias the estimate of the price index.

Using data from Miami, an index constructed using the standard repeat-sales estimation procedure is compared to a selection corrected regression estimate of house value changes. Indices based on the standard repeat-sales method are found to be biased upward during periods of economic growth and downward during periods of economic weakness—consistent with previous work by Gatzlaff and Haurin (1994). However, there is only weak evidence that standard index procedures tend to magnify the "true" cyclical movements of the price of the housing stock. Further testing using data from other localities is needed to yield definitive results.

Acknowledgments

This article was originally presented as a paper at the American Real Estate and Urban Economics Association National Meetings in Washington D.C. in January, 1995. The authors thank Caroline Kreimer for her technical assistance.

Notes

1. In 1991, homeownership accounted for 41.9% of the median household's total net wealth (Eller, 1994). Hartzell, Pittman, and Downs (1994) estimate the aggregate value of U.S. residential property in 1989 to be $8.7 trillion.
2. A number of responses to Mankiw and Weil are contained in a special issue of *Regional Science and Urban Economics* (1992).
3. Lancaster and Chesher (1981) address the question of whether samples drawn from a stock and samples drawn from a corresponding flow have similar properties. They provide a generalized version of the model which Gatzlaff and Haurin apply to housing.

4. This model can also be used to estimate an index of constant-quality house prices for varying locations.

5. Recall that the P are in natural logs.

6. Econometric problems related to heteroskedasticity of the repeat-sales method have been noted by Case and Shiller (1989) and Goodman and Thibodeau (1995).

7. The variance of ϵ_{it}^R is defined as $(\sigma^R)^2$, that of ϵ_{it}^O as $(\sigma^O)^2$, and the covariance as σ_{OR} (all assumed to be constant over time). Application of the Heckman procedure requires one of two assumptions. The model is identified if $\sigma_{OR} = 0$; or if offer prices depend on some explanatory variables not included in the reservation prices. It is likely that omitted explanatory variables yield a nonzero covariance (σ_{OR}); thus, the estimation technique requires the presence of some explanatory variables in only the offer equation.

8. Also, the information about when a once sold property sells again is not used in the repeat-sales method, because the second sale, if it occurs, is outside the sample range.

9. Of course the observed first sales not included in the repeat-sales data set remain available. As will be explained later, we use this "additional" information in our estimation of sample selection bias.

10. In the typical sequential estimation problem, a group of events is initially observed, then second events occur for only some of those cases experiencing a first event. In the repeat-sales approach, although a first sale occurs for many houses, the first sale data only enter the analysis once a second sale occurs. Thus, the condition for observing P_{it}^1 in (15) differs from the usual sequential selection analysis.

11. They are also defined in the user's manual for the econometric software program used in this study, LIMDEP.

12. An example of correlation would be if a property had a defect difficult for a buyer to recognize, but obvious once residence was established. This property would tend to sell frequently, but the cause would be unobservable.

13. This method takes advantage of the information contained in observations of first sales that are not followed by second sales in the sample period. Thus, the sample size of the first probit is the entire sample and "1"s are coded for any first sale, even if not followed by a second sale. The sample in the second probit consists of all properties at risk of a second sale, some of which sell, and others which do not. All never-sold properties (2,650) are eliminated from the second probit.

14. In the initial bivariate estimate where ρ is estimated, ρ did not converge; hence, $\rho = 0$ in the results reported. This bivariate approach continues to account for the truncation in the second-sale sample. Thus, the results in Panel B of Table 2 differ comparing the probit and bivariate probit methods.

15. The simple correlation coefficient for λ_1 and λ_2 is 0.03.

16. If the correlation among errors in the sale and price equations only occurs for the first-sale occurrence with the first-sale price and the second-sale occurrence and second-sale price, then the cross terms σ_{14} and σ_{23} will be 0. This implies that the coefficients of the lambdas will have opposite signs if the two remaining correlations have the same sign.

17. The local economic data were obtained from the University of Florida's Bureau of Economic and Business Research.

References

Bailey, M. J., R. F. Muth, and H. O. Nourse. "A Regression Method for Real Estate Price Index Construction." *Journal of the American Statistical Association* 58 (304) (1963), 933–942.

Case, B., and J. Quigley. "The Dynamics of Real Estate Prices," *Review of Economics and Statistics* 73 (3) (1991), 50–58.

Case, B., H. Pollakowski, and S. Wachter. "On Choosing Among House Price Index Methodologies," *AREUEA Journal* 19 (3) (Fall 1991), 286–307.

Case, K., and R. Shiller. "The Efficiency of the Market for Single-Family Homes," *American Economic Review* 79 (1) (March 1989), 125–37.

Dhrymes, P. J. "Limited Dependent Variables." In Z. Griliches and M. Intrilligator (eds.), *Handbook of Econometrics.* Amsterdam: Elsevier Science Publishers, 1986.

Eller, T. J. *Household Wealth and Asset Ownership: 1991.* U. S. Bureau of the Census, Current Population Reports. Washington: U.S. Government Printing Office, P70-34, 1994.

Fishe, R. P., R. P. Trost, and P. Lurie. "Labor Force Earnings and College Choice of Young Women: An Examination of Selectivity Bias and Comparative Advantage," *Economics of Education Review* 1 (1981), 169–191.

Gatzlaff, D., and D. Haurin. "Sample Selection and Biases in Local House Value Indices." Working paper, The Ohio State University, 1994.

Gatzlaff, D., and D. Ling. "Measuring Changes in Local House Prices: An Empirical Investigation of Alternative Methodologies," *Journal of Urban Economics* 35 (2) (1994), 221–244.

Goodman, A., and T. Thibodeau. "Heteroskedasticity in Repeat-Sale House Price Equations." Working paper, Wayne State University, 1995.

Greene, W. "Sample Selection Bias as a Specification Error: Comment," *Econometrica* 49 (3) (May 1981), 795–798.

Hartzell, D., R. Pittman, and D. Downs. "An Updated Look at the Size of the U.S. Real Estate Market Portfolio," *Journal of Real Estate Research* 9 (2) (Spring 1994), 197–212.

Haurin, D., and P. Hendershott. "House Price Indexes: Issues and Results," *AREUEA Journal* 19 (3) (Fall 1991), 259–269.

Heckman, J. "Shadow Prices, Market Wages, and Labor Supply," *Econometrica* 42 (1974), 679–694.

Heckman, J. "Sample Selection Bias as a Specification Error," *Econometrica* 47 (1979), 153–161.

Hendershott, P., and T. Thibodeau. "The Relationship between Median and Constant Quality House Prices: Implications for Setting FHA Loan Limits," *AREUEA Journal* 18 (3) (Fall 1990), 323–334.

Hosios, A. J., and J. E. Pesando. "Measuring Prices in Resale Housing Markets in Canada: Evidence and Implications," *Journal of Housing Economics* 1 (1) (1991), 1–15.

Ihlanfeldt, K. R., and J. Martinez-Vazquez. "Alternative Value Estimates of Owner-Occupied Housing: Evidence on Sample Selection Bias and Systematic Errors," *Journal of Urban Economics* 20 (3) (November 1986), 357–369.

Lancaster, T., and A. Chesher. "Stock and Flow Sampling," *Economic Letters* 8 (1981), 63–65.

Lee, Lung-Fei, and G. S. Maddala. "Sequential Selection Rules and Selectivity in Discrete Choice Econometric Models," *Econometric Methods and Applications II.* 1985, pp. 311–329.

Maddala, G.S. *Limited Dependent and Qualitative Variables in Econometrics.* Cambridge: Cambridge University Press, 1985.

Mankiw, G., and D. Weil. "The Baby Boom, the Baby Bust, and the Housing Market," *Regional Science and Urban Economics* 19 (2) (May 1989), 235–258.

Poirier, D. J. "Partial Observability in Bivariate Probit Models," *Journal of Econometrics* 12 (1980), 209–219.

Rosen, S. "Hedonic Prices and Implicit Markets: Product Differentiation in Pure Competition," *Journal of Political Economy* 82 (1) (1974), 34–55.

Tallis, G. M. "The Moment Generating Function of the Truncated Multi-Normal Distribution," *Journal of the Royal Statistical Society,* (Series B) 23 (1961), 223–229.

Tunali, I. "A Common Structure for Models of Double Selection." Working paper, University of Wisconsin–Madison, 1983.

Journal of Real Estate Finance and Economics, 14: 51–73 (1997)
©1997 Kluwer Academic Publishers

The Construction of Residential Housing Price Indices: A Comparison of Repeat-Sales, Hedonic-Regression, and Hybrid Approaches

RICHARD A. MEESE
Haas School of Business, University of California, Berkeley, CA 94720-1900

NANCY E. WALLACE
Haas School of Business, University of California, Berkeley, CA 94720-1900

Abstract

This article examines a number of hypotheses that underpin the repeat-sales and hedonic approaches to the construction of housing price indices, as well as the practical problems associated with the implementation of either approach. We also examine a hybrid procedure that combines elements of both the repeat-sales and hedonic-regression techniques. For our sample of individual home sales in Oakland and Fremont California over an 18-year period, repeat-sales methods are subject to sample selection bias; the maintained assumption of time constancy of implicit prices of housing attributes is violated; the repeat-sales estimator is extremely sensitive to influential observations; and the usual method used to correct for heteroskedasticity in repeat-sale housing returns is inappropriate in our sample. Hedonic techniques are better suited to contend with index number problems per se, as they can accommodate changing attribute prices over time. They also appear to give rise to more reliable estimates of price indices, as unusual observations have less effect on estimated price indices. Drawbacks of the hedonic approach include the usual concern with omitted attributes, and their effect on the estimated price index.

Key Words: repeat sales, hedonic models, price index estimation, housing prices

Introduction

The accurate measurement of real estate price change is important to our understanding of aggregate wealth and investment behavior, the efficiency of the housing market, and recent regional real estate cycles in the Northeast, Texas, and California. Indeed, financial economists frequently cite measurement error in real estate prices as the primary reason for their lack of focus on real estate markets (relative to the markets for stocks, bonds, and foreign exchange), despite the fact that real estate represents at least half of aggregate U.S. wealth. Likewise, macroeconomists working with optimizing models of aggregate behavior rarely explore the role that real estate price fluctuations play in the duration of regional and national business cycles.

It is unlikely that our understanding of regional business cycles will improve without refinements in the measurement of local housing price changes. For example, the most widely reported measure of real estate price trends is the National Association of Realtors quarterly publication of median sales prices of existing single-family homes from more than 100 metropolitan areas. A median sales price index makes no attempt to control for the types of homes sold during different phases of the business cycle, and is thus of limited use in the study of regional fluctuations.

Methods to control for variation in the types of homes sold over time include both the hedonic-regression and repeat-sales approaches to the construction of housing price indices. The construction of housing price indices using hedonic-regression models involves a two-step process. First, one estimates a regression of house sales price on a set of house attributes (e.g., square footage, a proxy for quality, number of bathrooms, etc.), and a constant term for each time period. These intercepts account for any trend in housing prices over the sample period, while the hedonic attributes control for the types of homes sold during any given time period.

The second step of the hedonic-regression approach is to use the estimates of the implicit attribute prices to construct a housing price index.[1] In what follows, we utilize a Fisher ideal price index; it is the geometric average of the Paasche (terminal period attribute weights) and Laspeyres (initial period attribute weights) price indices. The theory underlying the construction of price indices from hedonic-regression models first requires that attributes or characteristics of the heterogeneous good "housing" enter agents' utility functions rather than the housing itself. Rosen (1974) is the classic reference. Second, Triplett (1983) provides the necessary extension of index number theory to handle a composite good's characteristics and implicit characteristic prices.

Drawbacks to the hedonic-regression approach include ignorance of both the functional form of the relation and of the appropriate set of house characteristics to include in the analysis. Both problems can result in inconsistent estimates of the implicit prices of the attributes. Researchers have dealt with the functional form issue by using either flexible parameterizations of the model or nonparametric techniques.[2] The second drawback is more difficult to deal with, as it plagues all research in empirical economics. Consistent estimates of implicit hedonic prices will rely on the rather heroic assumption that all omitted variables are orthogonal to those included in the analysis.

In the repeat-sales methodology for constructing house price indices, researchers control for hedonic characteristics by examining only those properties that have sold more than once during the sample, *without* any change in house characteristics between sales. A modification to the original regression methodology of Bailey, Muth, and Nourse (1963), hereafter BMN, has recently been suggested by Case and Shiller (1987, 1989). The researcher codes the dates of the first and subsequent sales of the same house using dummy variables. An ordinary least-squares (OLS) regression of the logarithmic price change on the appropriately defined dummy variables results in a consistent estimate of average housing price change over the observation period.

Since the time between sales varies by property, the Case and Shiller (1987) modification to BMN involves a generalized least-squares (GLS) correction to account for the possibility of time-dependent error variances. In addition, Case and Shiller (1987) allow for a fixed variance component unrelated to the holding period between sales. The feasible GLS estimator proposed by the latter authors requires an auxiliary regression of the squared OLS residuals (obtained from a BMN repeat-sales regression) on a constant and the time between sales. Fitted values from this auxiliary regression are used to construct the weighted least-squares estimator in the usual manner. The procedure will result in more efficient parameter estimates (and consistent standard error estimates of the estimated coefficients) if the hypothesized error variance structure is correct.

The index number problem would appear not to plague the repeat-sales approach, as the attribute function (estimated implicit prices times the appropriate set of base-year attributes) drops out of the calculation of the price index. The repeat-sales price index for period t is obtained as the estimated GLS coefficient on the period t dummy variable, which is a minimum-variance weighted average of logarithmic price changes of properties that sold in all periods.

However, there are two important maintained hypotheses in the repeat-sales approach that are testable, if one has access to data on house attributes. The first is that the subsample of homes that sold more than once is representative of all home sales during the period. The second maintained hypothesis is that the implicit attribute prices are constant over time so that the attribute prices cancel in the construction of the housing price index. Both assumptions are easily testable; they amount to zero restrictions on a set of appropriately defined dummy variables in a general, dynamic, hedonic model of housing prices. In the next section, we describe the statistical tests of the two hypotheses, and report the test results.

In section 3, we compare a median sales price index to price indices generated by the repeat-sales approach, the hedonic-regression method, and a hybrid procedure that combines elements of the latter two methodologies. The hybrid approach is suggested by Quigley (1995); the additional structure which he imposes will again result in more efficient parameter estimates, provided the hypothesized error structure is correct.[3] We examine whether there are important qualitative differences between the four price indices when they are applied to the same data sets. We also consider additional problems associated with the implementation of the repeat-sales approach; these include the sensitivity of the estimated price index to influential observations, and the lack of conformity of the model's residuals to the assumption about disturbance variances. Section 5 summarizes our findings.

1. Test Methodology for Sample Selection Bias and Time Constancy of Implicit Prices

The first set of hypothesis tests which we consider are subsumed in the general hedonic model:

$$P_{i(t)} = \sum_{t=1}^{T} [\alpha_t D_t^1 + \beta\prime_t x_{i(t)} + x\prime_{i(t)} \Omega_t x_{i(t)} + \gamma\prime_t D_t^2 x_{i(t)} + D_t^2 x\prime_{i(t)} \Lambda_t x_{i(t)}] + \epsilon_{i(t)}, \qquad (1)$$

where $p_{i(t)}$ is the logarithm of the ith house sold in period t; D_t with a superscript 1 is a dummy variable for each time period of the analysis equal to 1 for period t and zero otherwise; D_t with a superscript 2 is a dummy variable equal to 1 for repeat sales observations and zero otherwise; $x_{i(t)}$ is a vector of the logarithm of house characteristics; $\epsilon_{i(t)}$ is a regression disturbance term; and all other Greek letters represent regression parameters to be estimated.[4] We use the notation $i(t)$ to denote individual observations, because the number of homes sold in any time period $i(t)$ differs for each period and is typically a function of the business cycle; i.e., we are NOT analyzing a panel data set. Equation (1) is a translog hedonic equation for house price that allows for separate intercepts for each time period, different slope coefficients for each period, and different slope coefficients for each time period for both single-sale and repeat-sale observations.

In the tests that follow, the x vector is composed of five attribute variables: the number of bathrooms, the ratio of bedrooms to total rooms, square footage, an index of house quality, and house age. Typically, all implicit attribute prices are positive, except for the ratio variable. In previous work (Meese and Wallace, 1993), we found that the ratio of bedrooms to total rooms produced a model with more defensible signs on its estimated coefficients than in a less constrained model where bedrooms and total room enter with separate coefficients. The total rooms variable is highly collinear with square footage. The ratio of bedrooms to total rooms variable gets at the idea that if you subdivide a house into too many bedrooms, it detracts from house value. We do not have a strong prior about the sign of the coefficient for the age variable, although it typically proxies for neighborhood effects (established community, older trees, etc.) and is hence positively priced. We report results of hypothesis tests for the five-variable model only. However, our conclusions are robust to six variable specifications (unconstrained bedroom and total room variables) as well.

We estimate several models that are subsumed in (1) for the cities of Oakland and Fremont California over the period 1970–1988 (see the Appendix 1 for sources). Our Oakland (Fremont) sample has 27,606 (23,408) total home sales observations, of which 3,342 (3,405) are repeat sales.[5]

Tests 1 and 2 examine the first implicit hypothesis of the repeat-sales approach, namely, that the repeat sales are representative of all homes sold during the sample period. In order to test this hypothesis, we consider two models subsumed in (1); we estimate both a five-variable translog (Test 1) and a five-variable log-linear (Test 2) specification.[6] Both models allow the two subsets of data to have different parameters. A small F-statistic is consistent with the null hypothesis that the dummy variable interaction terms are jointly zero (i.e., that both single-sale and repeat-sale houses have the same implicit prices.) We perform both a conventional F-test and a robust Chi-square test suggested by White (1980). The latter test allows for heteroskedasticity of unknown form in the disturbance vector ϵ.

Next we consider tests of the second maintained assumption of the repeat-sales approach, namely, that implicit attribute prices are constant over time. Test 3 compares a five-variable translog with separate intercepts and slopes for each year with a restricted model having 19 intercepts but common slope coefficients across observations. Test 4 compares a five-variable log-linear model with slope coefficients and an intercept that can change every year to a model that allows for a separate intercept each year, but common slope coefficients.

In addition to the four hypothesis tests, we report normality tests for the residuals of each model. The robust Chi-square procedure obviates the need to report a direct test for heteroskedasticity, and tests for serial correlation do not apply in the present context.

2. Empirical Results

Tables 1a and 1b contain the results of the four hypothesis tests for Oakland and Fremont, respectively. Columns correspond to Tests 1–4, and rows provide information about each

Table 1a. Hypothesis tests for equality of repeat- and single-sale implicit attribute prices (Tests 1 and 2), and equality of implicit attribute prices over time (Tests 3 and 4): City of Oakland.

Test[1]	1. Translog: Single vs. Repeat Sales	2. Log-linear: Single vs. Repeat Sales	3. Translog: Constancy of Parameters	4. Logarithm: Constancy of Parameters
Restrictions[2]	$527 - 272 = 255$	$198 - 108 = 90$	$399 - 39 = 360$	$114 - 24 = 90$
F-statistic	9.89	27.26	12.44	42.71
(p-value)	(0.00)	(0.00)	(0.00)	(0.00)
Chi-square	7875.8	3251.9	6184.	4228.
(p-value)	(0.00)	(0.00)	(0.00)	(0.00)
KS-Normality[3]	.21	.22	.21	.21
(p-value)	($< .01$)	($< .01$)	($< .01$)	($< .01$)
Time period[4]	1972–1988	1971–1988	1970–1988	1970–1988

All tests are based on 27,606 observations of which 3,342 are repeat sales with attributes that did not change between transactions.

1. For Test 1, the null hypothesis is that γ and Λ are jointly zero in (1); for Test 2, γ is zero conditional on Ω and Λ equal to zero; for Test 3, β and Ω are constant over time conditional on γ and Λ equal to zero; and for Test 4, β is constant over time conditional on Ω, γ, and Λ equal to zero.
2. The first number in the restriction row is the number of parameters in the unconstrained model, the second is the number of parameters in the constrained model, and the third is their difference (the number of linear constraints tested).
3. The Kolmogorov–Smirnov test of normality. The asymptotic formula for the significance levels 10%, 5%, and 1% are, respectively, $1.22/N^{.5}$, $1.36/N^{.5}$, and $1.63/N^{.5}$. For sample size $N = 23,947$, these numbers are .0079, .0088, and .0153 (see Lindgren, 1968). In all cases, the test statistic reported is for the unconstrained version of the model.
4. Repeat- versus single-sale tests are based on 17 or 18 years of data, since there are insufficient repeat-sales observations at the beginning of the sample to allow for separate coefficients in 1970 (log linear) and the 1970–1971 period (translog).

test. In all cases, we reject the hypothesis that the repeat- and single-sale observations have the same implicit prices; Tests 1 and 2 have marginal significance levels (p-values) of zero to three decimal places for both Oakland and Fremont. In our sample, the repeat-sales homes that did not change attributes are slightly smaller, and are in worse condition, than the average for single-sale homes.[7] The repeat-sales homes that did have attribute changes (about half of the repeat sales) tend to be slightly larger and in worse condition, than the average for single-sale homes; (see Table 2 for a comparison of attribute means and standard deviations for the three subsets of our sample).[8]

We always reject the null hypothesis that implicit prices remain constant over time (Tests 3 and 4). Here, p-values are again zero to three decimal places. The heteroskedasticity-consistent test statistics also reject the null of constant implicit prices over time. Tests for normality of the errors of any particular model reject the null of normality. In each case, we have more outlier observations than is consistent with normal distribution theory. However allowing for a fatter tail error distribution (e.g., by bootstrapping) is not likely to overturn our rejection of either null hypothesis, as the p-values for all test statistics are minuscule.

Table 1b. Hypothesis tests for equality of repeat- and single-sale implicit attribute prices (Tests 1 and 2), and equality of implicit attribute prices over time (Tests 3 and 4): City of Fremont.

Test[1]	1. Translog: Single vs. Repeat Sales	2. Log-linear: Single vs. Repeat Sales	3. Translog: Constancy of Parameters	4. Logarithm: Constancy of Parameters
Restrictions[2]	$527 - 272 = 255$	$198 - 108 = 90$	$399 - 39 = 360$	$114 - 24 = 90$
F-statistic	20.83	57.11	31.15	126.6
(p-value)	(.000)	(.000)	(.000)	(.000)
Chi-square	17,583.	9860.	14,220.	11,714.
(p-value)	(.000)	(.000)	(.000)	(.000)
KS-Normality[3]	.20	.20	NA	.19
(p-value)	(< .01)	(< .01)	( )	(< .01)
Time period[4]	1972–1988	1971–1988	1970–1988	1970–1988

All tests are based on 23,408 observations of which 3,405 are repeat sales with attributes that did not change between transactions.

1. For Test 1, the null hypothesis is that γ and Λ are jointly zero in (1); for Test 2, γ is zero conditional on Ω and Λ equal to zero; for Test 3, β and Ω are constant over time conditional on γ and Λ equal to zero; and for Test 4, β is constant over time conditional on Ω, γ, and Λ equal to zero.
2. The first number in the restriction row is the number of parameters in the unconstrained model, the second is the number of parameters in the constrained model, and the third is their difference (the number of linear constraints tested).
3. The Kolmogorov–Smirnov test of normality. The asymptotic formula for the significanfce levels 10%, 5%, and 1% are, respectively, $1.22/N^5$, $1.36/N^5$, and $1.63/N^5$. For sample size $N = 23,947$, these numbers are .0079, .0088, and .0153 (see Lindgren, 1968). In all cases, the test statistic reported is for the unconstrained version of the model.
4. Repeat- versus single-sale tests are based on 17 or 18 years of data, since there are insufficient repeat-sales observations at the beginning of the sample to allow for separate coefficients in 1970 (log linear) and the 1970–1971 period (translog).

We do, however, deal with the issue of outlier observations and their effect on estimated price indices in the next section.

In sum, we find evidence against both maintained hypotheses of the repeat-sales approach; we reject lack of sample selection bias in repeat-sales data sets and constancy of implicit attribute prices over time. This result obtains with either the full set of data, or the subset of repeat-sales observations.[9]

3. Differences in Estimated Price Indexes Constructed from the Same Data Sets

In this section, we consider whether sample selection bias and time variation in attribute prices are of practical importance, by comparing the price indices generated by the repeat-sales, hedonic, and a hybrid approach to a median sales price index using the same data sets. We test for differences in the covariance structure of the generated price series, and also address the issue of estimation efficiency. Repeat-sales indices are based on less information

Table 2a. Attribute means and standard deviations for repeat-sales sample without attribute changes, repeat-sales sample with attribute changes, and single-sale sample for Oakland.

Variables	Repeat-Sales Sample with no Change in Attributes (n = 3342)		Repeat-Sales Sample with Changes in Attributes (n = 4772)		Single-Sale Sample (n = 19,492)	
	Mean	Standard Deviation	Mean	Standard Deviation	Mean	Standard Deviation
Number of bathrooms	1.4	.59	1.5	.66	1.5	.64
Number of bedrooms	2.6	.75	2.8	.95	2.7	.88
Living area (sq. ft.)	1459	548.7	1624	628.4	1538	637.9
Number of rooms	5.8	1.24	6.2	1.39	5.9	1.46
Condition of property	2.3	.53	2.3	.62	3.7	.64
Age of property	42.1	16.5	41.6	15.6	41.6	17.5
Price (nominal dollars)	73,540.03	53,761.51	82,777.81	65,806.51	72,011.68	65,353.12

Table 2b. Attribute means and standard deviations for repeat-sales sample without attribute changes, repeat-sales sample with attribute changes, and single-sale sample for Fremont.

Variables	Repeat-Sales Sample with no Change in Attributes (n = 3405)		Repeat-Sales Sample with Changes in Attributes (n = 3064)		Single-Sale Sample (n = 16,939)	
	Mean	Standard Deviation	Mean	Standard Deviation	Mean	Standard Deviation
Number of bathrooms	1.8	.48	1.8	.54	2.0	.50
Number of bedrooms	3.3	.64	3.2	.69	3.4	.73
Living area (sq. ft.)	1469.1	430.6	1533.4	562.7	1614.4	539.8
Number of rooms	6.2	1.22	6.3	1.29	6.5	1.32
Condition of property	2.1	.53	2.1	.64	4.0	.58
Age of property	67.5	9.09	68.0	9.23	71.1	11.0
Price (nominal dollars)	89,484.83	58,826.19	90,801.93	69,465.61	100,650.35	99,985.54

than the indices generated by the hedonic regression, but they impose more structure on the disturbance covariance matrix. Hybrid indices exploit all the data and impose structure on the disturbance covariance matrix for the repeat transactions. The last issue which we examine in this section is the sensitivity of the repeat-sales, hedonic-regression, and hybrid procedures to influential observations.

Before getting to a comparison of the indices, we address several operational issues that arise during estimation of the indices. These include a description of the methodologies used for the auxiliary regression of the repeat-sales procedure, an explanation of the nonparametric regression procedure which we employ, and the underlying model for the hybrid price index procedure.

The repeat-sales price index is generated using Case and Shiller's (1987) methodology.[10] Their generalized least-squares technique requires an auxiliary regression of the squared residuals from the OLS fit of price change on a set of appropriately defined dummy variables to generate GLS weights.[11]

Another technical issue regarding the estimation of the repeat-sales price index is whether to include the constant term. The usual procedure is to regress the logarithm of all price changes (for homes selling at least twice) on a set of $(T - 1)$ dummy variables, where T is the number of time periods in the sample (76 quarters in our case.) Since the dummy variables are coded with -1 for an initial sale and $+1$ for a subsequent sale, the first column of the design matrix is omitted to avoid perfect multicollinearity (the row sum of all T variables would be zero). However, some authors include a constant term in the regression along with the appropriately defined dummy variables. Goetzman and Spiegel (1995) include a constant term, and argue that it controls for a homeowner's investment in property improvements prior to sale. Case and Shiller (1987, 1989) leave out the constant term in their published work.[12]

In Figure 1, we graph the Case and Shiller feasible GLS index (without a constant term) for the city of Oakland.[13] As a benchmark for comparison, we include the median sale price index (rationale provided below) in all figures where price indices are plotted. In Figure 1, we also graph the repeat-sales price index generated from the original Bailey, Muth, and Nourse OLS procedure, since we do not find evidence in favor of disturbance specification underlying the Case and Shiller GLS procedure (again see the discussion below.) The

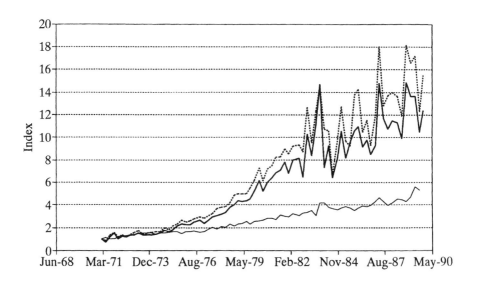

Figure 1. Repeat sales index: Oakland.

repeat-sales price index estimates are consistently higher than the median sales price index, so much so that they are not credible. The repeat-sales methodology suggests about a 12-fold increase in housing prices over our sample, while the median sales price index indicates an increase of about half that amount. The repeat-sales index is also highly variable relative to the median index.

The hedonic price index is generated using nonparametric estimates of the implicit attribute prices, as described in Meese and Wallace (1991). The nonparametric procedure that we utilize is locally weighted regression (LWR) (see Cleveland and Devlin, 1988). LWR can be used to estimate the attribute function $G(x)$ in the equation

$$P_{i(t)} - \overline{P_t} = G(x_{i(t)}) + u_{i(t)},$$

$$\overline{P_t} = \frac{1}{N(t)} \sum_{i(t)=1}^{N(t)} P_{i(t)}, \tag{2}$$

where $N(t)$ is the total number of home sales in period t. Since LWR requires stationary dependent and independent variables, we remove the trend in $p_{i(t)}$ by subtracting the quarterly mean of the dependent variable each quarter. The function G is estimated by running a weighted least-squares regression each time period, using a "window" of observations in a neighborhood of the "median" house sold each quarter. Weights are inverse functions of the Euclidean distance between the median house (standardized) attributes, and the attributes of other houses in the observation window.[14]

An important operational issue associated with LWR is the choice of window width (i.e., the percentage of all observations in the observation window). A small (large) window size corresponds to more (less) "implicit" parameters. LWR with a window size of 100% (i.e., one that uses all the data to estimate $G(x)$ at each point in the sample) is similar to parametric weighted least-squares with weights determined by the distance metric described above. Note that the researcher faces the usual bias—sampling variability tradeoff when determining window size. Fewer observations in the smoothing window is equivalent to more implicit parameters in the regression, and more implicit parameters improves the fit (decreases bias) at the expense of increased sampling variability. Our experiments suggest that a 30% window size provides for the best balance between bias and sampling variability.[15]

Having estimated (2) by LWR, the dynamic hedonic price index is then constructed by adjusting the quarterly average housing price by the LWR estimates of the implicit attribute prices for each quarter. Initial year and current year (median) attribute quantity weights are used to form the Paasche and Laspeyres price indices, respectively. The geometric average of these two price indices is the Fisher Ideal index noted earlier; it is plotted in Figure 2, again relative to the median sales price index.

The next procedure for constructing housing price indices is a hybrid approach suggested by Quigley (1995). This approach blends the repeat-sales method with a parametric hedonic regression. The value added is to posit a structure for the error variance of homes that sold more than once, and to exploit this structure while estimating the price index using ALL data points. Repeat sales allow the researcher to estimate a component of house price due to

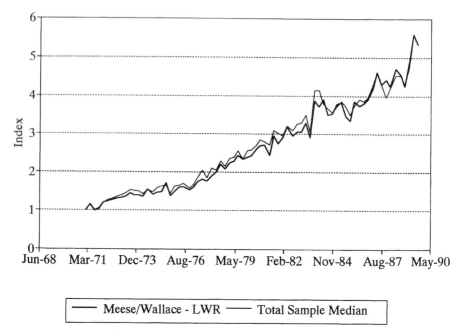

Figure 2. Fisher Ideal price index: Oakland.

idiosyncratic elements. These elements cannot be estimated from a data set consisting of single sales alone.

The structure of the error variance is derived from both a random walk assumption on housing price, and from previous empirical work:[16]

$$E(\epsilon_i(t) - \epsilon_i(\tau))^2 = [\delta(t - \tau) + \xi(t - \tau)^2]\sigma_\epsilon^2, \tag{3}$$

where $\epsilon_i(t)$ is the composite disturbance, τ is the date of the initial transaction, t the date of the subsequent transaction, δ and ξ are parameters, and σ^2 with subscript ϵ is the variance of $\epsilon_i(t)$. Case and Shiller (1987, 1989) specify $\xi = 0$ and find δ (statistically) greater than zero, while Quigley and Van Order (1995) find $\delta > 0, \xi < 0$, using data at a more aggregate level than is used in this study (i.e., metropolitan areas, as well as five census regions). We do not find support for either specification, as the estimated values of δ and ξ are indistinguishable from zero. In addition, plots of the square of $\epsilon_i(t)$ versus time between sales reveal a "U"-shaped pattern (see Figure 3). Since our residual patterns are inconsistent with disturbance variance specification (3), we provide both GLS and OLS variants of the Quigley index, along with the median sale price index, in Figure 4.

Since the "true" constant quality house price index is unobservable, we use the simple median sales price index as a benchmark to compare the more sophisticated repeat-sales, hedonic, and hybrid approaches. The median sales price index is the most widely used, and easiest to construct index of housing price change. The series in included in Figures 1, 2, and 4 as a reference series. We also provide a 95% confidence interval for the median sales

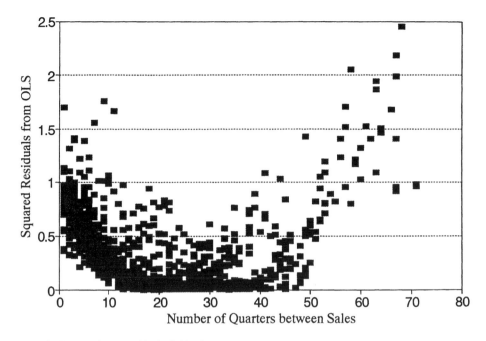

Figure 3. Repeat sales sq. residuals: Oakland.

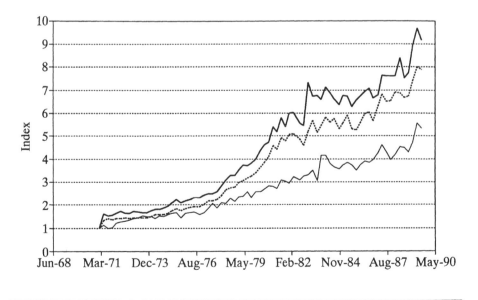

Figure 4. Hybrid index: Oakland.

price index generated from the full sample of home sales data in Figure 5.[17] Here we plot a single variant of each of our three price indices against the benchmark median index.

As noted earlier, the repeat-sales and the hybrid repeat-sales procedure do not produce reliable estimates of the price indices for the municipalities of Fremont and Oakland. The 19-year price increases obtained for Oakland and Fremont are in the neighborhood of 1200%. The other median and nonparametric hedonic regression price indices show house price appreciation of around 500% for Oakland and in excess of 700% for Fremont.

In Appendix 2, we highlight numerical problems that can arise when a researcher constructs a repeat-sales index on what we term "sparse" data sets. At first glance, it might appear that our sample of repeat-sales observations would be sufficiently large to yield a reliable estimate of a repeat-sales index over a 76-quarter period. We estimate 76 regression parameters using about 1700 repeat-sale observations per municipality, and this hardly amounts to over-fitting the data.[18] However, the repeat-sales approach draws on all possible sales events in our 76-quarter period. When viewed in this light, the problem becomes one of estimating a price index from $(76 * 75)/2 = 2,850$ different sales possibilities.[19]

Thus the repeat-sales approach is subject to two data problems. The first is the sparse nature of repeat sales at a municipality level (this causes the repeat-sales index to behave like a chained index), and the second is the sensitivity of the estimated price index in any quarter to a subsequent sample of anomalous home sales in a particular quarter. (For the remainder of the sample, the index jumps up by the amount of the average sales price in the unusual quarter.) Figure 1 illustrates this point. The repeat-sales price index for Oakland looks

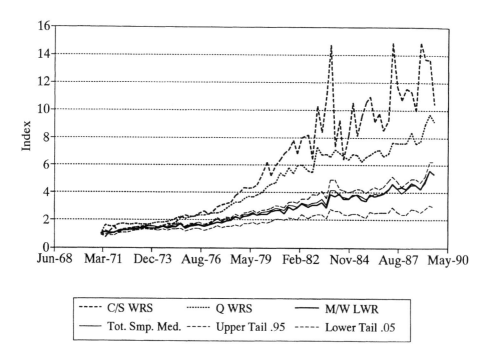

Figure 5. Comparison of price indices: Oakland.

reasonable for the early 1970s. Then the growth rate accelerates relative to the median sales price index. The problem plagues the OLS variant (the estimator originally proposed by BMN), either variant of our Case and Shiller procedure, and a robust repeat-sales estimator that down weights influential observations.[20]

The Quigley hybrid behaves more like the repeat-sales index than the nonparametric hedonic price index. It appears to overstate the 18-year house price appreciation in Oakland (Figure 4). Only the nonparametric hedonic price index provides a reasonable estimate of the trend increase in housing prices over our sample. The Fisher Ideal index falls within a 95% confidence interval of the median sales price index for the Oakland data set (Figure 5), but it remains below the lower bound of the median price index confidence interval for much of the Fremont data set (not shown). We now proceed with a more formal test of the equality of the Fisher Ideal and median price series.

In Table 3, Panels 1–2, we compare estimates of trend and autocorrelation in the median and Fisher Ideal price indices, and test the null hypothesis that the trend and autocorrelation structure of the two series are equal. These tests are based on the multivariate regression:

$$a(L)P_t^1 = a_0 + a_1 t + u_t^1,$$

$$b(L)P_t^2 = b_0 + b_1 t + u_t^2; \qquad (4)$$

$$\textit{where } a(0) = 1 = b(0), \quad (u_t^1, u_t^2) \textit{ are iid } N\!\left(0, \sum\right);$$

where P^i denotes the logarithm of the price index i, and L is the lag operator. Our first test is conducted using the (logarithmic) level of the price series. Here the null hypothesis is for the equality of the autoregressive (AR) polynomials $a(L) = b(L)$, and deterministic time trends, $a_1 = b_1$. Our second test is conducted using the logarithmic difference (growth rates) of the price indices. The null hypothesis is $a'(L) = b'(L)$ and $a_0 = b_0$, conditional on both $a_1 = 0 = b_1$, and $a'(L) = (1 - L)a(L)$ and $b'(L) = (1 - L)b(L)$; i.e., the AR polynomials apply to the first difference of the price series. The latter formulation assumes a stochastic trend in housing prices, while the former assumes a linear deterministic trend. We do not constrain the intercepts in the levels version of the test, but we do impose the constraint in the logarithmic first difference regressions.[21]

Tests for the equality of trend and autocorrelation structure are of interest, as it is the time-series properties of the generated price indices that are important for market efficiency tests. From a practical perspective, if there is no quantitative difference between the median sales price indices and the more sophisticated hedonic approaches, then government agencies can save a lot of resources by relying on the traditional median sales price index.

We first estimate the system (4) for the logarithmic level and logarithmic difference of the price indices with a maximal lag of four, to account for any seasonality in our quarterly series. In all cases, we can reject the hypothesis that a simpler three-lag model of the dependent variable is sufficient, so tests of the equality of trend and autoregressive coefficients are conditional on four lags of the dependent variable. In Table 3, we report likelihood ratio statistics for both hypothesis tests, their corresponding p-values, R^2, and a subset of the estimated coefficients and their t-ratios. The first panel of Table 3 refers to price index data in

Table 3: Panel 1. Tests for equality of the autocorrelation structure of estimated price indices: Oakland and Fremont indices in logarithmic levels (71 observations).

Price Index	Trend[1]	Likelihood Ratio Test[2]	P-Value	R^2
Oakland: Hedonic	.009 (3.29)	9.42	.093	.98
Oakland: Median	.008 (3.91)			.98
Fremont: Hedonic	.003 (2.00)	5.02	.413	.99
Fremont: Median	.002 (1.48)			.99

1. Maximum likelihood estimates for the system (4) with *t*-ratios in parentheses.
2. Null hypothesis: The coefficients on trend and lags 1–4 of the dependent variable are equal for the median and hedonic price indices. The statistic is asymptotically distributed as a Chi-square with five degrees of freedom.

logarithmic levels for Oakland and Fremont; the last panel of Table 3 refers to price index growth rates, again for Oakland and Fremont.

We do not find evidence of a difference in the trend and autocorrelation structure of the Fisher Ideal and median sales price indices for either municipality, whether the test is conducted in levels or differences (probability values range from .093 to .553). Figure 5 suggests that the Oakland LWR price index lies within the confidence interval around the median which is consistent with our tests; however, the Fremont LWR index lies outside the interval after February 1982, and thus appears at variance with our test results. Last, we attribute this possible inconsistency to the low power of our testing procedure, once we have accounted for trend (i.e., some of the intermediate lags are insignificantly different from zero). We chose not to compare trend and serial correlation between the LWR or median and the repeat-sales index or the hybrid repeat-sales index, given the evident divergence in these series, as shown in Figure 5.

4. Concluding Remarks

In this article, we document the shortcomings of repeat-sales price indices when they are constructed on municipality-level data sets. The indices suffer from sample selection bias and nonconstancy of implicit housing characteristic prices, and they are quite sensitive to small sample problems. Recent published applications of repeat-sales indices (e.g., Case and Shiller, 1987, 1989) use housing price data aggregated over larger geographic areas, so

Table 3: Panel 2. Tests for equality of the autocorrelation structure of estimated price indices: Oakland and Fremont indices in logarithmic differences (70 observations).

Price Index	Constant[3]	Likelihood Ratio Test[4]	P-Value	R^2
Oakland: Hedonic	.052 (5.06)	4.11	.533	.36
Oakland: Median	.051 (5.03)			.23
Fremont: Hedonic	.035 (3.50)	3.98	.553	.09
Fremont: Median	.041 (3.98)			.21

3. Maximum likelihood estimates for the system (4) with *t*-ratios in parentheses.
4. Null hypothesis: The coefficients on the constant and lags 1–4 of the dependent variable are equal for the median and hedonic price indices. The statistic is asymptotically distributed as a Chi-square with five degrees of freedom.

presumably, sample size issues are of less concern. In addition, the standard variance specification of repeat-sales approaches appears to be inappropriate for data at the municipality level. While the nonparametric regression technique that we use to construct housing price indices results in reliable, municipality-level indices, we fail to reject the null hypothesis that our index has a different trend and serial correlation than the median sales price index.

Given the low power of our test for the equivalence of trend and autocorrelation structure, and a marginal significance level of 9% for the Oakland test, we recommend that researchers interested in questions of housing market efficiency rely on the hedonic indices (at least at the municipality level.) The results of market efficiency tests are quite dependent on the autocorrelation structure of price change (housing return) series. Our results suggest that researchers interested in regional real estate cycles or just a reliable estimate of the local trend in housing price movements can rely on the simple median sales price index. The median index is inexpensive to compute, and is readily available from National Association of Realtors.

Appendix 1

We obtained our data from the California Market Data Cooperative. The data set consists of sales price and house attributes for homes sold in Oakland and Fremont California over the 1970–1988 period. Approximately 90% of all recorded individual home sales in the two municipalities over this period are included. The remaining 10% of the transactions have either missing data, or were not arms-length transactions.

Appendix 2

The Bailey, Muth, Nourse (1963) ordinary least-squares method to estimate real estate price indices in logarithmic form assumes the following specification for log price relatives:

$$r = z\phi + \mu, \tag{A.1}$$

where r is an n-dimensional column vector of the logarithms of the ratio of final transaction price to the initial transaction price, ϕ is a T-dimensional column vector of unknown logarithms of the index numbers to be estimated, z is an $n \times T$ matrix in which each transaction pair (each row) is represented with -1 in the period of the initial transaction and $+1$ in the period of the final transaction. All other elements of z are zeros. The base period, first column of the z matrix, is suppressed to avoid perfect collinearity. The elements of the residual vector, μ, are in logs and are assumed to be independent and identically distributed $N(0, \sigma^2)$.

The primary advantage of the BMN repeat-sales methodology is that it provides an efficient (minimum variance) estimator for a chained log price index. However, this advantage can only be exploited *if* the event space of all unique times between sales is well balanced. For example, consider a sample with three time periods. The possible events in this case are: (1) properties with the initial transaction in the base period, period 0, and the final transaction in period 1, (2) properties with the initial transaction in the first period and final transaction in the period 2, or (3) properties with the initial transaction in the base period and final transaction in period 2. Using BMN's notation, let $\bar{r}_{01}$ represent the mean returns for the n_{01} properties for case 1, $\bar{r}_{12}$ represent the mean returns for the n_{12} properties for case 2, and $\bar{r}_{02}$ represent the mean returns for the n_{02} properties for case 3. The least-squares estimator for the logarithm of the index number for periods one and two, respectively, are:

$$\hat{\phi}_1 = \frac{n_{01}(n_{02} + n_{12})\bar{r}_{01} + n_{02}n_{12}(\bar{r}_{02} - \bar{r}_{12})}{n_{01}(n_{02} + n_{12}) + n_{02}n_{12}} \tag{A.2}$$

$$\hat{\phi}_2 = \frac{n_{02}(n_{01} + n_{12})\bar{r}_{02} + n_{01}n_{12}(\bar{r}_{01} + \bar{r}_{12})}{n_{01}(n_{02} + n_{12}) + n_{02}n_{12}}$$

The variances of these index numbers are:

$$var(\hat{\phi}_1) = \frac{(n_{02} + n_{12})\sigma^2}{n_{01}(n_{02} + n_{12}) + n_{02}n_{12}} \tag{A.3}$$

$$var(\hat{\phi}_2) = \frac{(n_{01} + n_{12})\sigma^2}{n_{01}(n_{02} + n_{12}) + n_{02}n_{12}}.$$

Now consider the case in which there are no observations for properties that transacted with a time between sales from the base period to the second period (e.g., $n_{02} = 0$). In this case, due to sparseness of the data, the estimated logarithm of the index number becomes

$$\hat{\phi}_1 = \overline{r_{01}}; \qquad \hat{\Phi}_2 = \overline{r_{01}} + \overline{r_{12}}. \tag{A.4}$$

Similarly, when $n_{01} = 0$ the parameter vector becomes

$$\hat{\phi}_1 = \overline{r_{02}} - \overline{r_{12}}; \qquad \hat{\Phi}_2 = \overline{r_{02}}, \tag{A.5}$$

and when $n_{12} = 0$ the parameter vector is:

$$\hat{\phi}_1 = \overline{r_{01}}; \qquad \hat{\Phi}_2 = \overline{r_{02}}. \tag{A.6}$$

In all three of these outcomes, the estimated parameters are simple sums of the mean of the log price ratios for the events with positive frequencies. There is no variance weighting to the parameter estimates. In real-world data applications, the simple mean of a low frequency sample may provide a very poor representation of the true population mean return given the known sensitivity of sample means to outlier observations. Such outliers would effect the estimated logarithm of the index number for the relevant time period, and, because the index is chained, they also affect the indices of other periods in the sample.

Similarly unbalanced frequencies can lead to very different weights for the mean returns of each time interval and again very different estimates for the overall population price index. In Table A1, we compare the parameter estimates for the log indices for various sampling frequencies over the event space of the three possible times between sales. As is clear, the parameter estimates are very sensitive to the frequency counts in the event space. The relative weights for returns from period 1 to period 2, $\overline{r_{01}}$, vary from one-fifth to four-fifths. In the extreme case, when returns for the sales between the first period and the second period, n_{12}, or between the base period and the second period, n_{02}, are not observed, the estimated period 1 index, (ϕ_1), assigns a weight of one to $\overline{r_{01}}$.

For samples drawn over longer time intervals, such as our sample of 76 quarters, there are 2,926 unique events that must be spanned by the data. At the municipality level, we observe 1,759 (1,785) repeat-sales transactions for Oakland (Fremont), and there is not a balanced coverage of all possible times between sales. This leads to the problems

Table A1. Comparison of the effects of sample frequencies on estimated log index numbers.

Event Frequencies	Estimate of the logarithm of the index number for period 1(ϕ_1).	Estimate of the logarithm of the index number for period 2(ϕ_2).
$n_{01} = n_{02} = n_{12} = m$	$2/3\overline{r_{01}} + 1/3(\overline{r_{02}} - \overline{r_{12}})$	$2/3\overline{r_{02}} + 1/3(\overline{r_{01}} + \overline{r_{12}})$
$n_{02} = n_{12} = m$ $n_{01} = 2m$	$4/5\overline{r_{01}} + 1/5(\overline{r_{02}} - \overline{r_{12}})$	$3/5\overline{r_{02}} + 2/5(\overline{r_{01}} + \overline{r_{12}})$
$n_{01} = n_{12} = m$ $n_{02} = 2m$	$3/5\overline{r_{01}} + 2/5(\overline{r_{02}} - \overline{r_{12}})$	$4/5\overline{r_{02}} + 1/5(\overline{r_{01}} + \overline{r_{12}})$
$n_{01} = n_{02} = m$ $n_{12} = 2m$	$1/5\overline{r_{01}} + 4/5(\overline{r_{02}} - \overline{r_{12}})$	$3/5\overline{r_{02}} + 2/5(\overline{r_{01}} + \overline{r_{12}})$

exemplified in Table A1, where observed mean returns for some events are assigned large weights throughout the panel of log price indices. It is also very difficult to detect problems of this type using usual regression diagnostic techniques. For example, even in very extreme cases when there are no observations for $n_{02}, n_{03}, \ldots, n_{0T}$ transaction events, the design matrix has full rank and there is no indication that many of the estimated logarithms of index numbers are unweighted sums of means. Careful use of methods to identify influential observations (see Belsley, Kuh, and Welsh, 1980) and to evaluate the frequency counts by events is the only reliable means to identify whether the log of the price indices has been systematically overweighted by returns that are outliers.

Goetzman and Spiegel (1995) argue for the inclusion of an intercept in the BMN repeat-sales method. The formula for the parameter estimates for the logarithm of the index number for the three-period case shown above would be:

$$\hat{\phi}_{intercept} = \overline{r_{01}} + \overline{r_{12}} - \overline{r_{02}} \qquad (A.7)$$

$$\hat{\phi}_1 = \overline{r_{01}} - \overline{r_{12}}$$

$$\hat{\phi}_2 = 2\overline{r_{02}} - \overline{r_{01}} - \overline{r_{12}}.$$

The variances of these parameter estimates are:

$$var(\hat{\phi}_{intercept}) = \frac{(n_{01}n_{02} + n_{01}n_{12} + n_{12}n_{02})\sigma^2}{n_{01}n_{02}n_{12}}$$

$$var(\hat{\phi}_1) = \frac{(2n_{01}n_{12} + n_{01}n_{02})\sigma^2}{n_{01}n_{02}n_{12}}$$

$$var(\hat{\phi}_2) = \frac{(4n_{01}n_{12} + n_{02}n_{01} + n_{02}n_{12})\sigma^2}{n_{01}n_{02}n_{12}}.$$

An important difference with the intercept version of the BMN ordinary least-squares repeat-sales method is that samples in which $n_{01} = 0$, or $n_{02} = 0$, or $n_{12} = 0$ are no longer estimable if the intercept is included, because the z-matrix is rank deficient. Also, as is obvious from (A.7), the parameter estimates are no longer functions of the sales event frequencies and are now simple means of price relatives rather than variance-weighted averages of mean price relatives.

Given the assumptions made about the μ vector, the variance of the intercept version of the BMN least-squares estimators is always greater than the BMN estimator without an intercept. It should be noted however, that the variance of the estimators for the BMN least-squares estimators for the log price indices also increases as sample event frequencies fall to zero or when there are relatively more event observations in the early periods relative to the later periods. Thus, the relative efficiency of the BMN estimator is extremely sensitive to the observed event frequencies in a given sample.

All of the results reported above are for the ordinary least-squares version of the repeat sales methodology. The weighted least-squares version of the BMN methodology corrects for a time-dependent error variance component and a fixed variance component. The weighted least-squares method uses fitted values from an auxiliary regression of the squared OLS residuals on a constant and the time between sales to obtain weighted least-squares estimates of the logarithms of the index number. In Table A2, we examine the effects of sample event frequencies on the estimated logarithm of the index number, applying the Case and Shiller (1987) version of the weighted least-squares corrections. We use the same three-period transaction population that was considered in Table A1 and the same four possible event frequencies.

As shown, the weighted least-squares estimates of the logarithm of the index number are quite sensitive to the frequency counts in the event space of time between sales, and the relative weights are similar to those reported in Table A1 for the ordinary least-squares BMN estimates. The weighted least-squares estimates for the logarithm of the index numbers are identical to the ordinary least-squares estimates for the cases in which $n_{01} = 0$ (see (A.4)), or $n_{02} = 0$ (see (A.5)), or $n_{12} = 0$ (see (A.5)) respectively. Thus, even in the weighted least-squares case, parameter estimates that are unweighted sums of means are possible, and even likely, when there is sparse data coverage of all possible times between sales within the sample period.

Figure A1 shows the frequencies of influential observations in the Oakland repeat-sales samples. There are 166 observations in Oakland that exceed standard cutoff limits for influence on either the covariance of the estimated parameter vectors of log returns or the studentized residuals. The influential observations (the Fremont results are similar but are not reported) are plotted on both their "buy" date (time 1 sale) and their "sell" date (time

Table A2. Comparison of the effects of sample frequencies on estimated log index numbers.

(θ_0 is the parameter estimate for the fixed error variance component, and θ_1 is the parameter estimate for the time-dependent error variances)

Event Frequencies	Estimate of the logarithm of the index number for period 1(ϕ_1).	Estimate of the logarithm of the index number for period 2(ϕ_2).
$n_{01} = n_{02} =$ $n_{12} = m$	$\left(\dfrac{2\hat{\theta}_0 + 3\hat{\theta}_1}{3\hat{\theta}_0 + 4\hat{\theta}_1}\right)\overline{r_{01}} + \left(\dfrac{\hat{\theta}_0 + \hat{\theta}_1}{3\hat{\theta}_0 + 4\hat{\theta}_1}\right)(\overline{r_{02}} - \overline{r_{12}})$	$\left(\dfrac{\hat{\theta}_0 + \hat{\theta}_1}{3\hat{\theta}_0 + 4\hat{\theta}_1}\right)(2)\overline{r_{02}} + \left(\dfrac{\hat{\theta}_0 + 2\hat{\theta}_1}{3\hat{\theta}_0 + 4\hat{\theta}_1}\right)(\overline{r_{01}} + \overline{r_{12}})$
$n_{02} = n_{12} = m$ $n_{01} = 2m$	$\left(\dfrac{4\hat{\theta}_0 + 6\hat{\theta}_1}{5\hat{\theta}_0 + 7\hat{\theta}_1}\right)\overline{r_{01}} + \left(\dfrac{\hat{\theta}_0 + \hat{\theta}_1}{5\hat{\theta}_0 + 7\hat{\theta}_1}\right)(\overline{r_{02}} - \overline{r_{12}})$	$\left(\dfrac{\hat{\theta}_0 + \hat{\theta}_1}{5\hat{\theta}_0 + 7\hat{\theta}_1}\right)(3)\overline{r_{02}} + \left(\dfrac{2\hat{\theta}_0 + 4\hat{\theta}_1}{5\hat{\theta}_0 + 7\hat{\theta}_1}\right)(2)(\overline{r_{01}} + \overline{r_{12}})$
$n_{01} = n_{12} = m$ $n_{02} = 2m$	$\left(\dfrac{3\hat{\theta}_0 + 4\hat{\theta}_1}{5\hat{\theta}_0 + 6\hat{\theta}_1}\right)\overline{r_{01}} + \left(\dfrac{\hat{\theta}_0 + \hat{\theta}_1}{5\hat{\theta}_0 + 6\hat{\theta}_1}\right)(2)(\overline{r_{02}} - \overline{r_{12}})$	$\left(\dfrac{\hat{\theta}_0 + \hat{\theta}_1}{5\hat{\theta}_0 + 6\hat{\theta}_1}\right)(4)\overline{r_{02}} + \left(\dfrac{\hat{\theta}_0 + 2\hat{\theta}_1}{5\hat{\theta}_0 + 6\hat{\theta}_1}\right)(\overline{r_{01}} + \overline{r_{12}})$
$n_{01} = n_{02} = m$ $n_{12} = 2m$	$\left(\dfrac{3\hat{\theta}_0 + 5\hat{\theta}_1}{6\hat{\theta}_0 + 7\hat{\theta}_1}\right)\overline{r_{01}} + \left(\dfrac{\hat{\theta}_0 + \hat{\theta}_1}{6\hat{\theta}_0 + 7\hat{\theta}_1}\right)(2)(\overline{r_{02}} - \overline{r_{12}})$	$\left(\dfrac{\hat{\theta}_0 + \hat{\theta}_1}{5\hat{\theta}_0 + 7\hat{\theta}_1}\right)(3)\overline{r_{02}} + \left(\dfrac{2\hat{\theta}_0 + 4\hat{\theta}_1}{5\hat{\theta}_0 + 7\hat{\theta}_1}\right)(\overline{r_{02}} + \overline{r_{12}})$

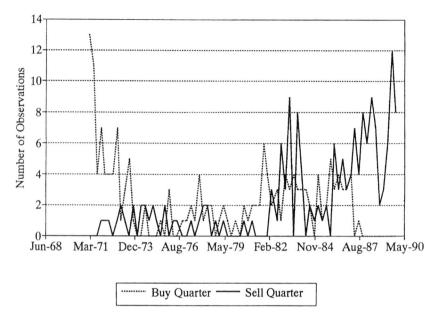

Figure A1. Influential observations: Oakland $n = 166$.

2 sale). As shown, the influential observations cluster at the beginning and end of each sample period and during the business cycle trough in 1982. Each of these three clusters corresponds to periods in which very few repeat sales transactions occurred, and cell frequencies are very small or are zero. The effect of these unbalanced frequency counts is to increase the weights for periods in which there are more data and in some cases by chaining unweighted mean returns for some events. At the municipality level, we find that the transaction frequencies for many possible events are small, increasing the likelihood that outliers can have significant effects on the chained indices.

Acknowledgments

The authors gratefully acknowledge financial support from the Center for Real Estate and Urban Economics, and the Berkeley Program in Finance. Research assistance was provided by Pierre Collin Dufresne and Christopher Downing.

Notes

1. Implicit attribute prices are calculated as the derivative of the hedonic price function with respect to the attribute of interest. For nonlinear models, these implicit attribute prices depend on both the regression parameters and current period values of dependent and independent variables.
2. Halvorsen and Pollakowski (1981) consider estimation of hedonic price equations using second-order Taylor series approximations, and Pace (1993) surveys the literature on nonparametric techniques.

3. The efficiency gain over Case and Shiller (1987) arises from the use of ALL the data to generate price indices. In our sample, repeat sales represent no more than 15% of all home sales observations over an 18-year period.

4. For notational simplicity, we write second-order terms using quadratic forms with symmetric parameter matrices. Clearly, redundant elements of Ω and Λ are not estimated.

5. For the repeat-sales sample which we employ below, there are not enough observations to permit the estimation of a model with regression slope parameters that vary each quarter. Estimation of a five-variable translog model requires one intercept, five linear, and 15 quadratic terms (for a total of 21 estimated parameters) for each time period. In 1970 (due to the sample start-up problem) and in some quarters associated with severe recessions, we do not have 21 observations. Instead we opt for an annual translog with interaction but not squared terms.

6. Clearly, we can test the log-linear model as a constrained version of the translog using standard procedures. Standard F and Chi-square tests (described below) both indicate that the translog specification is preferable, while model selection criteria such as those of Schwarz (1978) tend to favor the more parsimonious specification (see Meese and Wallace, 1991, for more detail).

7. The condition variable is a subjective (integer) index filled out by the listing real estate agent. The scale runs from 1 to 5, where 1 denotes the worst condition.

8. Clapp, Giaccotto, and Tirtiroglu (1991), Gatzlaff and Haurin (1993), and Quigley (1995), among others, provide additional examples of sample selection bias in repeat-sales samples.

9. P-values for the F- and the heteroskedasticity-robust Chi-square tests of the null hypothesis of time-constant parameters using only the subsample of repeat-sales observations are also zero to three decimal places.

10. For the Case and Shiller repeat-sales methodology, we use only those homes that sold at least twice during our sample period, and that had no change in any of our six measured attributes.

11. We also consider a variant of this technique that is less sensitive to residual outliers. The variation makes use of an auxiliary regression of the absolute value of the OLS residuals on the time between sales. This variant was suggested by Glejser (1969) and Davidian and Carrol (1987) in different contexts, and has been applied in the finance literature by Schwert and Seguin (1990). When we use this technique to estimate a repeat-sales price index for Oakland and Fremont, the resulting price index is qualitatively similar to the one generated by the results which we report for the original Case and Shiller methodology.

12. Our experiments with the repeat-sales methodology—when a constant term is included in the feasible GLS regression—did not remedy the problems with the index that we discuss below. Thus, we do not subject this variant of the repeat-sales price index to any further analysis (see Appendix 2 on the BMN methodology for further detail).

13. Due to space limitations, we provide figures for Oakland only. Plots of price indices for the city of Fremont display patterns quite similar to those for Oakland, and are not reported.

14. The distance metric is sensitive to units of measure, so all attributes are standardized prior to estimation of $G(x)$. In addition, LWR uses a tricube function to further down weight attributes $x_{i(t)}$ that are far away (in attribute space) from the median attributes $x_{m(t)}$ (see Cleveland and Devlin, 1988). This makes the procedure much less sensitive to outlier observations, i.e., home sale observations where house attributes are atypical of the median or average house sold in a given quarter.

15. We considered a grid of window sizes from 20% to 100%. The 30% window size resulted in a distribution of the 76 implicit attribute prices (attribute prices are calculated for each quarter of our data set) with sensible mean values and moderate variation.

16. The random walk assumption gives rise to an error variance that grows linearly with time between sales. The quadratic term is data driven. Equation (3) of the text is taken from Quigley (1995), equation (6).

17. We use an approximation for the distribution of the median that is likely to result in a conservative confidence interval, given the fat-tailed distribution of house prices in our sample.

18. Our Oakland (Fremont) sample consists of 3,342 (3,405) unique transactions for houses that transacted more than once and had no documented change in attributes between sales. These transactions account for 1,759 (1,785) pairs of transactions, since some properties transacted more than twice. The repeat-sales index methodology can only be applied to the home sale observations where no quality change has occurred.

19. For example, every element of the (75×75) design matrix $X'X$ corresponds to a unique combination of the first and subsequent sale(s) of the same house. If many of the (i, j) elements of $X'X$ are close to zero (e.g., there are few homes that sold first in period i and again in period j), then the repeat-sales index will be well approximated by a simple chaining index (see Appendix 2). Also, an unusual observation in a given

quarter (for example, a quarter with a high average house price) will affect all subsequent values of the price index by the same amount. This issue comes up in the original BMN article (see chart 1, p. 941, and the accompanying discussion). However, the fact that the estimated price index can be unreliable when estimated at a municipality level using over 1,700 repeat-sales observations is not intuitively obvious.
20. For the Oakland data set, standard regression diagnostics (e.g., Belsley, Kuh, and Welsch, 1980) indicate 166 (143) influential observations for Oakland (Fremont). Removing the influential observations or making use of a robust regression procedure that down weights these observations does not mitigate the peculiar behavior of the repeat-sales index. As noted earlier, it is the "sparseness" of the data that makes this index behave like an unweighted chained index.
21. Since we are testing for equality of both trend and autocorrelation structure, we test for equality of intercepts in the difference regressions to ensure that the two series being compared have the same growth rates.

References

Bailey, M. J., R. F. Muth, and H. O. Nourse. "A Regression Method for Real Estate Price Index Construction," *American Statistical Association Journal* (1963), 933–942.

Belsley, D. A., E. Kuh, and R. E. Welsh. *Regression Diagnostics: Identifying Influential Data and Sources of Collinearity.* New York: John Wiley & Sons, 1980.

Case, K. E., and R. J. Shiller. "Prices of Single Family Homes Since 1970: New Indexes for Four Cities," *New England Economic Review* (1987), 45–56.

Case, K. E., and R. J. Shiller. "The Efficiency of the Market for Single Family Homes," *American Economic Review* 79(1) (1989), 125–137.

Clapp, J. M., C. Giaccotto, and D. Tirtiroglu. "Housing Price Indices Based on All Transaction Compared to Repeat Sub-samples," *AREUEA Journal* 19(3) (1991), 270–286.

Cleveland, W. S., and S. J. Devlin. "Locally Weighted Regression: An Approach to Regression Analysis by Local Fitting," *Journal of the American Statistical Association* 83 (1988), 596–610.

Davidian, M., and R. J. Carrol. "Variance Function Estimation," *Journal of the American Statistical Association* 82 (1987), 1079–1091.

Gatzlaff, D. H., and D. R. Haurin. "Sample Selection and Biases in Local House Value Indices." Unpublished manuscript, 1993.

Glejser, H. "A New Test for Heteroskedasticity," *Journal of the American Statistical Association* 64 (1969), 316–323.

Goetzman, W., and M. Spiegel. "Non-Temporal Components of Residential Real Estate Appreciation," *The Journal of Real Estate Finance and Economics* 77 (1994), 199–206.

Halvorsen, R., and H. O. Pollakowski. "Choice of Function Form for Hedonic Price Equations," *Journal of Urban Economics* 10(1) (1981), 37–49.

Lindgren, B. W. *Statistical Theory.* London: the Macmillan Co., 1968.

Meese, R. A., and N. E. Wallace. "Nonparametric Estimation of Dynamic Hedonic Price Models and the Construction of Residential Housing Price Indices," *AREUEA Journal* 19 (1991), 308–332.

Meese, R. A., and N. E. Wallace. "Residential Housing Prices in the San Francisco Bay Area: New Tests of the Explanatory Power of Economic Fundamentals." Unpublished manuscript, 1993.

Pace, R. K. "Nonparametric Methods with Applications to Hedonic Models," *The Journal of Real Estate Finance and Economics* 7 (1993), 185–204.

Quigley, J. M. "A Simple Hybrid Model for Estimating Real Estate Price Indexes," *Journal of Housing Economics* 4 (1995), 1–12.

Quigley, J. M., and R. Van Order. "Explicit Tests of Contingent Claims Models of Mortgage Default," *Journal of Real Estate Finance and Economics* 12 (1995).

Rosen, S. "Hedonic Price and Implicit Markets: Product Differentiation in Pure Competition," *Journal of Political Economy* 82 (1974), 34–55.

Schwarz, G. "Estimating the Dimension of a Model," *Annals of Statistics* 6 (1978), 461–464.

Schwert, G. W., and P. J. Seguin. "Heteroskedasticity in Stock Returns," *Journal of Finance* 45 (1990), 1129–1156.

Triplett, J. E. "Concepts of Quality in Input and Output Price Measures: A Resolution of the User Value–Resource Cost Debate." In M. F. Foss, Ed., *The U.S. National Income and Product Accounts: Selected Topics* (*NBER Studies in Income and Wealth,* Vol. 47). Chicago: University of Chicago Press, 1983, pp. 269–311.

White, H. "A Heteroskedasticity-consistent Covariance Matrix Estimator and a Direct Test of Heteroskedasticity," *Econometrica* 48 (1980), 817–838.

Journal of Real Estate Finance and Economics, 14: 75–88 (1997)

Aggregation Bias in Repeat-Sales Indices

JONATHAN DOMBROW
University of Connecticut, School of Business Administration, Center for Real Estate and Urban Economic Studies, 368 Fairfield Road, U-41RE, Storrs, CT 06269-2041

J. R. KNIGHT
University of the Pacific, Eberhardt School of Business, 3601 Pacific Avenue, Stockton, CA 95211

C. F. SIRMANS
University of Connecticut, School of Business Administration, Center for Real Estate and Urban Economic Studies, 368 Fairfield Road, U-41RE, Storrs, CT 06269-2041

Abstract

The repeat-sales methodology has become a standard approach for estimating real estate price indices. This article examines the underlying assumptions inherent in the repeat sales model and provides an empirical test for both included and omitted variables as sources of aggregation bias. The results indicate that virtually all price indices may be biased, the degree of bias being dependent upon the number of variables examined and the instability of their parameters over time.

Key Words: price index, housing, aggregation bias, varying parameters, repeat sales

The repeat-sales method for measuring price changes of housing (Bailey, Muth, and Nourse, 1963; Case and Shiller, 1989) has recently been adopted by Fannie Mae and Freddie Mac in constructing their joint house price indices for cities and regions throughout the nation, and by Case, Shiller, and Weiss (1993) in building residential indices for futures and options trading. Its selection for these purposes has elevated repeat-sales technique to a position of preeminence among competing models, on practical if not theoretical grounds. The widespread and growing usage of the methodology underscores the need to investigate the assumptions that underlie its validity.

The repeat-sales method has flaws, many of which have been previously acknowledged in the literature. Most importantly, because change in age is perfectly collinear with the time between sales of a property, it cannot capture the depreciation effect (Bailey, Muth, and Nourse, 1963; Palmquist, 1980) and thus does not produce a "pure" price index. Also, by unnecessarily restricting the sample to properties that transact more than once, it fails to use the full information available in the data (Case and Quigley, 1991; Hill, Knight, and Sirmans, 1995).[1] The smaller samples associated with multiple transaction properties raise concerns about sample selection bias; properties that transact more than once may not be representative of all properties in the market (Clapp and Giaccotto, 1992). As the index period lengthens, a larger percentage of the population fits the multiple sale category.

This reduces sample selection bias but aggravates a problem of heteroskedasticity (Case and Shiller, 1989); price change variability is greater the longer the period between transactions. Another weakness of the repeat-sales technique is the concealed but implicit assumption of parameter stability over the duration of the index period, creating the potential for temporal aggregation bias.

The appeal of the repeat-sales model is its ability to control for constant quality across index periods by measuring the same asset in different periods, thereby putatively avoiding the variable selection and functional form selection issues that afflict the competing hedonic model (Griliches, 1971; Rosen, 1974; Goodman, 1978). But even this strength of the repeat-sales technique is open to question. Since the model derives from the hedonic method, all of the apparent weaknesses of the hedonic model apply equally to the repeat-sales model, but are merely hidden from view. This article demonstrates this fact in the case of variable selection, showing that the potential for aggregation bias exists with the repeat-sales model, whether property attributes are included or omitted. To show the effect of omitting important property characteristics within a repeat-sales sample, we investigate housing aspects that are generally significant in hedonic regressions, but that researchers typically overlook when constructing indices with the repeat-sales technique. We then show that bias can be present even if the property characteristic is measured and controlled.

This article is organized as follows. In the next section, we derive the repeat-sales model from the hedonic model and discuss the assumptions implicit in the repeat-sales model as typically formulated. Section 2 describes and specifies the housing attributes which we have chosen for our investigation. We present the results in section 3, graphically showing the result of ignoring our selected property characteristics in the repeat-sales context. Our summary and conclusions appear in Section 4.

1. The Repeat-sales Model and Aggregation Bias

The repeat-sales model is derived directly from the hedonic model. To see this, consider the usual hedonic pricing framework for an individual asset i at time t.

$$V_{it} = \sum_{j=1}^{k} \beta_{jt} X_{ijt} + \alpha_t T_t \tag{1}$$

Where V_{it} = Log of value of asset i at time t

β_{jt} = Value of attribute X_j at time t

X_{ijt} = Attributes of asset i at time t

α_t = Value associated with being sold at time t

T_t = Intercept for properties sold at time t.

Next assume that the property sells twice within the index period, the first transaction occurring at time f and the second at time s. Then

$$V_{is} - V_{if} = \left(\sum_{j=1}^{k} \beta_{js} X_{ijs} - \sum_{j=1}^{k} \beta_{jf} X_{ijf} \right) + (\alpha_s \dot{T}_s - \alpha_f T_f), \qquad (2)$$

which, under certain conditions, simplifies to the repeat-sales regression model of Bailey, Muth, and Nourse (1963):

$$V_s - V_f = \alpha T. \qquad (3)$$

The left-hand side is a vector of log price relatives for properties that have transacted more than once, and the right-hand side is a matrix, T, of zeros, ones, and negative ones, indicating no transaction, second sale, and first sale, respectively. There is a column of T for each time period except the base period, and each row of T represents the sales history of an individual property. Note in the repeat-sales regression that the matrix X has disappeared and that correspondingly the vector β is not estimated.

This vanishing act is quite convenient and vastly simplifies the estimation process. However, it is very important to keep in mind the conditions that permit the simplification. First, the property characteristics must not have changed between sales. Second, the marginal contribution of those characteristics to overall house price must be stable across periods. Violating either of these assumptions imparts bias to an index constructed from a repeat-sales regression. And both of these assumptions apply equally to all characteristics that contribute to property value, whether measured or unmeasured.

1.1. Sources of Aggregation Bias

If property attributes change between sales and the changes are not controlled for, the index is no longer a constant quality index; it is not possible in this case to separate the pure price change from the price change associated with the changing property attributes. Researchers understand this and typically control for changes in one of two ways. Most common is a careful screening of the data to ensure that the repeat-sales sample used to construct the index consists only of properties which experienced no characteristics changes between sales. The other means of controlling for attribute changes is to augment the right-hand side of the regression model (3) to include the characteristics that change.[2] Because it uses more of the information available in the data, this latter method is preferred, notwithstanding its less frequent use.

Even if the control for attribute change is perfectly implemented, however, recall that this is only one of two important conditions that must be met. The other, unchanged marginal values of these attributes across periods, is equally important. Unfortunately, as usually implemented, the repeat-sales model is ill-equipped to measure the value of property attributes, nor is it suited to measuring changes in those attribute values.

In a perfectly competitive market for the housing attributes (Olsen, 1969), a horizontal supply curve ensures that the long-run equilibrium attribute prices are unchanged. In this case, changing parameter values are not a concern. By contrast, the short-run supply curve for housing characteristics is perfectly vertical, reflecting the time necessary to construct housing assets of the demanded composition of attributes, or to alter the existing housing stock appropriately. In this case, changing parameter values are a major concern, as attribute price change is the only available market response to changing demand.

It is likely that the period-to-period supply curves for house price indices of typical interval (monthly, quarterly, or annual) fall somewhere on a continuum between these two extremes. Thus, the supply curve for housing attributes over the intermediate term is likely to be upward sloping, such that interperiod variation in parameter values is a natural consequence of changing consumer tastes for housing characteristics.

There are numerous ways in which the marginal values of the attributes could change across periods to produce an observed price change in the composite asset. But the repeat sales method compresses this information into a single number. Therefore, even if the measured characteristics in repeat sales are carefully screened and go unchanged between periods, the index is sensitive to attribute composition within the sample. For example, assume that the marginal contribution of an additional bathroom to overall house price rises significantly between two periods and that this is the only housing characteristic whose shadow price has changed. In this case, a repeat-sales sample composed of one-bathroom properties will show less interperiod price change than one composed of two-bathroom properties; and the bias is present even if no properties in the sample either add or reduce the number of bathrooms during the interval between sales.

Following this example further, consider the effect if bathrooms are omitted from the repeat-sales model so that the data are not screened on this variable and no measurements of bathroom quantity are taken at transaction points. One is tempted to say that it makes no difference if bathrooms are neither added nor removed between sales, but we see now that it can indeed matter. If a housing characteristic contributes to overall house value, and if either the characteristic or its shadow price change between sales, an index that does not control for this characteristic will be biased. This is true whether the researcher chooses to measure that particular characteristic or not. The severity of the bias is tied to the extent to which the characteristic is present in the sample and the extent to which it and/or its marginal value changes between periods. Understanding the derivation of the repeat-sales model from the hedonic model and the assumptions that underlie this derivation, we see that the repeat-sales model is not as free from variable selection and omitted variables concerns as one might think. The potential for aggregation bias exists for both included and omitted variables. Our current study focuses on these sources of aggregation bias in repeat-sales.

1.2. Testing for Aggregation Bias

Repeat-sales aggregation bias results from (1) misspecification (characteristics that contribute value to the composite asset are omitted from the model), and (2) parameter instability (the value of the characteristics changes during the index period.) The presence of each of these forms of bias can be tested with an F-test.

To test for omitted variables bias, assume that the traditional repeat-sales model is augmented with K property attributes but omits P additional characteristics that are also important. We construct the F-statistic

$$\mu_1 = \frac{(S_0 - S_1)/P}{S_1/(N - P - K)},$$

where S_0 is the sum of squares from the restricted model containing only the first K variables and S_1 the sum of squares from the unrestricted model containing all $K + P$ variables. If both the K and P elements of X are non-stochastic, μ_1 is distributed as an F-statistic with P and $N - K - P$ degrees of freedom.

Another F-test may be applied to test for parameter stability. Observe that in order for (2) to reduce to (3),

$$\left(\sum_{j=1}^{k} \beta_{js} X_{ijs} - \sum_{j=1}^{k} \beta_{jf} X_{ijf} \right)$$

must equal zero for all characteristics, j, $j = 1, \ldots, K$, and for all pairs of index periods, t, where s and f are two such periods contained in $t = 1, \ldots, T$. This null result will be true if $X_{ij1} = X_{ij2} = \ldots = X_{ijt}$ for all assets i, $i = 1, \ldots, N$, characteristics j, and time periods t, and if $\beta_{j1} = \beta_{j2} = \ldots = \beta_{jt}$ for all j and all t. The joint hypotheses suggested by parameter stability are tested with the statistic

$$\mu_2 = \frac{(Rb)'[R(X'X)^{-1}R']^{-1}Rb}{J\hat{\sigma}^2},$$

where R is a $J \times TK$ matrix imposing the J equality constraints, b the $TK \times 1$ vector of least squares parameter estimates, and $\hat{\sigma}^2$ the estimate of error variance. Under the null hypothesis of parameter stability, μ_2 is distributed as an F-statistic with J and $N - TK$ degrees of freedom. This test is appropriate to test for changes in the value, β_j, of the property characteristics, X_j, over the index period.

2. Variable Selection

In screening data based on physical characteristics, researchers control for only one source of aggregation bias, that which occurs when those screened characteristics change between sales. Overlooked by this method are two additional sources: that which accompanies inter-period changes in shadow prices of the measured or screened characteristics; and, that associated with changes in either the quantity or price of omitted variables.

Repeat-sales researchers typically control for changes in the X_{ijt} by first selecting variables to screen, and then screening the sample to ensure that there were no interperiod changes in those variables. We performed just such a careful screening on our sample, noting the many physical amenities that add to house value, such as swimming pools, patios, and fenced yards, to ensure that no major additions to the homes occurred between sales. In addition to rejecting properties that change characteristics between sales, we augment the right-hand side of the traditional repeat-sales equation with one variable that is normally considered by researchers in the screening process, the size of the home, and two that are generally ignored, financing arrangements and occupancy status. In this way, we illustrate the bias sensitivity of the repeat-sales technique to both included variables and omitted variables.

Selling price and the size of a home are highly correlated, and one may logically expect to find some degree of market segmentation. Differential pricing for a unit of size may arise from any of several supply and demand conditions that may affect homes of different sizes differently. Such conditions include new construction, demolition, population and demographic changes, zoning regulations, and interest rates. We proxy for possible market segmentation, therefore, by including a variable measuring square feet of living area in the model. To the extent that different sizes of homes follow different price paths, the coefficient for house size will vary from period to period, reflecting the composition of home sales in a given period. Though researchers typically screen physical characteristics, especially size, bias occurs not because an individual house changed size between sales, but rather because houses of different sizes are aggregated to form the repeat sales sample.

Just as researchers typically consider physical attributes in screening repeat-sales data, they typically ignore transactional attributes, even though differences in the nature of the transaction may introduce aggregation bias as well. The method chosen by the buyer to finance the transaction, and whether the house is vacant or occupied by the owner during the listing period are two aspects of a residence at the time of sale that undoubtedly affect the selling price, but that are not typically considered when screening data.

It is frequently possible for home buyers to finance their residential purchase at a rate lower than the market mortgage rate. Examples of such arrangements are seller financing, assumptions of existing loans with low face rates, and public housing assistance programs at the federal, state, and local levels. When such below-market financing is utilized in a transaction, at least part of the value of the benefit is capitalized into the selling price of the home. Residential appraisers recognize this value and appropriately adjust comparables that have benefited from "sweetheart" financing, but researchers almost uniformly disregard the effect of this transactional characteristic. Our data do not indicate the actual rates for owner financing, assumptions, or Mortgage Finance Authority loans at the time of sale. However, we assume that these rates are less than prevailing market rates, and include a dummy variable to capture the effects of below-market financing. We expect a positive coefficient, but the importance of the variable will differ from period to period as market conditions change.

The occupancy status at the time of each sale must also be considered an important transactional attribute to be explicitly measured. Vacant housing produces neither rental income nor housing services to its owner. This causes holding costs to be high, and induces the owner to sell at a discount. In spite of this apparent negative effect on house value, researchers, more often than not, fail to consider the impact of this transactional attribute. We screened rental housing from our sample to eliminate the complex effects of tax and investment considerations and of differential depreciation relative to owner-occupied housing (Shilling, Sirmans, and Dombrow, 1991). Our remaining sample contains only vacant homes and homes lived in by the owner at the time of sale. We include in our augmented repeat-sales model a binary variable to identify the vacancy status of a house at the time of sale.

The variables which we have chosen to examine here are not intended to provide a comprehensive examination, but rather merely to illustrate the existence of aggregation bias, stemming from both included and omitted variables, when the repeat sales approach is employed. Any variable that would appropriately be used in a hedonic regression is a variable that has the potential, whether the variable be included or omitted, to impart bias to a repeat sales regression. And the variables that would be appropriate in a hedonic regression differ depending on the purpose of the study and the data employed.

The data used in this study consist solely of detached single-family homes which sold at least twice during the period 1985–1993 in Baton Rouge, Louisiana. All observations and characteristics were obtained from the local Multiple Listing Service and were screened thoroughly to ensure that financing and tenancy status were the only measured characteristics to change between sales for a given home. Recognizing the potential problems associated with spatially aggregating across the entire SMSA, and attempting to avoid inducing any confounding aggregation bias, we identified a homogeneous subsection of the SMSA through discussions with local real estate professionals. The final sample consists of 419 pairs of repeat sales, including transactions that involve below-market financing, as well as observations of vacant homes at the time of sale. Descriptive statistics for the sample appear in Table 1, and the distribution of repeat sales pairs for the binary variables, financing, and occupancy is shown in Table 2.

Table 1. Descriptive statistics for a sample of 419 housing repeat sales: Baton Rouge, Louisiana, 1985–1993.

		Panel A: First Sale		
	Mean	Standard Deviation	Minimum	Maximum
Selling price	106,261	28,842	48,000	215,000
Square feet	2,182	388	1,413	3,498
Age	6.0	4.5	0	18
		Panel B: Second Sale		
	Mean	Standard Deviation	Minimum	Maximum
Selling price	110,521	27,679	59,700	220,000
Square feet	2,182	388	1,413	3,498
Age	9.1	4.7	1	23

Table 2. Repeat sales by financing and occupancy status: First versus second sale.

Panel A: Financing Status			
	First Sale		
Second Sale	Below Marker	Market	Total
Below market	8	31	39
Market	32	348	380
Total	40	379	419

Panel B: Occupancy Status			
	First Sale		
Second Sale	Owner Occupied	Vacant	Total
Owner occupied	197	150	347
Vacant	41	31	72
Total	238	181	419

3. Results

In order to establish the existence of bias in the traditional repeat sales approach, we estimated two models. The estimation results appear in Tables 3 and 4. Table 3 shows the time coefficients that result from estimating (3), the Traditional Repeat Sales (TRS) model. By augmenting the right-hand side with the variables under investigation, we estimated the unrestricted model, (2), to get the coefficient estimates in Table 4. We call this the Augmented Repeat Sales (ARS) model. With the estimates provided in both tables, we can test two restrictions of TRS: (1) that the variables omitted by TRS are unimportant,[3] and (2) that the value of characteristics remains unchanged across periods. The F-statistic for these restrictions is 1.82, significant at the 1% level. This result causes us to reject TRS in favor of ARS, and brings into question the validity of the assumptions upon which TRS rests.

Note from the t-statistics on the living area variables in Table 4 that size is significant in two of eight periods. A joint test for insignificance ($\beta = 0$) across all periods yields an F-statistic of 2.59. Size matters in explaining price changes. Differently sized homes follow different appreciation/depreciation paths, and the index value in any particular period is sensitive to the composition, with respect to size, of the sample transacting in that period. We also find that the value of size changes across periods; our F-test for parameter equality $\beta_1 = \beta_2 = \cdots = \beta_T$) is highly significant (2.81).

The financing variable is a dummy variable that takes the value 1 if below-market financing was used on the second sale, -1 if used on the first sale, and 0 otherwise. We would therefore expect a positive coefficient as the value of these favorable terms is capitalized

Table 3. Parameter estimates for traditional repeat-sales model.[a]

Variable	Parameter Estimate	t-statistic
YR 1986	−0.010	−0.61
YR 1987	−0.054	−3.59
YR 1988	−0.049	−2.96
YR 1989	−0.063	−4.11
YR 1990	−0.052	−3.41
YR 1991	−0.015	−0.98
YR 1992	0.042	2.72
YR 1993	0.099	6.27

[a] The repeat-sales model of Bailey, Muth, and Nourse (1963). See (3) in the text. Hedonic variables are not used in the regression of house price change.

into the sales price. We see that this is the case in every period save one. However, both of our *F*-tests for the financing variable are insignificant. We reject neither the joint hypothesis of insignificance nor the joint hypothesis of equality across periods.

The occupancy variable is defined in a manner similar to that of the financing variable. Here, a vacant home is marked by a one at the second sale and a minus one at the first sale. We see from the *t*-statistics that only two of the occupancy variables are significant at the 10% level, but note that all but one are negatively signed, as one would expect from the way the variable is coded. As was true with the financing variable, both of the joint *F*-tests for the occupancy variable are insignificant.

To further illustrate the aggregation bias that can occur, we prepare indices from the estimation results in Tables 3 and 4 and chart these indices. Since the time coefficients of TRS represent the cumulative percentage change in price from the base period, 1985, the TRS index flows directly from Table 3. To construct an ARS index, we must specify the characteristics of a constant quality house and then apply the coefficients for each time period from Table 4 to these characteristics.

Figure 1 compares the TRS approach with the ARS method for which a constant quality home is defined as being 2,200 square feet in size, and owner-occupied with market financing. Both indices indicate a price path characterized by rapid decline, slow decline, slow rise, rapid rise. Although the two indices indicate the same market trends, however, note that ARS follows a smoother path and lies consistently below TRS.

The effect of favorable financing is illustrated in Figure 2. Although only a few of the financing terms were individually significant in the regressions, the index that takes this variable into account is quite different from the market-financed ARS index. A few of the discrepancies appear large. From the graph, it is apparent that failing to consider the effect of favorable financing on some of the homes in a sample would generally result in a lower index; how much lower in any period would depend on the number of favorably financed homes in that period.

Table 4. Parameter estimates for augmented repeat-sales model.[a]

Variable[b]	Parameter Estimate	*t*-statistic
YR 1986	−0.172	−1.54
YR 1987	−0.107	−1.18
YR 1988	−0.020	−0.19
YR 1989	−0.063	−0.71
YR 1990	−0.261	−2.72
YR 1991	−0.126	−1.44
YR 1992	0.080	0.91
YR 1993	−0.147	−1.69
LIV 1986[c]	0.064	1.29
LIV 1987	0.024	0.60
LIV 1988	−0.025	−0.53
LIV 1989	−0.003	−0.07
LIV 1990	0.091	2.13
LIV 1991	0.043	1.09
LIV 1992	−0.024	−0.63
LIV 1993	0.110	2.76
V 1985	−0.038	−1.55
V 1986	−0.001	0.03
V 1987	−0.040	−1.73
V 1988	−0.002	−0.09
V 1989	−0.034	−1.44
V 1990	−0.047	−1.90
V 1991	−0.032	−1.23
V 1992	−0.025	−0.77
V 1993	−0.039	−0.96
BM 1985	0.017	0.47
BM 1986	0.048	0.72
BM 1987	0.023	0.76
BM 1988	0.029	0.72
BM 1989	0.047	1.25
BM 1990	0.042	0.91
BM 1991	0.094	2.57
BM 1992	−0.043	−0.92
BM 1993	0.026	0.40

[a] The augmented repeat-sales model incorporates hedonic variables on the right-hand side of the regression of house price change. See (2) in the text.

[b] Independent variables are as follows: YR 1986–YR 1993 mark the year of transaction with a −1 for first sale, +1 for second sale, and 0 otherwise; LIV 1986–LIV 1993 record the square feet of living area in each year in which a property transacts, signed negative if first sale and positive if second sale; V 1986–V 1993 record the occupancy status, −1 if vacant at first sale and +1 if vacant at second sale; BM 1986–BM 1993 capture special financing by coding transactions with −1 if below-market financing is obtained with first sale and +1 if below market financing is obtained at second sale.

[c] Parameter estimates reported for living area variables are actual estimates multiplied by 10^3.

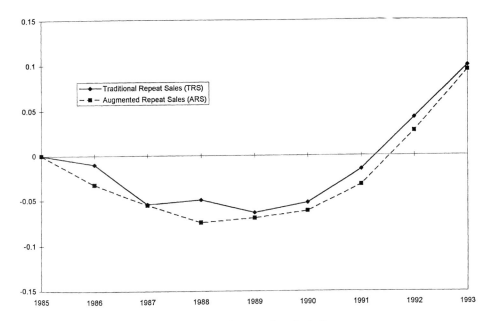

Figure 1. Comparison of traditional and augmented repeat-sales price indices.

Notes:
1. Traditional Repeat-Sales Index constructed using the methodology of Bailey, Muth, and Nourse (1963). See (3) in text.
2. Augmented Repeat-Sales Index constructed using hedonic variables for size, occupancy status, and financing status. Index shown is for a 2,200-square-foot home with owner occupancy and market financing at the time of both sales. See (2) in text.

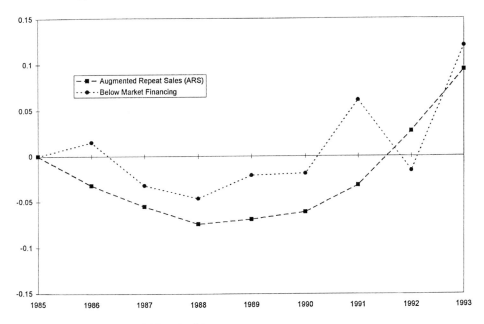

Figure 2. Illustration of potential financing bias.

Notes:
1. Augmented Repeat-Sales Index constructed as indicated in Figure 1.
2. Below Market Financing Index is also augmented with hedonic variables. In addition, it considers the effect of obtaining below-market financing at the time of the second sale.

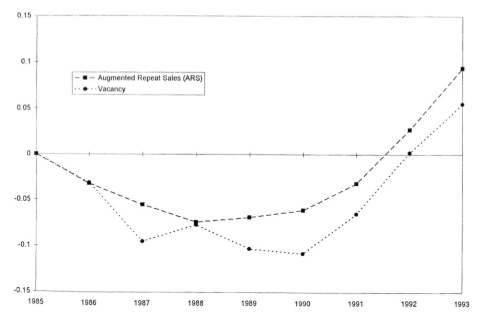

Figure 3. Illustration of potential vacancy bias.

Notes:
1. Augmented Repeat-Sales Index constructed as indicated in Figure 1.
2. Vacancy Index is also augmented with hedonic variables. In addition, it considers the effect of the dwelling's being vacant at the time of the second sale.

Figure 3 shows the impact of vacancy on the repeat-sales index. The vacancy index, which modifies the constant quality home by introducing a vacant status at the second sale, is consistently lower than that of the ARS index, which uses market financing of owner-occupied homes. The index is also consistent with expectations, since the differential diminishes in strong markets as holding costs are reduced. Since the vacancy bias appears to be systematic, it is clear that a repeat sales index is sensitive to the number of vacant homes selling for the second time in a particular period, and an index that ignores occupancy status would be too high.

Finally, in Figure 4, we show the effect of varying the size of the constant quality home assumed for the index. Recall from the regression results that the living area terms for the index period are both jointly not equal to each other and jointly not equal to zero. Therefore, there is a compound effect for size on a resulting repeat-sales index. Because the value of size varies from period to period, bias results from aggregating the sample over time. And because size is significant in explaining price change, bias results from the changing composition of the sample with respect to size in any given period. As is apparent from Figure 4, the price path followed by a small home (1,800 square feet) may be dramatically different from the price path followed by a large home (2,600 square feet).

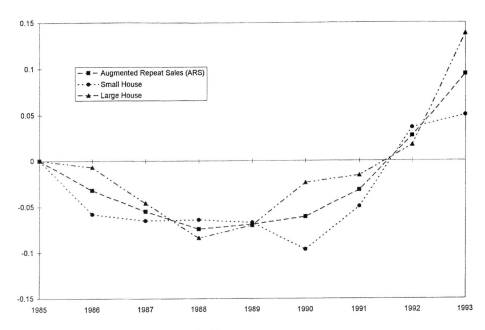

Figure 4. Illustration of potential dwelling size bias.

Notes:
1. Augmented Repeat-Sales Index constructed as indicated in Figure 1.
2. Small House and Large House Indices are also augmented with hedonic variables. In addition, they consider the effect of the dwelling's being smaller (1,800 square feet), or larger (2,600 square feet) at the time of both sales.

4. Conclusions

In discrediting the most compelling argument for the repeat-sales methodology, freedom from variable selection concerns, our results contain disquieting news for those who would employ the technique to construct house price indices. The method remains theoretically pure at the level of the individual asset, but as data are aggregated across time, space, and property attributes to compose an index, model specification becomes a relevant and important concern for the repeat sales model. Errors occurring at any stage of the aggregation process will generate bias in the resulting index. Moreover, decisions and results contingent on correctly measuring the index may also be invalidated.

We provide an empirical examination of the assumptions inherent in the traditional repeat-sales model via a comparison with an augmented repeat-sales approach that permits attribute values to change from period to period. Our results argue against assuming a constant rate of price change for all characteristics, and demonstrate the need both to measure individual characteristics and to allow for differential pricing. Augmenting the right-hand side of the repeat-sales regression partially mitigates the problem, but when one considers the daunting array of hedonic variables that might be included, it is quickly discovered that the varying parameters approach will have practical limitations. Adding one attribute to the model adds a column for each time period of the regression, such that the parameter space quickly becomes unmanageable, and difficult if not impossible to estimate.

Since house price indices are created from aggregate data, aggregation bias is difficult to avoid. The repeat-sales methodology provides no immunization from this affliction. When specifying their models, therefore, researchers should carefully consider the time, location, and property attribute sources of aggregation bias, and should recognize that the degree of bias will be sample dependent. The final sample selected for study should be the result of an analysis that considers the specific end use of the index to be created.

Notes

1. The joint maximum likelihood estimation technique for a combined hedonic/repeat-sales model of Hill, Knight, and Sirmans (1997) overcomes both of these problems.
2. See Shiller (1993) for a recent innovation in this method.
3. At the individual asset level, the assumption is that the characteristics of that asset remain unchanged. However, as the data are aggregated, the condition becomes that the characteristics are unimportant. If the characteristics are significant, then the index will be sensitive to changes in the aggregate level of the characteristics from period to period.

References

Bailey, M. J., R. F. Muth, and H. O. Nourse. "A Regression Method for Real Estate Price Index Construction," *Journal of the American Statistical Association* 58 (1963), 933–942.
Case, B., and J. M. Quigley. "The Dynamics of Real Estate Prices," *The Review of Economics and Statistics* 22 (1991), 50–58.
Case, K. E., and R. J. Shiller. "The Efficiency of the Market for Single Family Homes," *American Economic Review* 79 (1989), 125–137.
Case, K. E., R. J. Shiller, and A. N. Weiss. "Index-Based Futures and Options Markets in Real Estate," *The Journal of Portfolio Management* 19 (1993), 83–92.
Clapp, J. M., and C. Giaccotto. "Repeat Sales Methodology for Price Trend Estimation: An Evaluation of Sample Selectivity," *Journal of Real Estate Finance and Economics* 5 (1992), 357–374.
Goodman, A. C. "Hedonic Prices, Price Indices and Housing Markets," *Journal of Urban Economics* 5 (1978), 357–374.
Griliches, Zvi (ed.). *Price Indexes and Quality Change.* Cambridge, MA: Harvard, 1971.
Hill, R. C., J. R. Knight, and C. F. Sirmans. "Estimating Capital Asset Price Indexes," *The Review of Economics and Statistics* 19 (forthcoming, 1997).
Olsen, Edgar O. "A Competitive Theory of the Housing Market," *American Economic Review* 59 (1969), 612–622.
Palmquist, R. B. "Alternative Techniques for Developing Real Estate Price Indices," *The Review of Economics and Statistics* 62 (1980), 442–448.
Rosen, S. "Hedonic Prices and Implicit Markets: Product Differentiation in Pure Competition," *Journal of Political Economy* 82 (1974), 35–55.
Shiller, Robert J. "Measuring Asset Values for Cash Settlement in Derivative Markets: Hedonic Repeated Measures Indices and Perpetual Futures," *The Journal of Finance* 48 (1993), 911–931.
Shilling, J. D., C. F. Sirmans, and J. F. Dombrow. "Measuring Depreciation in Single-Family Rental and Owner-Occupied Housing," *Journal of Housing Economics* 1 (1991), 368–383.

Journal of Real Estate Finance and Economics, 14: 89–111 (1997)
© 1997 Kluwer Academic Publishers

Appraisals, Transaction Incentives, and Smoothing

PETER CHINLOY
American University, Washington, DC 20016-8044

MAN CHO
Fannie Mae, Washington, DC 20016-2899

ISAAC F. MEGBOLUGBE
Fannie Mae Foundation, Washington, DC 20016-2899

Abstract

This article is structured around three principal objectives. The first is to determine whether any incentives for appraisals support an underlying purchase offer, which may be termed a transaction bias. Appraisals that are lower than purchase prices could involve additional cost for justification and thus undermine the transaction. The second objective is to test whether appraisal data are smoothed or exhibit less volatility than purchase data. The article compares the volatility of separate appraisal and purchase data. Given separate appraisal and purchase time series, the third objective is to derive the implied optimal appraisal updating rule.

The model is applied to appraisal and purchase price indices for 3.7 million repeat transactions on mortgages bought by Fannie Mae and Freddie Mac by using monthly data from January 1975 to December 1993. The estimation procedure uses generalized autoregressive conditioned heteroskedastic (GARCH) analysis to take account of persistence in means and volatility in the house price time series. The article draws three principal conclusions. First, appraisals are systematically higher than purchase data, a first-moment differential. Second, appraisal smoothing does not occur generally. Third, the appraisal updating rule for the United States appears to involve error correction whereby underappraisals from pervious periods are eventually adjusted.

Key Words: appraisal smoothing, appraisal bias, house price indices, house price volatility

This article is structured around three principal objectives. The first is to determine whether any incentives exist for an appraisal to support an underlying purchase offer for real estate. This transaction incentive bias might lead to average appraisals that exceed average purchase prices. Downward appraisals could involve additional cost for justification and thus undermine the transaction. The second objective is to determine whether appraisals are smoothed or exhibit less volatility than purchase data when time-series tests are applied. In the absence of complete purchase data, appraisers may extrapolate from current information and cause smoothing or suppression of volatility. Given separate appraisal and purchase time series, the third objective is to derive an optimal updating rule for appraisal.

To manage default risk, mandatory appraisals are part of mortgage underwriting. Even without formal regulation, mortgage lenders require appraisals to validate a purchase price or to value collateral on a refinancing. Institutional investors, plan sponsors, and other real estate portfolio holders rely on appraisals to construct valuations and returns.

Many participants in the real estate market, including sales agents, mortgage brokers, lenders, and property and asset managers, are paid only if a transaction is executed. Appraisers face an asymmetric cost function, with higher costs of validation and documentary support for an appraisal below a purchase price as compared with one above the purchase price. This transaction incentive to overappraise can lead to an upward aggregation bias from combining purchase and appraisal data into a single price index.[1]

The test procedures for transaction incentives and smoothing use the first and second moments of appraisal and purchase price distributions. In forming their expectations, participants incorporate conditional means and variances of appraisals and purchase prices. This article focuses on mortgages purchased by Fannie Mae and Freddie Mac. The monthly observations extend from January 1975 to December 1993. At the end of 1994, the two agencies had purchased mortgages with outstanding balances of over $1 trillion, or one-third of all such debt, and accounted for more than 40% of the flow of mortgage purchases. The real estate collateral supporting the mortgages accounts for one-quarter of the household wealth in the United States.[2] Paired repeat transactions are constructed for two consecutive sales of a house and two consecutive appraisals with no corroborating purchase data. The transactions are usually constructed when a house undergoes a mortgage refinancing. The number of paired repeat transactions is 3.7 million. Of 16 regional and transaction-type subindices constructed, none contains fewer than 100,000 observations over the 228 months in the sample.

This article draws three principal empirical conclusions. First, appraisals tend to be higher than purchase prices. Comparing the appraisal and purchase price on the same house at the same time yields a robust conclusion. Appraisals are about 2% higher than purchases. Second, results on appraisal smoothing are mixed. Some evidence of smoothing appears both nationally and regionally in the Northeast and Midwest. The South and West, however, demonstrate less evidence of smoothing. Small sample sizes of comparables and heterogeneous beliefs among appraisers appear to outweigh smoothing tendencies in the latter two regions. Appraisal and purchase prices do not appear to have the same probability distributions.

Third, volatility and time-series representations of house price indices differ by region. With persistent volatility, turbulence in the real estate market prevails. Appraisal data differ from purchase data in volatility, leading to aggregation errors in combining such data with purchases.

The appraisal series applies to a cross-section of agents with heterogeneous beliefs and information. A time series for a single appraiser could well indicate appraisal smoothing after controlling for differences between appraisers. The underlying indication is that the heterogeneous beliefs and information differences are considerable, suggesting an efficiency gain from an automated appraisal procedure.

The first-moment analysis indicates a transaction incentive in appraisal. The second moment volatility analysis suggests that appraisal smoothing is not universal. Any analysis of appraisal data, including use in measures of real estate performance and returns, must account for both first and second moments of the underlying price distribution.

1. Real Estate Price Indices

Behavioral models specify how appraisers use market information in valuations. Quan and Quigley (1991) and Geltner (1993) specify an appraisal as the weighted average of the current price and the lagged appraisal. The weights are parameters to be estimated, depending on variance components for marketwide and transaction-specific effects, or temporal aggregation and seasonals. Ross and Zisler (1991) develop an autoregressive integrated moving average (ARIMA) representation of appraisal data. If appraisals involve autoregressive, integrated moving average updating, valuation depends on a series of lagged appraisals.

The approach in this study involves conditional means and variances of price distributions that follow generalized autoregressive conditional heteroskedasticity (GARCH), as in Bollerslev (1986). The conditional variances of house prices vary over time and between appraisal and purchase data and thus allow a test for smoothing. The approach complements the weighting and updating procedure of appraisers by estimating marketwide and property-specific variance components and not restricting them to a constant value. The procedure permits direct identification and estimation of the weights and minimizes the risk of error in real estate investment and construction of optimal portfolios.

The logarithm of the price of house i at time t $(t = 0, \ldots, T)$ is $\ln H_{it} = P_t + M_{it}$, where P_t is the desired index of general real estate prices and M_{it} denotes the error term. The error combines a random walk Gaussian showing an intertemporal volatility around the price index and the white noise representing cross-sectional dispersion in property valuation. In repeat-sales price construction, the capital gain between dates s and t for property i is

$$H_{it} - \ln H_{is} = P_t - P_s + M_{it} - M_{is}$$

$$= \sum_{j=1,}^{T} \beta_j D_{ij} + \vartheta_i \tag{1}$$

where the second equality is a stochastic specification. This procedure is applied by Case and Shiller (1989), Shiller (1993), and Lekkas, Quigley, and Van Order (1993). The D_{ij} are time dummy variables with $D_{ij} = -1$ for $j = s$, $D_{ij} = +1$ for $j = t$, and $D_{ij} = 0$ otherwise. The coefficients β_j, $j = 0, \ldots, T$ of the time dummies are the levels of the general price index, with $\beta_0 = 0$ by construction. With repeat sales, the characteristics of the property are held constant, but stochastic factors may affect the property. The error ϑ_i takes the form

$$E[M_{it} - M_{is}] = 0$$

$$E[M_{it} - M_{is}]^2 = \gamma_1(t - s) + \gamma_2(t - s)^2 + \gamma_3, \tag{2}$$

where the γ elements are parameters. The length of holding $t - s$ affects the volatility of the property-specific component. The weighted generalized least-squares methods produce efficient estimates of the parameters β_j, $j = 0, \ldots, T$. In a first stage, (1) is estimated with house capital gains $\ln H_{it} - \ln H_{is}$ regressed on time dummy variables. The residuals from the regression are recovered as e_{li}. A second-stage regression of e_{li}^2 on $(t - s)$ and $(t - s)^2$ permits estimates of γ. These estimates are used in a heteroskedastic transformation of (1). From a reestimation of (1), estimates of $\beta = (\beta_0, \ldots, \beta_T)$ are obtained.

The general price index is obtained from the β parameters as

$$P_t = P_0 \exp(\beta_t), \tag{3}$$

where

$$\beta_t = \ln\left(\prod_{i\epsilon L(t)}(H_{it}/(H_{is}\exp(-\beta_s)))\right)^{1/n(t)}. \tag{4}$$

Here, $n(t)$ is the number of properties transacting in period t, and $L(t)$ the set of properties transacting at t. The estimated coefficient is the ratio of the logarithm of the geometric mean of prices for properties transacting in period t to an estimate of the logarithm of the geometric mean in the base period.

The parameters are expressed in logarithmic form, and the index is an exponential transformation with $E[\exp(\beta)] \neq \exp(E(\beta))$. If the estimate b of β is distributed normally with mean β and variance σ_β^2, $\exp(b)$ is distributed lognormally with mean $\exp[\beta + 1/2\sigma_\beta^2]$.[3] In (3), a small-sample bias correction is

$$\exp(b) = \exp(\beta)[1 + (1/2)\hat{\sigma}_\beta^2], \tag{5}$$

where $\hat{\sigma}_\beta^2$ is a consistent estimate of σ_β^2 enabling the entire price series P_t to be constructed. This procedure produces a general price index P_t with one parameter β_t for each time period. This set of T prices comes from an initial group of N properties, where $N > T$.

In repeat-sales data, sufficient transactions are required to estimate accurately each time period parameter. To make the problem manageable and tractable, a two-stage procedure is developed. The first stage produces individual property repeat-sales data. The growth rate of the general price index is $p_t = (P_t - P_{t-1})/P_{t-1}$; it depends on the parameter estimates b of β, which themselves may exhibit a persistent or systematic pattern.

The first-stage estimates b for the price index parameters using (1)–(5). The second stage involves specifying a process for the b and the associated capital gains $p = (p_0, \ldots, p_T)$. The two-stage procedure assumes a recursive and block-diagonal structure of the conditional means and variances. This constraint could be removed by estimating the means and variances of the overall structure directly, but requires diagonalizing a matrix equal in dimension to the number of observations.

For the second-stage estimation of the nonconstant variances of growth in prices, participants have expectations about market behavior. Participants have an information set I_{t-1} about the market up to $t - 1$. Based on I_{t-1}, participants form expectations about the conditional mean and variance of house price growth, which are set respectively at m_t and v_t^2. The actual capital gain p_t is the conditional mean plus an error ε_t or

$$p_t = m_t + \varepsilon_t. \tag{6}$$

The error is $\varepsilon_t = v_t z_t$, the product of the conditional standard deviation and z_t, the standard normal variate, with zero mean and unit variance. If E_{t-1} is the expectation operator using information set I_{t-1},

$$E_{t-1}[\varepsilon_t] = 0 \qquad E_{t-1}[\varepsilon_t^2] = v_t^2, \tag{7}$$

and the variance of capital gains v_t^2 is nonconstant over time.

These variable variance forms have generally not been applied to real estate data because of limited time series. They have, however, been used extensively in financial markets. A specification that has been shown to fit data for stocks, bonds, foreign exchange, and derivatives is the generalized autoregressive conditional heteroskedastic (GARCH) form:

$$v_t^2 = \sigma_0 + \sigma_1 \varepsilon_{t-1}^2 + \sigma_2 v_{t-1}^2. \tag{8}$$

This specification is GARCH(1,1), since it includes one lag on the squared error and one lag on the conditional error variance. A shock—or unanticipated capital gain or loss—has an impact on subsequent variances. The parameter σ_1 measures the persistence of a shock. Suppose that there has been a recent downturn in a real estate market, such as for housing. Capital gains are less than expected. Houses decline in price when increases had been expected. In (6), $p_{t-1} < m_{t-1}$, and the disturbance term ε_{t-1} is negative and relatively large. This situation is a shock to the volatility. In the next period, participants include a squared shock term ε_{t-1}^2 in calculating the conditional expectation of the variance of capital gains in period t. If $\sigma_1 = 0$, such shocks do not affect the next period's variance. In addition, if $\sigma_2 = 1$, the variance is constant as in classical econometric specifications.

When separate data sets are available, a price index A_t from appraisal data need not be identical to P_t obtained from (1)–(8). An analogous series of expectations about conditional means and variances by appraisers leads to the appraisal index A_t. This index has first-moment parameters, β_{At}, and second-moment parameters, σ_A. The corresponding variance of the appraisal growth is $v_{A,t}^2 = \sigma_{A0} + \sigma_{A1}\varepsilon_{t-1}^2 + \sigma_{A2}v_{t-1}^2$. Sequential and separate testing of the two sets of first and second moment parameters yields statistical inference on transaction incentives and smoothing.

Specifically, if

$$\beta_t = \beta_{At} \qquad t = 0, \ldots, T \tag{9}$$

there is no transaction incentive bias. The conditional mean of the growth rate of an index using only purchase data is identical to that using only appraisal data. If

$$\sigma = \sigma_A \tag{10}$$

for the three parameters in (8), no appraisal smoothing occurs. Given shocks and lags, the resulting conditional variances for appraisal and purchase data are identical. This test (10) permits appraisal smoothing to occur in a flexible variance structure.

There are reasons for both lower and higher volatility in appraisal data as compared with purchases. Appraisal smoothing and extrapolation from recent data lower the variance. Appraisers may be influenced by clientele effects, reputation, or reliability. An appraiser generating volatile data could lose lender or portfolio holder business. At the same time, appraisals limited to a small sample of comparables not randomly selected almost surely exhibit more volatility than marketwide purchase prices.

2. Hypothesis Testing

The implementation of the transaction incentive test calls for stacking the initial capital gains observations between dates s and t. The gains have the deterministic component

$$\ln H_t - \ln H_s = \beta_t D_t - \beta_s D_s + \beta_{At} D_t J - \beta_{As} D_s J. \tag{11}$$

Here, H_t is either the purchase or appraisal observation, $D_t = 1$ for a transaction at date t, and 0 otherwise; and $J = 1$ for an appraisal, and 0 for a purchase. The error in capital gains, the dependent variable—capital gains—has a form analogous to (2). The stacking allows testing for first-moment aggregation of real estate data. A real estate index containing both purchase and appraisal data is valid in its first moments if

$$
\begin{aligned}
\beta_t &= \beta_{At} & t &= 0, \ldots, T & &\text{(aggregation)} \\
\beta_{At} &> \beta_t & t &= 0, \ldots, T & &\text{(transaction incentives)}.
\end{aligned}
\tag{12}
$$

The alternative hypothesis is that mean appraisals exceed mean purchase prices, with a transaction incentive. In this case, an aggregation bias arises from consolidating purchase and appraisal data.

As a moral hazard incentive to complete the deal, the transaction bias suggests that appraisals systematically exceed purchase prices. An appraiser faces asymmetric costs from overstating versus understating. Undervaluation involves costs of additional verification and the risk of the deal failing if the seller refuses to make concessions. Other first-moment errors in appraisal are aggregation bias where valuations at different time intervals are ascribed to a specific date, and seasonal clustering because such evaluations, which often occurs at the end of the year.

With separate appraisal and purchase data and a second-moment conditional heteroskedastic specification, a test for smoothing can be carried out. Let there be a criterion $\lambda \subset [\lambda_{\min}, \lambda_{\max}]$, which is a benchmark ranging over a predetermined interval. Searching over the interval, an appraisal price series is smoothed relative to its underlying purchase analogue when

$$\sigma_{A1} + \sigma_{A2} < \lambda, \sigma_1 + \sigma_2 > \lambda \qquad \text{for any } \lambda \subset [\lambda_{\min}, \lambda_{\max}]. \tag{13}$$

Less volatility and persistence are observed in the appraisal series when both are compared to a benchmark.[4] The test for appraisal smoothing permits market participants to have nonconstant expectations about the conditional variances v_t of capital gains. The appraisal smoothing test has no analogue in financial markets. Though focused on real estate, it could be applied to other illiquid assets such as jewelry and objects of art. Table 1 presents the time-series test procedures.

Another advantage of separate appraisal and purchase time series is the ability to construct an optimal updating rule. The rule is based on due diligence tests on the separate time series. A unit root test determines the degree of stationarity in the time series and whether appraiser updates are based on price levels or their growth rates. If purchase and appraisal

Table 1. Transaction incentives and appraisal smoothing tests.

Hypothesis Test	Parameter Restriction	Test Equation
First moment		
Unbiased	$\beta = \beta_A$	(12)
Transaction incentives	$\beta_A > \beta$	
Second moment		
Appraisal smoothing	$\sigma_{A1} + \sigma_{A2} < \lambda, \sigma_1 + \sigma_2 > \lambda$	
	for any $\lambda \subset [\lambda_{min}, \lambda_{max}]$.	(13)

prices are cointegrated, then optimal updating involves an error correction. Appraisers make adjustments depending on whether they have overvalued or undervalued in the recent past. Causality tests determine whether purchases cause appraisals and therefore can be viewed as exogenous in the updating function.

3. Data

The data are monthly price series from January 1975 to December 1993 for housing that acts as collateral for mortgages purchased by Fannie Mae and Freddie Mac. As part of their mortgage underwriting procedures, both agencies obtain data on property location, including street address, ZIP code, and state. The sample includes only single-family, single-unit dwellings. Condominium units, cooperatives, planned unit developments, and two- to four-unit dwellings are excluded. Properties whose mortgages carry full federal default protection insured by the Federal Housing Administration and the Veterans Administration are likewise excluded. For confidentiality and security purposes, variables in the mortgage application and house characteristics on the appraisal are not available.[5] Mortgages are limited to first liens and do not include home equity loans, second mortgages, or loans where the priority claim is unknown. An observation is a repeat-sales pairing where, for a given property, a mortgage has been purchased on two separate occasions by either agency during the sample period. The purchase series is the observation of two consecutive sales. The appraisal series is based on pairs of refinancings.

After pairing and cleaning by eliminating incomplete data, 3.7 million observations remain over the 228-month sample period. The data are divided between purchase observations in which two sales prices are observed and appraisal observations in which no sales prices are observed. In two hybrid cases, one sales price is observed. The mixed categories have a purchase and appraisal and an appraisal and purchase.

Alternative house price series cannot easily generate a national or regional index or contain measurement errors. The Society of Real Estate Appraisers collects data on house prices on a city-by-city basis, and aggregation into a national or regional index is difficult. The National Association of Realtors produces median prices for homes subject to compositional mix biases. Higher priced houses tend to sell during an upturn, with a market weighting toward less expensive houses during a downturn. The Bureau of the Census publishes quality-adjusted aggregate house price indices but focuses on new construction.[6]

Table 2. Repeat transactions: Fannie Mae and Freddie Mac mortgage purchases, 1975–1993.

	(1) Purchase–purchase	(2) Appraisal–appraisal	(3) Purchase–appraisal	(4) Appraisal–purchase	(5) Total
United States	752,562	955,904	1,744,640	298,967	3,753,073
Midwest	170,433	251,829	446,821	73,813	942,896
Northeast	161,490	158,229	357,041	66,773	743,533
South	194,199	118,111	360,168	55,872	728,350
West	226,440	427,735	580,610	102,509	1,337,294

Purchase: a mortgage purchased by either agency, involving sale of a property.
Appraisal: a mortgage purchased by either agency, not involving sale of a property.

The data are divided into the four census regions: Midwest, Northeast, South, and West. In addition to the national data, there are 16 subsamples for the four types of transaction index and four regions. Table 2 presents the number of observations on each of the 16 index types.

Four figures are provided to delineate house price movements based on purchase and appraisal indices from different geographical areas. Figure 1 displays regional purchases and

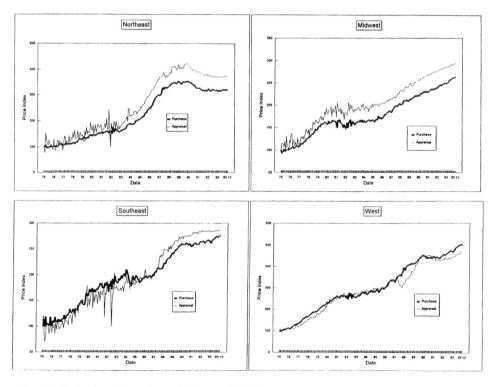

Figure 1. Regional purchase and appraisal house price indices (Monthly, January 1975–December 1993).

appraisal indices for house prices. Two conclusions emerge in the Midwest and Northeast. First, the appraisal index lies above the purchase index throughout the sample period. Second, the appraisal index appears more volatile than the purchase index, especially between 1975 and 1985. Smoothing is less of a problem than the volatility induced by small sample size and heterogeneous beliefs among appraisers. The same qualitative conclusions apply to the South, although, in the first half of the sample period, the appraisal index sometimes falls below the purchase index. The West exhibits crossover points between the two, although one index is above the other for several years at a time and appraisal volatility is less pronounced. For the United States housing market, shown in Figure 2, the appraisal index exceeds the purchase index from 1977 onward, with the differential increasing.

Figure 3 presents the data as annual regional growth rates. House price volatility declines in all regions of the country after 1983. Midwest prices increase in a tight range between zero and 5% annually after 1983 and never reach the negative range. The appraisal index in the Northeast is volatile during the 1970s but dampens during the 1980s.

From Figure 4, United States house price growth fluctuates during the 1970s and peaks in 1978. This is the year in which an all-time record of 4 million resale house transactions took place in response to inflationary expectations and property tax cut anticipations.[7] The appraisal index generally shows a higher growth rate than the purchase index. In some years,

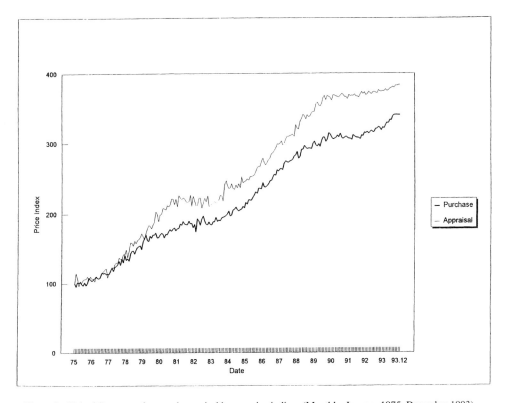

Figure 2. United States purchase and appraisal house price indices (Monthly, January 1975–December 1993).

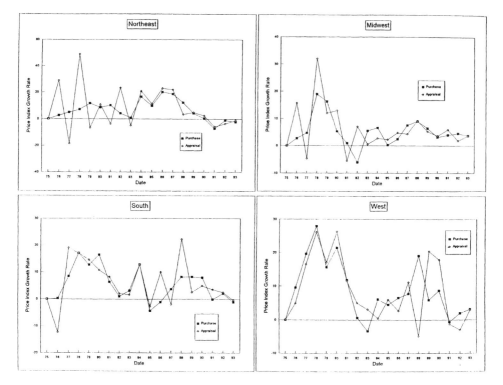

Figure 3. Regional house price appreciation (Annual, 1975–1993).

appraisal index generally shows a higher growth rate than the purchase index. In some years, prices on the appraisal index increase by over 20%, but the purchase index increases by several fewer percentage points. Since 1983, the two indices have moved closer together, though at more sluggish rates. House price growth has been trending downward on both indices and has remained barely positive during the 1990s. Over time, appraisal data have become tighter as they have approached the purchase index.

House price movements may be related to systematic variables, including real estate transaction volume and mortgage rates and the term structure. Macroeconomic factors similar to those used in arbitrage pricing of stocks by Chen, Roll, and Ross (1986) and, for real estate investment trusts, by Chan, Hendershott, and Sanders (1990) are applied to the sample of houses. The list of these factors is $Z_1, \ldots, Z_K$. The Z variables are changes in rates of expected inflation, the slope of the term structure, mortgage risk structure, the rate of unexpected inflation, the total return on the Standard & Poor's 500 index, and the volume of house transactions in the relevant appraisal or purchase category. The objective is to adjust the house price data so that the shocks and errors ε_t are completely unanticipated after correction for real estate and macroeconomic variables, including inflation and interest rates.

The expected inflation rate is from an autoregression of the monthly growth rate of the Consumer Price Index. A multicollinearity test indicated a condition number of less than 20 with 12 lags in the inflation autoregression.[8] The test indicates that it is possible to include

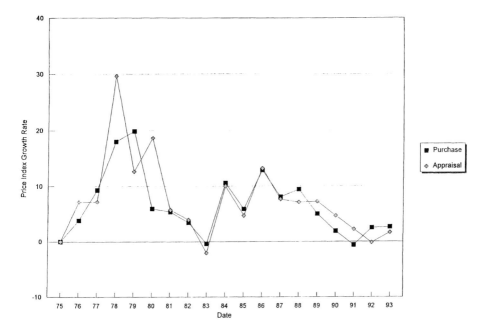

Figure 4. United States house price appreciation (Annual, 1975–1993).

a monthly lag length up to 12 without severe multicollinearity. The rate of expected inflation is the fitted value from the 12-month autoregression. The rate of unexpected inflation is the difference between the actual and expected inflation rates.

Interest rate effects are included through the term and risk structures. The term structure premium is the difference between the yield on ten-year Treasury bonds and that on relatively riskless three-month Treasury bills. The mortgage risk premium is the difference between the yield on 30-year amortization fixed-rate mortgages and the ten-year Treasury bond yield. The rationale is that 30-year mortgages are usually priced as a margin against ten-year Treasury bonds. The term structure premium prices the yield curve into house capital gains. The risk premium is for holding a mortgage, as opposed to a Treasury bond. The lender carries prepayment and potentially some residual default risk.

Housing may be integrated with other capital markets, such as the stock market. To test this integration, the total return—capital gains and dividends—on the Standard & Poor's 500 stock index is included as an explanatory variable.

4. Specification and Empirical Results

4.1. Transaction Incentives

The first stage of estimation is to estimate parameters β for the separate indices and to use an F-test to determine whether the parameters are the same across index specifications. There are four separate data sets: for purchase, appraisal, and two hybrids. There are six pairwise

Table 3. First-moment transaction incentive tests (*F*-statistics, 228 numerator, infinite denominator degrees of freedom).

	Midwest	Northeast	South	West
Purchase–Purchase vs. Appraisal–Appraisal	4.62	4.03	12.25	19.01
Purchase–Purchase vs. Purchase–Appraisal	2.77	5.87	16.20	9.10
Purchase–Purchase vs. Appraisal–Purchase	2.59	2.59	7.94	20.33
Appraisal–Appraisal vs. Purchase–Appraisal	4.45	4.45	12.95	27.17
Appraisal–Appraisal vs. Appraisal–Purchase	2.03	2.04	6.30	7.30
Purchase–Appraisal vs. Appraisal–Purchase	2.94	2.94	13.52	34.67

Results are for the six pairwise aggregations of the repeat indices.

tests for comparing whether the parameters of the indices are the same. Table 3 reports the results. With four separate regions and six index pairs, there are 24 separate *F*-tests.

With the critical value of *F* at 1.25 at 1% significance for 200 numerator and infinite denominator degrees of freedom, purchase and appraisal data are not identical—at least to first moments. The purchase-appraisal test statistic is 4.62, indicating a difference between the two data series. The test statistics for aggregating to a combined purchase-appraisal index range between 4.62 to 19.01, depending on the region. There are transaction incentive differentials between the two indices. The aggregation conditions fail for the other pairs as well. The results suggest that aggregation errors can arise from mixing purchase and appraisal data into one index.

Table 4. Appraisal and purchase on the same transaction.

	Midwest	Northeast	South	West	National
Negative Appraisal					
$< -10\%$	0.33	0.52	0.33	0.28	0.35
$-10\% \leq (A - P)/P < -5\%$	0.74	0.97	0.63	0.61	0.71
$-5\% \geq (A - P)/P < -1\%$	2.64	2.86	2.10	2.33	2.42
$-1\% \geq (A - P)/P < 0\%$	1.69	1.45	1.41	1.77	1.57
Negative Subtotal	5.40	5.80	4.47	4.99	5.05
$0\%(A = P)$	33.81	29.40	25.01	36.20	30.68
Positive Appraisal					
$0\% < (A - P)/P \leq 1\%$	26.39	21.00	25.78	25.36	25.02
$1\% < (A - P)/P \leq 5\%$	25.79	29.70	31.52	23.30	27.79
$5\% < (A - P)/P \leq 10\%$	5.34	8.04	8.09	5.94	6.86
$> 10\%$	3.29	6.06	5.13	4.20	4.59
Positive Subtotal	60.81	64.80	70.72	58.80	64.26
Total	100.00	100.00	100.00	100.00	100.00

Data are 600,000 Fannie Mae purchase-money mortgages during 1993. Both a purchase price and an appraisal are observed. The data are the frequency distribution of the percentage differences between the appraisal and purchase price on the same house. Negative appraisals occur when the valuation A falls below the purchase price P, or $(A - P)/P < 0$.

As a check of robustness, purchases and appraisals on the same house were compared. A purchase transaction requires an appraisal to validate the price. The sample is 600,000 mortgages purchased by Fannie Mae during 1993 when the purpose was purchase of a house rather than refinancing. Table 4 presents the results of this cross-sectional comparison. An appraisal is positive when it exceeds the purchase price and negative when it falls below the purchase price.

The results corroborate first moment differentials between appraisals and purchases. In 64% of the cases, the appraisal at the date of the transaction exceeds the purchase price. In another 31% of the cases, appraisals are identical to the purchase price to the dollar. In only 5% of the cases is the appraisal less than the purchase price. Overall, the mean appraisal price is 1.8% higher than the mean purchase price.

Both time-series and cross-sectional data suggest the possibility of transaction incentives. A positive appraisal provides a signal to an incompletely informed buyer that a property is undervalued, thus reducing the risk of fallout or not completing the purchase. A negative appraisal requires additional verification cost for the appraiser and jeopardizes referrals from lenders and brokers. The results have implications for using appraisal data for constructing price and rate-of-return indices. Comparisons with other real estate price series must be made cautiously, since the various purposes of appraisal are not identical. For example, although the Russell–NCREIF index is determined by appraisals, its intention is to mark properties to market rather than for loan procurement.

4.2. Appraisal Smoothing

In the second stage of the two-stage estimation procedure, appraisal smoothing tests are applied to the second moments. From the estimated β, the relevant price indices use the exponential corrections in (3)–(5). Capital gains p of the resulting price indices are then obtained. Under the restriction of block-diagonality between the first and second moments of the house price distribution, smoothing tests are performed. While this moment separability occurs, the second moments vary over the time-series observations.

The capital gains p may be influenced by macroeconomic variables that produce systematic effects. Any errors tested for persistence and smoothing must first by purged of the influence of financial and real estate market variables. The procedure used is the two-step method of Engle and Ng (1993), Glosten, Jagannathan, and Runkle (1993), and Nelson (1992). The first step determines an unpredictable shock residual from a regression of the growth rate of house prices on the $Z_1, \ldots, Z_K$ variables. The second step involves an autoregression of these unpredictable shock residuals under a persistent volatility specification.

The regression on the $Z_1, \ldots, Z_K$ variables is

$$p_t = \alpha_0 + \sum_{i=1}^{K} \alpha_i Z_{it} + v_t, \tag{14}$$

with error v_t. Residuals from this equation are $u_t = p_t - p_t^*$, where p_t^* is the fitted value. The residual is house price growth corrected for macroeconomic trends but subject to local market conditions and other shocks. The actual estimation is for an AR(2), where the residual embodies two lags and its error obeys a GARCH(1,1) process. The residual regression is

$$u_t = \gamma_0 + \gamma_1 u_{t-1} + \gamma_2 u_{t-2} + \varepsilon_t, \tag{15}$$

where the ε_t in (15) has zero mean and variance $v_t^2 = \sigma_0 + \sigma_1 \varepsilon_{t-1}^2 + \sigma_2 v_{t-1}^2$. Parameter estimates of these σ elements are obtained for each of the four indices. The system (14) and (15) is estimated simultaneously. Table 5 presents the results for the macroeconomic variables, residual lags, and GARCH(1,1) parameters. Asymptotic t-statistics are expressed in parentheses, and asterisks indicate coefficients significant at the 1% level.

In general, the macroeconomic variables do not have significant effects on house prices for either purchase or appraisal purposes. The only significant coefficients are on inflation variables. House price growth appears to be dampened by changes in expected inflation but increases with unexpected inflation.

The residuals—or house price growth corrected for macroeconomic factors—exhibit positive serial correlation. The one lag autoregressive coefficient γ_1 ranges between 0.21 and 0.45 and is significant at the 1% level in nine of the ten cases. This finding of positive serial correlation in house prices is similar to that observed by Case and Shiller (1989). They find a positive serial correlation of 0.4 for city data. The two lag autoregressive coefficients γ_2 are generally positive. In four cases, the coefficients are positive and range from 0.17 to 0.24, with no negative and significant effects. The results suggest short-term positive autocorrelations without an immediate tendency toward mean reversion, which would occur with negative coefficients, although these coefficients cover only two markets.

The GARCH coefficients for σ_1 and σ_2 indicate that house prices exhibit persistent volatility. If the coefficients on σ_2 for the lagged variance v_{t-1}^2 are equal to 1 and the coefficients on σ_1 for the lagged squared shock ε_{t-1}^2 are equal to zero, there is no GARCH structure, and the conventional constant variance applies. This situation does not apply in any region or in the United States. Instead, capital gain volatility in the housing market is persistent.

Table 6 presents the tests for appraisal smoothing. Entries are asymptotic t-statistics for the test that the sum of the two GARCH parameters is equal to the value in the first column. The sum $\sigma_1 + \sigma_2$ for each index is compared with a benchmark λ ranging between 0.9 and 1.1. Smoothing occurs when the sum of the volatility coefficients for appraisal is lower than those for purchase, or $\sigma_{A1} + \sigma_{A2} < \lambda, \sigma_1 + \sigma_2 > \lambda$.

The first column in Table 6 reports values for λ. The entries in the remaining columns in Table 6 are t-statistics. For any λ, a negative and significant test statistic for the appraisal index A_t and a positive and significant test statistic for the purchase index P_t indicate appraisal smoothing. One-tailed critical values of the t-statistic at 1% and 2.5% significance levels are 2.6 and 2.0, respectively. Appraisal smoothing occurs in the Northeast at a benchmark of $\lambda = 0.99$, with coefficients of 5.1 for purchase and -3.1 for appraisal. For the United States market at the same benchmark, the two coefficients are 1.4 for purchase and -2.0 for appraisal and indicate moderate smoothing. The test statistics for the appraisal index are numerically smaller than for the purchase index. Similar moderate appraisal smoothing that fails the benchmark test occurs in the Midwest.

Table 5. House prices: macroeconomic responses, autoregressive structure, and GARCH (1, 1) effects (t-statistics in parentheses).

	US P_t	US A_t	NE P_t	NE A_t	MW P_t	MW A_t	S P_t	S A_t	W P_t	W A_t
Intercept (*E + 02)	0.5 (6.2)	0.4 (4.9)	0.2 (1.8)	0.2 (1.6)	0.4 (0.1)	0.4 (7.3)	0.3 (2.5)	0.1 (1.7)	0.6 (5.6)	0.5 (4.7)
Expected inflation change	-1.1 (0.5)	-1.8 (0.8)	1.0 (0.3)	0.0 (0.0)	0.0 (0.0)	-0.8 (0.6)	1.3 (0.6)	1.6 (0.7)	-5.6* (2.2)	-1.4 (0.3)
Unanticipated inflation	0.5 (0.8)	0.7 (1.1)	-0.9 (0.7)	1.0 (1.4)	-0.3 (0.7)	-0.1 (0.3)	0.5* (4.6)	-0.2 (0.4)	0.8 (1.4)	0.3 (0.4)
Term structure change	1.5 (0.8)	0.3 (0.2)	1.3 (0.7)	0.3 (0.2)	0.4 (0.0)	0.1 (0.1)	-1.0 (0.6)	-0.6 (0.6)	1.5 (1.0)	-1.7 (1.0)
Mortgage risk structure change	-8.4 (1.7)	-3.4 (0.5)	2.9 (0.4)	8.8 (0.7)	6.6 (0.2)	-10.6 (1.6)	1.4 (0.2)	1.0 (0.1)	8.2 (1.8)	-0.1 (0.1)
Standard & Poor's 500 total return	-0.01 (0.2)	-0.04 (1.7)	0.02 (0.7)	-0.04 (0.8)	0.01 (0.0)	-0.04 (2.1)	0.03 (1.0)	0.03 (1.3)	-0.02 (0.4)	-0.49 (1.2)
House transaction volume lagged	-0.1 (1.5)	-0.9 (2.3)	-0.3 (0.4)	-1.2 (2.3)	-0.2 (0.1)	-0.2 (1.0)	0.5 (0.7)	-0.4 (1.3)	-1.2 (1.2)	-1.1 (1.7)
γ_1 House price residual lagged	0.43* (6.2)	0.41* (5.1)	0.21* (2.8)	0.28* (3.4)	0.34 (1.0)	0.45* (6.1)	0.32* (3.9)	0.59* (6.8)	0.20* (2.5)	0.21* (2.6)
γ_2 House price residual lagged twice	0.10 (1.3)	0.18* (2.4)	-0.05 (0.7)	0.17* (2.0)	0.15 (0.4)	0.24* (3.4)	0.09 (1.2)	0.25* (2.9)	-0.11 (1.5)	0.08 (0.9)
σ_1 ARCH(1) ε_{t-1}^2	0.15* (2.4)	0.11* (2.9)	0.22* (2.7)	0.16* (2.7)	0.16* (3.7)	0.13 (0.4)	0.18* (4.6)	0.19* (4.0)	0.15* (2.0)	0.16* (2.1)
σ_2 GARCH(1) v_{t-1}^2	0.84* (50)	0.88* (32)	0.80* (12)	0.83* (28)	0.87* (2.9)	0.82 (50)	0.88* (50)	0.82* (28)	0.85* (12)	0.85* (17)
R^2	0.19	0.14	0.11	0.18	0.14	0.30	0.16	0.31	0.16	0.07

Note: asymptotic t-statistics in parentheses, with change coefficients multiplied by E-03. Asterisks denote statistical nonzero significance at the .01 level.

Table 6. Benchmark tests for appraisal smoothing.

λ	United States		Northeast		Midwest		South		West	
	P_t	A_t	P_t	A_t	P_t	A_t	P_t	A_t	P_t	A_t
0.9	42.4	97.1	35.4	18.2	136.3	78.2	24.7	22.5	83.7	42.6
0.925	31.0	69.6	27.0	12.3	101.2	57.2	21.4	19.6	62.1	32.4
0.95	19.6	42.1	18.6	6.4	66.1	36.3	18.0	16.7	40.5	22.2
0.975	8.2	14.6	10.2	0.5	31.0	15.3	14.7	13.8	18.9	10.0
0.98	5.9	9.0	8.5	−0.7	24.0	11.1	14.0	13.2	14.6	10.0
0.99	1.4	−2.0	5.1	−3.1	10.0	2.8	12.7	12.0	6.0	6.0
1.00	−3.2	−13.0	1.7	−5.4	−4.1	−5.6	11.3	10.8	−2.6	1.9
1.01	−7.7	−24.0	−1.6	−7.8	−18.1	−14.0	10.0	9.7	−11.2	−2.2
1.02	−12.3	−35.0	−5.0	−10.2	−32.1	−22.4	8.6	8.5	−19.9	−6.3
1.025	−14.6	−40.5	−6.7	−11.4	−39.2	−26.6	8.0	7.9	−24.2	−8.3
1.05	−26.0	−68.0	−15.1	−17.3	−74.2	−47.5	4.6	5.0	−45.8	−18.4
1.075	−37.4	−95.5	−23.5	−23.2	−109.3	−68.5	1.3	2.1	−67.3	−28.6
1.1	−48.8	−123.1	−31.9	−29.1	−144.4	−89.4	−2.1	−0.8	−88.9	−38.8

Note: One-tailed critical values of the *t*-statistic at 1% and 2.5% significance levels are 2.6 and 2.0, respectively.

The South and West reveal more volatility in the appraisal index. In the West, where the purchase index is more dampened than the appraisal index, reverse smoothing is not rejected at the 5% level. The λ = 1 row shows benchmark test statistics of −2.6 for purchase and 1.9 for appraisal. Appraisers induce more volatility into house prices than in the underlying purchase series. The South exhibits a different volatility pattern. In this region, both test statistics remain positive until λ is greater than unity.

4.3. Appraiser Behavior

The tests permit a determination of appraiser behavior. With unit roots in the time series, restrictions are imposed on the stationarity of the process. Under cointegration, there is a long-term relationship between appraisal and purchase data that should be incorporated into appraisal rules. Under causality, the structure of aggregation of appraisals and the exogeneity of purchase data can be determined.

The unit root test is carried out on both the price level of the index P_t and its growth rate p_t. The price series is stationary and has a unit root when $\beta_{UP} = 1$ in

$$P_t = \beta_{U0} + \beta_{UP} P_{t-1} + \beta_{Ut} t + \sum_{i=1}^{M} \beta_i \Delta P_{t-i}, \tag{16}$$

with a similar condition holding for p_t. A stronger version of the unit root test adds a zero time trend or $\beta_{Ut} = 0$. Given monthly data, the lag length M is set at 12. Table 7 displays estimates of the unit root tests. The upper panel presents price levels P_t and the lower panel growth rates p_t.

Table 7. Appraisal and purchase indices: unit root tests (test statistics).

	Purchase			Appraisal		
(1)	(2)	(3)	(4)	(5)	(6)	(7)
		Weak	Strong		Weak	Strong
Price levels	$\beta_{UP} = 1$	$\beta_{UP} = 1$	$\beta_{UP} = 1$ $\beta_{Ut} = 0$	$\beta_{UP} = 1$	$\beta_{UP} = 1$	$\beta_{UP} = 1$ $\beta_{Ut} = 0$
Northeast	0.9744	−2.26	55.59	0.9687	−1.04	105.22
Midwest	0.9553	−1.87	106.43	0.9280	−1.67	105.38
South	0.9279	−2.06	106.10	0.8808	−1.71	104.44
West	0.9431	−2.36	106.73	0.9213	−3.41	106.88
United States	0.9363	−2.29	106.69	0.9422	−2.17	106.67
Growth rates						
Northeast	0.1187	−2.70	1.59	−1.9388	−5.09	7.20
Midwest	−0.1015	−2.88	0.39	−2.4752	−6.23	9.67
South	−1.2546	−4.49	3.84	−1.9159	−4.24	4.50
West	0.1421	−2.68	3.61	0.0498	−3.33	2.61
United States	−0.2923	−2.94	1.55	−0.2731	−3.18	3.00
Critical Values		t(ADF)	$F(2, \infty)$		t(ADF)	$F(2, \infty)$
		5%:7.9	5%:7.3		5%:7.9	5%:7.3
		1%:13.3	1%:8.4		1%:13.3	1%:8.4

Columns (3) and (6) provide Augmented Dickey–Fuller (ADF) test statistics for a weak unit root where $\delta_P = 1$. The stronger version with the time trend zero is presented in columns (4) and (7). The critical values of the test statistics are reported in the last row. For price levels of purchase and appraisal indices, the null hypothesis is not accepted; accordingly, there is no stationarity in the series. Such is the result for all five regions and for both the weak and strong versions of the test. In growth rates, the dependent variable in (16) is replaced by $p_t = (P_t − P_{t-1})/P_t$, and the test is that $\beta_{UP} = 0$.

As demonstrated by the results in the lower panel of Table 7, growth rates in the purchase and appraisal indices have a unit root and are stationary. In nine of the ten cases, the unit root is accepted under both criteria. The weak test of unity of the first difference in house price growth and the stronger test that adds a time trend confirm the hypothesis. The only exception is for appraisal data in the Midwest. The appraisal and purchase growth rates have a unit root and are integrated of order one, following Engle and Granger (1987).

With the growth rates of house prices stationary, appraisal and purchase data can be tested for cointegration. In the case of a long-term relationship between purchase and appraisal prices, the time series are cointegrated. The level of cointegration provides indications of the explicit functional form used by appraisers. Appraisers set their valuations based on recent purchase data, adjusting for any errors in previous periods. If they overappraised properties recently, they reduce future appraisals after taking account of the transaction incentive. The optimal appraisal depends on lagged adjustments or error corrections. Cointegration and its extent are testable as is the nature of the appraisal function. Cointegration is tested by applying a unit root test to the equation.

Table 8. Purchase and appraisal price cointegration.

	Endogenous	Exogenous	β_{C1}	Weak $\beta_{C1} = 1$	Strong $\beta_{C1} = 1, \beta_{Ct} = 0$
Northeast	Purchase	Appraisal	−0.6959	−362.92	2.84
	Appraisal	Purchase	−1.7344	−585.16	6.80
Midwest	Purchase	Appraisal	−0.9266	−412.29	3.89
	Appraisal	Purchase	−1.9518	−631.69	11.67
South	Purchase	Appraisal	−1.7737	−593.57	7.89
	Appraisal	Purchase	−2.0678	−656.50	6.46
West	Purchase	Appraisal	−0.5368	−328.87	2.35
	Appraisal	Purchase	−0.7154	−367.10	4.23
United States	Purchase	Appraisal	−0.7475	−373.96	2.75
	Appraisal	Purchase	−0.6533	−353.80	2.44
Critical Values				t(ADF) 5%:7.9 1%:13.3	$F(2, \infty)$ 5%:7.3 1%:8.4

$$e_t = \beta_{C0} + \beta_{C1}e_{t-1} + \sum_{j=2}^{12} \beta_{Cj}\Delta e_{t-j+1} + \beta_{Ct}t, \tag{17}$$

where the e_t are the residuals of the regression of p_t on a_t.

Table 8 presents test statistics for cointegration. The null hypothesis is that purchase and appraisal indices are not cointegrated; the alternative is that they are cointegrated. The variable listed as exogenous is the regressor in computing the residual, the change of which is the dependent variable for the test. The null hypothesis is that the residual in the regression of purchase on appraisal house price growth rates has a unit root. If so, purchase and appraisal growth rates are not cointegrated. Appraisers do not have a long-term relationship with purchase data in mind when developing valuations. The alternative, which calls for rejecting residual regression unit roots, is that the growth rates are cointegrated. In this case, appraisers link valuations with purchase information.

In nine of the ten cases, the hypothesis of unit roots in the residual regression is not accepted. Appraisal growth rates are cointegrated with purchase growth rates. Only in the appraisal index for the Midwest—the same case where a unit root failed—is there an exception.

With the growth rates exhibiting stationarity and cointegration, the variables can be tested for Granger causality to determine the optimal updating in the appraisal function. The direction of causality provides information as to the level of feedback in appraisal. If appraisals cause purchases, sellers look at recent valuations in determining which transaction prices to accept. If purchases cause appraisals, then appraisers set their valuations off against recent purchase data. Causality could run in both directions.

The growth rate of purchase house prices is $p_t = (P_t - P_{t-1})/P_{t-1}$. The corresponding growth rate based on appraisals is $a_t = (A_t - A_{t-1})/A_{t-1}$. Causality is tested by determining significance of lagged appraisals in the purchase equation and lagged purchases in the appraisal equation in a vector autoregression. Included also is a term c, a residual after regressing the current value of one dependent variable on the other and the macroeconomic

Table 9. Tests for causality of appraisal and purchase prices.

	(1) Endogenous	(2) Exogenous	(3) F (c included)	(4) F (c excluded)
Northeast	Purchase	Appraisal	7.93	3.14
	Appraisal	Purchase	5.64	6.33
Midwest	Purchase	Appraisal	6.98	7.21
	Appraisal	Purchase	6.15	10.90
South	Purchase	Appraisal	2.22	3.13
	Appraisal	Purchase	7.48	8.76
West	Purchase	Appraisal	1.80	1.88
	Appraisal	Purchase	7.62	1.88
United States	Purchase	Appraisal	7.45	1.91
	Appraisal	Purchase	12.35	4.53
			F (1%) 2.37	F (1%) 2.37,
			F(5%) 3.32	F(5%) 3.32

variables Z, following the Granger representation theorem. The vector autoregression is

$$P_t = \gamma_{PC} P_{t-1} + \sum_{i=1}^{M} \alpha_{Pi} p_{t-i} + \sum_{j=1}^{M} \beta_{Aj} a_{t-j} \tag{18}$$

$$a_t = \gamma_{AC} A_{t-1} + \sum_{i=1}^{M} \alpha_{Ai} p_{t-i} + \sum_{j=1}^{M} \beta_{Pj} a_{t-j}. \tag{19}$$

Appraisals do not cause purchases when $\alpha_{Pi} \neq 0$, $\beta_{Aj} = 0$. Purchases do not cause appraisals when $\alpha_{Aj} = 0$, $\beta_{Pj} \neq 0$. The causality equations are tested with c included and excluded.

Table 9 presents the Granger causality test statistics. The null hypothesis is for no causality; that is, the exogenous variable does not cause the endogenous variable. Columns (3) and (4) contain the F-test statistics, respectively, with the c adjustments included and excluded. Causality occurs if the test statistic exceeds the critical values indicated in the last two rows, and occurs in eight of the ten cases. In all five cases where appraisals are the dependent variable and c is included, purchase causality is supported. The implication is that purchase data can be viewed as exogenous in the appraisal function.

With unit root, cointegration, and Granger causality tests, the time-series structure of the optimal appraisal updating function can be clarified. The function is in growth rates which are stationary. Error corrections are necessitated by the fact that purchase and appraisal growth rates are cointegrated. The error corrections are $b_t = a_t - p_t$, where a_t is the appraisal price growth and p_t is the purchase price growth. The general form of appraisal updating is

$$a_t = \delta_A a_{t-1} + \delta_P p_t + \sum_{i=1}^{12} \delta_i b_{t-1}. \tag{20}$$

Table 10. Appraisal error-correcting updating with dependent variable a_T.

	Northeast	Midwest	South	West	United States
Intercept	0.0236	0.0100	0.0172	0.0072	0.0058
	(2.92)*	(3.47)*	(2.92)*	(3.48)*	(3.21)*
a_{t-1}	−0.8517	−0.5152	−0.1200	−0.1309	−0.0435
	(2.99)*	(3.51)*	(1.08)	(1.27)	(0.45)
p_t	0.2120	0.1295	0.3049	0.1396	0.2092
	(0.75)	(0.94)	(1.69)	(1.65)	(2.64)*
b_{t-1}	0.2456	−0.1621	−0.4206	−0.1425	−0.4725
	(0.84)	(1.13)	(2.31)*	(1.61)	(5.50)*
b_{t-2}	−0.4940	−0.4443	−0.3155	−0.0886	−0.3354
	(5.79)*	(5.57)*	(3.93)*	(1.45)	(4.72)*
b_{t-3}	−0.0134	−0.2596	−0.4019	−0.0371	−0.2245
	(0.15)	(3.00)*	(4.82)*	(0.61)	(2.97)*
b_{t-4}	−0.0169	−0.3021	−0.2945	−0.0875	−0.0340
	(0.19)	(3.47)*	(3.35)*	(1.45)	(0.44)
b_{t-5}	0.0495	−0.2205	−0.1889	−0.0038	−0.0949
	(0.56)	(2.47)*	(2.11)*	(0.06)	(1.24)
b_{t-6}	0.1049	−0.0673	−0.0788	0.0115	0.0515
	(1.189)	(0.76)	(0.87)	(0.19)	(0.67)
b_{t-7}	−0.0092	−0.1758	−0.0586	0.0140	−0.0139
	(0.10)	(1.97)*	(0.65)	(0.24)	(0.18)
b_{t-8}	−0.0041	−0.1552	−0.1302	0.0300	−0.0085
	(0.05)	(1.77)	(1.50)	(0.51)	(0.11)
b_{t-9}	0.0078	−0.1496	0.1634	−0.0869	−0.0720
	(0.09)	(1.73)	(1.91)	(1.47)	(0.96)
b_{t-10}	0.057	0.0365	0.017	−0.006	−0.005
	(0.902)	(2.109)**	(1.643)	(1.004)	(0.679)
b_{t-11}	0.0100	−0.100	−0.0824	0.0251	0.0213
	(0.15)	(1.23)	(1.14)	(0.44)	(0.34)
b_{t-12}	−0.0385	−0.0032	0.0510	0.1046	−0.0084
	(0.67)	(0.06)	(0.83)	(2.01)	(0.17)
R^2	0.43	0.38	0.40	0.15	0.31

There are 12 monthly lags on the error corrections, and the difference in growth rates between appraisal and purchase prices is included. This appraisal form differs from conventional specifications that include only lagged appraisal or purchase values.

Table 10 presents estimates for the appraisal updating function. Asterisks denote significant *t*-statistics at the 1% level. There is negative serial autocorrelation or mean reversion in appraisals. The lagged appraisal coefficient is negative in all four regions and the country, and significant in the Northeast at −0.85 and the Midwest at −0.51. Current purchases are positively correlated with appraisals for the United States at 0.21. In the regional markets, the coefficients are positive but not significant.

The first lagged error correction b_{t-1} is generally significant and negative. With a negative coefficient on any error-correction term, subsequent appraisals are reduced when an appraiser overestimates. There is a reverting tendency. If appraisers overestimated the market in the past, they compensate by current lower appraisals. The mean-reverting tendency in appraisal comes from first-order negative autocorrelation and the error corrections. Over-appraisals in the recent past are counterbalanced by lower growth rates.

The appraisal updating function for the United States appears to be

$$a_t = \delta_P p_t + \delta_1(a_{t-1} - p_{t-1}) + \delta_2(a_{t-2} - p_{t-2}) + \delta_3(a_{t-3} - p_{t-3}), \tag{21}$$

using current purchase prices and three lagged error corrections. By comparison, Ross and Zisler (1991), in an autoregressive integrated moving average (ARIMA) context, find that the Russell–NCREIF index is AR(1), first-order autoregressive. A real estate return index produced by Evaluation Associates is MA(2), a second-order moving average.[9] For the Evaluation Associates index, an appraisal autoregression produces significant coefficients on the second and fourth lags. The weighted-average appraisal updating in growth form used by Quan and Quigley (1991) is $a_t = \delta_A a_{t-1} + \delta_P p_t^*$, where p_t^* is the current expected purchase price growth.

5. Concluding Remarks

The long-run relationship between appraisal and purchase is supported by tests of cointegration and unit roots. Error corrections in the interaction between appraisal and purchase enter the appraisal function. The error correction has a natural interpretation as the percentage difference between the appraisal and purchase price. Appraisers make adjustments based on whether they have overappraised or underappraised in the recent past.

For reasons of confidentiality and because of the processing costs of collecting and matching records, individual house characteristics are not always available. Legislative provisions, including redlining restrictions, may prohibit prices for locations and characteristics to be used. At the same time, repeat-sales data may be self-selective, and the prices and quantities of the underlying characteristics need not be constant over time.

Lenders rely on appraisals to justify loan decisions. If adjustments can be made in appraisal series either through error correction or modification of the mean for transaction incentive or variance for smoothing, the process of appraisal can be made more efficient and mechanized. Institutional investors rely on appraisal data in the commercial return series, such as the Russell–NCREIF index, to benchmark their series. The results on smoothing have more direct consequences. Accurate estimates of variance in house prices are necessary for pricing the value embedded in these underlying mortgages. Appraisals provide estimates of the variance distributions as transactions, but not of the mean price. In addition, indices constructed from purchase-appraisal repeats will overestimate house price changes over time.

There are two implications for the use of appraisals in the aggregation of purchase and appraisal data and in determining when such valuations might not be necessary. First, existing indices of real estate prices are aggregates of purchase and appraisal data. The underlying hypothesis is that purchase and appraisal prices draw from separate distributions; the data appear to bear out this hypothesis. Appraisal first moments are higher than purchase first moments and are accompanied by second-moment differences as well. Cases remain when such an aggregation is unavoidable because of data constraints such as those associated with commercial real estate markets. The results provide an estimate of the aggregation bias to correct indices that use purchase and appraisal data. In cases where portfolio lenders must mark mortgages to market, a corrected index of combined appraisal and purchase data would increase accuracy.

Second, the estimates provide guidance on situations when appraisals may not be necessary. If the variance of appraisal growth is low during a period and volatility is dampened, a borrower who has recently refinanced may not need an appraisal for a second refinancing. Conversely, if recent volatility has been high, an appraisal for the second refinancing is warranted.

Acknowledgment

We are grateful to Jesse Abraham, Tim Bollerslev, Charles Calhoun, John Clapp, Carmelo Giaccotto, Ken Kroner, Thomas Thibodeau, Tyler Yang, Peter Zorn, and three referees for comments and suggestions.

Notes

1. In the commercial market, the Frank Russell Company–National Council of Real Estate Investment Fiduciaries (Russell–NCREIF), Evaluation Associates, Liquidity Fund, and Prudential Insurance Company produce time series of aggregate real estate returns. Stephens, Li, Abraham, Lekkas, Calhoun, and Kimner (1995) report on a residential house price index that uses repeat sales, for mortgages purchased by Fannie Mae and Freddie Mac.
2. These data are as of the end of the fourth quarter of 1994, from the Flow of Funds of the Board of Governors of the Federal Reserve System. The Board of Governors of the Federal Reserve System, in its Survey of Consumer Finances, indicates the dominance of house equity in wealth in the 1986, 1989, and 1992 data sets. The Flow of Funds reports on the total mortgage indebtedness of households.
3. The result follows by expanding $\exp(b)$ around $E[b] = \beta$ to obtain $\exp(b) = \exp(\beta) + (b - \beta)\exp(\beta) + (1/2)(b - \beta)^2\exp(\beta)$ in a Taylor series to second order. The results follow from rearranging and are discussed in Kennedy (1985, p. 36). An alternative specification instead of with σ_β^2 is with σ_t^2 an estimate of the variance across properties at time t.
4. This is a strong form test of appraisal smoothing designed to highlight cases with volatility differences between the appraisal and purchase series. A weaker test that involves less distinction between the two series, particularly in their level of integration, is the inequality restriction $\sigma_{A1} + \sigma_{A2} < \sigma_1 + \sigma_2$. This restriction can be tested as a sample space constraint by using linear programming procedures.
5. Automated documentation processing in the Automated Underwriting System at Fannie Mae and the Loan Prospector program for Freddie Mac permit an originator to complete the application on a computer as opposed to in traditional hard-copy form. These loan folders may ultimately become available to the agencies but remain protected from secondary markets and investors.
6. The Bureau of the Census in its Current Construction Reports series adjusts for quality. The adjustment is limited to new houses in the C-27 series on the Price Index for New One-Family Homes Sold.

7. California, with 10% of the U.S. population at the time, accounted for 15% of the total resale house transactions in 1978 with (600,000 transactions) in advance of the 1978 Proposition 13 tax reductions.
8. The condition number is the square root of the ratio of the largest to the smallest eigenvalues of the matrix of independent variables. Although there is no a priori basis for determining how large a condition number must be as an indication of collinear data, numbers greater than 30 are generally viewed as evidence of moderate to strong linear relations among explanatory variables. For this argument and further details on condition number see Belskey, Kuh, and Welsch (1980, pp. 100–105).
9. Ross and Zisler (1991, pp. 184–186) estimate and discuss these models. The Russell–NCREIF index is constructed by the Frank Russell Company, Tacoma, Washington, based on the performance of properties owned by tax-exempt real estate funds. The Evaluation Association index is constructed by equally weighting 33 tax-exempt real estate funds.

References

Bollerslev, T. "Generalized Autoregressive Conditional Heteroskedasticity," *Journal of Econometrics* 31(1986), 307–327.

Belsley, D. A., D. Kuh, and R. E. Welsch. *Regression Diagnostics: Identifying Influential Data and Sources of Collinearity.* New York: John Wiley & Sons, 1980.

Case, K. E., and R. J. Shiller. "The Efficiency of the Market for Single-Family Homes," *American Economic Review* 79 (1989), 125–137.

Chan, K. C., P. H. Hendershott, and A. B. Sanders. "Risk and Return on Real Estate: Evidence from Equity REITs," *Journal of the American Real Estate and Urban Economics Association* 18 (1990), 431–452.

Chen, N.-F., R. Roll, and S. A. Ross. "Economic Forces and the Stock Market: Testing the APT and Alternative Asset Pricing Theories," *Journal of Business* 59 (1986), 383–403.

Engle, R. F. "Autoregressive Conditional Heteroskedasticity with Estimates of the Variance of United Kingdom Inflation," *Econometrica* 50 (1982), 987–1008.

Engle, R. F., and C. Granger. "Co-Integration and Error Correction: Representation, Estimation, and Testing," *Econometrica* 55 (1987), 251–276.

Engle, R. F., and V. C. Ng. "Measuring and Testing the Impact of News on Volatility," *Journal of Finance* 48 (1993), 1749–1778.

Geltner, D. "Temporal Aggregation in Real Estate Return Indices," *Journal of the American Real Estate and Urban Economics Association* 21 (1993), 141–166.

Glosten, L. R., R. Jagannathan, and D. E. Runkle. "On the Relation between the Expected Value and the Volatility of the Nominal Excess Return on Stocks," *Journal of Finance* 58 (1993), 1779–1801.

Kennedy, Peter. *A Guide to Econometrics.* Cambridge, MA: MIT Press, 1985.

Lekkas, V., J. M. Quigley, and R. Van Order. "Loan Loss Severity and Optimal Mortgage Default," *Journal of the American Real Estate and Urban Economics Association* 21 (1993), 353–372.

Nelson, D. "Conditional Heteroskedasticity in Asset Returns: A New Approach," *Econometrica* 59 (1992), 347–370.

Quan, D., and J. Quigley. "Price Formation and the Appraisal Function in Real Estate Markets," *Journal of Real Estate Finance and Economics* 4 (1991), 127–146.

Ross, S. A., and R. Zisler. "Risk and Return in Real Estate," *Journal of Real Estate Finance and Economics* 4 (1991), 175–190.

Shiller, R. J. "Measuring Asset Values for Cash Settlement in Derivative Markets: Hedonic Repeated Measures Indices and Perpetual Futures," *Journal of Finance* 48 (1993), 911–931.

Stephens, W., Y. Li, J. Abraham, V. Lekkas, C. Calhoun, and T. Kimner. "Conventional Mortgage Home Price Index," *Journal of Housing Research* 6 (1995), 389–418.

Journal of Real Estate Finance and Economics, 14: 113–132 (1997)
©1997 Kluwer Academic Publishers

A Bayesian Approach to the Construction and Comparison of Alternative House Price Indices

CHIONG-LONG KUO
Price Waterhouse LCC, 1616 North Fort Myer Drive, Arlington, VA 22209-3100

Abstract

Several repeat-sales models have been advanced over the years for estimating real estate price indices. This article proposes a general model which incorporates earlier works as special cases and compares the alternative repeat-sales models using posterior odds ratios as criteria. While the existing literature estimates the real estate indices from the sampling point of view, in this article indices are constructed and then compared using a Bayesian approach. In general, the two-error term models outperform the one-error models. The model with a nontemporal component proposed by Goetzmann and Spiegel is found to be superior in three out of four cities. There is a significant discrepancy among the returns and indices obtained from different models.

Key Words: Bayesian approach, house price indices

Due to the infrequent trading and the heterogeneous quality of real estate assets, the median price as published by the National Association of Realtors or the simple average of all the sales prices in each period is an inaccurate measure of temporal housing price movement. To construct a good real estate price index, two approaches have been adopted: the hedonic method and the repeat-sales method.

The hedonic method specifies the common independent characteristics of all houses and includes these attributes in the regression analysis (see, e.g., Palmquist, 1979 and Thibodeau, 1995). The house price index is obtained either from the coefficients of time dummy variables in a single regression or by computing the value of a standard house from the coefficients of the hedonic variables for each period.

The repeat-sales method uses prices of houses sold at least twice to estimate the indices. Unlike the hedonic method, the repeat-sales method makes no use of prices of houses sold only once in the sample period. Baily, Muth, and Nourse (1963, hereafter BMN) present a repeat-sales model, assuming that the change in log price for an individual house is equal to the change in the corresponding log market index plus an error. By assuming the errors to be i.i.d., they interpret the estimated coefficients of time dummies to be the desired price index. Case and Shiller (1987) refine BMN's model by adding a Gaussian random walk into the regression error term. They use a three-stage regression procedure to estimate a weighted repeat-sales index. Webb (1988) also assumes that the return on a house follows a random walk, but that the error does not include the additional i.i.d. noise as in Case and Shiller (1987). Therefore, a weighted regression is performed, and the houses with longer duration between sales are given less weight for the estimation of the price index. Goetzmann (1992) assumes that the market returns are i.i.d. and normally distributed. He uses a two-step method to obtain the biased James and Sten estimator.[1] His first step estimates the ratio of the variance of property-specific error relative to the variance of the random walk market index. The estimated variance ratio is then used in the second step to obtain the maximum likelihood estimate of the price index. Goetzmann and Spiegel (1995) propose a repeat-sales model that separates housing returns into nontemporal and temporal components. They find that including an intercept in the regression to represent the nontemporal component makes a significant difference in two out of four cities.

Hybrid models that utilize both single sales and multiple sales data to construct house price indices have been advanced by Case and Quigley (1991), Hill, Knight, and Sirmans (1995), and Quigley (1995). In Case and Quigley (1991), three equations that model repeat sales of unchanged properties, repeat sales of improved properties, and single sales are "stacked" as a single equation and estimated by a two-step generalized least-squares procedure. Quigley (1995) improves upon Case and Quigley (1991) by modeling an explicit error structure, in which the variance of house price is a quadratic function of the elapsed time between sales. Hill et al. (1995) present a model with a stationary AR(1) error and employ a maximum likelihood method to construct the real estate price index using both single and repeat-sales data.

House price indices have been evaluated using several statistics. Crone and Voith (1992) use a mean-squared prediction error and a mean-absolute prediction error to evaluate the accuracy of indices estimated from five methods: mean-sales-price, median-sales-price, two hedonic methods, and the repeat-sales method. Gatzlaff and Ling (1994) compare four index methods; i.e., (1) median-sales price, (2) restricted hedonic, (3) repeat-sales, and (4) the assessed-value technique, using a signal-to-noise ratio suggested by Case and Shiller (1987) to measure the precision of competing index models.

This article proposes a general model in which the specification of the error term incorporates those of the BMN (1963) model, the Case–Shiller (1987) model, the Webb (1988) model, the Hill et al. model (1995), and the Goetzmann–Spiegel (1995) model. The alternative indices are constructed using a Bayesian framework. The alternative real estate indices are then compared using the posterior odds ratio as criteria. This article adds to the existing literature in two respects. First, real estate price indices are estimated using a Bayesian approach; thus, the unknown true indices are treated as random variables. Second, the alternative models are compared using the posterior odds ratio as a criterion.

The next section develops the Bayesian methodologies for estimating and comparing the alternative indices. In section 2, the posterior odds ratio is constructed to compare the alternative models. Section 3 applies this methodology to sales data of single-family homes in Atlanta, Chicago, Dallas, and San Francisco. Section 4 is the conclusion.

1. A General Model for Estimating Real Estate Index

Suppose house i is sold at time t for the kth time in the data set. Assume that the log price of house i's kth sale at time t, y_{ikt}, is given by:

$$y_{ikt} = \alpha_i + (k-1)\gamma + \beta_t + \eta_{it}, \tag{1}$$

where α_i is the ith house-specific effect, γ is the time-independent return associated with each sale, and β_t is the log price index at time t. The time-independent rerun associated with the first sale is absorbed in the house-specific effect α_i. In the data set, there are n houses that sold and N total sales. Each house was sold at least twice during the $T + 1$ periods considered ($N \geq 2n$). The log index of the base period (period 0) is set to 0. The error term η_{it} represents the discrepancy between the individual house price and the citywide price level. The sources of this discrepancy may include an error associated with each transaction and a persistent idiosyncratic error due to house maintenance and neighborhood quality. Therefore, we assume that the error η_{it} is composed of an i.i.d. noise term and an AR(1) process, that is,

$$\eta_{it} = u_{it} + v_{it} \qquad u_{it} \sim \text{i.i.d. } N(0, \sigma_u^2) \tag{2}$$

$$v_{it} = \rho v_{i,t-1} + \epsilon_{it} \qquad \epsilon_{it} \sim \text{i.i.d. } N(0, \sigma_\epsilon^2), \tag{3}$$

where u_{it} is assumed to be independent of ϵ_{js} for all $i, j = 1, \ldots, n$, and $t, s = 0, 1, \ldots, T$. For the ith house, there are k_i sales occurring at time $(t_{i1}, t_{i2}, \ldots, t_{iki})$. On the other hand, there are n_t houses $(i_{t1}, i_{t2}, \ldots, i_{tn_t})$ sold at time t. The autoregressive error term v_{it} is assumed to have a zero initial condition at time period $t_{i1} - m$; i.e., $v_{i,t_{i1}-m} = 0$ for each house i. v_{it} reduces to a stationary process when $|\rho| < 1$ and $m \to \infty$. The value for m is chosen large, so that, for $|\rho| < 1$ and not too near 1, the distribution of v_{it} is almost exactly that implied by the stationary unconditional distribution. Yet, with this initial condition for the AR(1) process, the model can apply to mildly explosive ($|\rho| \geq 1$) as well as nonexplosive ($|\rho| < 1$) situations.[2] Results may depend on m, and various values of m are selected to check for the sensitivity of the outcomes. Under these specifications, the variance of the sth sale price for house i, $\text{Var}(\eta_{it_{is}})$, and covariance of the rth sale and the sth sale, ($r < s$), for the house unit i, are:

$$\text{Var}(\eta_{it_{is}}) = \sigma_u^2 + \text{Var}(v_{it_{is}}) \tag{4}$$

$$\text{Cov}(v_{it_{ir}}, v_{it_{is}}) = \rho^{(t_{is}-t_{ir})} \, \text{Var}(v_{it_{ir}}) \tag{5}$$

$$\text{Var}(v_{it_{is}}) = \begin{cases} \dfrac{1 - \rho^{2(t_{is}-t_{i1}+m)}}{1 - \rho^2} \sigma_\epsilon^2 & \text{if } \rho \neq 1 \\ (t_{is} - t_{i1} + m)\sigma_\epsilon^2 & \text{if } \rho = 1 \end{cases}. \tag{6}$$

The above modeling of the error term is a generalization of BMN (1963), Case and Shiller (1987), Hill et al, (1995), Webb (1988), and Geotzmann and Spiegel (1995). For $\gamma = 0$, it reduces to the BMN model when $\sigma_\epsilon^2 = 0$; to the Case and Shiller (1987) model when $\rho = 1$; to the Hill et. al. (1995) model when $\sigma_u^2 = 0$; and to the Webb (1988) model when $\rho = 1$ and $\sigma_u^2 = 0$. For $\gamma \neq 0$, it reduces to the Goetzmann and Spiegel (1995) model when $\rho = 0$. The model can be written in matrix form as:

$$Y = X_\alpha \alpha + X_\gamma \gamma + X_\beta \beta + \eta, \tag{7}$$

where Y is an $N \times 1$ vector of log sales prices, α is an $n \times 1$ vector of house effects, and β is a $T \times 1$ vector of log market indices.

There are $(T + n + 4)$ unknown parameters, $(\alpha, \gamma, \beta, \rho, \sigma_u^2, \sigma_\epsilon^2)$, in the model. We first make a transformation of variable from σ_ϵ^2 to $z \equiv \sigma_\epsilon^2/\sigma_u^2$. A priori, it is assumed that $(\alpha, \beta, \ln(\sigma_u^2))$ are independent of (γ, ρ, z) and are locally uniform so that:

$$p(\alpha, \gamma, \beta, \rho, z, \sigma_u^2) \propto \sigma_u^{-2} p(\gamma, \rho, z), \tag{8}$$

where $p(\gamma, \rho, z)$ is the prior of (γ, ρ, z).

We assume that, a priori, (γ, ρ, z) are independent of each other. Since we have no prior information on the distribution of the variance ratio z, a reasonable assumption is $Pr(1/q \leq z \leq 1) = Pr(1 \leq z \leq q)$ for $q \geq 1$. Thus, the probability for $1/z \in [1, q]$ is also equal to that for $1/z \in [1/q, 1]$. This assumption is equivalent to that $w = \ln(z)$ is symmetric around 0. We experiment with alternative distributions of z such that its log, w, is a mean zero double exponential distribution[3] with parameters 1 and 3, and a mean zero normal distribution with standard deviation equal to 1 and 5. When $\ln(z)$ is a mean zero double exponential distribution, the probability density of z is

$$f(z) = \begin{cases} 0.5\lambda z^{\lambda-1} & 0 < z \leq 1 \\ 0.5\lambda z^{-\lambda-1} & z \geq 1 \end{cases}. \tag{9}$$

Equation (9) implies that z is uniformly distributed in $(0, 1)$ when $\lambda = 1$.

There have been extensive discussions regarding the choice of priors for autoregressive models in the literature.[4] The focus of the controversy is whether to choose a flat prior or a Jeffrey's prior for the autoregressive parameter. In our model, Jeffrey's prior would be extremely complicated. It would be difficult for a reader with a different prior to unravel the effect of Jeffrey's prior from the posterior and to combine it with his own prior in order to make an inference. From the perspective of reporting the likelihood, a simple prior such as a flat prior is preferable. Another unappealing feature of the Jeffrey's prior is its dependence on sample size. For these two reasons, the prior of ρ is assumed to be uniformly distributed in $(0, 2)$. I also assume a flat prior for γ in $(-0.5, 0.5)$.

The effects of different priors on the posterior depend on the distributions of the prior and the likelihood. If the posterior is sharply peaked, the inference is not likely to be sensitive to the choice of the prior unless the prior is also sharply peaked. As shown in section 3, the posteriors of ρ and z are both highly concentrated.

Multiplying (8) by the likelihood function of Y, we have the joint posterior distribution for the parameters,

$$p(\alpha, \gamma, \beta, \rho, \sigma_u^2, z \mid Y) \propto p(\gamma, \rho, z)(\sigma_u^2)^{-N/2-1}|\Omega|^{-1/2}$$
$$\exp\{-(1/2)\sigma_u^{-2}(Y - X_\alpha\alpha - X_\gamma\gamma - X_\beta\beta)'\Omega^{-1}(Y - X_\alpha\alpha - X_\gamma\gamma - X_\beta\beta)\}, \tag{10}$$

where Ω is the block-diagonal covariance matrix of the error term η divided by σ_u^2.

Integrating (10) with respect to α and σ_u^2 yields:

$$p(\beta, \gamma, \rho, z \mid Y) \propto p(\gamma, \rho, z)|\Omega|^{-1/2}|X_\alpha'\Omega^{-1}X_\alpha|^{-1/2}h^{-(N-n)/2}$$

$$\left\{1 + \frac{1}{h}(\beta - \hat{\beta})'X_\beta'M_\alpha'\Omega^{-1}M_\alpha X_\beta(\beta - \hat{\beta})\right\}^{-(N-n)/2}, \tag{11}$$

where

$$\hat{\beta} = (X_\beta'M_\alpha'\Omega^{-1}M_\alpha X_\beta)^{-1}X_\beta'M_\alpha'\Omega^{-1}M_\alpha Y$$

$$M_\alpha = I_N - X_\alpha(X_\alpha'\Omega^{-1}X_\alpha)^{-1}X_\alpha'\Omega^{-1}$$

$$h = (Y - X_\gamma - X_\beta\beta)'M_\alpha'(Y - X_\gamma - X_\beta\beta),$$

and I_N is an $N \times N$ identity matrix.

If γ, z, and ρ are known, the posterior distribution of β is a multivariate t-distribution with $(N - n - T)$ degrees of freedom, mean $\hat{\beta}$, and variance-covariance matrix

$$\text{Cov}(\beta \mid \gamma, z, \rho, Y) = \frac{h}{(N - n - T - 2)}(X_\beta'M_\alpha'\Omega^{-1}M_\alpha X_\beta)^{-1}. \tag{12}$$

Integrating β out of (11) gives

$$p(\gamma, \rho, z \mid Y) \propto p(\gamma, \rho, z)|\Omega|^{-1/2} \mid X_\alpha'\Omega^{-1}X_\alpha \mid^{-1/2} h^{-(N-n)/2} \mid X_\beta'M_\alpha'\Omega^{-1}M_\alpha X_\beta \mid^{-1/2}. \tag{13}$$

Denoting the right-hand side of (13) by $g(\gamma, \rho, z)$, the posterior means and variance-covariance matrix of log index β are given by:

$$E(\beta \mid Y) = \frac{1}{c_1}\int_{-0.5}^{0.5}\int_0^2\int_0^\infty \hat{\beta}g(\gamma, \rho, z \mid Y)\,dz\,d\rho\,d\gamma \tag{14}$$

$$\text{Cov}(\beta \mid Y) = \frac{1}{c_1}\int_{-0.5}^{0.5}\int_0^2\int_0^\infty [\text{Cov}(\beta \mid \gamma\rho, z, Y)$$

$$+ (\hat{\beta} - E(\beta \mid Y))(\hat{\beta} - E(\beta \mid Y))']g(\gamma, \rho, z)\,dz\,d\rho\,d\gamma, \tag{15}$$

where

$$c_1 = \int_{-0.5}^{0.5}\int_0^2\int_0^\infty g(\rho, z)\,dz\,d\rho\,d\gamma. \tag{16}$$

The log index β conditional on (γ, ρ, z) is close to a normal distribution, since it is a t-distribution with many degrees of freedom. The posterior mean of the real estate price index, $E(e^\beta \mid Y)$, can thus be well approximated by

$$E(e^\beta \mid Y) \approx \frac{1}{c_1} \int_{-0.5}^{0.5} \int_0^2 \int_0^\infty e^{E(\beta|\gamma,\rho,z,Y)+0.5\,\mathrm{Var}(\beta|\gamma,\rho,z,Y)} g(\gamma, \rho, z)\, dz\, d\rho\, d\gamma. \qquad (17)$$

Since the marginal posterior distribution of the index obtained by integrating out (γ, ρ, z) is also close to a normal distribution, $E(e^\beta \mid Y)$ can be approximated by

$$E(e^\beta \mid Y) \approx e^{E(\beta|Y)+0.5\,\mathrm{Var}(\beta|Y)}. \qquad (18)$$

In the sampling approach, if the estimator β is normally distributed with mean β and variance $\mathrm{Var}(\hat{\beta})$, the unbiased estimator for e^β is $e^{\beta-0.5\mathrm{Var}(\hat{\beta})}$. Therefore, even in the case where the point estimators for the log index β are the same for both the sampling approach and the Bayesian approach, the point estimators for the index e^β would still be different by a factor of $e^{0.5*(\mathrm{Var}(\beta|Y)+\mathrm{Var}(\beta))}$. This difference would disappear as the sample size goes to infinity.

The posterior marginal distribution for ρ is

$$p(\rho \mid Y) = \frac{1}{c_1} \int_{-0.5}^{0.5} \int_0^\infty g(\rho, z) dz\, d\gamma. \qquad (19)$$

Similarly, we can compute the marginal distribution for the variance ratio z.

2. Comparing Alternative Models

This section compares six alternative hypotheses:

$$
\begin{aligned}
H_1: \quad & 0 < z < \infty, \quad 0 < \rho < 2, \quad \gamma = 0 \\
H_2: \quad & 0 < z < \infty, \quad \rho = 1, \quad \gamma = 0 \\
H_3: \quad & \sigma_u^2 = 0, \quad 0 < \rho < 2, \quad \gamma = 0 \\
H_4: \quad & z = 0, \quad \gamma = 0 \\
H_5: \quad & \sigma_u^2 = 0, \quad \rho = 1, \quad \gamma = 0 \\
H_6: \quad & 0 < z < \infty, \quad \rho = 1, \quad -0.5 < \gamma < 0.5.
\end{aligned}
$$

H_1, H_2, and H_6 have two error components (u_{it} and v_{it}), while the other three models have only one error component v_{it}. H_1 is the model presented in section 1; H_2 is the Case and Shiller (1987) model; H_3 is the Hill et. al. (1995) specification extended to allow for the explosive case; H_4 is the BMN model; H_5 is the Webb (1988) model; and H_6 is the Goetzmann and Spiegel (1995) model.

The random walk models (models 2 and 5) suggest that the individual house price tends to wander away from the market level, where the variance of the deviation grows linearly with time. Thus, the assessment value of an individual house based on its previous transaction price and a market index would be subject to greater error when the elapsed time since previous sale is longer. The BMN model implies that the deviation of a house price from the market mean level only comes from the associated transaction, and is independent of the time interval between sales. Models 1 and 3 permit the idiosyncratic error to be autocorrelated rather than a random walk. A stationary idiosyncratic error means that the larger the deviation of the house value from the market level, the more likely the value will return to the market mean level. An explosive idiosyncratic error means that the speed at which an individual house values wanders away from the market level is even faster than that implied by a random walk model. While the case for ρ to be much greater than unity is unlikely, a mildly explosive error process may be attributed to rapid changes in neighborhood quality or in house condition.

Model 6 distinguishes itself from the other models by the inclusion of a time-independent return component γ. The existence of a positive γ implies that index estimated from a model neglecting to account for the time-independent return will be upward biased. The more frequently houses are traded, the greater is the bias.

The posterior probability associated with hypothesis H_i is

$$p(H_i \mid Y) = p(H_i)p(Y \mid H_i)/p(Y). \tag{20}$$

If the prior probabilities for all the six hypotheses are the same ($p(H_1) = 1/6$), then the posterior odds ratio $p(H_i \mid Y)/p(H_j \mid Y)$ is equal to the Bayes factor $p(Y \mid H_i)/p(Y \mid H_j)$, the ratio of predictive densities. The predictive density for model 1 is

$$p(Y \mid H_1) = (2\pi)^{-N/2} \int_{-0.5}^{0.5} \int_0^2 \int_0^\infty g(\gamma = 0, \rho, z) \, dz \, d\rho. \tag{21}$$

To derive the posterior distribution of β and ρ for models 2, 5, and 6, one simply substitutes the appropriate assumptions for (γ, ρ, z) into the formulae in section 1. Thus,

$$p(Y \mid H_2) = (2\pi)^{-N/2} \int_0^\infty g(\gamma = 0, \rho = 1, z) \, dz. \tag{22}$$

$$p(Y \mid H_4) = (2\pi)^{-N/2} g(\gamma = 0, z = 0) \tag{23}$$

$$p(Y \mid H_6) = (2\pi)^{-N/2} \int_{-0.5}^{0.5} \int_0^\infty g(\gamma, \rho = 1, z) \, dz \, d\gamma. \tag{24}$$

For models 3 and 5, the variance of η_{it_s} becomes

$$\text{Var}(\eta_{it_s}) = \begin{cases} \dfrac{1 - \rho^{2(t_{is} - t_{i1} + m)}}{1 - \rho^2} \sigma_\epsilon^2 & \text{if } \rho \neq 1 \\ (t_{is} - t_{i1} + m)\sigma_\epsilon^2 & \text{if } \rho = 1, \end{cases} \tag{25}$$

and Ω is defined as the variance-covariance matrix of the error term η divided by σ_u^2. Following the procedures in section 1, one can derive the posterior density for ρ and β. The posterior density of ρ is now

$$p(\rho \mid Y) \propto |\Omega|^{1/2} |X_\alpha' \Omega^{-1} X_\alpha|^{-1/2} h^{-(N-n)/2} |X_\beta' M_\alpha' \Omega^{-1} M_\alpha X_\beta|^{-1/2}. \tag{26}$$

Denoting the right-hand side of (26) by $f(\rho)$, the predictive densities for models 3 and 5 are, respectively,

$$p(Y \mid H_3) = (2\pi)^{-N/2} \int_0^2 f(\rho)\, d\rho \tag{27}$$

$$p(Y \mid H_5) = (2\pi)^{-N/2} f(1). \tag{28}$$

The posterior distribution of ρ and z depends on the initial condition period m in model 1 and model 3, where $\rho \in (0, 2)$. Although $\operatorname{var}(\eta_{it})$ is a function of m (see (4)), it can be verified that β, $\operatorname{Cov}(\gamma, \beta \mid z, \rho, Y)$, $g(\gamma, \rho, z)$ and $f(\rho)$ do not depend on m when $\rho = 1$ as in models 2, 5, and 6. The irrelevance of m is consistent with the random walk property that past information, including the initial condition period, is not useful in predicting future price movement.

To measure the difference between two return series, we define a normalized distance function. Let return series A and B be $\theta^A = (\theta_1^A, \theta_2^A, \ldots, \theta_T^A)$ and $\theta^B = (\theta_1^B, \theta_2^B, \ldots, \theta_T^B)$, respectively. Let the norm of a return series θ, denoted by $\|\theta\|$, be the average absolute return of the series, e.g., $\|\theta^A\| = \frac{1}{T}\sum_{i=1}^T |\theta_i^A|$. Define the distance between return series A and B to be the norm of their difference $\theta^A - \theta^B$. The distance $\|\theta^A - \theta^B\|$ is then divided by the average norm of these two return series and multiplied by 100 to obtain a normalized distance, which is denoted by $d_n(\theta^A, -\theta^B)$, where:

$$d_n(\theta^A, \theta^B) = \frac{\|\theta^A - \theta^B\|}{0.5 * (\|\theta^A\| + \|\theta^B\|)} * 100. \tag{29}$$

3. Empirical Results

In this section, the above methodology is applied to the Case and Shiller (1987) data. The data set contains sales prices and dates (quarterly) of single-family homes in four metropolitan areas: Atlanta, Chicago, Dallas, and San Francisco from 1971 to 1986. Each house sold twice during that period and had no apparent quality change between sales. The numbers of these repeat-sale houses in Atlanta, Chicago, Dallas, and San Francisco were 8,945; 15,530; 6,669; and 8,066, respectively.

We take the posterior mean of log index, $E(\beta \mid Y)$, as the point estimator for the log index, because it is the Bayes estimator under a quadratic loss function. Let θ_t be the return at time $t(\theta_t = \beta_t - \beta_{t-1})$, and θ_t be the estimated return at time $t(\theta_t = E(\beta_t \mid Y) - E(\beta_{t-1} \mid Y))$. Define $\theta = (\theta_1, \theta_2, \ldots, \theta_T)$, $\bar{\theta} = \frac{1}{T}\sum_{t=1}^T \theta_t$ and $\sigma_\theta = (\frac{1}{T}\sum_{t=1}^T(\theta_t - \bar{\theta})^2)^{1/2}$. From the estimated return series, one can compute its arithmetic average $\bar{\theta}$, absolute average $\|\theta\|$, and standard deviation σ_θ.

The computation for models 1 and 3 is performed for a sequence of initial condition periods m.[5] We compute θ, $\|\theta\|$, σ_θ, $E(\rho \mid Y)$, $E(z \mid Y)$, and $p(Y \mid H)$ for each m, and the distance between return series for successive choices of m. The computational results show that all of the above statistics converge as m increases. In what follows we report the results for the cases when m equals to 1, 300, and 10,000.

Table 1 reports the posterior odds between alternative models. We compute the posterior odds ratio in favor of model i relative to the Case–Shiller model:

$$K_{i2} = p(Y \mid H_i)/p(Y \mid H_2) \qquad i = 1, 2, 3, 4, 5, 6. \tag{30}$$

The posterior odds criteria show that the Goetzmann–Spiegel model has the best performance for Atlanta, Chicago, and Dallas; while model 1 has the best performance for San Francisco. The Goetzmann–Spiegel model has significantly higher posterior odds ratios than the Case–Shiller model for all four cities, suggesting that it is preferable to include a non-temporal component in the model. The posterior means of the nontemporal return are 2.16%,

Table 1. Posterior odds ratio for alternative models.

m	K_{12}	K_{22}	K_{32}	K_{42}	K_{52}	K_{62}
			Atlanta			
$m = 1$	1.52E + 06	1	2.30E − 116	5.14E − 165	6.72E − 577	5.12E + 16
$m = 300$	5.57E + 07	1	9.28E − 121	5.14E − 165	6.72E − 577	5.12E + 16
$m = 10000$	0.001095	1	9.28E − 121	5.14E − 165	6.72E − 577	5.12E + 16
			Chicago			
$m = 1$	0.008385	1	3.56E − 117	7.15E − 255	2.10E − 861	1.04E + 20
$m = 300$	0.006281	1	2.52E − 126	7.15E − 255	2.10E − 861	1.04E + 20
$m = 10000$	0.001237	1	2.52E − 126	7.15E − 255	2.10E − 861	1.04E + 20
			Dallas			
$m = 1$	0.005178	1	3.02E − 41	1.43E − 123	5.54E − 294	9.45E + 29
$m = 300$	0.005178	1	4.20E − 45	1.43E − 123	5.54E − 294	9.45E + 29
$m = 10000$	0.005178	1	4.20E − 45	1.43E − 123	5.54E − 294	9.45E + 29
			San Francisco			
$m = 1$	1.77E + 40	1	4.80E + 29	5.15E − 105	2.11E − 197	3.67E + 22
$m = 300$	8.12E + 40	1	4.88E + 29	5.15E − 105	2.11E − 197	3.67E + 22
$m = 10000$	8.12E + 40	1	4.88E + 29	5.15E − 105	2.11E − 197	3.67E + 22

Notes: K_{i2}, equal to $p(H_i|Y)/p(H_2|Y)$, is the posterior odds ratio in favor of model i relative to the Case–Shiller model. m is the time period such that $v_{i,t_{i1}-m} = 0$. For models 1, 2, and 6, the prior of $\ln(z)$ is assumed to be a double exponential distribution with parameter 1.

1.83%, 3.50%, 2.66% for Atlanta, Chicago, Dallas, and San Francisco, respectively, and the respective 95% highest posterior density (HPD) intervals are (1.68%, 2.65%), (1.45%, 2.26%), (2.90%, 4.11%), and (2.15%, 3.20%).[6] The nontemporal return is significantly positive in all four cities, which is consistent with the fact that the posterior odds ratio of the Goetzmann–Spiegel model relative to the Case–Shiller model is much greater than unity.

The two-error models, models 1, 2, and 6, outperform the one-error models except for San Francisco. For San Francisco, the three one-error models are still dominated by model 1, but model 3 has higher posterior probabilities than the Case–Shiller model and the Goetzmann–Spiegel model. Among the one-error models, the AR(1) model has the highest posterior odds, with the BMN model next; the Webb model is least supported by the data.

In order to make a choice between an AR(1) error model and a random walk model, comparison has to be made between model 4 and model 5 for the one-error structure, and between model 1 and model 2 for the two-error structure. In the one-error structure, the AR(1) error model has much higher posterior odds than in the random walk model. However, in the two-error structure, the comparison is not conclusive. Among the 12 cases (four cities and three choices of m), the Case–Shiller model outperforms model 1 in seven cases. Therefore, one may want to favor the Case–Shiller model over model 1. However, if we average the posterior odds ratios across the 12 cases, we find that model 1 outperforms the Case–Shiller model. This is due to the fact that, when the posterior odds of model 1 relative to the Case-Shiller model are smaller than 1, they are not very small relative to 1, but when the posterior odds support model 1 over the Case–Shiller model, they are much greater than 1, especially in San Francisco. Thus, there is good reason to favor the two-error AR(1) model over the Case-Shiller model. More data may be needed to make further comparisons of the two-error AR(1) model and the Case–Shiller model.

Table 2 presents the posterior odds ratios, the posterior means, and the HPD intervals for the two-error models with different priors of the variance ratio z. As can be seen from the table, the posterior odds ratios and the estimates of z are insensitive to the choice of priors for z. Therefore, we present the empirical results in Table 1 and Tables 3 through 6, assuming that $ln(z)$ has a double exponential distribution with parameter 1.

Table 3 provides the summary statistics of the estimated return series for $m = 300$. It also shows the average of the estimated standard deviation of the true return denoted by $\bar{\sigma}_\theta = \frac{1}{T} \sum_{t=1}^{T} \hat{\sigma}_{\theta_t}$, where $\hat{\sigma}_{\theta_t}^2$ is the posterior variance of the true return θ_t. The posterior covariance matrix of θ is equal to $L^{-1}\text{Cov}(\beta \mid Y)(L')^{-1}$, where L is a $T \times T$ lower triangular matrix of ones. The economic implications of σ_θ and $\bar{\sigma}_\theta$ are different. σ_θ is the temporal variability of the real estate returns captured in estimates $\hat{\theta}$. It measures the temporal risk in the housing market. $\bar{\sigma}_\theta$ is the average of the estimated one-period variances of the true return. It measures the variability of the deviation of true θ from $\hat{\theta}$.

In three out of four cities (except in Atlanta), the BMN model (model 4) has the highest $\bar{\sigma}_\theta$. It also has the highest $\|\hat{\theta}\|$ and σ_θ in Atlanta, Dallas, and San Francisco. The tendency for the BMN model to have a higher $\|\hat{\theta}\|$, σ_θ, and $\bar{\sigma}_\theta$ is due to its oversimplified specification of the error structure. The more complicated error structures in other models absorb a bigger proportion of the variation in housing price than the one i.i.d. error structure does. The Webb model has the highest average return in all of the four cities, indicating a possible overestimation in using the one-error random walk error structure. The Goetzmann–Spiegel

Table 2. Posterior odds ratios, posterior means of z, and HPD intervals of z for alternative priors of z.

Prior	K_{12}	K_{22}	K_{62}	Posterior Mean of z	HPD Interval of z
			Atlanta		
prior 1	5.E + 07	1	5.12E + 16	0.156	(0.135, 0.178)
prior 2	1.74E + 06	1	5.75E + 16	0.158	(0.140, 0.176)
prior 3	2.60E + 06	1	5.39E + 16	0.157	(0.136, 0.179)
prior 4	3.97E + 08	1	4.85E + 16	0.156	(0.135, 0.177)
			Chicago		
prior 1	0.006281	1	1.04E + 20	0.140	(0.124, 0.156)
prior 2	0.005407	1	1.02E + 20	0.141	(0.125, 0.151)
prior 3	0.005804	1	1.03E + 20	0.140	(0.124, 0.156)
prior 4	0.006764	1	1.05E + 20	0.139	(0.124, 0.155)
			Dallas		
prior 1	0.006929	1	9.45E + 29	0.189	(0.158, 0.222)
prior 2	0.008942	1	1.08E + 30	0.192	(0.160, 0.225)
prior 3	0.007425	1	9.92E + 29	0.190	(0.159, 0.223)
prior 4	0.006297	1	8.86E + 29	0.188	(0.161, 0.215)
			San Francisco		
prior 1	8.12E + 40	1	3.67E + 22	0.285	(0.238, 0.331)
prior 2	6.51E + 41	1	4.60E + 22	0.290	(0.235, 0.348)
prior 3	7.04E + 40	1	3.80E + 22	0.286	(0.231, 0.340)
prior 4	3.08E + 40	1	3.29E + 22	0.282	(0.228, 0.336)

Notes: For model 1, m in the initial condition $v_{i,t_{i1}-m} = 0$ is assumed to be 300. Prior 1 and prior 2 are the double exponential distributions with parameter 1 and 3 for $\ln(z)$, respectively. Prior 3 and prior 4 are the mean zero normal distributions with standard deviation 1 and 5 for $\ln(z)$, respectively.

model has a much lower average return in all four cities. This is due to the existence of a significantly positive nontemporal return.

Case and Shiller (1987) and Gatzlaff and Ling (1994) use a signal-to-noise ratio to measure the precision of estimated price indices. It is defined as the ratio of the standard deviation of the estimated return series to the average standard error of the estimates. The higher the signal-to-noise ratio, the more precise the estimated index. The corresponding signal-to-noise ratio in the Bayesian approach proposed here is $\sigma_\theta / \overline{\sigma}_\theta$. From Tables 1 and 3, we see that the signal-to-noise ratio principle is not consistent with the posterior odds criteria in comparing alternative models. If the true returns are the same in each period, then, given the same average standard error, one would expect an estimated return series with a lower signal-to-noise ratio to be better than another series with a higher signal-to-noise ratio. The estimated signal-to-noise ratio may be higher or lower than the true signal-to-noise ratio.

Table 3. Summary statistics for the estimated return series.

	$\bar{\theta}$	$\|\hat{\theta}\|$	min	max	σ_θ	$\bar{\sigma}_\theta$	SNR
Atlanta							
model 1	1.672	2.295	−5.458	10.62	2.468	1.534	1.609
model 2	1.67	2.335	−5.815	11.06	2.527	1.535	1.647
model 3	1.662	2.409	−6.137	12.661	2.731	1.535	1.779
model 4	1.665	2.435	−6.091	12.871	2.771	1.545	1.793
model 5	1.681	2.422	−6.174	7.909	2.561	1.644	1.558
model 6	1.557	2.238	−5.833	10.926	2.513	1.528	1.645
Chicago							
model 1	1.688	2.054	−2.461	5.132	1.806	1.141	1.582
model 2	1.688	2.054	−2.443	5.434	1.806	1.14	1.584
model 3	1.678	2.032	−3.631	5.434	1.818	1.127	1.613
model 4	1.693	2.092	−2.891	5.45	1.88	1.222	1.538
model 5	1.697	2.094	−4.01	5.919	1.86	0.97	1.917
model 6	1.583	1.966	−2.359	5.412	1.764	1.137	1.552
Dallas							
model 1	2.116	2.96	−4.942	7.499	2.775	2.008	1.382
model 2	2.164	2.958	−4.926	7.488	2.763	2.01	1.375
model 3	2.208	3.082	−6.534	15.471	3.355	1.985	1.691
model 4	2.195	3.302	−9.555	16.462	3.672	2.134	1.721
model 5	2.219	2.751	−5.339	9.725	2.573	1.817	1.416
model 6	1.981	2.793	−4.003	7.644	2.644	1.983	1.334
San Francisco							
model 1	2.567	3.011	−3.842	12.572	2.856	1.776	1.608
model 2	2.585	3.018	−4.553	11.098	2.808	1.831	1.534
model 3	2.561	2.996	−3.303	13.308	2.901	1.739	1.669
model 4	2.541	3.16	−4.972	14.794	3.29	1.905	1.727
model 5	2.63	3.021	−3.12	10.536	2.859	1.65	1.733
model 6	2.456	2.924	−4.566	10.415	2.779	1.812	1.534

Note: m in the initial condition $v_{i,t_{i1}-m} = 0$ is assumed to be 300. $\bar{\theta}$, $\|\hat{\theta}\|$, min, max, and σ_θ are, respectively, the average, absolute average, minimum, maximum, and standard deviation of the estimated return series θ. $\bar{\sigma}_\theta$ is the average of the estimated standard error of the true return series. SNR ($= \sigma_\theta/\bar{\sigma}_\theta$) is the signal-to-noise ratio. For model 1, 2, and 6, the prior of $\ln(z)$ is assumed to be a double exponential distribution with parameter 1. Except for SNR, all the numbers are expressed in percent (%).

Therefore, the signal-to-noise ratio is not a good measure of the precision of the estimated index.

Table 4 reports the posterior mean and 95% HPD interval for ρ. The posterior distributions of ρ are highly concentrated. The posterior distributions for ρ in Atlanta, Chicago, and

Dallas are concentrated around unity. Thus the posterior odds ratio for mode 1 is lower than unity in Chicago and Dallas for all m and in Atlanta for m equal to 10,000. For Atlanta, when $m = 1$ and 300, the 95% HPD intervals do not cover the unity case although the posterior means are 1.021 and 1.006, respectively. In these two case, model 1 outperforms the Case–Shiller model even though the posterior mean of ρ seems close to unity. The sharp peak in the posterior of ρ suggests that the empirical results based on the flat priors for ρ are not sensitive to different choices of priors.

Table 5 presents the normalized distance between the alternative quarterly return series. The normalized distances between return series vary from 0.36% to 55.8%. In Atlanta, Chicago, and Dallas, the smallest distance between a pair of return series is the distance between the return series for models 1 and 2. The distances between the return series for model 5 and the other models tend to be large, especially between model 5 and 4. In most cases, the normalized distances is higher than 10%, indicating that the choice of model used to estimate the intertemporal variation of the market return is important.

The index for the Case–Shiller model is plotted in Figure 1. The differences between the index series for the Case–Shiller model and those for other models are plotted in Figures 2 through 5. These figures show that the differences between the indices for the

Table 4. Posterior mean and 95% HPD interval for ρ.

m	model 1			model 3		
	Mean	95% HPD	Interval	Mean	95% HPD	Interval
			Atlanta			
$m = 1$	1.02126	1.01419	1.02719	0.74765	0.70786	0.79022
$m = 300$	1.00628	1.00388	1.00884	0.64098	0.59796	0.68967
$m = 10000$	0.99971	0.9985	1.00244	0.64098	0.59796	0.68967
			Chicago			
$m = 1$	1.00336	0.99864	1.00655	0.81361	0.79814	0.83577
$m = 300$	1.0007	0.996	1.00389	0.7312	0.71395	0.75622
$m = 10000$	0.99727	0.99498	1.00179	0.7312	0.71395	0.75622
			Dallas			
$m = 1$	0.99914	0.99092	1.00655	0.86222	0.8444	0.88357
$m = 300$	0.9942	0.97342	0.92263	0.79238	0.76961	0.81957
$m = 10000$	0.99293	0.98637	1.00236	0.79238	0.76961	0.81957
			San Francisco			
$m = 1$	0.94882	0.93996	0.95980	0.90521	0.89711	0.91900
$m = 300$	0.90653	0.88841	0.92432	0.84635	0.82855	0.86059
$m = 10000$	0.90653	0.88919	0.92433	0.84635	0.82855	0.86059

Note: m is the time periods such that $v_{i,t_{i1}-m} = 0$. For model 1, the prior of $\ln(z)$ is assumed to be a double exponential distribution with parameter 1.

Table 5. Normalized distance between alternative quarterly return series.

	model 1	model 2	model 3	model 4	model 5	model 6
			Atlanta			
model 1	0					
model 2	5.845	0				
model 3	17.761	12.834	0			
model 4	17.615	14.869	8.993	0		
model 5	37.696	34.348	36.267	44.425	0	
model 6	9.828	7.435	15.723	17.508	35.301	0
			Chicago			
model 1	0					
model 2	0.355	0				
model 3	14.242	14.011	0			
model 4	13.455	13.346	14.697	0		
model 5	31.19	31.003	22.37	36.133	0	
model 6	7.615	7.596	14.993	15.799	30.912	0
			Dallas			
model 1	0					
model 2	0.845	0				
model 3	19.149	19.914	0			
model 4	24.653	25.015	17.847	0		
model 5	30.936	31.003	35.207	52.067	0	
model 6	14.537	14.182	26.182	30.916	34.011	0
			San Francisco			
model 1	0					
model 2	10.267	0				
model 3	7.359	17.19	0			
model 4	23.851	24.263	27.004	0		
model 5	33.105	35.128	29.899	55.755	0	
model 6	15.769	10.303	22.074	29.541	33.237	0

Note: m in the initial condition $v_{i,t_{i1}-m} = 0$ is assumed to be 300. The normalized distance is the absolute average of the difference between two return series, divided by the average norm of these two return series, and then multiplied by 100. For models 1, 2, and 6, the prior of $\ln(z)$ is assumed to be a double exponential distribution with parameter 1.

Goetzmann–Spiegel model and those for other models tends to grow with time. This makes the Goetzmann–Spiegel index dramatically different from other indices. The normalized distance between the alternative log index series (see Table 6) varies from 0.013% to 9.497%. The distance between index series is in general much smaller than that between quarterly return series. The normalized distances between the index series other than the Goetzmann–Spiegel index are all less than 5%, but the distances between the Goetzmann–Spiegel index and other indices are mostly larger than 5%, with a high of 13.225% in Dallas.

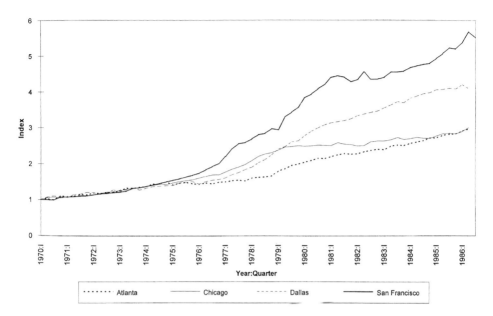

Figure 1. Indices for the Case–Shiller model from 1970:I to 1986:III (1970:I = 1).

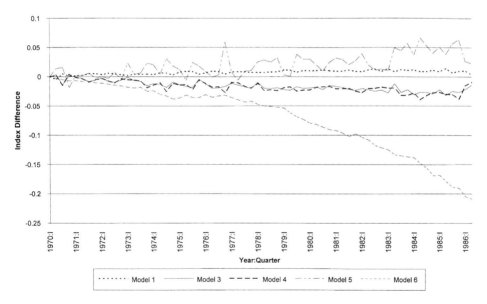

Figure 2. Index difference between the alternative models and the Case–Shiller model for Atlanta (alternative indices minus Case–Shiller index).

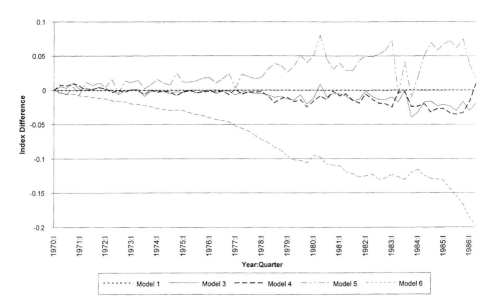

Figure 3. Index difference between the alternative models and the Case–Shiller model for Chicago (alternative indices minus Case–Shiller index).

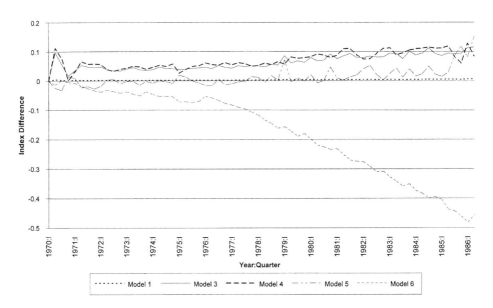

Figure 4. Index difference between the alternative models and the Case–Shiller model for Dallas (alternative indices minus Case–Shiller index).

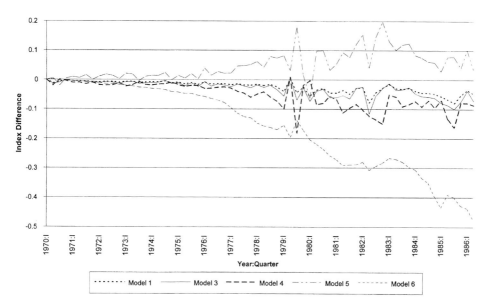

Figure 5. Index difference between the alternative models and the Case–Shiller model for San Francisco (alternative indices minus Case–Shiller index).

As shown in Table 5, the normalized distances between models 1 and 2 for Chicago and Dallas are less than 1% where the Case–Shiller model dominates the two-error AR(1) model. However, in Atlanta and San Francisco, where the two-error AR(1) model is favored, the normalized distance is greater than 5%. Based on the posterior odds ratio criteria and the normalized distance, the two-error AR(1) model seems to perform better than the Case–Shiller model.

When faced with alternative models, one may be reluctant to choose one model and discard the others due to weak evidence or even conflicting conclusions. In this case, a weighted return series can be constructed from the return series of the competing models, using the corresponding posterior probabilities as weights (see Moulton, 1991).

We noted in section 1 that the unbiased estimators for the sampling and the Bayesian price indices would differ by a factor of $e^{0.5*(\mathrm{Var}(\beta|Y)+\mathrm{Var}(\beta))}$ even if the unbiased estimators for the log index β were the same. The minimum, maximum, and average $\mathrm{Var}(\beta \mid Y)$ across the sample time periods and all six models are (0.0375%, 0.532%, 0.0625%), (0.0149%, 0.256%, 0.0238%), (0.220%, 0.767%, 0.256%), and (0.0231%, 0.491%, 0.0517%) for Atlanta, Chicago, Dallas, and San Francisco, respectively. The magnitude of $\mathrm{Var}(\beta \mid Y)$ is negatively correlated with the sample size in the corresponding city. Overall, given the sample size in the data set, the effects of $\mathrm{Var}(\beta \mid Y)$ on the price indices are insignificant.

Case and Shiller (1987) employ a three-stage weighted least-squares method to estimate the real estate price index. In this article, a Bayesian approach is used to estimate the index. The normalized distance between the quarterly return series estimated using these two different methods for the Case–Shiller model are 2.34%, 1.73%, 3.37%, and 4.73% for

Table 6. Normalized distance between alternative log index series.

	model 1	model 2	model 3	model 4	model 5	model 6
			Atlanta			
model 1	0					
model 2	0.749	0				
model 3	2.357	1.611	0			
model 4	2.423	1.677	0.282	0		
model 5	1.572	1.996	3.496	3.575	0	
model 6	7.018	6.287	4.758	4.701	8.154	0
			Chicago			
model 1	0					
model 2	0.013	0				
model 3	0.651	0.648	0			
model 4	0.699	0.697	0.34	0		
model 5	1.96	1.954	2.464	2.542	0	
model 6	5.347	5.352	4.867	4.851	7.189	0
			Dallas			
model 1	0					
model 2	0.2	0				
model 3	3.705	3.905	0			
model 4	4.014	4.214	0.633	0		
model 5	1.191	1.2	3.677	4.13	0	
model 6	9.222	9.027	12.916	13.224	9.497	0
			San Francisco			
model 1	0					
model 2	0.841	0				
model 3	0.269	1.097	0			
model 4	1.067	1.82	0.888	0		
model 5	2.431	1.673	2.663	3.472	0	
model 6	4.351	5.134	4.133	3.558	6.722	0

Note: m in the initial condition $v_{i,t_{i1}-m} = 0$ is assumed to be 300. The normalized distance is the absolute average of the difference between two log index series, divided by the average norm of these two log index series, and then multiplied by 100. For models 1, 2, and 6, the prior of $\ln(z)$ is assumed to be a double exponential distribution with parameter 1.

Atlanta, Chicago, Dallas, and San Francisco, respectively. For the annual return series, the corresponding normalized distances are 0.25%, 0.09%, 0.53%, and 0.34%, respectively. The normalized distances between the return series estimated using these two different methods increases as the autocorrelation parameter in the generalized model deviates from unity.

4. Conclusions

In this article, a general Bayesian framework for constructing house price indices is proposed. Six alternative models are examined: the two-error AR(1) model; the Case–Shiller model; the one-error AR(1) model; the BMN model; the Webb model; and the Goetzmann–Spiegel model.

The posterior odds ratio test suggests that the three two-error models dominate the three one-error models. The Geotzmann–Spiegel model has the highest posterior odds in three out of four cities, and the two-error AR(1) model has the highest posterior odds in San Francisco. The Geotzmann–Spiegel model outperforms the Case-Shiller model in all four cities, suggesting that it is preferable to include the nontemporal return component in the model for constructing price index. Among the three one-error term models, the AR(1) model has the best performance. The BMN and the Webb model follow in performance, respectively. Although the one-error AR(1) model outperforms the one-error random walk model, the performances of the two-error AR(1) model relative to the Case–Shiller model are mixed.

The posterior density of the autocorrelation parameter for the two-error AR(1) model is highly concentrated around unity in three out of four cities; however, the 95% HPD interval of the autocorrelation parameter may not contain unity. When the 95% HPD interval does not contain 1, the Case–Shiller model is dominated by the two-error AR(1) model.

The existing literature uses the signal-to-noise ratio to measure the accuracy of the real estate index. The empirical evidence shows that the criteria for comparing alternative models by a posterior odds ratio contradict the criteria of the signal-to-noise ratio. This study suggests that the signal-to-noise ratio is not a good measure of the precision of the estimated index and is not a valid criterion for evaluating alternative models.

We define a normalized distance to measure the difference between each pair of return series. The normalized distance is much smaller for the log index series than for the quarterly return series. There could be a significant discrepancy among alternative return series or index series. Therefore, the choice of alternative models is important.

Acknowledgments

The author thanks Kurt Fisher, Robert Shiller, Christopher A. Sims, Thomas G. Thibodeau (the editor), and two anonymous referees for helpful comments.

Notes

1. The biased James and Stein estimator was first proposed in James and Stein (1961).
2. Zellner and Tiao (1964, p. 764) provide an alternative specification of the initial condition for an AR(1) error process, allowing for explosive and nonexplosive evolution. In our context and notation, their specification would be $V_{it_{il}} = M + \epsilon_{it_{il}}$, where M is a parameter.
3. The probability density function for a double exponential distribution with mean μ is $f(w) = 0.5\lambda e^{-\lambda|w-\mu|}$, where $\lambda > 0$ is a parameter.

4. See Sims (1988), Sims and Uhlig (1991), and a special issue of the *Journal of Applied Econometrics* (1991) for discussions.
5. Specifically, we choose *m* to be 1, 50, 100, 150, 200, 300, 400, 500, 600, 800, 1000, 1500, 2000, 2500, 3000, 3500, 4000, 5000, 6000, 7000, 8000, 9000, and 10000.
6. The different priors of the variance ratio z have little effect on the posterior mean and HPD interval of γ. The difference in the estimates due to a different prior is less than 0.01%.

References

Bailey, M. J., R. F. Muth, and H. O. Nourse. "A Regression Method for Real Estate Price Index Construction," *Journal of the American Statistical Association* 58 (1963), 933–942.

Box, George E. P., and G. C. Tiao. *Bayesian Inference in Statistical Analysis*. Reading, MA: Addison-Wesley, 1973.

Case, B., and J. M. Quigley. "The Dynamics of Real Estate Prices," *The Review of Economics and Statistics* 73 (1991), 50–58.

Case, K. E., and R. J. Shiller. "Prices of Single Family Homes since 1970: New Indexes for Four Cities," *New England Economic Review* (1987), 45–56.

Crone, T. M., and R. P. Voith, "Estimating House Price Appreciation: A Comparison of Methods," *Journal of Housing Economics* 2 (1992), 324–338.

Gatzlaff, D. H., and D. C. Ling. "Measuring Changes in Local House Prices: An Empirical Investigation of Alternative Methodologies," *Journal of Urban Economics* 35 (1994) 221–244.

Goetzmann, W. E. "The Accuracy of Real Estate Indices: Repeat Sale Estimators," *Journal of Real Estate Finance and Economics* 5 (1992), 5–53.

Goetzmann, W. E., and M. Spiegel. "Non-Temporal Components of Residential Real Estate Appreciation," *Review of Economics and Statistics* 77 (1995), 199–206.

Hill, R. C., J. R. Knight, and C. F. Sirmons. "Estimating Capital Asset Price Indexes." *The Review of Economics and Statistics* (in press).

James, W., and C. Stein. "Estimation with Quadratic Loss." In J. Neyman (ed.), *Proceedings of the 4th Berkeley Symposium on Mathematical Statistics and Probability,* Vol. 1. Berkeley, CA.: University of California Press, 1961, pp. 361–379.

Moulton, B. R. "A Bayesian Approach to Regression Selection and Estimation, with Application to a Price Index for Radio Services," *Journal of Econometrics* 49 (1991), 169–193.

Palmquist, R. B. "Hedonic Price and Depreciation Indexes for Residential Housing: A Comment," *Journal of Urban Economics* 6 (1979), 267–271.

Quigley, J. M. "A Simple Hybrid Model for Estimating Real Estate Price Indexes," *Journal of Housing Economics* 4 (1995) 1–12.

Sims, C. A. "Bayesian Skepticism on Unit Root Econometrics," *Journal of Economics and Dynamic Control* 12 (1988), 463–474.

Sims, C. A. and H. Uhlig. "Understanding Unit Rooters: A Helicopter Tour," *Econometrics* 59 (1991), 1591–1599.

Thibodeau, T. G. "House Price Indices from the 1984–1992 MSA American Housing Surveys," *Journal of Housing Research* 6 (1995), 439–481.

Webb, C. "A Probabilistic Model for Price Levels in Discontinuous Markets." In W. Eichhorn (ed.) *Measurement in Economics*. Heidelberg: Physic-Verlag, 1988.

Zellner, A. and G. Tiao. "Bayesian Analysis of the Regression Model with Autocorrelated Errors," *American Statistical Association Journal* 59 (1964) 763–778.

Journal of Real Estate Finance and Economics, 14: 133–154 (1997)
©1997 Kluwer Academic Publishers

Short Holds, the Distributions of First and Second Sales, and Bias in the Repeat-Sales Price Index

MARION STEELE
Department of Economics, University of Guelph and Centre for Urban and Community Studies, University of Toronto

RICHARD GOY
Department of Consumer Studies, University of Guelph

Key Words: house price, price index, repeat sales, opportune buyer

1. Introduction

The last two decades have seen vast swings in house prices which have distorted the distribution of wealth and have created major problems for lenders. These swings make it important to have good, simple price indices for analysis, and over the last decade researchers have used Bailey, Muth, and Nourse's (1963) repeat-sales method to fill this need. The repeat-sales method is a generalization of the old chain index, using as its basic building block the fact that, when the same asset sells twice, the change in its price is a quality-adjusted price change, and a sample of such price changes can be used to yield a quality-adjusted price index. Case and Shiller reintroduced the repeat-sales method to the literature, using an amended version in their work on house prices (1989, 1990). Recently, it also has been used (Pesando, 1993; Goetzman, 1993) to study price movements in the markets for modern prints and paintings.

A major problem for the use of repeat-sales prices is the possibility that such prices are exceptional. The repeat-sales sample is, by construction, confined to assets selling relatively frequently, and this sample selection will yield a biased index if price changes in the sample are different from those of all transacting assets. Haurin and Hendershott (1991) note this might be the case for houses if repeat-sales properties are starter homes which appreciate relatively quickly. Shiller's (1993b) hedonic repeat-sales estimator addresses this issue by generalizing the repeat-sales estimator to allow for different rates of price change among assets with different characteristics. Clapp and Giaccotto (1994) have applied and extended this to housing.[1]

A different approach to the bias issue is taken by Goetzman and Spiegel (1995). They argue that repeat-sales properties *change* in a special way between sales. In particular, home improvement occurs which is not associated with the length of time that the property is held, but with the act of selling. Thus, one component of the change in the price of a repeat-sales house arises because of a change in the characteristics of the house—possibly, like painting and other cosmetic improvements, a change which is not observed. This component is nontemporal, and therefore must be eliminated in the construction of any price index.

We approach the issue of bias from another tack. We are concerned not so much with the characteristics of repeat-sales *properties* or the change in those properties, as with the nature of the repeat-sales *prices* and the economic agents holding repeat-sales properties. Like Goetzman and Spiegel (1995), we are concerned with the nontemporal component of the price change in the repeat-sales properties, but unlike them, we view the critical aspect of investments in repeat-sales properties to be their relatively short holding period. In any given sample of transacting properties, the subsample sold twice in the sample period will tend to have a shorter holding period than the sample as a whole. This is especially true if the sample range of time is short, as in our sample, which covers only 1988 to 1990. Further, it seems plausible that short holds are more important during price booms when sales are high—such as the years 1988 and 1989 in our data—than during periods of falling, stagnant, or slowly growing prices when sales are low.[2]

Why should a short holding period be associated with an observed price change which is biased as an indicator of market price change? This is the case, because it tends to indicate an opportune buyer. The housing market is a fertile field for such a buyer (Goetzmann and Spiegel, 1995). Search theory tells us that the law of one price does not hold in markets such as that for housing where search is costly because of the heterogeneity of the product. Price discovery is costly. Heterogeneity also leads to illiquidity. For these reasons, there will tend to be substantial dispersion of actual prices around the true equilibrium price of a house. Well-informed buyers can engage in profitable arbitrage—purchasing an asset selling below its true value and later selling it at its true price, or higher.[3] It is possible that well-informed participants are primarily motivated by expectations that they will profit from rising prices, but they may use their special knowledge to purchase bargains as the vehicle for their arbitrage through time. If repeat-sales properties are held by such buyers, the first sale of a repeat-sales pair will tend to occur below the mean of the price range for houses of the same observed characteristics and the second sale will tend to occur at the mean or above. Putting this point more formally, the distribution of the disturbance term in the hedonic regression will vary according to whether a sale is a first sale of a repeat-sale pair, a second sale, or not.

In this article, we test for the existence of bias in first transactions, "purchases," and in second transactions, "sales" prices. We seek the answer to the simple question: does the fact that a transaction is the first of a repeat pair (with a short holding period) have an effect on price? We find that the answer is yes in our data: the first transaction in a repeat pair occurs at a statistically significant discount (and the second at a slight, but not statistically significant premium). A major contribution of this note is the use of this simple test and the empirical finding supporting the hypothesis of bias. This test does not appear in the literature. It was not available to Goetzman and Spiegel (1995), because they did not have detailed characteristics data.

We then derive the expression for the bias in the repeat-sales price index. We show that where the bias in the *change in prices* is constant, the bias in the *index* will vary from one quarter to the next, because the bias in the index depends not only on (a) the bias in the second transaction minus the bias in the first transaction, but also on (b) the distributions of first and second transactions. The information about the impact of these distributions is summarized in an easily derived vector which we call the R vector. We use it to demonstrate the potentially large impact of variations in these distributions on the bias in the repeat-sales regression coefficients and the repeat sales index.

The existence of the bias which we have identified in our hedonic data apparently implies that the Repeat-Sales (RS) estimator should be amended. The amendment is a simple one: include an intercept in the RS regression. Goetzman and Spiegel (1995) have made this amendment, and they find a large intercept indicating a large bias. Shiller (1993a, p. 139) has shown, however, that under certain conditions in a heterogeneous market the intercept in an Intercept Repeat-Sales (IRS) regression will be a component of the truly temporal change in price. This implies that (a) the intercept in an IRS regression in a period of rising prices will overstate the bias, and (b) an index computed assuming that the intercept represents only nontemporal change in price will understate the rise in prices. Shiller's point is borne out in our data. We find that the estimate of bias derived from an IRS regression is much higher than the direct estimate of bias obtained from the hedonic regression.

We also find that in our data transactions are highly imbalanced—almost no first sales take place during the quarters around the peak in prices, while many second sales occur then. We find that bias in our RS index is negligible in early quarters—when first sales dominate—and increases monotonically to become substantial by the final quarters, when almost all sales are second sales. This varying bias is more damaging to the usefulness of the repeat-sales indices than a constant bias.

As a supplement to the evidence of our data, we also include a reanalysis of data in Bailey, Muth, and Nourse's (BMN) seminal article (1963). Their subsample of fast repeats over an extended period of time suggests a bias which is greater than that indicated in our data. These data also cast some light on which of the various explanations for bias is the most compelling.

On the basis of our results, we recommend that authors estimating repeat-sales indices report summary information about the distribution of first and second sales in the form of the vector R developed below, so that readers can gauge the potential bias in the index.[4] We recommend that authors stick with the non-intercept version of the repeat-sales index, because of the evidence that the intercept version overstates the nontemporal component of price change and understates price increases. We caution authors to reconsider the use of GLS estimators which give relatively heavy weight to fast repeats, because these are the most likely to be contaminated by bias.

2. Are Repeat-Sales Prices Biased?

2.1. An Amended Hedonic Specification

To answer the question of whether or not repeat sales are biased, we first set out a widely used hedonic specification for houses, the semi-logarithm specification, in which the dependent variable is the log of price, and regressors are *one,* the characteristics of the property and dummy variables for time, so that the implicit marginal prices of characteristics are constrained to rise at the same rate over time. Specifically, we assume that

$$P_i = \alpha + X_i\beta + \lambda_2 D2_i + \lambda_3 D3_i + \ldots \lambda_T DT_i + u_i, \tag{1}$$

where P_i is the natural log of the price in *transaction i*; X_i is a $1 \times k$ vector of characteristics of the property sold in transaction i; DT_i takes the value one if transaction i occurs in period T, and zero otherwise; β is a $k \times 1$ vector of parameters; and $\alpha, \lambda_2, \lambda_3, \ldots, \lambda_T$ are scalar parameters. The disturbance term u_i is iid with mean zero and incorporates the effects of omitted characteristics and the effects of the omitted interaction between characteristics and time, as well as random error in price.

We now amend the standard model to allow the nature of the transaction to affect the distribution of the disturbance term. We hypothesize that the first sale or second sale of a repeat-sales pair occurs at a discount or premium relative to other transactions. Our view is not that there is anything different about a repeat-sale *property,* but rather that the involvement in a transaction of a relatively short-hold investor indicates that the transaction has likely occurred towards one of the tails of the price distribution. Thus, we drop the assumption that the u_i's are identically distributed and replace it with the following assumptions:

$$u_{i_f} = \gamma_f + \varepsilon_{i_f}$$

$$u_{i_s} = \gamma_s + \varepsilon_{i_s}$$

$$u_{i_o} = -\frac{0.5\pi}{1 - \pi}(\gamma_f + \gamma_s) + \varepsilon_{i_o},$$

where u_{i_f} is the disturbance for the ith transaction if it is the first sale of a repeat-sales pair, u_{i_s} is the disturbance if the ith transaction is the second sale of a repeat-sale pair, u_{i_o} is the disturbance if the ith transaction is not part of a repeat-sale pair, π is the proportion of all transactions in the sample data range which are one of a repeat pair, and ε_{i_f}, ε_{i_s}, ε_{i_o} are white noise terms.[5] Substituting in (1),

$$P_i = \alpha + X_i\beta + D_i\lambda + (\gamma_f + \varepsilon_{i_f})F_i + (\gamma_s + \varepsilon_{i_s})S_i + \left(-\frac{0.5\pi}{1 - \pi}(\gamma_f + \gamma_s) + \varepsilon_{i_o}\right)O_i,$$

and accordingly,

$$P_i = \alpha - \frac{0.5\pi}{1 - \pi}(\gamma_f + \gamma_s)O_i + X_i\beta + D_i\lambda + \gamma_f F_i$$
$$+ \gamma_s S_i + F_i\varepsilon_{i_f} + S_i\varepsilon_{i_s} + O_i\varepsilon_{i_o}, \tag{1a}$$

where D_i is the $1 \times (T - 1)$ vector of time dummies, and F, S, and O are 1, 0 dummies for first of a repeat pair, second of a repeat pair, and other, respectively. Because these dummies are linearly dependent (1a) cannot be estimated, and so, using the fact $O_i = 1 - (F_i + S_i)$, we rewrite it as:

$$P_i = \alpha' + X_i\beta + D_i\lambda + \delta_f F_i + \delta_s S_i + F_i\varepsilon_{i_f} + S_i\varepsilon_{i_f} + O_i\varepsilon_{i_o}, \tag{1b}$$

where

$$\delta_f = \gamma_f + \frac{0.5\pi}{1-\pi}(\gamma_f + \gamma_s), \delta_s = \gamma_s + \frac{0.5\pi}{1-\pi}(\gamma_f + \gamma_s)$$

and $\alpha' = \alpha - \frac{0.5\pi}{1-\pi}(\gamma_f + \gamma_s).$

Note that $\delta_s - \delta_f = \gamma_s - \gamma_f$, that is, the difference between coefficients of S and F equals the bias in the change in the price of a repeat-sale property.

2.2. Data

We apply our analysis to data on Multiple Listing Service (MLS) house prices for the years 1988–1990 from Kitchener-Waterloo. Prior to the sample period, 1988–1990, the average MLS price rose strongly—by about 85% from the beginning of 1985 to the beginning of 1988, reaching a peak in May 1990, about 40% above its beginning, 1988 value. It has fallen quite substantially since then. The dating and pattern of the boom are very similar to those in Los Angeles, but the extent of the increase is substantially greater—almost precisely the same as that in the 1980s' boom in Boston (Cf. Case and Shiller, 1994).

The sample used in the regressions consists of records for 9,811 transactions of semi-detached and single houses, all sold through MLS. Virtually all information on structure and lot variables given in the MLS records is used in the definition of characteristics, on the grounds that listing real estate agents should be good judges of what affects purchase decisions and house prices. Most variables are standard, but "size," is total living area in thousands of square feet, found by summing the square footage in individual rooms (but not halls and closets). Certain rooms in our sample—recreation, laundry, and game rooms—are typically found in basements, and this low quality space distorts the size variable. The effect of this is offset by the inclusion of dummy variables for these rooms, which are expected to have negative effects.[6]

Most important of all, we include variables to capture our maintained hypothesis in (1b) that repeat sales occur at a discount or premium: FIRST (= F in (1b)) equals 1 if a price is for the first sale in a repeat-sales pair, and SECOND (= S in (1b)) equals one for a second sale. Testing the null hypothesis that the difference between the coefficients of these two dummy variables is zero amounts to testing the null of no bias in the repeat-sales price change. On the grounds that a discount or premium may vary with the interval between sales—the holding period, H—we also include interaction variables, FIRSTH (FIRST*H) and SECONDH (SECOND*H).

2.3. Results for the Amended Constrained Hedonic Regressions

Results for the amended model are shown in Table 1. The $\bar{R}^2$, at 0.84 is quite high for a parametric hedonic specification. Signs and quantitative effects are generally highly plausible,

Table 1. Results for constrained hedonic regression with sales characteristics variables.

Variable	Parameter Estimate	t-statistic	Parameter Estimate	t-statistic
Intercept	11.3634	612.460	11.3631	612.461
Bedrooms	0.0324	12.970	0.0324	12.977
Other Rooms	0.0156	11.764	0.0156	11.765
Living Area	0.0893	4.909	0.0889	4.886
Living Area^2	0.0332	5.510	0.0333	5.530
Lot Area	0.0137	17.857	0.0137	17.844
Lot Area^2	−0.000087	−3.317	−0.000087	−3.295
Large Lot	−0.0018	−2.131	−0.0018	−2.158
Rec. Room	−0.0239	−6.576	−0.0239	−6.600
Family Room	0.0156	4.256	0.0156	4.238
Games Room	−0.0226	−2.719	−0.0225	−2.705
Den	0.0381	7.895	0.0381	7.892
Laundry	−0.0152	−2.275	−0.0152	−2.275
Kitchen(2)	−0.0337	−3.843	−0.0338	−3.851
Full Baths	0.0566	20.324	0.0566	20.334
Half Baths	0.0411	15.118	0.0411	15.132
Basement(unf)	−0.0031	−0.957	−0.0030	−0.954
Basement W/O	0.0130	3.133	0.0130	3.138
Garage (one)	0.0315	10.586	0.0316	10.612
Garage (2+)	0.1254	28.609	0.1254	28.613
Fireplaces (no)	0.0560	18.805	0.0560	18.807
Pool (inground)	0.0379	5.380	0.0379	5.385
Pool (above gd)	0.0115	1.745	0.0113	1.702
UFFI	−0.0326	−2.644	−0.0329	−2.672
UFFI (removed)	0.0024	0.215	0.0025	0.223
Central Air	0.0356	11.151	0.0356	11.167
Electric BB	−0.0254	−3.725	−0.0255	−3.733
Oil Heat	−0.0162	−4.135	−0.0161	−4.113
Bungalow	0.0052	0.968	0.0051	0.956
1 ½ Storey	−0.0258	−3.885	−0.0259	−3.899
2+ Storey	0.0570	10.502	0.0570	10.491
Side Split	0.0266	4.078	0.0265	4.065
Back Split	−0.0079	−1.299	−0.0080	−1.322
Semi-det.	−0.0859	−14.504	−0.0860	−14.513
Age (1–5)	−0.0900	−17.824	−0.0901	−17.837
Age (6–15)	−0.1594	−30.109	−0.1597	−30.150

a heartening result in view of what might be regarded as the foolhardy strategy of including such a large array of variables. In any case, our primary concern is not with coefficients of *house* characteristics but rather with the coefficients of characteristics of the *sale*. The results indicate that the first sale of a repeat-sales pair is not like other sales—it takes place at an estimated discount of about 2.0%. The effect is highly significant using a two-tailed test; the results are even stronger if a one-tail test, consistent with the opportune buyer hypothesis, is used. A second sale is estimated to take place at a slight premium, only about 0.2% and is not statistically significant. The bias, $\gamma^* = \gamma_s - \gamma_f$, in the change in

Table 1. Results for constrained hedonic regression with sales characteristics variables. (*Continued*)

Variable	Parameter Estimate	t-statistic	Parameter Estimate	t-statistic
Age (16–30)	−0.1481	−25.287	−0.1482	−25.310
Age (31–50)	−0.1859	−26.758	−0.1861	−26.785
Age (51+)	−0.2734	−38.188	−0.2736	−38.214
Brick Veneer	0.0351	4.644	0.0351	4.644
Vinyl/Alum.	−0.0165	−1.840	−0.0168	−1.874
Stone	0.0579	5.020	0.0577	5.004
Frame	−0.0741	−5.693	−0.0745	−5.719
Brick/Wood	0.0153	1.880	0.0154	1.900
Brick/Alum.	0.0200	2.680	0.0199	2.671
Solid Mason	0.0435	4.950	0.0436	4.955
Unemploy (%)	−0.0024	−2.442	−0.0024	−2.456
Incid. of Pov.	−0.0004	−1.582	−0.0004	−1.555
CBD (inv.)	−0.0149	−4.972	−0.0148	−4.947
CBD (log)	0.0280	6.333	0.0280	6.321
Indust (inv.)	−0.0137	−8.111	−0.0137	−8.121
Indust (log)	−0.0274	−8.472	−0.0275	−8.502
Pop. Density	−0.0021	−7.191	−0.0021	−7.117
First	−0.0201	−3.552	−0.0353	−2.888
FirstH			0.0030	1.394
Second	0.0016	0.296	−0.0105	−0.954
SecondH			0.0025	1.263
Quarter 2	0.0409	7.894	0.0413	7.959
Quarter 3	0.0737	13.634	0.0743	13.713
Quarter 4	0.1059	18.595	0.1068	18.664
Quarter 5	0.1731	32.239	0.1740	32.262
Quarter 6	0.2278	39.754	0.2288	39.747
Quarter 7	0.2260	39.670	0.2268	39.662
Quarter 8	0.2525	43.172	0.2532	43.147
Quarter 9	0.2748	48.143	0.2753	48.092
Quarter 10	0.2684	42.156	0.2685	42.018
Quarter 11	0.2346	36.046	0.2345	35.857
Quarter 12	0.1920	25.436	0.1918	25.300
$\bar{R}^2$	0.8412		0.8412	
n	9811		9811	

log price of repeat-sales properties, as compared with single-sale properties, is estimated to be 0.0217, with a standard error of 0.0079. Thus, we estimate that the repeat-sale properties rose 2.19% more in price over their holding period than other properties. Note that the premium is, plausibly, higher than this for opportune buyers alone, because some short holders may be ordinary purchasers who sell shortly after purchase because of an unexpected job change, an unexpected change in consumption demand, or discovery of a lemon. If three-quarters of the short holds are simply the manifestation of mistakes and unexpected changes and if the average premium for all short holds is 2%, then the average premium for opportune buyers is 8%.

Consistent with the assumptions of the model, we hypothesize that the longer the holding period of a repeat-sale property, the more like all prices the repeat-sale pair will be. The second regression in Table 1 provides evidence on this point. As hypothesized, each quarter of holding period is estimated to reduce bias, but the reduction is very slight—a mere 0.00045—and far from statistical significance (standard error is 0.0030). From the second regression, the estimated bias for properties held one year is 0.0230 (s.e. 0.0085); for holds of two years, it is almost as large, 0.0212 (s.e. 0.012).[7]

3. Implications for the Repeat-sales Regression

3.1. The Amended Repeat-sales Regression Specification

Bias in the change in price of a repeat-sales pair, as incorporated into the amended hedonic regression model (1b), implies a repeat-sales regression specification with an intercept. To see this, consider transactions involving only properties which sell twice in the sample period. Let j_f refer to the first transaction of the jth *property* and j_s refer to the second transaction of property j. Then, assuming that the set of properties selling twice is confined to those with unchanged characteristics between sales, from (1b) we derive

$$
\begin{aligned}
P_{j_s} - P_{j_f} &= \gamma_s - \gamma_f + \lambda_2(D2_{j_s} - D2_{j_f}) + \lambda_3(D3_{j_s} - D3_{j_f}) \\
&\quad + \cdots + \lambda_T(DT_{j_s} - DT_{j_f}) + \varepsilon_{j_s} - \varepsilon_{j_f} \\
&= \gamma_s - \gamma_f + \lambda_2 Q2_j + \lambda_3 Q3_j + \cdots + \lambda_T QT_j + w_j,
\end{aligned}
\tag{2}
$$

where $Q\tau_j = 1$ if $D\tau_{j_s} = 1$

$\qquad\quad\ = -1$ if $D\tau_{j_f} = 1$

$\qquad\quad\ = 0$ otherwise, for $\tau = 2, \ldots, T$,

and where $w_j = \varepsilon_{j_s} - \varepsilon_{j_f}$. Note that $\gamma_s - \gamma_f$, the intercept, equals the bias in the repeat-sales price change. Note also that (2) may be rewritten as

$$
A = (i Q) \binom{\gamma^*}{\lambda} + w,
\tag{2a}
$$

where there are m repeat-sales properties, A is the $m \times 1$ vector of changes in log price, i is a $m \times 1$ vector of ones, Q is the $m \times (T - 1)$ matrix of -1, 0, 1 dummies, γ^* is a scalar equal to $\gamma_s - \gamma_f$, λ is the $T - 1$ vector of coefficients, and w is an $m \times 1$ vector of disturbances.

The maintained hypothesis that transaction which are one of a repeat-sales pair occurs at a discount or premium—that is, $\gamma_f \neq 0$ and $\gamma_s \neq 0$—implies $\gamma^* \neq 0$ unless $\gamma_f = \gamma_s$. This, in turn, implies that an unbiased repeat-sales regression includes a constant term; we term this an Intercept Repeat-Sales (IRS) regression. Such a regression has been estimated by Goetzman and Spiegel (1995). Shiller (1993a), however, has shown that the econometrics cannot distinguish between an intercept which is a true nontemporal component of price change, as in the model (2), and an intercept which is part of the temporal component of price change. In general, the estimated intercept from an intercept repeat regression will be the sum of a nontemporal and a temporal component. Model (2a) is still useful, however, because it allows us to gauge the effect on the price index of any hypothesized nontemporal component of the change in price in a repeat-sales pair. This effect is not obvious a priori. We derive an expression for it below.

3.2. Derived Bias in the Standard Repeat-sale Regression Coefficients

If (2) and (2a) are the true model, but a model without an intercept is estimated, estimates of the vector λ are biased. The expression for bias is an application of the well-known (e.g., Greene, 1993) expression for omitted-variable bias; the omitted "variable" in the standard (RS) regression is one (i.e., the intercept is omitted). Let $\tilde{\lambda}$ be the OLS estimator of λ using the RS regression. Then, the bias in this estimator is given by

$$E(\tilde{\lambda}) - \lambda = (Q'Q)^{-1}Q'i\gamma^* = R\gamma^* \quad \text{where} \quad R = (Q'Q)^{-1}Q'i. \tag{3}$$

Clearly, while the amount of bias depends on the value of γ^*, it also depends on Q. What is its nature? It reflects the distribution of first and second sales over the sample range. Notice that $Q'i$ is a $(T - 1)$ vector in which the τth element equals the number of second transactions minus the number of first transactions in period τ. It is convenient to refer to first transactions as purchases and second transactions as sales. If the number of sales balances the number of purchases in period τ, the τth element will be zero. If the vector is zero, bias will be zero. The $(T - 1)$th element of this vector cannot be zero, however, because, by construction, only sales—not purchases—can occur in period T. This implies that, in general, if $\gamma^* \neq 0$, bias will be nonzero.

Some examples are illuminating. As an aid to the reader, we show the omitted dummy vector, labeled $Q1$, as well as Q. Consider example 1, in which the sample range is four quarters, and sales and purchases are balanced except in the first and last quarters (when, by construction, they cannot be): in the first quarter there are two purchases, in each of the second and third there is perfect balance (one purchase and one sale), and in the fourth there are two sales. Three-quarters of the repeats are very fast (i.e., holding period is one quarter). Thus, $Q1$ and Q are

$$
Q1 \qquad\qquad Q
$$

$$
\begin{bmatrix} -1 \\ -1 \\ 0 \\ 0 \end{bmatrix}
\qquad
\begin{bmatrix} 1 & 0 & 0 \\ 0 & 0 & 1 \\ -1 & 1 & 0 \\ 0 & -1 & 1 \end{bmatrix}
$$

This yields

$$E \begin{bmatrix} \tilde{\lambda}_2 - \lambda_2 \\ \tilde{\lambda}_3 - \lambda_3 \\ \tilde{\lambda}_4 - \lambda_4 \end{bmatrix} = \begin{bmatrix} 0.5 \\ 1.0 \\ 1.5 \end{bmatrix} \gamma^*.$$

Here, the bias for the fourth-quarter log price index number is *three times* the bias for the second-quarter log price index number.

Our second example is a more unbalanced one. Almost all purchases occur in the first and second quarter, and almost all sales in the last quarter. The base quarter, the first quarter, has the least activity of any quarter. One-half of the repeats are very fast (holding period one quarter).

Specifically,

$$Q1 \qquad Q$$

$$\begin{bmatrix} -1 \\ 0 \\ 0 \\ 0 \\ 0 \\ 0 \end{bmatrix} \quad \begin{bmatrix} 0 & 0 & 1 \\ -1 & 0 & 1 \\ -1 & 0 & 1 \\ -1 & 1 & 0 \\ 0 & -1 & 1 \\ 0 & -1 & 1 \end{bmatrix}.$$

This yields

$$E \begin{bmatrix} \tilde{\lambda}_2 - \lambda_2 \\ \tilde{\lambda}_3 - \lambda_3 \\ \tilde{\lambda}_4 - \lambda_4 \end{bmatrix} = \begin{bmatrix} -0.25 \\ 0.25 \\ 1.00 \end{bmatrix} \gamma^*.$$

In this case, the second quarter coefficient is *negatively* biased.

These examples demonstrate that if repeat-sale properties change in price relatively more or less than single-sale properties which are the same in measurable characteristics, the extent of the bias in any index coefficient is potentially highly sensitive to the pattern of first and second sales. We now apply this analysis to our data.

3.3. Results for Bias in the Standard Repeat-sales Regression

3.3.1. The repeat-sales subsample. Repeat sales account for 1,158 transactions in our sample. Of these, 178 transactions, or 15.4% of the total, were eliminated because the property involved changed between transactions. Deducting these as well as transactions of properties selling more than twice within the data range, or selling twice in the same quarter, yields 944 sales which are one of a repeat-sales pair; this is 9.6% of the total sample used in the hedonic regression. Gross of properties which changed between sales, repeat (i.e., second) sales are 6% of transactions. This ratio is quite high in view of the data range of only three years. Putting this in perspective, Clapp, Giaccotto, and Tirtiroglu (1991) found repeat-sales to be 25% of all transactions over a seven-year range. Mark and Gold-berg (1984) found 32% over a 23-year range.[8] Case and Shiller (1989) found a ratio of only 4% over a 16-year interval. Means and standard deviations of selected characteristics for all sales and repeat sales are shown in Table 2. As is usual for repeat-sales subsamples,

Table 2. Means and standard deviations for repeat-sales sample and all houses.

	Repeat-Sales		All-houses	
	Mean	Standard deviation	Mean	Standard deviation
Sales price[a]	140606	44157	151712	51247
Real Price[b]	123960	37744	134080	44269
Bed Rooms	3.048	0.584	3.165	0.590
Other Rooms	3.425	1.133	3.547	1.150
Living Area	1.119	0.315	1.176	0.334
Living Area^2	1.351	0.801	1.494	0.924
Lot Area	5.727	2.900	6.311	3.651
Lot Area^2	41.201	76.746	53.165	142.403
Large Lot	0.262	2.661	0.299	3.246
Rec. Room	0.645	0.479	0.628	0.483
Family Room	0.243	0.429	0.316	0.465
Games Room	0.015	0.120	0.022	0.146
Den	0.068	0.252	0.071	0.256
Laundry	0.036	0.187	0.034	0.181
Kitchen (2)	0.020	0.138	0.020	0.139
Full Baths	1.407	0.535	1.492	0.576
Half Baths	0.487	0.543	0.522	0.570
Basement (unf)	0.290	0.454	0.328	0.469
Basement W/O	0.072	0.259	0.094	0.292
Garage (one)	0.464	0.499	0.421	0.494
Garage (2+)	0.169	0.375	0.235	0.424
Fireplace (no.)	0.397	0.494	0.460	0.498
Pool (in ground)	0.025	0.157	0.031	0.173
Pool (above ground)	0.038	0.191	0.035	0.183
UFFI	0.007	0.082	0.010	0.097
UFFI (removed)	0.020	0.138	0.012	0.108
Central Air	0.196	0.397	0.202	0.401
Electric BB	0.030	0.171	0.034	0.182
Oil Heat	0.165	0.371	0.154	0.361
Bungalow	0.210	0.407	0.197	0.398
1 ½ Storey	0.124	0.330	0.104	0.306
2+ Storey	0.307	0.461	0.329	0.470
Side Split	0.042	0.201	0.069	0.253
Back Split	0.098	0.297	0.096	0.294
Semi-detached	0.146	0.353	0.125	0.331
Age (1–5)	0.182	0.386	0.186	0.389
Age (6–15)	0.254	0.435	0.238	0.426

Table 2. Means and standard deviations for repeat-sales sample and all houses. (*Continued*)

	Repeat-Sales		All-houses	
	Mean	Standard deviation	Mean	Standard deviation
Age (16–30)	0.199	0.400	0.223	0.416
Age (31–50)	0.175	0.380	0.145	0.352
Age (51+)	0.145	0.352	0.113	0.317
Brick Veneer	0.271	0.444	0.260	0.438
Vinyl/Alum.	0.067	0.251	0.049	0.216
Stone	0.015	0.120	0.018	0.132
Frame	0.016	0.124	0.012	0.109
Brick/Wood	0.093	0.290	0.101	0.302
Brick/Alum.	0.453	0.498	0.475	0.499
Solid Mason	0.054	0.226	0.057	0.232
Unemploy (%)	5.678	1.661	5.505	1.571
Incid. of Pov	.11.071	5.740	10.705	5.876
CBD (inv. of dist.)	0.922	1.028	0.829	0.906
CBD (log of dist.)	-0.424	0.747	-0.488	0.688
Indust (inv. of dist.)	1.865	2.174	1.811	2.135
Indust (log of dist.)	0.037	1.134	0.063	1.122
Pop. Density	8.730	4.953	8.708	5.166
First	0.500	0.500	0.048	0.214
FirstH	2.389	3.071	0.245	1.225
Second	0.500	0.500	0.048	0.214
SecondH	2.384	3.068	0.245	1.229
Quarter 2	0.105	0.307	0.121	0.326
Quarter 3	0.105	0.307	0.102	0.302
Quarter 4	0.079	0.270	0.082	0.275
Quarter 5	0.099	0.298	0.110	0.312
Quarter 6	0.086	0.280	0.085	0.279
Quarter 7	0.079	0.270	0.088	0.283
Quarter 8	0.082	0.275	0.080	0.271
Quarter 9	0.077	0.267	0.087	0.282
Quarter 10	0.086	0.280	0.060	0.238
Quarter 11	0.063	0.242	0.055	0.228
Quarter 12	0.037	0.189	0.036	0.186

[a]Nominal dollars
[b]Deflated using constrained hedonic price index (1988: 1 = 1.00), computed using regressions without sales characteristics variables.

repeat-sale properties are somewhat more modest than properties in the total sample. The price in terms of 1988, first-quarter dollars[9] is 7% less. Differences for pure size measures are quite small—for example, square feet of living area is only 5% less—but differences in the incidence of luxury characteristics are large: for example, the incidence of two-car garages is 30% less.

3.3.2. The distributions of first and second sales. Critical for our purpose, because of the role which they play in the bias expression, are the distribution of first and second sales. These are shown in Figure 1, along with the distribution of total sales. The very nature of

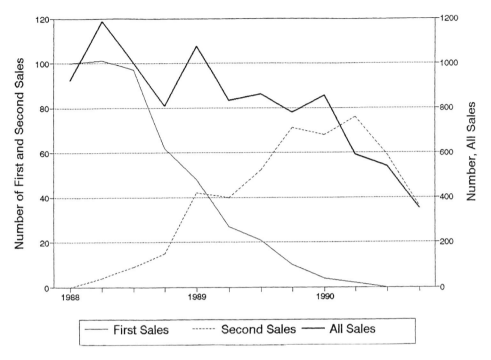

Figure 1. Number of MLS Sales First Sales, Second Sales and All.

constraints imposed by the selection of the repeat-sales subsample, especially for a period as short as 12 quarters, implies that first sales will tend to occur disproportionately towards the beginning of the period, and second sales disproportionately towards the end of the period. In our sample, however, it is clear that the imbalance is much greater than is forced by the constraints implicit in the sample selection. First sales fall off greatly towards the end of 1988 and virtually stop before the end of 1989, shortly before the peak of the boom in first quarter of 1990. Second sales peak one quarter after prices do, and fall off in the later part of 1990 in much the same way as do all sales. Note that the second sales distribution is much closer to uniform than is the first sales distribution.

3.3.3. Estimated bias in the repeat-sales coefficients.

Table 3 shows the estimated $\mathbf{R}\gamma^*$, the estimate of the bias vector given in (3), and the unadjusted and adjusted index. As can be seen, estimated bias in the price index coefficients is very small for the first coefficient, λ_2, but is substantial and positive for the last one, λ_{12}. At the price peak, the adjusted index is 129.4 (down from the unadjusted index level of 133.1), so that the percentage increase from base to peak is 3.7 percentage points less than that shown by the unadjusted index. At the end of the period, the difference is 3.9. It is difficult to label the last difference anything less than substantial, in view of the adjusted estimated price increase of just 20.9%.

3.3.4. Estimates of the intercept repeat-sales index.

An alternative estimate of γ^*, the bias in the price change of a repeat-sale pair, is (see (2)) the estimated intercept in the IRS regression. If this intercept is an unbiased estimate of γ^*, then the estimated coefficients of

Table 3. Bias vector and adjusted repeat-sales indices.

Quarter	R	$R\gamma*$ (bias)	RS (Repeat sales index unadjusted) (1988:1=100)	RSadj (Repeat sales index, adjusted using $R\gamma*$) (1988:1=100)	IRS (Intercept repeat sales index) (1988:1=100)
1 (1988:1)	n.a	n.a	100.0	100.0	100.0
2 (1988:2)	0.0730	0.0016	101.2	101.0	100.8
3 (1988:3)	0.1604	0.0035	106.4	106.0	105.6
4 (1988:4)	0.2653	0.0058	108.7	108.0	107.4
5 (1989:1)	0.6515	0.0142	119.9	118.2	116.4
6 (1989:2)	0.7994	0.0174	123.4	121.3	119.0
7 (1989:3)	0.9588	0.0208	124.6	122.0	119.3
8 (1989:4)	1.1399	0.0248	126.9	123.8	120.5
9 (1990:1)	1.3007	0.0283	133.1	129.4	125.5
10 (1990:2)	1.3300	0.0291	130.9	127.2	123.2
11 (1990:3)	1.3679	0.0297	128.6	124.9	120.9
12 (1990:4)	1.4680	0.0319	124.8	120.9	116.8

Note: R is defined in (3). RSadj and IRS are computed from coefficients in Table 4.

the $-1, 0, 1$ dummies are bias-free estimates of log-price index numbers. As noted above, the argument of Shiller (1993a) suggests, however, that the intercept will be upward biased as an estimate of γ^*. In Table 4 are shown the results for the amended regression. The estimated intercept and accordingly, the estimated bias, is 0.0454, more than two standard errors larger than the bias estimated by the constrained hedonic regression in Table 1. Consistent with this, the IRS index is substantially below the original RS index in later quarters (the IRS index at the peak is 125.5, as compared to 133.1 for the RS index) and implausibly lower than the constrained hedonic index (see Table 3 and Figure 2). The IRS index substantially

Table 4. Regression results for repeat sales and intercept repeat sales.

Variable	Repeat-sales Regression		Intercept repeat-sales Regression	
	Parameter Estimate	Standard Error	Parameter Estimate	Standard Error
Intercept			0.04544	0.00940
Quarter 2	0.01168	0.01216	0.00836	0.01189
Quarter 3	0.06158	0.01214	0.05430	0.01195
Quarter 4	0.08303	0.01303	0.07097	0.01296
Quarter 5	0.18125	0.01226	0.15164	0.01345
Quarter 6	0.21044	0.01341	0.17412	0.01510
Quarter 7	0.22002	0.01317	0.17645	0.01571
Quarter 8	0.23833	0.01246	0.18653	0.01622
Quarter 9	0.28598	0.01314	0.22688	0.01773
Quarter 10	0.26912	0.01261	0.20869	0.01755
Quarter 11	0.25187	0.01345	0.18971	0.01838
Quarter 12	0.22159	0.01676	0.15489	0.02141
S.E.R	0.088		0.086	

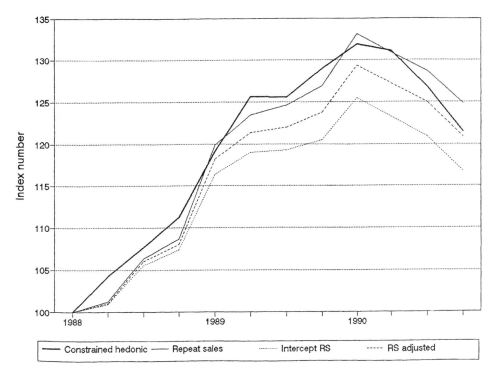

Figure 2. Constrained hedonic and repeat sales indices.

overcorrects for bias. This supports the view that the estimated intercept in an IRS regression is likely to be, in large part, a temporal component of price change. Accordingly, abandoning the orthodox RS specification is at best unwarranted.

3.3.5. Evidence from BMN.   We have argued that the opportune buyer rationale for the existence of bias in the price change of repeat-sales properties implies that the bias should be greater the shorter the period that a property is held. We found this relationship in our constrained hedonic regression (see section 2), but it was not statistically significant, and so we did not base our adjusted index on it.[10] Fortunately, a reinterpretation of data in BMN provides further suggestive evidence on the impact of short holds. Computations from these data are shown in Table 5. Fortuitously, BMN provide chain index results; the database for this index, of course, consists of pairs of sales occurring in adjacent years, so that the holding period is a minimum of one quarter and a maximum of seven quarters.[11] Thus, this database is very short holds. A comparison of price changes shown by BMN's chain index and those shown by their RS index is a comparison between the price increases of *very* short holds and those of *somewhat* short holds.

   BMN's motivation for the use of the RS regression rather than the chain index was to reduce variance, and indeed it did so in their application. But the mean increase in price also was reduced, and this is not a prediction of the theory. For the whole period, the mean simple annual rate of price increase is 15.4% for the chain index and only 6.5% for the RS

Table 5. Rate of price change, 1938–1959, fast repeats and all repeats, BMN data.

Year	Number of first and second sales (1)	Rate of change in price index		Difference ((2) − (3)) (4)
		Fast repeats (2)	All repeats (3)	
		%	%	
1937	52			
1938	35	−6.0	−1.0	−5.0
1939	60	166.0	−3.0	169.0
1940	65	−46.0	9.4	−55.4
1941	70	73.3	1.9	71.4
1942	77	44.0	31.8	12.2
1943	59	−27.0	7.8	−34.8
1944	103	5.3	−0.7	5.9
1945	109	15.1	15.9	−0.8
1946	128	19.1	20.0	−0.9
1947	105	23.4	11.4	12.0
1948	90	9.4	10.7	−1.3
1949	67	−5.4	14.7	9.2
1950	64	23.0	26.2	−3.3
1951	70	0.9	3.9	−3.0
1952	64	−2.0	3.1	−5.1
1953	50	3.8	−1.0	4.8
1954	39	−15.7	−2.0	−13.7
1955	47	14.3	6.5	7.8
1956	31	15.1	9.4	5.7
1957	44	−9.5	−9.5	0.0
1958	38	0.5	2.3	−1.8
1959	44	−15.9	−16.3	0.3
Mean, 1938–1959		15.4	6.5	8.9
Mean, 1944–1959		6.5	5.4	1.0

Source: Computed from data in Bailey, Muth, and Nourse (1963, table, p. 940), "Fast repeats" here refers to their index computed using the "chain link method." "All repeats" here refers to their index computed using the "regression method."

index (see Table 5). Even when the early years are eliminated, confining the comparison, as BMN suggest, to 1944 and later, the mean increase shown by the chain (fast-repeat) index is greater (6.5% versus 5.4%). Putting it in other terms, setting 1994 = 100, the index is 187 in 1959, using fast repeats only, and 174, using all repeats. This suggests that the change in the price of RS properties is more upward biased as an indicator of the true price change in transacted properties for short- than for long-hold repeats.

Consider also the relation of the sign of the differences to the volume of sales. Assume that fast repeats are dominantly those of opportune buyers in hot markets, when volume is rising and dominantly lemons or mistakes when volume is falling. Then, the difference between the price change given by the fast-repeat index and that given by the all-repeat index will be positive in years in which volume rises and negative in years in which it falls. In fact, in eight of 11 years of rising volume here, the difference is positive. The probability of eight or more positive signs occurring by chance alone is only 0.11.[12] In seven of the 11 years of falling volume, the difference is negative; the probability of seven or more positive signs occurring by chance alone is 0.27. Together, these results provide some support for the hypothesis that the price change of very short holds is not only biased but has a bias systematically related to the direction of sales volume.

4. Alternative Reasons for the Bias in the Price Change of Repeat-Sale Properties

We have hypothesized that the actions of opportune buyers, taking advantage of price dispersion—in Case and Shiller's (1987) terminology, "price risk"—result in upward bias in the price change in repeat-sales properties as an estimator of quality-adjusted price change. We found such a bias in our hedonic regressions. Goetzman and Spiegel (1995) favor an alternative explanation for bias—home improvement—and also note the existence of price risk. A third, fourth, and fifth explanation are also possible.

The third explanation is that the bias may be an artifact of timing, in interaction with the strong upward trend in prices in our data set. [13] A sale in our data set can only be a "first sale" if its corresponding second sale occurs before the end of the three years. Suppose that the holding period is random and has the same probability distribution for all properties. Then, a property which sells on the first day of quarter one has a higher probability of selling again before the end of the three years than a property selling on the last day of quarter one. This proposition holds for all quarters. Thus, first sales which have mates within the three years will tend to occur early in any quarter. Analogously, second sales will tend to occur late in any quarter. If, for example, first sales on average occur in the first month and second sales in the third month, and if the average rate of increase is 1% per month, there will be a bias of about 2%.

A difficulty with this explanation, in our data set, is that it requires that the average holding period for properties with first sales a quarter or two before the peak be the same as the average holding period for properties with first sales two years before the peak. These averaging holding periods are not observed (because of the three-year truncation) but examination of the distributions of sales in Figure 1 suggests that they are not the same.[14]

The fourth explanation, one for a *downward* bias,[15] is a "lemons' " hypothesis. Houses with flaws which are undiscoverable until ownership will tend to be put up for sale when the flaws are revealed. Lemons will thus be overrepresented among houses for sale, and especially among houses with a relatively short holding period (i.e., fast turnover rate).[16] Full characteristics discovery will be easier for the purchaser at the second sale than for the purchaser at the first sale of the lemon's life, because a quick second sale acts as a signal of lemonness, while the first sale, by the builder, does not. Consequently, the price will fall. At the third sale, especially if it occurs very soon after the first, the lemon signal will be stronger still (assuming that buyers are aware of the sales history of the house), so that the lemon discount may be expected to increase. Thus, both the change in price between first and second sale, and that between second and third sale, will be downward biased. These discounts are nontemporal, because they are associated not with the passage of time but with characteristics discovery. To the extent that this phenomenon is important, it will at least partially offset any positive bias induced by the presence of opportune buyers. Its net effect may be expected to be greater in slow markets than in hot ones, because of the likelihood that opportune buyers tend to be absent from such markets.

The fifth explanation, another one for downward bias, is forced sales. In general, when the market turns down, the sales which occur will tend to be at higher prices than those of the entire stock (Hendershott and Kane, 1995). This may be characterized as the tendency for "winners" to sell (Abraham and Schauman, 1991). At the same time, there will be some sales of nonwinners, because some *sellers* of nonwinners will find it difficult to hold and sell later, rather than sell now. Homeowners undergoing a job transfer or raising cash for a divorce settlement, and cash-strapped institutions selling foreclosed property will be biased towards selling now. On average, one would expect these sales to occur after shorter holding periods than all sales, because the reasons for the sale are unexpected. The price change of these properties will be downward-biased as an estimate of the quality-adjusted price change of all properties which sell (although they may not be, as an estimate of the price change of the total stock.) Repeat-sales properties with a second sale in a downturn are thus apt to be short-hold properties, sold because of an unexpected event, and falling in value more than other sold properties.

In our view, the most compelling explanations for bias—especially in rising markets—are the opportune-buyer and the home-improvement ones. Both are consistent with the fact that in our sample—and typically in repeat-sales samples—repeat-sale properties are of lower quality than the average property sold. Specifically, in our sample, repeat-sale properties are somewhat smaller and have a much lower incidence of luxury characteristics. Since our repeat-sale sample is confined to properties which do not measurably change in between sales, by even so much as an additional plumbing fixture, the home improvement story rests, in our view, on the proposition that houses which are of *measurably* low quality are more likely to have *unmeasurable* improvements, such as redecoration of a living room, than are measurably higher quality properties. We do not find this persuasive. At the same time, lower than average quality seems consistent with the opportune-buyer explanation. Such a buyer, counting on a fast resale, will wish to buy a house which is relatively liquid and which does not present financing problems. Few opportune buyers have the capital strength to purchase a bargain if its price is two million dollars. It is relevant here that Gatzlaff and Ling (1994), who eliminated the fastest repeats from their sample, found that the average value in their remaining repeats sample was *higher* than the average value of all transactions.

The suggestive evidence on fast repeats both from our sample and from BMN also suggests that the opportune-buyer explanation is more compelling. Shorter holds are associated with greater bias. This is consistent with the behavior of opportune buyers, but because improvements take time, not so consistent with the home-improvement explanation.

Some reconciliation of the two explanations does seem possible: the bargain which attracts the opportune buyer may exist partially because other potential buyers are turned off by quite trivial problems, such as unprunned shrubbery, dirty walls, rooms jammed with furniture, and a generally shabby appearance. The opportune buyer who makes a house more saleable by removing old, excess furniture is in some sense improving the house, and certainly painting the house improves it. The opportune-buyer and home-improvement explanations cannot be entirely disentangled.

5. Concluding Remarks

Our analysis shows how differences in the disturbance term for first and second sales of a repeat-sales pair can result in bias in the change in the price of repeat-sales properties as an estimator of the change in the true price. We find evidence confirming the existence of this bias, a nontemporal component of price change, in our hedonic regression. Goetzmann and Spiegel (1995) hypothesized that such a bias exists but did not test for its existence, directly, using a hedonic regression.

We hypothesize that the source of this bias is the presence of opportune traders who tend to hold properties for a short time. We find suggestive evidence in our data and in BMN's data that the bias is greater for fast repeats than for other repeats. The existence of a difference is broadly consistent with Hendershott and Kane's suggestion (1995) and Gatzlaff and Haurin's (1994) evidence that the prices of transacting properties change differently from the prices of nontransacting property.

The effect of the price-change bias on the repeat-sales index can apparently be eliminated simply by including an intercept in the repeat-sales regression (Goetzmann and Spiegel, 1995) and computing the repeat-sales index ignoring the intercept. Unfortunately, however, Shiller has shown (1993a) that, in a heterogeneous market, an intercept may incorporate temporal as well as nontemporal price change, and the Goetzmann and Spiegel procedure will then overstate the nontemporal component and result in a downward-biased price index. We find evidence for such overstatement—*substantial* overstatement—in our data. Adopting the Goetzmann and Spiegel procedure is apt to produce a cure worse than the disease.

What should prudent producers and users of RS price indices do? They should consider the possibility that their indices may be contaminated and compute the effect of any given price change bias on their index using the vector **R** derived in this article. We have shown that, for a *given, fixed,* nontemporal component of the price change of repeat-sales properties, the *bias in the RS index varies* from period to period, depending on the pattern of first and second sales. The **R** vector—which is simply the coefficient vector obtained when a column of ones is regressed on the repeat sales regressors—translates the fixed component of price change into variable index bias. In our data, this computation shows that the bias for the early quarters is close to zero but that the bias for the last quarter is over three percentage points. In effect, this vector summarizes relevant information about the pattern of first and single sales. It indicates the degree of vulnerability of a repeat-sales index to bias. We recommend that it be computed as standard practice.

An important implication of the suggestive evidence on short holds is that various GLS estimators (e.g., Case and Shiller, 1989; Goetzmann, 1993; Quigley, 1995) should be reassessed. These estimators weight short-hold repeats more heavily than long-hold repeats, on the grounds that price change of short-hold repeats has lower variance. Our evidence suggests that the price of this lower noise may be greater bias. This price may be too high. GLS methods should be used warily, or they should be amended, or, following Gatzlaff and Ling (1994), very short holds should be eliminated from the data set.

Appendix: Further Details on the Data

Kitchener-Waterloo is a city of about 300,000 with its economic base in manufacturing and with two large universities, located in southwestern Ontario about 75 miles from Toronto.

Each record contains price, structure and lot information, dwelling address, and MLS map district. Eliminated from the original sample were 22 transactions for which lots were very large (over an acre and a half), and records related to defaulting sales.[17] Also eliminated were ten transactions involving properties sold twice in the same quarter, and 26 transactions involving properties sold more than twice. Clapp and Giaccotto (1992) adduce convincing evidence that such properties are typically lemons largely because results of these regressions are used to estimate bias in repeat-sales indices which also do not use these observations.

Excluded from "size" are living areas in halls, bathrooms, and some closets. Living area defined in this way is about two-thirds of the living area based on the standard measure (outside dimensions), so long as all rooms are above ground. Lot area is measured in thousands of square feet. "Large lot" equals zero if less than one-half acre, and actual area otherwise. UFFI is a dummy variable equal to 1 for houses insulated using urea formaldehyde foam. UFFI (removed) equals 1 for houses which have had UFFI removed. Offers to purchase commonly include a clause requiring vendors to certify that UFFI is absent.

Neighborhood variables are derived from Census Tract data for 1986. School information is not included because school quality does vary substantially. Accessibility variables are street distances to the Central Business District and to the closest industrial area, respectively.

Properties which changed between transactions were identified using the MLS records. Changes leading to exclusion were changes to the number of bathrooms or rooms, the addition of a pool, garage, fireplace or recreation room, changes to number of bathroom fixtures, changes in the dimensions of any room or the lot. This plausibly led to substantially more exclusions than would have been the case if assessment data had been used, as in Clapp, Giaccotto, and Tirtiroglu (1991). In Ontario, reassessments are not triggered by adding a fixture to a bathroom or finishing part of a basement for use as a recreation room.

Acknowledgments

We are grateful to two anonymous referees for ideas, corrections, and advice, to Karl E. Case for his stimulating and useful discussion at the AREUEA meetings, to David de Meza, David Prescott, and Clive Southey for ideas and suggestions, to John Goodman for insightful comments on a related article, and to the Kitchener-Waterloo Real Estate Board for providing us with their machine readable data. Any errors are ours alone.

Notes

1. A still more general approach to problems in the repeat-sales index is to integrate it with the hedonic model. Case and Quigley's (1991) is the first of several articles taking this approach.
2. A point implicit in Shiller's example (1993a, p. 139).
3. An opportune sale seems less likely than an opportune buy, because the former *requires* only that the agent need be able to spot a bargain house (a house listed at a bargain price), while the latter requires that the agent need be able to spot and capture a high-bidding *purchaser.* Ask prices are published, but bid prices are not, in housing markets, in contrast to the stock market where both prices are published.
4. Few authors report any information on the distributions of sales. An exception is Bailey, Muth, and Nourse, who report number of sales by year, although they do not distinguish between first and second sales.
5. This set of assumptions implies that $E(u_i) = 0$. This can be seen by noting that the proportion of all transactions that are the first sales of a repeat-sale pair is 0.5π (and similarly for second sales) so that

$$E(u_i) = 0.5\pi(\gamma_f + \varepsilon_{i_f}) + 0.5\pi(\gamma_s + \varepsilon_{i_s})$$

$$- (1 - \pi)\left(\frac{0.5\pi}{1 - \pi}\right)(\gamma_f + \gamma_s) + (1 - \pi)\varepsilon_{i_o} = 0.$$

6. Further data details are given in the appendix. See also Goy and Steele (1994).
7. The estimated bias falls to zero when the holding period is greater than 13 years. This extrapolation goes so far beyond the sample range, and its standard error is so large, that the estimate is unreliable.
8. Computed from Mark and Goldberg (p. 33): total number of sales (8,488) minus total number of housing units involved (5,765) equals number of repeat-sales (2,723) divided by total number of sales times 100 equals 32%. Using the data on p. 36, presumably after third sales and units with quality change were deleted, gives 29%, and the ratio computed from p. 47 is 26%.
9. The price index used is from the constrained hedonic regression without the four sales characteristic variables.
10. The short range of time for our sample, in any case, means that all repeats are relatively short holds in the context of standard repeat-sales data sets.
11. The middle of this range, four quarters, is substantially less than the average in our data set.
12. This assumes that the number of positive differences may be treated as a binomial random variable; this requires serial independence.
13. This point is due to David de Meza. Also see Geltner (1993) for analysis of the effect of frequency of observation on measured price change.
14. However, at the AREUEA meetings, Karl Case reported that, when he reestimated repeat-sales indices using a longer time period, positive bias was introduced.
15. I am indebted to a referee for this explanation, an extension of the explanation in Clapp and Giaccotto (1992) for the relatively low level of prices of RS properties.
16. Clapp and Giaccotto (1992) identified lemonness especially with houses with an especially high turnover rate in their sample—those selling three or more times—and thought the phenomenon of sufficient importance to eliminate them for their sample.
17. The MLS records relate to agreements to purchase. An examination of all repeat-sales properties held less than seven months revealed 35 cases in which the "first" sale did not close (i.e., the agreement of purchase went into default). Almost all of these cases were found among properties with intervals between "sales" of three months or less.

References

Abraham, J. M., and W. S. Schauman. "New Evidence on House Prices from Freddie Mac Repeat Sales," *AREUEA Journal* 19 (3) (1991), 333–352.

Bailey, M. J., R. F. Muth, and H. O. Nourse. "A Regression Method for Real Estate Price Index Construction," *American Statistical Association Journal* 58 (1963), 933–942.

Case, B., and J. M. Quigley. "The Dynamics of Real Estate Prices," *Review of Economics and Statistics* 83 (1991), 50–58.

Case, K. E., and R. J. Shiller. "Prices of Single Family Homes Since 1970: New Indices for Four Cities," *New England Economic Review* (1987), 45–56.

Case, K. E., and R. J. Shiller. "The Efficiency of the Market for Single-Family Homes," *American Economic Review* 79(1) (1989), 125–137.

Case, K. E., and R. J. Shiller. "Forecasting Prices and Excess Returns in the Housing Market," *AREUEA Journal* 18(3) (1990), 253–273.

Case, K. E., and R. J. Shiller. "A Decade of Boom and Bust in the Prices of Single-Family Homes: Boston and Los Angeles, 1983 to 1993," *New England Economic Review* (Federal Reserve Bank of Boston) (1994), 40–50.

Clapp, J. M., C. Giaccotto, and D. Tirtiroglu. "Housing Price Indices Based on All Transactions Compared to Repeat Subsamples," *AREUEA Journal* 19(3) (1991), 270–285.

Clapp, J. M., and C. Giaccotto. "Estimating Price Trends for Residential Property: A Comparison of Repeat Sales and Assessed Value Methods," *Journal of Real Estate Finance and Economics* 5 (1992), 357–374.

Clapp, J. M., and C. Giaccotto. "Price Indexes Based on the Hedonic Repeat Sales Method: Application to the Housing Market." Centre for Real Estate and Urban Economics Studies, University of Connecticut, 1994.

Gatzlaff, D. H., and D. R. Haurin. "Sample Selection and Biases in Local House Value Indexes," Department of Insurance, Real Estate and Business Law, The Florida State University, Tallahassee, 1994.

Gatzlaff, D. H., and D. C. Ling. "Measuring Changes in Local House Prices: An Empirical Investigation of Alternative Methodologies," *Journal of Urban Economics* 35(2) (1994), 221–244.

Gau, G. W., and K. Wang. "The Tax-Induced Holding Periods of Real Estate Investors: Theory and Empirical Evidence," *Journal of Real Estate Finance and Economics* 8 (1994), 71–85.

Geltner, D. "Temporal Aggregation in Real Estate Return Indices," *AREUEA Journal* 21(2) (1993), 141–166.

Goetzmann, W. N. "Accounting for Taste: Art and the Financial Markets Over Three Centuries," *American Economic Review* 83(5) (1993), 1370–1376.

Goetzmann, W. N., and M. Spiegel. "Non-temporal Components of Residential Real Estate Appreciation," *Review of Economics and Statistics* 77 (1995), 199–206.

Goy, R., and M. Steele. *Alternative Constant-Quality Price Indexes for Modest Houses and Condominiums in Kitchener-Waterloo* Ottawa: Canada Mortgage and Housing Corporation, 1994.

Greene, W. H. *Econometric Analysis, 2nd ed.* New York: Macmillan, 1993.

Haurin, D. R., and P. H. Hendershott. "House Price Indexes: Issues and Results," *AREUEA Journal* 19(3) (1991), 259–269.

Hendershott, P. H., and E. J. Kane. "U. S. Office Market Values During the Past Decade: How Distorted Have Appraisals Been?" *Real Estate Economics* 23(2) (1995), 101–116.

Mark, J. H., and M. A. Goldberg. "Alternative Housing Price Indices: An Evaluation," *Journal of the American Real Estate and Urban Economics Association* 12(1) (1984), 30–49.

Pesando, J. E. "Art as an Investment: The Market for Modern Prints," *American Economic Review* 83(5) (1993), 1075–1089.

Quigley, J. "A Simple Hybrid Model for Estimating Real Estate Indexes," *Journal of Housing Economics* 4(1) (1995), 1–12.

Shiller, R. J. *Macro Markets* Oxford: Clarendon Press, 1993a.

Shiller, R. J. "Measuring Asset Values for Cash Settlement in Derivative Markets: Hedonic Repeated Measures Indices and Perpetual Futures," *The Journal of Finance* 48 (1993b), 911–931.

Turnbull, G. K., and C. F. Sirmans. "Information, Search and House Prices," *Regional Science and Urban Economics* 23(4) (1993), 545–557.

Journal of Real Estate Finance and Economics, 14: 155–171 (1997)
© 1997 Kluwer Academic Publishers

Bias and Precision of Estimates of Housing Investment Risk Based on Repeat-Sales Indices: A Simulation Analysis

DAVID GELTNER
Department of Finance, College of Business Administration, University of Cincinnati, P. O. Box 210195, Cincinnati, OH 45221-0195

Abstract

A simulation analysis is reported which examines the bias and precision of estimates of housing investment risk based on small sample indices of housing returns. The trade-off between smoothing bias (due to temporal aggregation in the index) and noise bias (induced by random estimation error) is examined in the housing return total volatility, beta, and autocorrelation statistics of the index returns. The study compares the performance of three different specifications of the repeat-sales index, under assumptions of either an informationally efficient or inefficient housing market, and at two levels of estimation data availability. Findings suggest that regression-based repeated-measures indices may be useful at a more micro-level (e.g., at the neighborhood level or for specific housing types) than has hitherto been employed.

Key Words: housing investment, repeat-sales indices, risk and return

This article reports the findings of a simulation analysis of the bias and precision of estimates of investment risk based on small sample indices of housing market returns. The study focuses on the return-index sample second moments of interest to investors, including the return own-variance or "total volatility," the covariance with an exogenous innovations series or "beta," and the first-order autocorrelation in the returns. The former two statistics are measures of investment risk, while the autocorrelation relates to the predictability of the investment returns and the informational efficiency of the housing market. This study has several specific objectives:

1. Simultaneous consideration of two sources of second-moment bias, "smoothing" (caused by temporal aggregation in the index construction) as well as "noise" (caused by random estimation error). The article focuses on the *trade-off* between these two sources of second-moment bias in several different specifications of the repeat-sales regression-based index, based on small samples of houses.
2. Consideration of small sample sizes both in terms of a small number of individual houses or valuation observations on which the index is based and a small number of historical time periods available in the data. This is motivated by the practical desire to push the development of empirically based subindices of housing market returns to more micro-levels of disaggregation (e.g., indices by neighborhood and type of house).

3. Consideration of the precision as well as the bias of the index second moments as estimators of the true sample second moments realized in a given historical period. Precision of the second-moment estimates is important in judging the reliability and confidence bounds of investment-risk estimates.

4. Examination of the above-described questions under both efficient and inefficient housing market assumptions. As we are unsure to what degree housing markets are informationally efficient, it is of interest to examine how informational efficiency in the underlying housing market affects the nature of the error in our measurement of investment risk in the observable index.

The technique used to examine these questions is that of simulation analysis. While simulation analysis is in some respects not as general as a more purely analytical approach, it has the advantage of "transparency"—helping to clarify the nature of the statistical issues being examined. Furthermore, the parameter values examined in this simulation have been chosen to reflect realistic values, so it is hoped that the quantitative findings contained herein will be of some practical value to those engaged in the empirical study of housing investment risk.

1. Background

In recent years, the development of indices of housing returns has spawned growing interest in applying quantitative methods of investment analysis to housing assets. Transactions-based indices that control for differences across time in the quality of the transacting houses, such as the regression-based repeated-measures indices pioneered by Bailey–Muth–Nourse (1963) and Case–Shiller (1989), are gaining increased use for analyzing housing equity and mortgage investment risk. Shiller (1993a) has proposed using such housing indices as the basis of publicly traded futures contracts that would enable direct hedging of housing investment risk.

In analyzing investment risk, and in developing hedging strategies, the second moments of the returns across time are crucially important statistics that can be derived historically from such indices. Of course, there are problems with using the returns time-series second moments observed directly from housing indices. Investment analysts have become increasingly sensitive to the effects which the infrequent trading of unique individual houses has on the second moments observed in such indices.

As a result of the infrequent trading problem, there are two important and distinct sources of bias and error in estimated or reported housing return indices which do not occur in indices of more liquid securities and which can seriously affect the returns sample second moments observed in the index. The first type of error is commonly referred to as "smoothing." Smoothing is caused fundamentally by temporal aggregation of house prices, and results in second moments (own-variance and covariance) that are biased toward zero. It also injects positive bias into the first-order autocorrelation of the returns series, and results in the index value changes lagging in time behind the true underlying housing market value changes.[1] Smoothing will generally not greatly affect the contemporaneous correlations observed between housing subindices (e.g., between New York and California houses), assuming that the smoothing is similar in the two subindices.

The second type of error is often referred to as "noise." Noise is caused fundamentally by purely random valuation or observation error at the individual property level, with the associated coefficient estimation error in regression-based indices. As noise is purely random, it has no theoretical effect on the expected value of the "beta" estimated from the housing index, or contemporaneous covariance between housing and an exogenous series of innovations. However, noise reduces the precision of the beta estimate, and will bias toward zero the correlation coefficient between housing subindices. Noise also biases upward the estimated volatility (own-variance) of the index returns, and injects a negative bias into the first-order autocorrelation of the returns. In this impact on the own-variance and autocorrelation, noise has an effect opposite to smoothing, and so the two sources of error will tend to partially or totally offset one another in these moments when they are simultaneously present in the index.

Not only do smoothing and noise tend to have opposite effects on the measurement of some of the index-return second moments that are of interest to investors, but index construction strategy often faces a trade-off between these two types of error. In order to reduce noise, one must include as many individual house transactions as possible in estimating the index value as of each point in time. Yet, given thin trading, to include more individual property transactions requires going back farther in time to encompass more transactions. This increases the temporal aggregation and resulting smoothing error.

Both smoothing and noise can be analyzed statistically, and it is often possible to approximately correct for the theoretical bias in index-return second moments. Nevertheless, the problem with the precision of empirical estimates remains. Furthermore, correction of second-moment bias is complicated by the interaction of the two sources of error which, as noted, tend to offset and mask one another. In practice in the current literature, housing index-return statistics second moments are often not corrected for smoothing and noise.

The remainder of this article is organized into four sections. Section 2 describes the housing indices which we will examine. Section 3 describes the simulation analysis procedure. Section 4 presents the results of the simulation analysis, and section 5 summarizes and concludes the article.

2. The Housing Indexes

While simple median price indices are widely reported in the popular and trade literature, academic study of housing prices generally employs relatively sophisticated, regression-based indices. Fundamentally, the purpose of the regression model is to control for the quality differences across the transacting houses, so as to be able to use the observed transaction prices as observations (with random error) of the true underlying housing market index value. The two major types of models that have been used in recent years are hedonic models and repeat-sales models. The former control for the quality differences by quantifying quality descriptors of each house (hedonic regressors). The latter control for the quality differences by limiting the estimation database to houses which have sold at least twice, so that what is modeled by the regression becomes the relative changes in the prices of the same house across time.[2]

In the present study, the repeat-sales model will be used to represent the housing indices, for two reasons. First, the repeat-sales model is structurally simpler and so causes less "muddying of the waters" for purposes of focusing on the second-moment bias and precision issues that are of interest to us here.[3] Second, it seems that the repeat-sales approach is to date finding more widespread practical use than the hedonic approach, as it has been adopted by FNMA/FHLMC in their Joint Agency Housing Index. This index is published regularly at the national, regional, and metropolitan levels (see Stephens et al., 1993), and has already experienced considerable academic and professional usage.

In this article we will examine by simulation the bias and precision characteristics of the returns time- series sample second moments based on the repeat-sales regression-based index. We will consider several different specifications of the regression and procedures for trading off smoothing bias versus noise bias.[4]

2.1. Housing Index Specifications and Procedures To Be Examined

To understand the different housing index construction procedures to be examined here, it will be helpful to consider a stylized simple database consisting of eight houses ($N = 8$), each of which has sold exactly twice during a four-year time sample (1990–1993, $T = 4$). In particular, let us assume that one house sold (for the first time) at the end of every third calendar month (March, June,...) during the first two years of the sample (1990–1991). Each house was held exactly two years and then sold for the second time at the end of every third month beginning with March 1992, through December 1993. Let $b^i_{y \cdot m}$ and $s^i_{y \cdot m}$ represent the natural log of the price of the first and second transactions, respectively, of house "i" ($i = 1, \ldots, 8$), where the subscript denotes the year and month of each transaction. Then, we can construct the 8×1 dependent variable vector, P, consisting of the eight price relatives, as follows:

$$
P = \begin{bmatrix}
-b^1_{90.3} + s^1_{92.3} \\
-b^2_{90.6} + s^2_{92.6} \\
-b^3_{90.9} + s^3_{92.9} \\
-b^4_{90.12} + s^4_{92.12} \\
-b^5_{91.3} + s^5_{93.3} \\
-b^6_{91.6} + s^6_{93.6} \\
-b^7_{91.9} + s^7_{93.9} \\
-b^8_{91.12} + s^8_{93.12}
\end{bmatrix}. \tag{1}
$$

In all of the housing index construction methods which we will consider, a vector of price relatives observations such as (1) will be regressed onto a series of time-dummy variables. The historical housing return index will be constructed from the estimated coefficients on the time-dummy variables. The general form of the regression is as follows:

$$P = Dc + E. \tag{2}$$

In this model, the dependent variable, P, is the $N \times 1$ vector of observed transaction price relatives, where N is the number of observed repeat-sale pairs in the database, as for example $N = 8$ in (1) above. E is the $N \times 1$ vector of random disaggregate price relative observation errors, assumed to be distributed iid normal with zero mean. The definition of the matrix of time-dummy variable observations, the regressors D, is what distinguishes each of the three index construction procedures which we shall consider. The time-dummy coefficient estimates which form the basis of the housing index are estimated by OLS: ($\hat{c} = (D'D)^{-1}D'P$).

The first housing index construction approach which we will examine will be labeled the "classic uncorrected repeat-sales regression" model (CURSR). This is the traditional repeat-sales regression specification, first developed by Bailey–Muth–Nourse (BMN), without any correction for smoothing. This is the most widely employed approach in the existing literature. Among the approaches considered here, the CURSR index involves the greatest degree of effective temporal aggregation of individual property valuations across time, and therefore makes the maximum use of the available price observation data to minimize noise in the index. This is done at the expense of taking on more smoothing bias.

In the classic uncorrected RSR model, the design matrix, D, in (2) is an $N \times (T - 1)$ matrix, whose $T - 1$ columns consist of one dummy variable for each year in the time sample after the first year for which transaction observations are available. Under this specification, we let the dummy variables assume a value of $+1$ in each year after the year in which the house is first sold up to and including the year in which the second sale occurs, and 0 otherwise. The coefficient vector then gives the house index individual period-by-period returns (first differences of the log-value levels of the index) for each period (after the first). In our eight-house, four-year example from (1) above, the matrix D in (2) would be given by the following 8×3 matrix:

$$D = \begin{bmatrix} 1 & 1 & 0 \\ 1 & 1 & 0 \\ 1 & 1 & 0 \\ 1 & 1 & 0 \\ 0 & 1 & 1 \\ 0 & 1 & 1 \\ 0 & 1 & 1 \\ 0 & 1 & 1 \end{bmatrix}. \tag{3}$$

The eight rows in D correspond to houses 1–8 in (1), and the three columns are the year dummy variables corresponding to years 1991, 1992, and 1993, respectively, from left to right. In this example, we have an average of two transaction-pair observations per year (eight repeat sales in four years, giving: $n = N/T = 2$), and each transaction is equally weighted in the design matrix, no matter when during the year it took place.

The second specification which we shall examine in the simulation analysis will be labeled the "time-weighted RSR" model (TWRSR), because we will modify the design matrix to take into account when during each year the transaction occurred. This specification was first suggested by Bryan and Colwell (1982), and has recently been employed by Goetzmann (1992). This specification requires relatively precise knowledge of the date (within each year) on which each transaction took place. In this specification, the dummy variable for year "y" has a fractional value between 0 and 1, corresponding to the proportion of the year during which the property was "held" (i.e., proportion of the year after the first transaction and before the second transaction). Thus, if a property was bought at the end of June 1991, then the observed value of the 1991 dummy variable for that house is 0.50. If the same house is then sold at the end of September 1993, then the value of the 1992 dummy variable for that house is 1.00; while the value for the 1993 dummy variable is 0.75. In our eight-house example from (1), the design matrix D in (2) for the time-weighted RSR model would be given by (4) below.

The TWRSR return index is still obtained directly, as in the CURSR approach, as the elements of the estimated coefficient vector: $\hat{c} = (D'D)^{-1}D'P$ (only with D now defined as in (4)).

$$D = \begin{bmatrix} 1 & .25 & 0 \\ 1 & .50 & 0 \\ 1 & .75 & 0 \\ 1 & 1 & 0 \\ .75 & 1 & .25 \\ .50 & 1 & .50 \\ .25 & 1 & .75 \\ 0 & 1 & 1 \end{bmatrix} \tag{4}$$

By weighting later price observations within each year greater than earlier observations, the TWRSR specification reduces temporal aggregation and thereby reduces the smoothing bias in the second moments of the return index. However, this smoothing correction is obtained at a cost in that the unequal weighting of the price observations causes the TWRSR specification to make less efficient use of the data than does the CURSR for the purpose of filtering out random transaction error, or noise. Thus, the time- weighted specification will have less smoothing bias, but more noise bias, in its returns second moments, in comparison with the classic uncorrected specification.

The third approach to building a housing returns index (and second approach to reducing smoothing bias in the second moments of the housing return index) which we shall examine does not involve a different specification of the repeat-sales regression per se. The classical uncorrected RSR model is applied, but to a higher frequency definition of the data. Then, the return index is developed as a higher order first difference from the resulting log-value-level index. We will label this third index construction procedure the increased-frequency RSR model (IFRSR).

For example, suppose that we ultimately desire to use an annual frequency return index. Then we might apply the classical uncorrected RSR model at the quarterly frequency instead of annual frequency. D in (2) would be defined as in (3), only with each time dummy variable (column in D) corresponding to a calendar quarter instead of to a calendar year, as in (5) below.[5]

$$D = \begin{bmatrix} 1 & 1 & 1 & 1 & 1 & 0 & 0 & 0 & 0 & 0 & 0 & 0 \\ 1 & 1 & 1 & 1 & 1 & 1 & 0 & 0 & 0 & 0 & 0 & 0 \\ 1 & 1 & 1 & 1 & 1 & 1 & 1 & 0 & 0 & 0 & 0 & 0 \\ 1 & 1 & 1 & 1 & 1 & 1 & 1 & 1 & 0 & 0 & 0 & 0 \\ 0 & 1 & 1 & 1 & 1 & 1 & 1 & 1 & 1 & 0 & 0 & 0 \\ 0 & 0 & 1 & 1 & 1 & 1 & 1 & 1 & 1 & 1 & 0 & 0 \\ 0 & 0 & 0 & 1 & 1 & 1 & 1 & 1 & 1 & 1 & 1 & 0 \\ 0 & 0 & 0 & 0 & 1 & 1 & 1 & 1 & 1 & 1 & 1 & 1 \end{bmatrix} \tag{5}$$

From the estimated coefficients in the $\hat{c}$ vector, we would derive a quarterly log-value-level index. We would then take the calendar year differences of this quarterly index to define our annual-frequency returns index. (Or, equivalently, we could just sum the four quarterly returns in each calendar year to obtain the annual returns index.)

The IFRSR procedure was employed by Case–Shiller (1989). It is similar in effect to the TWRSR in that price observations occurring later within any calendar year are effectively weighted more than those occurring earlier. The weighting, however, is not linear as in the TWRSR, but tends instead to weight all fourth-quarter observations equally, with effectively very little weight placed on any price observations from quarters other than the fourth. Thus, the IFRSR procedure acts much like the TWRSR model in that smoothing bias in the returns second moments is reduced at the expense of reduced ability to filter out random transaction error, leading to greater noise bias. While the IFRSR requires more knowledge about the dates of transactions than the CURSR, it does not require as precise knowledge as the TWRSR.

3. The Simulation Model and Analysis

A simulation model has been developed to examine the effects of smoothing and noise on the bias and precision of estimates of housing capital-returns sample second moments based on the above-described index construction procedures applied to small samples. We examine annual frequency return moments when the length of the return time sample is taken to be 15 years. So we have only 15 data points in the time series. We consider two levels of data availability regarding house transaction price observations. The "observation-poor" scenario has an average of $n = 60$ observations (transaction pairs) per year, while the "observation-rich" scenario is characterized by $n = 180$ observations per year. While both of these levels of data availability are much lower than what is available in typical metropolitan-level housing indices, these numbers are consistent with the objective of exploring how far we can push these types of indices toward developing more specific micro-level subindices for specific neighborhoods and house types.

In the simulation study, 100 different underlying "simulated histories," each of 15 years duration, were generated randomly. Each of these 100 repetitions may be thought of as a "trial," or "sample" drawn with replacement. Although the index-return moments to be examined are at the annual frequency, the underlying information used in the simulation analysis is generated at the monthly frequency, so as to approximate an environment of continuous time.

The simulated histories in the index analysis are based on corresponding underlying simulated histories of information arrival. Each of the 100 underlying information histories is drawn independently from an identically distributed random variable representing the arrival over time of "news," or information innovations, relevant to the value of housing within the 15-year history. To be more specific, let I_m be the new information that arrives in month "m" relevant to the value of all houses. For each of the 100 histories, the values of I_m are generated for at least 15 years worth of months (180 months) as iid drawings from a normal (0, .025) random variable.[6] Each trial starts with a new random number "seed," so each 15-year history is independent of the others. We can label the underlying information series for history "h" as: $\{I_m\}_h$, where $m = 1, \ldots, 180$ (at least), and $h = 1, \ldots, 100$. Each of the information histories is thus generated from a white noise process with no deterministic drift and a theoretical monthly standard deviation of 2.5% (implying theoretical annual standard deviation of 8.66%). $\{I_m\}_h$ is the exogenous "news" (or, information innovation) history which will underlie all house prices and values during the "hth" 15-year return sample history.

In each simulated 15-year history, the realized "true" underlying housing market returns are derived from this news series. Let us label these true annual housing returns within a given history as r_y, for years $y = 1, \ldots, 15$. We also define a number of individual houses and generate random individual house transaction price observations based on the true market values but also containing random "error" representing individual transaction "noise." It is from this individual house transaction price data (including errors) that we develop within each simulated history the estimated index returns, labeled r_y^*, using the various index construction methods described in section 2. For example, the vector, r^*, consisting of the 15 annual r_y^* estimated index-return observations for the CURSR or TWRSR indices is given directly from the OLS regression of the individual house transaction price relatives onto the annual time dummy variables:

$$r^* \equiv \hat{c} = (D'D)^{-1}D'P.$$

These estimated index returns (r_y^*) are the only index returns that would be able to be derived and observed in the real world. We would therefore not be able to know for sure in the real world how the estimated index returns and their time-series sample statistics compared to the true historical index returns and statistics. However, in the simulation, we can make this comparison exactly. Comparing the observable sample second moments of the $\{r_y^*\}_h$ series with those of the corresponding unobservable true series $\{r_y\}_h$ is indeed the purpose of the simulation analysis.

The simulation analysis reported here includes two alternative assumptions about the nature of the underlying true housing market capital-returns generation process. One assumption is that true returns are generated from a "white noise" process, with no deterministic drift and no autocorrelation. This would be approximately consistent with an assumption that the housing market is "weak-form" efficient, in an informational sense, similar to most public securities markets. The other assumption is that the true returns are generated by an ARMA process which results in considerable "memory" or "inertia" in the returns (reflected by positive first-order autocorrelation in the annual true market returns). This would be consistent with an assumption that the housing market is "sluggish" and "adaptive" in its incorporation of new information into market prices.

Under the efficient market assumption, it is assumed that the true returns each month fully reflect the news that month:[7]

$$r_m \equiv I_m. \tag{6a}$$

Under the sluggish market assumption, it is assumed that the news which arrives in month "m" gradually filters through to the housing market values (some in month "m," some one month later, some one quarter later, and some one year later), and that the market gradually adapts its perceptions of value to the arrival of new information. This results in an ARMA specification with both moving average and autoregressive components in the true market return-generating process, based on the underlying white noise news:[8]

$$r_m \equiv (0.25)I_m + (0.25)I_{m-1} + (0.25)I_{m-3}$$
$$+ (0.25)I_{m-12} + (0.3)r_{m-1} + (0.2)r_{m-12} \tag{6b}$$

These two ways in which the true housing market returns are generated are, of course, mutually exclusive. (There can be only one "truth" in any one "history.") The simulation analysis is therefore run separately under both market assumptions (but using, in each case, the same underlying information histories). Thus, while the true housing market returns history in trial h, $\{r_y\}_h$, will be different, depending on which market assumption is employed, the underlying information history for trial h, $\{I_m\}_h$ will be the same under both market assumption scenarios.

In generating the individual house transaction price observations which underlie the development of the estimated return indices, a number, N, of individual houses are defined, each of which is assumed to have a true value each month equal to the current market value described above.[9] That is, for any individual house "j" ($j = 1, \ldots, N$) at month "m": $V_m^j = V_m = V_{m-1} + r_m$, where V_m^j is j's true log value at the end of month m, V_m is the true market index realized log value at that time, and r_m is the market return for month m, generated as described above. However, the observed transaction price of property j as of month m (assuming that j happened to transact that month), labeled V_m^{j*}, will differ from the true value, due to random transaction price "error" (or "noise"):

$$V_m^{j*} = V_m + e_m^j. \tag{7}$$

The random error or noise component, e_m^j, is drawn from the iid normal $(0, \sigma)$ random number generator. For the simulations presented here, it is assumed that : $\sigma = 0.1$, roughly averaging 10% of property value.[10]

The number of individual properties in the simulation, N, is defined so as to examine the effect of the average number of transaction-pair price observations available per year, labeled "n." It is assumed that the average length of time between the first and second sale of each house is five years, and that each house in the index database transacts exactly twice (providing one price-relative observation) during the 15-year sample history from which the index will be constructed (within each of the 100 trials). Thus, $N = (15 + 1)n$. [11] It is further assumed that the exact time when each house transacts is random, and transaction time is generated for each of the 100 trials by an iid random number generator. [12]

Within each simulated 15-year history, the estimated housing index returns are computed using the individual house transaction price observation information described above and the index construction methods described in section 2. In particular, the three repeat-sales regression-based specifications and procedures (CURSR, TWRSR, and IFRSR) are applied to develop the housing indices. Each of the three indices is constructed based on the same realized random transaction price errors. This holds constant the realized random disaggregate errors (which are exogenous to the index construction method) across the index construction methods, thereby facilitating comparisons across the index construction methods.

The sample second moments which we are interested in measuring are those of most interest to investors studying the risk characteristics of housing. In particular, we examine the annual-frequency time-series sample moments of the 15-year simulated histories: (1) the annual return volatility (or square root of the time-series sample variance); (2) the beta (normalized contemporaneous covariance with exogenous innovations); and (3) the first-order autocorrelation coefficient:

$$\text{STD}[r_y] = \sqrt{\text{VAR}[r_y]} = \sqrt{(1/(14)) \sum_{y=1}^{15} (r_y - \bar{r}_y)^2} \qquad (8)$$

$$\text{BETA}[r_y, I_y] = \frac{\sum_{y=1}^{15} (r_y - \bar{r}_y)(I_y - \bar{I}_y)}{\sum_{y=1}^{15} (I_y - \bar{I}_y)^2} \qquad (9)$$

$$\text{AUTO}[r_y] = \frac{\sum_{y=2}^{15} (r_y - \bar{r}_y)(r_{y-1} - \overline{r_{y-1}})}{\sum_{y=2}^{15} (r_y - \bar{r}_y)^2} \qquad (10)$$

The purpose of the simulation analysis is to compare the true value of these sample second moments with those computed based on the RSR-derived estimated returns indices, within 15-year historical samples. To clarify, let $\text{MOMENT}[r_y]_h$ refer to the value of any one of the sample moments defined above (i.e., STD, BETA, or AUTO) observed for the true housing market returns in trial h, and let $\text{MOMENT}[r_y^*]_h$ refer to the same moment for the estimated index returns in trial h. Then, we wish to examine the relationship between MOMENT$[r_y^*]_h$ and MOMENT$[r_y]_h$ across the $h = 1, \ldots, 100$ trials. The central tendency of this relationship across the 100 trials represents the bias in the estimated moment, and the dispersion in the relationship represents the precision.

4. Results of the Simulation Analysis

The results of the simulation analysis described above are reported and discussed in this section. Tables 1 and 2 show, for each index construction method, the mean, standard

Table 1. Comparison statistics for estimated housing index vs. true second-moments observation-rich case (minor noise).

| | Results of 100 Trials of 15 years each Avg 180 repeat-sales observations per year ($N = 2880, T = 16$) | | | | | |
| | Efficient Market | | | Sluggish Market | | |
	CURSR Index	TWRSR Index	IFRSR Index	CURSR Index	TWRSR Index	IFRSR Index
VOL:						
Mean	0.84	1.05	1.00	0.93	1.07	1.02
Standard deviation	0.15	0.12	0.12	0.08	0.09	0.08
Range	0.59–1.08	0.89–1.27	0.83–1.17	.79–1.06	.97–1.15	0.91–1.13
BETA:						
Mean	0.54	0.96	0.91	0.35	1.02	0.86
Standard deviation	0.18	0.13	0.11	0.23	0.12	0.12
Range	0.19–0.79	0.77–1.14	0.73–1.07	−0.05–0.70	0.83–1.18	0.67–1.05
AUTO:						
Mean	0.17	−.01	−.01	0.08	−.05	−.04
Standard deviation	0.24	0.17	0.16	0.10	0.11	0.12
Range	−.22–0.61	−.28–0.28	−.28–0.24	−.04–0.22	−.24–0.13	−.21–0.16
CORR:						
Mean	0.63	0.90	0.90	0.82	0.96	0.95
Standard deviation	0.16	0.05	0.06	0.08	0.02	0.03
Range	0.29–0.83	0.81–0.97	0.81–0.97	0.69–0.93	0.92–0.99	0.90–0.99

All moments are time-series sample moments for the annual frequency returns within the 15-year samples, as defined in (8)–(10).

VOL refers to the ratio of the estimated index volatility (square root of the own-variance) divided by the true market volatility: STD$[r_y^*]_h$/STD$[r_y]_h$.

BETA refers to the ratio of the estimated index beta (contemporaneous covariance with exogenous information innovations series) divided by the true market beta: COV$[r_y^*, I_y]_h$/COV$[r_y, I_y]_h$.

AUTO refers to the difference of the estimated index first-order autocorrelation coefficient minus the true market first-order autocorrelation coefficient: CORR$[r_y^*, r_{y-1}^*]_h$ − CORR$[r_y, r_{y-1}]_h$.

CORR refers to the contemporaneous correlation between the estimated index returns and the true market index returns over the 15-year sample: CORR$[r_y^*, r_y]_h$.

The "Mean," "Standard Deviation," and "Range" of the above comparison statistics, reported in the table, are taken across the 100 independent trials ($h = 1, \ldots 100$). "Range" refers to the 5th–95th percentile range.

Table 2. Comparison statistics for estimated housing index vs. true second-moments observation-poor case (major noise).

	Results of 100 Trials of 15 years each Avg 60 repeat-sales observations per year ($N = 960, T = 16$)					
	Efficient Market			Sluggish Market		
	CURSR Index	TWRSR Index	IFRSR Index	CURSR Index	TWRSR Index	IFRSR Index
VOL:						
Mean	0.87	1.10	1.07	0.94	1.11	1.11
Standard deviation	0.15	0.14	0.17	0.09	0.11	0.13
Range	0.64–1.10	0.89–1.32	0.86–1.41	0.79–1.06	0.96–1.28	0.94–1.31
BETA:						
Mean	0.52	0.96	0.89	0.36	1.03	0.88
Standard deviation	0.19	0.15	0.17	0.24	0.16	0.21
Range	0.18–0.81	0.73–1.19	0.62–1.21	−0.10–0.78	0.83–1.21	0.52–1.15
AUTO:						
Mean	0.12	−.05	−.06	.05	−.12	−.13
Standard deviation	0.25	0.20	0.21	0.11	0.14	0.18
Range	−.27–0.55	−.38–0.26	−.34–0.27	−.13–0.23	−.36–0.09	−.47–0.15
CORR:						
Mean	0.59	0.87	0.82	0.82	0.94	0.90
Standard deviation	0.17	0.08	0.10	0.09	0.04	0.07
Range	0.21–0.82	0.72–0.96	0.61–0.95	0.68–0.93	0.84–0.98	0.77–0.97

All moments are time-series sample moments for the annual frequency returns within the 15-year samples, as defined in (8)–(10).

VOL refers to the ratio of the estimated index volatility (square root of the own-variance) divided by the true market volatility: $STD[r_y^*]_h/STD[r_y]_h$.

BETA refers to the ratio of the estimated index beta (contemporaneous covariance with exogenous information innovations series) divided by the true market beta: $COV[r_y^*, I_y]_h/COV[r_y, I_y]_h$.

AUTO refers to the difference of the estimated index first-order autocorrelation coefficient minus the true market first-order autocorrelation coefficient: $CORR[r_y^*, r_{y-1}^*]_h - CORR[r_y, r_{y-1}]_h$.

CORR refers to the contemporaneous correlation between the estimated index returns and the true market index returns over the 15-year sample: $CORR[r_y^*, r_y]_h$.

The "Mean," "Standard Deviation," and "Range" of the above comparison statistics, reported in the table, are taken across the 100 independent trials ($h = 1, \ldots 100$). "Range" refers to the 5th–95th percentile range.

deviation, and the 5–95 percentile range of a comparison between the estimated index versus the true market sample second moments, across the 100 simulated histories.

The mean relates to the bias in the estimated moments, while the standard deviation and range relate to the precision of the estimated moments. In the case of the volatility and beta, the comparison measure being examined (labeled VOL and BETA) is the ratio of the estimated index to the true market value of the sample moment. In the case of the first-order autocorrelation, the measure being examined (labeled AUTO) is the arithmetic difference between the estimated index and the true market values of the sample moments. Thus, the "ideal" (no bias) value for the mean across the trials is 1.00 for the VOL and BETA measures, and 0 for the AUTO measure. The "ideal" value for the standard deviation and range is for these measures to be as small as possible (greater precision).

In addition to the three second moments discussed above, the tables also report the results for the simple contemporaneous correlation between the estimated index-returns series and the true market-returns series within the 15-year trials. This correlation is a good general measure of the temporal fit of the estimated index. Obviously, the higher the average correlation, the better.

In general, the results displayed in Tables 1 and 2 are consistent with our a priori qualitative understanding of the effect that smoothing and noise have on the three index specifications. For example, the findings that the CURSR volatility is biased modestly on the low side, the beta more so, and the autocorrelation biased positive are consistent with the results suggested by Geltner (1993). The presence of random noise at the disaggregate property level in both the transaction prices and times acts to increase to some extent the volatility and to reduce the positive autocorrelation as compared to the theoretical values suggested by Geltner. The smoothing-corrected specifications (TWRSR, IFRSR) obtain much more accurate estimates of the beta, and a notably better temporal fit (higher contemporaneous correlation with the true returns). While these specifications display greater sensitivity to noise, this does not appear to pose a great problem even in the observation-poor scenario with $n = 60$. For example, the overestimation of volatility and underestimation of autocorrelation is barely more than 10%, which is hardly greater than the corresponding (but opposite direction, that is, underestimation and overestimation, respectively) bias on the part of the CURSR.

The quantitative results reported in Tables 1 and 2 allow a practical appreciation of the relative strengths and weaknesses of the different index construction methods, together with a quantitative appreciation for the amount of data necessary to obtain reasonably accurate estimates of the returns second moments of investment interest. The results also highlight the effect which the informational quality of the housing market (efficient or sluggish) has on these problems and trade-offs.

To obtain a visual glimpse into the impact which the return errors discussed above have on the housing value index in a "typical history," Figure 1 displays the housing market value history traced out by the three index specifications for a single example 15-year simulated history. Figure 1 also shows the true underlying housing market during that history (solid line). The dashed lines show the three estimated indices.[13] The example history shown in Figure 1 is fairly typical of the efficient market, observation-poor scenario trials. There is slightly less smoothing apparent in the CURSR in Figure 1 than occurs on average, and slightly more random noise in the IFRSR. Smoothing in the CURSR is apparent in Figure 1 only slightly during years 7–11. The overall visual impression left by Figure 1 suggests that all of the RSR specifications examined here generally do a pretty good job of depicting the ups and downs as well as the general trend of the housing market, even with as few as an average of 60 repeat-transaction observations per index period.[14]

5. Summary and Conclusions

A brief study of the results of the simulation analysis contained in Tables 1 and 2 suggests several findings of interest, summarized below.

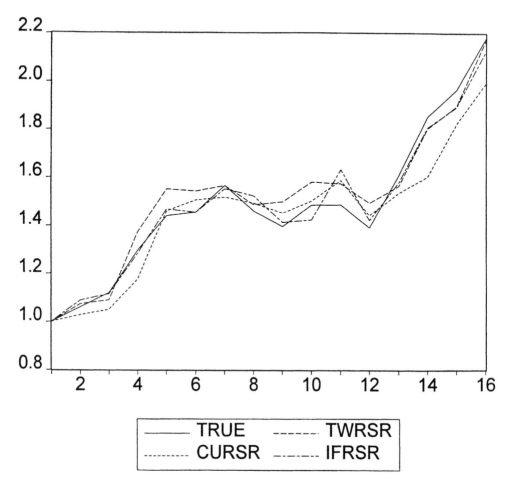

Figure 1. Example simulated history, showing true (solid line) and estimated housing market value levels under the efficient market, observation-poor scenario.

1. No single index specification dominates in all situations.   As seen in Tables 1 and 2, as a result of the trade-off between smoothing and noise, no one of the three index construction specifications tested is most accurate in all situations or for all of the moments considered. The traditional (CURSR) specification exhibits serious smoothing bias in the beta, but tends to provide the best estimates of total volatility and autocorrelation with low data availability when the housing market is sluggish. The smoothing-corrected specifications provide good estimates of beta even with low data availability, and provide a better temporal fit to the true returns. Although the smoothing-corrected specifications are susceptible to noise at low levels of data availability, the resulting overestimation of the total volatility and under-estimation of the autocorrelation of the housing returns typically remains within about 10% of the true values even with data availability as low as an average of 60 transaction-pair observations per index period.

2. Useful housing subindices can be developed at more micro-levels. By generating more than one index specification and/or using the most appropriate specification for examining each of the various moments of interest, it appears that reasonably accurate estimates of housing-return second moments are possible at the level of 60 disaggregate valuation observations per period. As the typical history portrayed in Figure 1 suggests, the three index specifications tested here should typically provide a usable picture of the "essence" of what was really going on in the housing market. As most real-world index development and application to date has taken place with far more data than this, the implication is that there may be substantial scope for pushing the development of subindices to more micro-levels (e.g., neighborhood and house-type indices).

3. Precision considerations. Overall, the precision of the estimates of the housing return second moments of interest to investors appears quite reasonable in our simulation. Precision is naturally a bit worse in the observation-poor scenario, but even with only 60 repeat observations per period the standard errors of the moment estimates were generally well below half the mean value of the moment being estimated. A notable exception is first-order autocorrelation, which is more difficult to precisely estimate because of its low true value even in the sluggish market case. Interestingly, the smoothing-corrected specifications for the housing indices do not appear to sacrifice precision in most cases.

4. Efficiency of the housing market has little impact on smoothing and noise. The smoothing-correction procedures examined here seem to generally work about as well under the efficient and inefficient market assumptions, if anything slightly better in the inefficient market. Smoothing in the volatility is a less severe problem to begin with, using the CURSR under the inefficient market, although smoothing in the beta appears to be somewhat more severe with the CURSR when the market is inefficient.

Finally, a caveat should be noted in conclusion. The specific quantitative results portrayed here should be construed as "upper bounds," on the level of return second-moment estimation accuracy and reliability achievable by regression-based indices of housing returns. In an effort to focus on the several issues of interest here, we have assumed away some problems that arise in constructing real-world indices. For example, we have ignored the heteroskedasticity problem, and by approximating continuous time with monthly intervals (basic time period one-twelfth the index time period), we have ignored a minor amount of temporal aggregation smoothing. Perhaps more seriously, we have ignored the sample selection, specification, and observation errors which can plague real-world hedonic and repeat-sales indices. Nevertheless, the simulation presented here goes farther than previous studies in attempting to include and model all of the real-world phenomena that are important in affecting the time-series second moments of housing indices.

Acknowledgments

The author would like to thank John Clapp, David Downs, Norm Miller, Tom Thibodeau, and two anonymous referees for their comments. The author alone is responsible for any errors.

Notes

1. Geltner (1993) points out that, under certain regularity conditions, the pure effect of temporal aggregation-induced smoothing will cause the own-variance of the returns to be underestimated by one-third, the beta to be underestimated by one-half, and the autocorrelation to be overestimated by 25%.
2. See Clapp and Giacotto (1992) for a discussion of the relationship between the hedonic and repeat-sales specifications. More recently, Shiller (1993b) has proposed a hybrid of these two approaches, the "hedonic repeated measures" model, which is found by Clapp and Giacotto (1994) to present many of the advantages of both approaches.
3. In effect, in a simulation of an hedonic index, one would have to create artificial hedonic variables, an extra step that can be avoided by working with the repeat-sales model. Such an extra step would only be useful for purposes of examining the effect of specific types of omitted-variables or errors-in-variables problems, issues which are beyond the scope of the present article. Another way to look at our use here of repeat-sales models is the following. In our simulated repeat-sales environment, there is (by construction) no omitted or incorrectly observed "hedonic" component. (That is to say, all of our fictitious houses are defined to be "truly" identical.) Thus, in effect, we are simulating the level of results that would obtain from either a "perfect" hedonic model (with no specification error or errors in variables), or a "perfect" repeat-sales model (in the sense of having no sample-selection bias or unobserved home improvements, etc.). Thus, one may view the present analysis as pertaining to an "ideal" econometric model, whether that be an hedonic or repeat-sales or some hybrid specification. The three alternative repeat-sales specifications to be examined here are distinguished only by the way in which the time-dummy variables are defined, and therefore have obvious corresponding specifications in the hedonic framework.
4. To simplify the analysis and focus attention onto the smoothing and noise issues of interest here, we will ignore two issues which have been treated extensively in the previous repeat-sales literature, namely, the best estimation procedure to deal with heteroskedaticity (e.g., GLS with proportional or affine weights) and whether to use arithmetic instead of geometric averaging across properties to compose the index value at each point in time. Thus, our simulation is constructed so that there is no heteroskedasticity, and we shall work entirely in log values, so that the geometric average index (arithmetic average of log values) is assumed to be appropriate. Either of these assumptions could be relaxed, but at the expense of muddying the waters for the smoothing/noise focus of the present analysis.
5. Similarly, if you ultimately wanted to use a quarterly index, you would initially estimate a monthly index, and so on.
6. Actually, more than 15 years of information history must be generated for each simulated history, because one of the housing-return-generating processes requires "looking back" in time at past news (e.g., "sluggish" housing market assumption).
7. The annual returns are, by definition, the sum of the monthly returns in each year, or the first difference of the end-of-year log values:

$$r_y = \sum_{m=12(y-1)+1}^{12y} r_m = V_y - V_{y-1}$$

where r_y is the annual true return and V_y is the end-of-year realized log-value level of the true housing market index.
8. The presence of the autoregressive terms in (6b) raises a starting value problem. In practice, five years of "prehistory" prior to the commencement of the used histories were generated, with the initial values of the lagged autoregressive terms on the RHS of (6b) being assumed to equal the corresponding news value at the beginning of the prehistorical period.
9. Thus, we assume away any idiosyncratic component to the true individual house return. This is to avoid the heteroskedasticity complication noted earlier.
10. There is some evidence, at least for commercial real estate, that 10% is a typical magnitude of disaggregate valuation error standard deviation (see Webb, 1994; Geltner–Graff–Young, 1994.) Such an error magnitude would also appear to be roughly consistent with RSR-based evidence from housing studies. For example, the

nontemporal component of the variation in home prices (one-half of the intercept value in the second-stage regression of the squared first-stage residuals onto time between sales) reported by Goetzmann (1993) ranged from 0.0029 (San Francisco) to 0.0049 (Atlanta, based on $\alpha/2$ in Goetzmann's Table 3). This would imply (after taking square roots) a standard deviation of the pure price noise component from 5.4% to 7.0% of the house price. Thus, if anything, the simulation here may be slightly overstating the typical magnitude of noise.
11. To get 15 years of annual return observations we need 16 years of valuation data.
12. To be more precise, for each house, both the first and second sale times (months) are obtained from a Poisson arrival process with "arrival rate" parameter 1/60 (reflecting average time between sale of five years). If a house does not randomly have two sales within the 16-year historical observation period, then that house is thrown out of the sample, and another house is simulated, until N houses with random repeat transactions within the 16-year window are accumulated.
13. All the indices shown in Figure 1 are computed as the antilog of the accumulated returns, and set arbitrarily equal to unity at the end of year 1.
14. Note that the randomness of transaction times means that there will inevitably be some periods of time with significantly fewer transaction observations than the overall average. However, the repeat-sales methodology is relatively robust to such data shortfalls, as it does not rely solely on transactions occurring within each period to determine the return during that period.

References

Bailey, M., R. Muth, and H. Nourse. "A Regression Method for Real Estate Price Index Construction," *Journal of the American Statistical Association* 58 (1963), 933–942.

Bryan, T. and P. Colwell. "Housing Price Indexes." C. F. Sirmans (ed.), In *Research in Real Estate, Vol. 2,* Greenwich, CT: JAI Press, 1982.

Case, K. and R. Shiller. "The Efficiency of the Market for Single Family Homes," *American Economic Review* 79 (1) (1989), 125–137.

Clapp, J. and C. Giacotto. "Estimating Price Indices for Residential Property: A Comparison of Repeat-Sales and Assessed Value Methods," *Journal of the American Statistical Association* 87 (June 1992), 300–306.

Clapp, J. and C. Giacotto. "Price Indexes Based on the Hedonic Repeat-Sales Method: Application to the Housing Market," Paper presented at the Annual Meeting of the A.R.E.U.E.A., Washington DC, January 1995, University of Connecticut Center for Real Estate Working Paper, October 1994.

Geltner, D. "Temporal Aggregation in Real Estate Return Indices," *AREUEA Journal* 21(2) (Summer 1993), 141–166.

Geltner, D., R. Graff, and M. Young. "Random Disaggregate Appraisal Error in Commercial Property: Evidence from the Russell–NCREIF Database," *Journal of Real Estate Research* 9(4) (Fall 1994), 403–420.

Goetzmann, W. "The Accuracy of Real Estate Indices: Repeat-Sale Estimators," *Journal of Real Estate Finance & Economics* 5(1) (March 1992), 5–54.

Goetzmann, W. "The Single Family Home in the Investment Portfolio," *Journal of Real Estate Finance & Economics* 6(3) (May 1993), 201–222.

Shiller, R. *Macro Markets: Creating Institutions for Managing Society's Largest Risks.* Oxford: Clarendon Press, 1993a.

Shiller, R. "Measures of Asset Values for Cash Settlement in Derivative Markets: Hedonic Repeated Measures Indices and Perpetual Futures," Journal of Finance 48 (July 1993b), 911–931.

Stephens, W., Y. Li, J. Abraham, V. Lekkas, C. Calhoun, and T. Kimner. "Agency Repeat Transactions Index." FNMA/FHLMC/Urban Institute Working Paper, December 1993.

Webb, R. B. "On the Reliability of Commercial Appraisals: An Analysis of Properties Sold from the Russell–NCREIF Index (1978–1992)." *Real Estate Finance* 11(1) (Spring 1994), 62–65.

Journal of Real Estate Finance and Economics, 14: 173–187 (1997)

Frequency of Transaction and House Price Modeling

BRADFORD CASE
Yale University, New Haven, Connecticut

HENRY O. POLLAKOWSKI
Boston College, Boston, Massachusetts

SUSAN M. WACHTER
The University of Pennsylvania, Philadelphia, Pennsylvania

Abstract

This article examines the characteristics and price behavior of repeatedly transacted properties. Using data from four U.S. counties, we estimate hedonic price models of properties grouped by transaction frequency, and compare estimated standard deviations and estimated appreciation rates by group.

For each of four counties studied, we find that estimated house price appreciation is systematically higher among properties that transact more frequently. One possible explanation for this result is that purchasers make property improvements that are not adequately reflected in the available data.

We also find that estimated standard deviations of the disturbance term show a marked decrease as the frequency of transaction increases. Since frequently transacting properties are not found to be systematically more homogeneous than seldomly transacting properties, we do not attribute this to any increase in homogeneity for frequently transacting properties, but rather to the length of time elapsed between transactions of properties.

The findings of this article suggest that repeat-sales price models may need to be adjusted to account for cross-sectional variation in transaction probabilities—that is, the selectivity of the subsample of properties that transacted (or transacted repeatedly) during any finite study period.

Key Words: price indices, repeat sales, hedonics

1. Introduction

An unsettled issue in the empirical literature on modeling price indices is whether frequently sold properties are representative of properties that do not transact or transact only once during the sample period. The exploration of this question has important implications for the interpretation and use of repeat-transactions price indices. This is the case, because these indices are, out of necessity, based on properties that transact at least, and often more than, two times during the sample period. To gain insight on this issue, we examine the characteristics and price behavior of repeatedly transacted properties by transaction frequency. Using a rich data set from four different counties distributed across the U.S., this article investigates whether mean appreciation rates and their reliability vary with frequency of transaction and hypothesizes plausible sources for possible variations in these measures.

2. Why Transaction Frequency Matters

The construction of area-wide price indices, whether repeat-transactions, hedonic, or hybrid, typically assumes uniformity of mean rates of price appreciation and standard deviations of disturbance terms, independent of the frequency of transaction. Case, Pollakowski, and Wachter (1994) suggest, however, that the repeat-transactions model may yield estimates of the standard deviation of the disturbance term that are biased downward. Case and Shiller (1987) note that the standard deviation of the disturbance term associated with a particular property may be positively related to the length of time elapsed between transactions of that property. One explanation for this is that both buyers and sellers tend to have better information regarding the true market value of a given property if the time elapsed since the last transaction of that property is relatively small. Conversely, after a relatively long holding period, both buyers and sellers tend to have weaker information regarding the true market value of the property, and thus are more likely to agree on a transaction price that differs substantially from the market value.[1]

A property type hypothesis may provide an additional explanation of the association of lower standard deviations of disturbance terms with frequency of property transaction. This association would occur, even in the absence of increased information with shorter holding periods, if there were a group of properties whose characteristics increased both their probability of transaction and their homogeneity. Several researchers hypothesize that "starter homes"—generally defined as relatively small and with fewer amenities—may be both more homogeneous and more likely to transact than larger homes with more amenities. Moreover, some properties may be less likely to transact, because their occupants have invested in the development of "specific capital"—that is, improvements or modifications that are valued highly by the current owner but that may be valued slightly by other prospective owners. To the extent that either is so, the standard deviation of the disturbance term (that is, the variation in the unexplained or random component of transaction prices) may be smaller for frequently transacting properties than for seldom transacting properties, reflecting the greater homogeneity of the frequently transacting data set.

Estimated appreciation rates of repeatedly sold properties also may be unrepresentative of the universe of properties. Repeatedly sold properties may differ from non-transacting or single-sale properties in ways that affect their measured appreciation rates. Lock-in effects may discourage mobility and the sale of homes due to mortgage prepayment constraints. This may give rise to a sample selection bias in which homes that depreciate in value are less likely to be sold. In addition, sample selection bias may occur if some properties transact more frequently, because they appeal to a class of "fixer-uppers" who purchase a property for investment purposes, improve it to increase its market value, and then resell it to repeat the process with another property.[2] If properties transact less frequently as a result of lock-in effects or more frequently as the result of a "fixer-upper" process, then measured market values of frequently transacting properties may increase more rapidly relative to the rest of the housing stock.[3]

Most importantly, perhaps, measured rates of appreciation may vary with frequency of property transactions, reflecting upgrades in the quality of frequently transacting properties; that is, there may be a nontemporal component of property appreciation rates. Unobserved heterogeneity of quality may vary with frequency of sale. This could occur if, as the evidence suggests, a house purchase is associated with improvement and remodeling expenditures. This may be important in the measurement of price appreciation, since it may be impossible to construct a pure price index of unchanged repeatedly transacted properties. To minimize this problem, repeat-sales indices are often constructed by first eliminating properties for which changes are observed. Unidentified modifications that remain, however, may significantly bias measured appreciation rates. If repeated sales occur and if modifications vary with the frequency of transaction, this bias may vary with the frequency of property transactions.

In this analysis, we use data from four quite different counties to differentiate among the sources of variation in both the estimated standard deviation of the disturbance term and the estimated mean appreciation rate. Specifically, properties in each county are divided into groups on the basis of the number of times that the property transacted during the study period. We then estimate identically specified hedonic price models on each group of properties by frequency of transaction and compare estimated standard deviations and estimated appreciation rates by frequency of transaction for each county. By using identical specifications, we control for model specification as a possible source of differences in the estimated standard deviation of the disturbance term and estimated appreciation rate. We also estimate nearly identically specified hedonic price models across each of four widely differing counties. We hope to minimize idiosyncratic data as a possible source of differences by conducting the analysis using data across these counties.[4]

3. The Characteristics of Repeatedly Sold Properties

As noted, several researchers have suggested that smaller or "starter" homes are more likely than larger properties to transact in any given period, because they tend to be purchased by a succession of first-time buyers who then sell them soon thereafter as they move to larger, newer, and otherwise higher quality residences. If this hypothesis is true, then properties that transact relatively frequently should be smaller in land area and living area, be older, and have fewer bathrooms and other rooms, on average, than properties that transact relatively infrequently. In addition, properties that transact more frequently may be more homogeneous—that is, have smaller standard deviations in their measured characteristics—than properties that transact less frequently. They also may show less investment in specific capital and fewer modifications than less frequently transacted properties. In the following, we examine sample statistics to determine whether these characteristics are observed.

The analysis employs data on all identifiable single-family residential properties in the four counties reported in the databases studied. Specifically, the data sets employed in this analysis provide sale-price and date information on all transactions of single-family residential properties, plus attribute data on all such properties (transacting and non-transacting), during a specified study period in each of four counties:

- San Francisco, California: August 1977–December 1989.
- Contra Costa, California (outer suburbs of the San Francisco–Oakland metropolitan area): August 1977–December 1989.

- Dade, Florida (Miami metropolitan area): October 1974–December 1989.
- Fairfax, Virginia (outer suburbs of the Washington metropolitan area): January 1977–December 1988.

These four counties were selected for the analysis, because data on property characteristics, transaction prices, transaction dates, and property addresses were available for a relatively long study period. In addition, as Table 1 indicates, the counties vary widely in terms of several key measures, which implies that any findings that hold consistently across counties can be considered broadly representative rather than unique to a particular metropolitan area or a particular type of housing market.

For each of the four counties, data on property transactions were obtained from county deed transfer files, while property attribute data were obtained from county property tax assessment records for the year in which the property transacted.[5] The two types of data were merged by property tax identification number to create a master data set containing one record for each property transaction (with property characteristics data for the corresponding year), plus one record (containing property characteristics data for the most recent year) for each non-transacting property.[6]

Tables 2–5 present summary statistics for unchanged properties in each county, grouped by the number of times that each property transacted during the study period. The first column of Table 2, for example, presents the sample mean, standard deviation, and number of valid (non-missing) observations by property attribute for the 33,513 single-family houses in San Francisco that did not transact at all during the study period, while the second column presents identical information for the 38,172 properties that transacted once during the same period.

For properties that transacted more than once during the study period, Tables 2–5 present data only for properties whose primary attributes remained unchanged between transactions.[7] For example, in Table 2, 17,386 properties transacted twice in San Francisco during the study period, and 4,356 properties transacted three times. Table 2 presents summary statistics for 31,116 transactions of properties that transacted twice and remained unchanged between transactions and 9,848 transactions of unchanged properties that transacted three times, etc.

Table 1. Sample statistics by county.

County	San Francisco	Contra Costa	Dade	Fairfax
Census division	Pacific	Pacific	South Atlantic	South Atlantic
Metropolitan type	Urban	Suburban	Urban/Suburban	Suburban
Land area	1,900	4,400	NA	2,500
Living area	1,400	1,500	1,800	1,700
Age (years)	47	23	19	5
Full baths	1.3	1.8		1.9
Half baths	0.03	0.12		0.61
Total rooms	5.8	7.2		7.1
Bedrooms			1.8	
Number of properties	94,885	134,429	153,666	230,802

Table 2. Summary statistics on property characteristics: San Francisco County.

Number of Transactions	0	1	2	3	4	5	6	7	8
Land area									
sample mean	2,064	2,085**	1,765**	1,555**	1,476**	1,479	1,261**	1,494**	1,264
standard deviation	404	521**	628**	629**	610**	634**	445**	530*	318*
valid observations	30,506	34,504	29,096	9,156	2,973	796	196	49	9
Living area									
sample mean	1,440	1,467**	1,451**	1,368**	1,328**	1,287	1,110**	1,055	882
standard deviation	515	545**	565**	527**	518**	555**	374**	331	230
valid observations	32,595	36,860	29,634	9,569	3,153	847	196	56	9
Age (years)									
sample mean	N/A	43.2	47.8**	51.2**	52.7**	55.6**	54.8	58.8	68.8**
standard deviation	N/A	19.5	20.9**	19.4**	19.2*	20.7**	22.2**	14.7**	7.7**
valid observations	N/A	35,766	28,862	9,030	2,858	767	186	49	9
Full baths									
sample mean	1.31	1.35**	1.35	1.29**	1.25**	1.26	1.16**	1.24	1.00**
standard deviation	0.59	0.63**	0.64**	0.57**	0.54**	0.53**	0.44**	0.45	0.00**
valid observations	32,738	37,076	29,944	9,664	3,196	852	196	56	9
Half baths									
sample mean	0.002	0.04	0.03	0.01	0.01	0.02	0.02	0	0
standard deviation	0.04	0.21	0.18	0.11	0.11	0.15	0.12	0	0
valid observations	33,513	38,172	31,116	9,848	3,208	857	196	56	9
Total rooms									
sample mean	5.76	5.85**	5.81**	5.67**	5.67	5.52**	5.02**	5.21	5.44
standard deviation	1.35	1.38**	1.43**	1.38**	1.45**	1.49**	1.07**	1.02	0.53**
valid observations	32,566	36,749	29,462	9,428	3,112	839	196	56	9
Number of properties	33,513	38,172	17,386	4,356	1,143	252	49	12	2

*Sample mean or standard deviation differs from the corresponding estimate reported in the cell immediately to the left at the 95% confidence level.
**Sample mean or standard deviation differs from the corresponding estimate reported in the cell immediately to the left at the 99% confidence level.
Note: Table shows data for unchanged repeat-transacting properties only.

The summary statistics presented in Tables 2–5 lend strong support to the first part of the property type hypothesis, that frequently transacting properties tend to be smaller than seldom transacting properties. For example, in San Francisco (Table 2), average land area declines fairly steadily from 2,085 square feet for properties transacting once to 1,264 square feet for unchanged properties transacting eight times; average living area declines from 1,467 square feet for single-transacting properties to 882 square feet for properties transacting eight times; average number of bathrooms declines from 1.35 to 1.00; and average total number of rooms generally declines from 5.85 to 5.44. The same results generally hold true for the other counties included in the analysis, as shown in Tables 2–5.[8]

It has been hypothesized that frequently transacting properties can be expected to be more homogeneous than seldom transacting properties. Interestingly, the sample standard deviations presented in Tables 2–5 do not lend strong support to this hypothesis, and tend to refute it in some cases. For example, in San Francisco (Table 2) the only characteristic

Table 3. Summary statistics on property characteristics: Contra Costa County.

Number of Transactions	0	1	2	3	4	5	6
Land area							
sample mean	4,486	4,447**	4,377**	4,302**	4,207**	4,031**	3,908
standard deviation	363	397**	431**	459**	528**	634**	753**
valid observations	5,434	99,933	23,028	7,941	2,066	491	100
Living area							
sample mean	1,472	1,571**	1,503**	1,458**	1,448	1,376**	1,280
standard deviation	509	544**	540*	519**	546**	542*	553
valid observations	5,482	103,184	24,946	8,755	2,250	515	114
Age (years)							
sample mean	N/A	23.0	23.3	23.8	24.9*	21.9**	25.6*
standard deviation	N/A	14.6	14.7*	15.2**	15.6**	15.5	12.0**
valid observations	N/A	11,318	10,664	4,276	1,204	230	72
Full baths							
sample mean	1.66	1.80**	1.75**	1.73**	1.72	1.62**	1.47*
standard deviation	0.60	0.60*	0.59**	0.59	0.60	0.58**	0.59
valid observations	5,483	104,115	25,164	8,791	2,258	515	120
Half baths							
sample mean	0.18	0.15	0.03	0.03	0.04	0.02	0.05
standard deviation	0.42	0.36	0.17	0.16	0.19	0.15	0.22
valid observations	5,523	109,607	28,092	9,832	2,554	570	120
Total rooms							
sample mean	6.82	7.23**	7.05**	6.94**	6.89	6.64**	6.10**
standard deviation	1.63	1.77**	1.79*	1.73**	1.73	1.85**	1.62*
valid observations	5,452	100,303	23,080	7,959	2,078	491	100
Number of properties	5,523	109,607	14,926	3,548	685	119	21

*Sample mean or standard derivation differs from the corresponding estimate reported in the cell immediately to the left at the 95% confidence level.
**Sample mean or standard deviation differs from the corresponding estimate reported in the cell immediately to the left at the 99% confidence level.
Note: Table shows data for unchanged repeat-transacting properties only.

that tends to show increasing homogeneity as transaction frequency increases is the number of bathrooms. In Contra Costa (Table 3), in fact, the standard deviation of land area (for unchanged properties) increases quite steadily as the number of transactions increases, a result directly contrary to that hypothesized.

In short, the summary statistics presented in Tables 2–5 indicate that frequently transacting properties do not appear to be systematically more homogeneous than seldom transacting properties, but that they do appear to be systematically smaller, at least compared to properties that transact just once or a few times.[9] This finding suggests that any observed tendency of the estimated standard deviation of the disturbance term to decline as the frequency of transaction increases cannot be attributed with confidence to any increase in homogeneity for frequently transacting properties.

As noted, a second hypothesis concerning the probability of transaction suggests that properties may transact less frequently, because their owners have made changes that can

Table 4. Summary statistics on property characteristics: Dade County.

Number of Transactions	0	1	2	3	4	5	6	7	8
Living area									
sample mean	1,680	1,770**	1,908**	1,757**	1,767	1,663**	1,671	1,645*	1,562**
standard deviation	670	676*	711**	650**	641**	597**	569**	552**	510**
valid observations	32,473	47,274	81,820	24,830	19,725	9,479	6,667	3,932	2,360
Age (years)									
sample mean	N/A	19.7	18.0**	20.4**	18.2**	20.7**	19.7**	21.0**	20.9
standard deviation	N/A	16.7	15.5**	14.5**	13.7**	13.1**	12.7**	12.4**	12.4
valid observations	N/A	43,844	82,400	24,935	19,779	9,494	6,673	3,925	2,360
Bathrooms									
sample mean	1.67	1.79**	1.91**	1.79**	1.82**	1.72**	1.73	1.69**	1.63**
standard deviation	0.71	0.69**	0.70*	0.68**	0.66**	0.65*	0.62**	0.64**	0.61**
valid observations	32,464	47,271	81,784	24,827	19,721	9,484	6,667	3,932	2,360
Bedrooms									
sample mean	2.89	2.36**	0.99**	1.58**	1.73**	1.94**	2.11**	2.28**	2.37*
standard deviation	0.85	1.49**	1.52**	1.62**	1.61**	1.52**	1.48**	1.40**	1.33**
valid observations	32,640	47,571	82,458	24,953	19,783	9,504	6,673	3,932	2,360
Number of properties	32,673	59,881	42,671	8,838	5,313	2,086	1,230	632	342

*Sample mean or standard deviation differs from the corresponding estimate reported in the cell immediately to the left at the 95% confidence level.
**Sample mean or standard deviation differs from the corresponding estimate reported in the cell immediately to the left at the 99% confidence level.
Note: Table shows data for unchanged repeat-transacting properties only.

be considered investments of specific capital in the property. Although the summary statistics do not address this issue directly, the hypothesis can be tentatively investigated using the data presented in Table 6. Specifically, if changes in primary property characteristics can be considered indicative of investments in specific capital,[10] then the proportion of properties that change between transactions can be expected to decline as transaction frequency increases.[11] The data for Fairfax County presented in Table 6 supports this hypothesis, but the data for San Francisco and Dade counties tend to refute it (Contra Costa shows no consistent pattern). For example, in San Francisco the proportion of properties modified between transactions increases from just 10.5% for twice-transacting properties to 24.6% for properties transacting three times, 29.8% for those transacting four times, and more than 30% for properties transacting five times or more during the study period. These results also suggest that a property's probability of modification increases with frequency of sale for observed characteristics.

4. Hedonic Price Model Results

The estimated standard deviation of the disturbance term and estimated appreciation rate for a given model are affected by two sets of factors: the quality of the model specification,

Table 5. Summary statistics on property characteristics: Fairfax County.

Number of Transactions	0	1	2	3	4	5
Land area						
sample mean	2,577	2,581	2,444**	2,308**	2,264*	1,987**
standard deviation	809	811	811	771**	804**	531**
valid observations	43,809	98,616	44,396	14,077	1,467	51
Living area						
sample mean	1,522	1,692**	1,665**	1,593**	1,535**	1,400**
standard deviation	508	576**	567**	529**	520**	307**
valid observations	41,685	99,486	44,929	14,187	1,469	51
Age (years)						
sample mean	N/A	5.22	5.55**	5.88**	6.04	6.38
standard deviation	N/A	7.57	7.43**	7.29**	7.35*	7.67
valid observations	N/A	99,246	44,763	14,155	1,469	51
Full baths						
sample mean	1.76	1.94**	1.92**	1.86**	1.81**	1.73
standard deviation	0.65	0.64*	0.63**	0.63**	0.65**	0.67
valid observations	41,700	99,730	44,991	14,213	1,468	51
Half baths						
sample mean	0.46	0.64	0.66	0.67	0.70	0.78
standard deviation	0.62	0.61	0.63	0.64	0.66	0.76
valid observations	54,607	107,370	47,388	14,933	1,528	51
Total rooms						
sample mean	6.77	7.18**	7.06**	6.88**	6.73**	6.51
standard deviation	1.63	1.62*	1.60*	1.53**	1.46**	1.21*
valid observations	41,593	99,153	44,736	14,144	1,471	51
Number of properties	54,630	107,412	51,305	15,814	1,589	52

*Sample mean or standard deviation differs from the corresponding estimate reported in the cell immediately to the left at the 95% confidence level.
**Sample mean or standard deviation differs from the corresponding estimate reported in the cell immediately to the left at the 99% confidence level.
Note: Table shows data for unchanged repeat-transacting properties only.

Table 6. Percentage of properties modified between transactions.

Frequency of Transaction	Two Transactions	Three Transactions	Four Transactions	Five Transactions	Six Transactions	Seven Transactions	Eight Transactions
San Francisco	10.5%	24.6%	29.8%	32.0%	33.3%	33.3%	43.8%
Contra Costa	5.9	7.6	6.8	4.2	4.8	N/A	N/A
Dade	0.3	2.8	5.4	8.2	9.3	11.1	13.5
Fairfax	7.6	5.5	3.8	2.0	N/A	N/A	N/A

Note: This table indicates the percentage of transaction pairs in each frequency-of-transaction group for which there was a significant modification in primary property attributes between transactions. For example, in San Francisco County, there was a significant modification in primary property attributes between transactions for 10.5% of transaction pairs involving properties transacting exactly twice during the study period, and for 24.6% of transaction pairs involving properties that transacted exactly three times during the study period.

and the actual standard deviation and mean appreciation rate of the underlying data. In order to focus attention on the second of these two sets of factors, we control for the quality of the model specification by estimating, as far as possible, an identically specified hedonic price model for each group of data (defined by the number of times that each property transacted during the study period) in each county included in the analysis. Since the model specification was identical across groups defined by transaction frequency and almost so across counties as well, a fairly simple specification was employed, generally using property attributes that are common to all four county data sets.[12] The hedonic price model used employs a semi-logarithmic specification, expressing the natural logarithm of transaction price as a function of land area (except in Dade County); living area; building age; number of full bathrooms, half bathrooms, and total rooms (bedrooms in Dade County); and a series of quarterly dummies for each quarter during the study period for that county (excluding the initial quarter).

Following estimation, these models can be compared on the basis of four commonly used indicators of the performance of a house price appreciation model, three focusing on the quality of the model specification and the degree of cross-sectional variation in housing prices, and the fourth focusing on the rate of house price appreciation:

1. The first and most important indicator is the estimated standard deviation of the disturbance term (s_ϵ, also called "root mean squared error").
2. The second indicator is the width of a 95% confidence interval drawn around the predicted price of a representative property in that county. The width of the confidence interval is a function of two important factors: (1) the estimated standard deviation of the disturbance term, and (2) the estimated variance-covariance matrix. Thus, the width of the confidence interval is likely to vary with the estimated standard deviation of the disturbance term to some extent, although not to a corresponding degree.
3. The third indicator is the square of the correlation coefficient estimated between actual and predicted prices for properties in each frequency-of-transaction group.
4. Separately, we investigate whether price appreciation varies with sale frequency, using the fourth indicator presented in this analysis, the average (quarterly) increase in the estimated house price appreciation index computed from each hedonic price model. The average quarterly increase is thus used to investigate systematic differences in estimated appreciation rates among the groups of properties defined by transaction frequency.

The results of the hedonic price models estimated for each county are presented in Tables 7–10. Each table shows the number of transactions of properties in each frequency-of-transaction group; for example, Table 7 shows that in San Francisco the number of observations included in each group of properties varies from more than 17,000 observations for single-transacting and double-transacting properties to just a few hundred transactions of properties that transacted five times.[13]

The second column of Tables 7–10 presents the estimated standard deviation of the disturbance term for each group of properties defined by frequency of transaction.[14] In every county, this indicator shows a marked decrease as the frequency of transaction increases: for example, in San Francisco (Table 7) the estimated standard deviation of the disturbance

Table 7. Summary of model results by number of transactions for San Francisco County.

Number of Times Property Transacted		Standard Deviation of Disturbance Term	Width of 95% Confidence Interval	Squared Correlation Between Y and $\hat{Y}$	Average Quarterly Increase in Index
1	$n = 17,442$	54.9%	260%	60.9%	2.7%
2	$n = 18,226$	40.5%	176%	52.7%	2.5%
3	$n = 9,585$	35.7%	153%	52.2%	3.0%
4	$n = 3,148$	31.6%	137%	54.0%	3.5%
5	$n = 730$	28.4%	139%	61.7%	4.5%

term decreases from 55% for single-transacting properties to less than 30% for the most frequently transacting properties. As noted, part of this decrease may be attributable to the different sample sizes for each group of properties. It is important to note, however, that, for San Francisco, the estimated standard deviation for twice-transacting properties is much lower than that for single-transacting properties (41% versus 55%) even though the sample sizes for these two groups are quite similar.

This observation and, more generally, the magnitude of the decline in the estimated standard deviation of the disturbance term suggest that the major source of difference is systematic difference in the actual underlying standard deviation of the disturbance term. This may be attributable either to a shorter holding period between transactions (that is, increased information available to both buyers and sellers on the true market value of the property) or to property type homogeneity. However, we reject the latter property type explanation, given its inconsistency with the finding, discussed in the previous section, of less observed homogeneity (in terms of property attributes and market prices) among frequently sold properties.

The third column of Tables 7–10 presents the width of a 95% confidence interval estimated around the predicted price of a representative property in each county.[15] As noted, the width of the confidence interval depends on two relevant factors: (1) the estimated standard deviation of the disturbance term, and (2) the estimated variance-covariance matrix of the

Table 8. Summary of model results by number of transactions for Contra Costa County.

Number of Times Property Transacted		Standard Deviation of Disturbance Term	Width of 95% Confidence Interval	Squared Correlation Between Y and $\hat{Y}$	Average Quarterly Increase in Index
1	$n = 9,333$	56.9%	329%	57.0%	3.2%
2	$n = 7,736$	46.4%	291%	53.5%	3.0%
3	$n = 2,535$	41.2%	292%	49.4%	3.3%
4	$n = 616$	38.6%	227%	50.5%	3.6%

Table 9. Summary of model results by number of transactions for Dade County.

Number of Times Property Transacted		Standard Deviation of Disturbance Term	Width of 95% Confidence Interval	Squared Correlation Between Y and Ŷ	Average Quarterly Increase in Index
1	n = 54,771	38.3%	178%	47.0%	1.1%
2	n = 29,524	27.3%	134%	43.7%	1.2%
3	n = 10,084	24.1%	121%	44.3%	1.3%
4	n = 2,504	20.8%	108%	48.0%	1.7%
5	n = 565	18.3%	164%	59.0%	2.1%

coefficient estimates. In each county, the confidence interval narrows markedly from properties that transacted just once during the study period to properties that transacted three or four times; this narrowing appears to be related primarily to the estimated standard deviation of the disturbance term.[16]

The fourth column of Tables 7–10 shows the square of the correlation coefficient between actual and predicted prices for properties in each frequency-of-transaction group. In each county, the correlation coefficient declines from single-transacting properties to properties transacting three times, but then increases for properties transacting three or more times. For properties transacting three or more times, this result is as expected; as the number of transactions increases, and as the degree of unexplained variation in market prices (that is, the standard deviation of the disturbance term) decreases, the hedonic price models should generally do a better job of predicting market prices for individual properties.

The last column of Tables 7–10 shows the average quarterly increase in the price index estimated for each group of properties defined by frequency of transaction. These present quite an interesting pattern: the measured average rate of price appreciation is generally lowest for seldom transacting properties, increasing steadily for properties that transacted more than twice during the study period.[17] For example, in San Francisco (Table 7) the average estimated quarterly increase in the price index is just 2.7% and 2.5%, respectively,

Table 10. Summary of model results by number of transactions for Fairfax County.

Number of Times Property Transacted		Standard Deviation of Disturbance Term	Width of 95% Confidence Interval	Squared Correlation Between Y and Ŷ	Average Quarterly Increase in Index
1	n = 42,054	32.1%	135%	50.2%	1.6%
2	n = 16,348	23.0%	94%	49.1%	2.4%
3	n = 3,738	18.0%	76%	61.7%	2.5%
4	n = 264	12.3%	70%	68.3%	4.0%

for single- and double-transacting properties, increasing to 3.0% for properties transacting three times, 3.5% for properties transacting four times, and 4.5% for properties transacting five times.

This pattern suggests that the observed rate of house price appreciation is systematically higher among properties that transact more frequently. The observed difference in house price appreciation rates is common to all counties. A possible explanation for the systematic difference in appreciation rates between seldom transacting and frequently transacting properties is that purchasers make property improvements that are not adequately reflected in the available data, and that therefore appear as increases in the house price appreciation rate.

This observed phenomenon may also arise if households are "locked-in" to homes that decline in value. In addition, the more frequently transacted starter and fixer-upper homes may appreciate more rapidly and/or may attract more capital investment, in the form of unobserved or observed improvements.

5. Conclusions

In this article, we examine the estimated standard deviation of disturbance term and estimated mean-appreciation-rate characteristics of house price indices, segmented by transaction frequency. Major findings are:

1. Frequently transacting properties tend to be smaller than seldom transacting properties, lending some support to the property type distinctiveness hypothesis that the probability that a property transacts is related to the structural, locational, and neighborhood characteristics of that property. However, frequently transacting properties tend to be less homogeneous than seldomly transacted properties.[18]
2. Estimated standard deviations of the disturbance term show a marked decrease as the frequency of transaction increases. Thus the repeat-transactions model may yield an estimated standard deviation of the disturbance term that is downward biased as a measure of the cross-sectional variation of house prices for less frequently transacting properties.
3. The rate of measured house price appreciation is systematically higher among properties that transact more frequently.

The combined findings on less homogeneity and lower standard deviations for repeatedly transacted properties are consistent with better market data that result when there are shorter lags between sales. The findings on systematic differences in measured appreciation rates are consistent with the explanation that repeatedly transacted properties reflect property improvements that are not adequately reflected in the available data. The higher appreciation rate findings are also consistent with the hypothesis that repeatedly transacted properties form a separate group of houses with higher than average appreciation rates net of modification. This may be due to lock-in effects that discourage sale of homes that depreciate in value. Evidence that repeatedly transacted homes are significantly smaller also suggests that there may be a group of "starter" or "fixer-upper" houses with higher measured appreciation rates and higher probability of sale.

The systematic differences in house price appreciation patterns between frequently transacting and seldom transacting properties observed in this analysis suggest (1) that properties exhibiting different transaction frequencies may constitute different housing submarkets that should be analyzed separately, and (2) that, if properties are not to be analyzed separately, the analytical methodology should take into account the systematic differences in transaction probability or frequency. One approach is that illustrated in this article: house price appreciation patterns can be estimated separately for different subsamples of the housing stock (for example, Case–Shiller weighted repeat-sales models could be estimated separately for properties transacting twice, three times, etc.). Alternatively, following Goetzmann and Spiegel (1995), a constant term could be included in the repeat-sales model to account for changes in property value caused by systematic unmeasured property improvements associated with transaction frequency but not with time.

Another promising approach to improving empirical analysis of property transactions is the censored regression technique illustrated by Gatzlaff and Haurin (1993), following Heckman (1979), which involves the specification of a first-stage model of the probability of transaction. While Gatzlaff and Haurin focus on intertemporal variation in transaction probability, the findings of this article emphasize that the probability-of-transaction model may also need to account for cross-sectional variation in transaction probabilities—that is, the selectivity of the subsample of properties that transacted (or transacted repeatedly) during any finite study period.

Notes

1. The relationship between the holding period and the standard deviation of the disturbance term implies that the repeat-transactions model suffers from heteroskedasticity and that each pair of transactions should be weighted by the inverse of the holding period to correct for this source of heteroskedasticity. The same source of heteroskedasticity affects the hedonic and hybrid models, but the explicit correction advocated by Case and Shiller cannot be implemented where the holding period is unknown—that is, where only one property transaction is observed.

2. This investment behavior could represent a market response to expected returns on certain property improvements: specifically, investors either identify properties on which any above-named improvement would have a relatively high return (i.e., properties that are substandard in general relative to surrounding properties), or they identify properties that need a certain type of improvement that itself has a relatively high return (e.g., properties with roofs, bathrooms, kitchens, or other specific components that are substandard relative to otherwise similar properties). Like the starter-homes hypothesis, this hypothesis suggests that frequently transacting properties would tend to be older, smaller, and in poorer condition relative to seldom transacting properties. By itself, however, this hypothesis does not suggest any clear expectation regarding the relative homogeneity of each group of properties: improvements designed to increase the market value of the property (as opposed to development of specific capital) would tend to increase the homogeneity of the frequently transacting housing stock if the tastes of potential buyers are homogeneous and constant, but conversely might make the frequently transacting stock more heterogeneous if the tastes of potential buyers are heterogeneous or changing. Note also that this hypothesis implies that the frequency of transaction for fixer-uppers would exceed that of comparable other properties by just one transaction (or, more accurately, by the number of owner-investors required to transform the property from a fixer-upper to a standard unit).

3. If "fixer-upper" houses are both more likely to appreciate in value and more likely to be repeatedly sold, market segmentation by property type may cause the assumption that there exists one price index valid for all single-family housing within an area to be violated.

4. It should be noted that this methodology does not enable a definitive comparison of the standard deviation of the disturbance term, because in practice the estimated standard deviation of the disturbance term may be related to the number of observations. To control for this difference, identically sized samples could be drawn from each group of observations separated by number of transactions.

5. The data for San Francisco, Contra Costa, and Dade counties were purchased from TRW–REDI Property Data, a Fort Lauderdale, Florida-based data vendor that collects and compiles data from county deed transfer and assessment records. The data for Fairfax County were purchased directly from the county.

6. Compiling the property transaction and assessment databases required a significant amount of work. First, records from the two data sources—deed transfer records providing transaction price and date information and tax assessment records providing property attributes—were merged by property identification number. Second, single-family residential properties were identified on the basis of land use and zoning codes as well as data on number of units; and properties with unreasonably large or small values and observations on other variables (land area, living area, age, bathrooms, total rooms, bedrooms) that suggested that they were not single-family were eliminated. Third, records were sorted by transaction date (if any) and, after any duplicate records were eliminated, properties were grouped by frequency of transaction. Fourth, consecutive transactions of repeat-transacting properties were identified as changed or unchanged on the basis of values of primary property attributes (land area, living area, age, bathrooms, total rooms, bedrooms) recorded at the time of each transaction. Finally, primary attributes that were available in all (or most) counties studied were identified for the hedonic-regression analysis.

7. Summary statistics were generally comparable for properties whose primary attributes changed between transactions, but these are not shown for simplicity and because smaller numbers of observations made summary statistics less reliable.

8. Interestingly, non-transacting properties appear to be smaller, on average, than properties that transacted at least once during the study period, in contrast with the general pattern observed for transacting properties. This result may indicate the existence of a group of relatively small properties that do not transact frequently. For example, some small properties are likely to be occupied by older householders, who are similar to "starter households" in that they do not require substantial living space. Unlike starter households, however, older households may be relatively immobile, preferring to remain in a smaller property rather than to transact frequently.

9. Nonetheless, it remains possible that the estimated standard deviation of the disturbance term is smaller in repeatedly transacted properties due to their greater homogeneity. This would occur if these properties were more homogeneous than the larger, more valuable seldom transacted properties in attributes that we do not measure.

10. This is certainly a strong assumption, but the lack of data on improvements makes it necessary to use changes in recorded property attributes as the only available proxy for investments of specific capital.

11. Unfortunately, with the available data it is impossible to evaluate changes in the characteristics of non-transacting or single-transacting properties, which are most likely to have been modified according to the specific-capital hypothesis.

12. The exception to this was Dade County, which was included in the hedonic specification even though data on attributes identical to other counties were not available.

13. The number of transactions used in estimating the hedonic price models is substantially fewer than the total number of transactions, because transactions for which any of the regressor variables were missing had to be excluded from the estimation.

14. It is useful to keep in mind that the estimated standard deviation of the disturbance term is relatively large, because the constraint that the hedonic price model be identically specified across counties meant that the best possible model specification could not be developed for any county.

15. It is useful to keep in mind that the width of the confidence interval is relatively large for two reasons: (1) the arbitrarily chosen 95% confidence level is fairly high, and (2) the constraint that the hedonic price model be identically specified across counties meant that the best possible model specification could not be developed for any county.

16. For properties transacting more than three or four times, however, the confidence interval begins to widen, reflecting the variance-covariance matrix of models estimated on relatively small samples of frequently transacting properties.

17. While the difference in average appreciation rates is not statistically significant at conventional levels of confidence, the consistency of the pattern across all counties supports this interpretation. The result contradicts the authors' earlier findings (1991) for one district of Fairfax County, where the average quarterly house price appreciation rate was lower for repeat-transacting properties as a group than for single-transacting properties.
18. This suggests that the observed difference in the estimated standard deviation of the disturbance term is attributable to shorter holding periods between transactions (that is, increased information available to both buyers and sellers on the true market value of the property) rather than to property type distinctiveness.

References

Bailey, M. J., R. F. Muth, and H. O. Nourse. "A Regression Method for Real Estate Price Index Construction," *Journal of the American Statistical Association* 58 (1963), 933–942.

Bryan, T. B., and P. F. Colwell. "Housing Price Indices," *Research in Real Estate* 2 (1982), 57–84.

Case, B., and John M. Quigley. "The Dynamics of Real Estate Prices," *Review of Economics and Statistics* 73 (1991), 50–58.

Case, B., Henry O. Pollakowski, and Susan M. Wachter. "On Choosing Among House Price Index Methodologies," *Journal of the AREUEA* 19 (1991), 286–307.

Case, K. E., and Robert J. Shiller. "The Efficiency of the Market for Single-Family Homes," *American Economic Review* 79 (1989), 125–137.

Case, K. E., and R. "Prices of Single-Family Homes Since 1970: New Indices for Four Cities," *New England Economic Review* (September/October 1987), 45–56.

Clapp, J. M., and C. Giaccotto. "Estimating Price Trends for Residential Property: A Comparison of Repeat Sales and Assessed Value Methods," *Journal of the American Statistical Association* 87 (1991), 300–306.

Clapp, J. M., and C. Giaccotto. "Repeat Sales Methodology for Price Trend Estimation: An Evaluation for Sample Selectivity," *Journal of Real Estate Finance and Economics* 5 (1992), 357–374.

Clapp, J. M., C. Giaccotto, and D. Tirtiroglu. "Housing Price Indices: Based on All Transactions Compared to Repeat Subsamples," *Journal of the AREUEA* 19 (1991), 270–285.

Fama, E. F. *Foundations of Finance*, New York: Basic Books.

Gatzlaff, D. H., and D. R. Haurin. "Sample Selection and Biases in Local House Value Indexes," Paper presented at the annual conference of the American Real Estate an Urban Economic Association, January 1993.

Goetzmann, W. N. "The Single Family Home in the Investment Portfolio," *Journal of Real Estate Finance and Economics* (July 1993), 201–222.

Goetzmann, W. N. and M. Spiegel. "Non-temporal Components of Residential Real Estate Appreciation," *Review of Economics and Statistics* 77 (1995), 199–206.

Halvorsen, R., and H. Pollakowski. "Choice of Functional Form for Hedonic Price Equations," *Journal of Urban Economics* 10 (1981), 37–49.

Heckman, J. "Sample Selection Bias as a Specification Error," *Econometrica* 47 (1979), 153–161.

Meese, R., and N. Wallace. "Non-Parametric Estimation of Dynamic Hedonic Price Models and the Construction of Residential Housing Price Indices," *Journal of the AREUEA* 19 (1991), 308–332.

Mills, E. S., and B. W. Hamilton. *Urban Economics*. Glenview, Illinois: Scott, Foresman and Company, 1984.

Rosen, S. "Hedonic Prices and Implicit Markets: Product Differentiation in Pure Competition," *Journal of Political Economy* 82 (1974), 34–55.

Shiller, R. J. "Measuring Asset Values for Cash Settlement in Derivative Markets: Hedonic Repeated Measures Indices and Perpetual Futures," *The Journal of Finance* 48 (1993), 911–931.

Stambaugh, R. F. "On the Exclusion of Assets from Tests of the Two Parameter Model," *Journal of Financial Economics* 10 (1982), 237–268.

Journal of Real Estate Finance and Economics, 14: 189–202 (1997)
©1997 Kluwer Academic Publishers

Evaluating the Usefulness of the American Housing Survey for Creating House Price Indices

KATHERINE A. KIEL
Department of Economics, Northeastern University, Boston, MA 02115

JEFFREY E. ZABEL
Department of Economics, Tufts University, Medford, MA 02155

Abstract

The American Housing Survey (AHS) is a valuable source of information on houses and occupants over time. The AHS has several advantages over sales data for use in the creation of price indices: it is readily available, has frequent observations over time and space, has data from the late 1970s through the mid-1990s, includes houses that do not sell, as well as those that do, and has information on the occupants. The drawbacks include: a time lag between the interview and the release of the data, data suppression issues, owner-stated house values, and a lack of neighborhood information. In this study, we use the metropolitan version of the AHS, which has been supplemented with the original survey data as well as Census tract data for three cities over 14 years to examine whether the AHS can be used to create indices. Indices are estimated using hedonic, repeat valuation, and hybrid techniques, overcoming some of the problems inherent in the estimation of indices. We find that the data-suppression issues and the owner-stated house values are not problematic. The biggest drawback of the AHS is its lack of objective information on neighborhood quality.

Key Words: American Housing Survey, house price indices

1. Introduction

The American Housing Survey (AHS) is an important source of information on houses and occupants, containing data covering almost 20 years for metropolitan areas across the United States. It has been used in the past to create house price indices (e.g., Thibodeau, 1989, 1992), but it is not clear how accurate these are relative to sales-based indices. The AHS has several advantages in the development of indices: the data are easily obtained by researchers; and the survey covers more than 60 MSAs since 1974, contains information on houses that do not sell as well as those that do, follows the same houses over time, and has information about the current occupants. However, its drawbacks include: a time lag between the interview and the release of the data, data suppression issues such as top-coding and bracketing, a lack of objective neighborhood information, and owner-stated values rather than sales prices.[1]

In this study, we use the metropolitan version of the AHS for three cities over 14 years to analyze how useful the data are for creating indices and consider each of the drawbacks listed above. The problems with data suppression and the lack of neighborhood variables are eliminated by accessing proprietary data, which allows us to look at the raw data, and to attach Census tract information to each housing unit. We find that, while top-coding and bracketing have little impact on house price indices, the lack of neighborhood characteristics does have a major effect.

The issue of owner accuracy has been addressed by several researchers (see Goodman and Ittner, 1992, for a survey). We have used the same data set to test for owner accuracy and find that the average owner overstates the value of his house by 5.0% (Kiel and Zabel, 1995a). The differences between owner-stated values and sales prices are tested, and are found not to be related to house, market, or owner characteristics. These results suggest that hedonic equations based on owners' valuations will provide unbiased estimates of the changes in house prices and are consistent with Kiel and Carson's (1990) findings. In this article, we take the next step, creating indices based on both sale prices and owners' valuations using transaction prices. We find that the differences are small and insignificant, confirming the earlier findings. However, there are substantial differences when comparing indices based on owners' valuations for the full data set and for the subset of observations where houses sell. This is evidence that transactions are not a random sample of the population of all houses, suggesting that indices based on sales data may be biased.

There are three methods for estimating house price indices: hedonics, repeat sales, and hybrid models; we consider variations of these based on valuation data. The hedonic method can be problematic if the functional form is misspecified, or if there are missing independent variables. It also can suffer from sample selection bias if houses that sell are different from those that do not, a problem that all sales-based indices face. This is exacerbated in the repeat sales approach, which requires the house to sell more than once and to not undergo any changes in its physical or locational characteristics. Hybrid models can incorporate some of the missing information, and can be specified to allow for changes in housing characteristics and prices over time. However, using owner-stated, value-based data sets to estimate hedonic or hybrid repeat value indices can eliminate several of these drawbacks, since they include houses which sell (once or more often) as well as those that do not, and can incorporate changes in many of the characteristics which influence house values.

In the next section, we present the data used in this study. In section 3, we discuss the advantages and disadvantages of the AHS for creating house price indices and how we eliminate some of these drawbacks. In section 4, we describe the different ways of creating the indices which we will estimate. In the fifth section, we provide the empirical results and comparisons with other available indices, then conclude in the sixth section.

2. Data

The main data source used for this study is the Metropolitan Statistical Area (MSA) American Housing Survey (AHS). Beginning in 1974, the AHS contains detailed information on particular houses through time, including the current owner's evaluation of the house price, house characteristics, and self-reported information on the house's current occupants. The Chicago, Denver, and Philadelphia MSAs are used for this study. The AHS surveys a given MSA every three to four years. Thus, there are data for five different years for each of the three MSAs that are used in this study:[2]

Chicago: 1975, 1979, 1983, 1987, 1991

Denver: 1976, 1979, 1983, 1986, 1990

Philadelphia: 1975, 1978, 1982, 1985, 1989

For each survey date, owners are asked to estimate how much their property (house plus lot) would sell for if it were for sale. Data on the sales prices of houses that sold in the previous 12 months were first provided in 1978. Since we will use both owners' valuations and sales prices when estimating indices, the initial survey year for each MSA is excluded in this study. A house from the AHS was included in the sample only if there was a regular occupied interview, the unit was owner-occupied, and sat on a lot of less than ten acres. Because of possible miscodings, a house sold within 12 months prior to the interview is dropped if the owner's valuation is more than 200% or less than 50% of the sales price.

An important component of house values that is not well quantified in the AHS is information relating to neighborhood quality, as it focuses on the occupant's evaluation of a self-defined neighborhood. However, detailed information on neighborhood characteristics is available in the Summary Tape Files (STF) for the decennial Censuses. The STF provides summary information for different geographical units, including census tracts and sample data that are weighted to represent the total population. The tract information includes the median age, the percent of individuals aged 25 or older who have graduated from high school, average household income, and residential property vacancy rates. These serve as proxies for various neighborhood characteristics that affect house prices.

To merge this data with the AHS, it is necessary to have information on the location of each house. However, the publicly available AHS data only provide information on whether a house is in the MSA's central city, although, for more recent years, a "zone" variable is recorded as well. This variable identifies a "socio-economically homogeneous area" with more than 100,000 residents. Since this does not greatly differentiate regions within the metropolitan area, it is unlikely to allow for accurate neighborhood quality information. Also, this geographic unit is not available in the STF.

The internal AHS files, however, identify the census tract in which each house is located, and, through special arrangements, we had access to these propriety data. A census tract is defined as a homogeneous area in regard to the characteristics of the population, their economic status, and living conditions. A tract generally has between 2,500 and 8,000 residents. Knowing the census tract in which the house is located allows for more accurate neighborhood characteristics to be assigned to each house.

The information from the 1980 and 1990 STFs is merged with the AHS data by census tract. We use the 1990 STF data for the 1989–1991 surveys, weighted averages of the 1980 and 1990 STF data for the 1982–1987 surveys, and 1980 STF data for the 1978–1979 surveys.[3]

3. Advantages and Disadvantages of Using the AHS to Create Indices

Using the AHS to create indices has several potential problems, as well as several advantages. In this section, we will examine whether the survey can be used, and if so, what data are required. We look first at the publicly available AHS data set, focusing on the issues of owner accuracy, sample selection bias, and additional information available relative to sales data. Then, the additional information gained by accessing the raw data is considered, to see if this is necessary when utilizing the survey data.

3.1. Publicly Available AHS Data

Since it is common to report the owner's valuation of the house in surveys, it is important to know if the reported values can be used as proxies for prices. Others have tested the accuracy of owners' house value estimates. As presented in Table 1 of Goodman and Ittner, Kish and Lansing (1954) find that owners overstate values by 4%; Kain and Quigley (1972) and Follain and Malpezzi (1981) find an undervaluation of 2%; Robins and West (1977) find an overstatement of 5%; and Ihlanfeldt and Martinez-Vazquez (1986) find an overvaluation of 16%. Goodman and Ittner, using the 1985 and 1987 waves of the national version of the AHS, conclude that the average homeowner overestimates the value of his home by 6% and that the average absolute error is 14% of sales price. This error in measurement is not correlated with house, owner, or market characteristics which suggests that price indices should not be "seriously flawed" and that the rates of change in house values should be unbiased.[4]

Table 1. Variable names and definitions.

LNSALE	natural log of the sales price of the house
LNVALUE	natural log of the owner-estimated value of the house
CNTRLCTY	$=1$ if the house is in the central city of the MSA, $=0$ otherwise
HOUSEAGE	the age of the house in years
HOUSEAGE2	the square of the age of the house in years
GARAGE	$=1$ if the house has a garage, $=0$ otherwise
BEDS	number of bedrooms in the house
FULLBATH	number of full bathrooms in the house
AIRCOND	$=1$ if the house has either central or room air conditioning, $=0$ otherwise
#PERSONS	number of individuals in the household
MARRIED	$=1$ if the head of household is married, $=0$ otherwise
INCOME	household income in tens of thousands of 1990 dollars
NONWHITE	$=1$ if the head of household is not white, $=0$ otherwise
MEDINCOME	median income in the house's census tract in tens of thousands of 1990 dollars
MEDAGE	median age of individuals in the house's census tract
%NONWHITE	percent of nonwhite individuals in the house's census tract
%HS	percent of individuals over 25 who have completed high school in the house's census tract
%BLUECOLL	percent of blue collar workers in the house's census tract
%TURNED	percent of houses in the census tract that have changed hands in the last five years
%VACANT	percent of housing units vacant in the house's census tract
%LOWOCC	percent of houses in the census tract with less than one occupant per room
TENURE1	$=1$ the household moved into the unit in the 12 months prior to survey, $=0$ otherwise
TENURE15	$=1$ if household in unit 1 to 5 years, $=0$ otherwise
TENURE510	$=1$ if household in unit 5 to 10 years, $=0$ otherwise

In order to verify Goodman and Ittner's results over time, we examine the AHS for the accuracy of owner-reported values for three cities over a time span of 14 years (Kiel and Zabel, 1995a). Our results are quite similar to Goodman and Ittner's. However, we do find that length of tenure affects owner accuracy, with newer owners being less accurate. While this evidence supports the use of the AHS for creating house price indices, a more direct test would be to compare indices based on sales and owners' valuation data for observations where houses sell. This is done in section 5.

An advantage of the AHS is that it gives values for houses whether or not they sell, thus eliminating the likelihood of sample selection bias. Ihlanfeldt and Martinez-Vazquez test for potential sample selection bias in sales-price-based data using Heckman's (1978) two-step method and find no evidence of sample selection bias. Jud and Seaks (1994) estimate the model developed by Clapp and Giaccotto (1992) and find that sample selection may indeed be a problem. Goodman and Ittner and Kiel and Zabel (1995a) also use Heckman's procedure and conclude that sample selection bias is not likely to be a problem with the AHS. In section 5, a further test for selection bias is carried out by comparing changes in indices, using the full data set and the subsample of houses that sell.

3.2. Proprietary Data

We have access to the internal version of the AHS, which allows us to add neighborhood information to the data set. If these variables do affect values or sales prices, then excluding them from hedonic regressions will likely create problems in index estimation. Kiel and Zabel (1995b) estimate house value regressions, including measures such as the median income and age and the percent of nonwhite and blue collar workers in the census tract, and find that these variables have a great deal of explanatory power. As most housing data sets do not include this type of variable, estimating indices with and without neighborhood indicators will shed light on the cost of excluding them. Indices are also estimated with the publicly available AHS neighborhood quality variables, and the results are compared.

For privacy reasons, the owners' valuations and sales prices for the more expensive houses are top-coded in the public-use version of the AHS. Homes that cost more than $150,000 in 1978, $300,000 in the 1979–1983 period, and $250,000 since 1984 are considered expensive and are therefore top-coded. The proprietary data is not top-coded. Thus, we can see how this might affect the estimation of indices.

Owners' valuations are bracketed in the public-use version of the AHS prior to 1984, but the actual value is given in the proprietary data. We create a variable using the midpoint of the interval and compare this with the continuous owners' valuation variable to determine if bracketing affects the estimate of the price index.[5]

4. Estimating House Price Indices

In this section, we develop a number of indices estimated from hedonic regressions, repeat valuation models, and hybrid models, based both on owner-provided values and sales prices.

This will allow us to determine whether the AHS can be used to develop indices, and if so, what data are required. These indices will be estimated and compared in the following section.

The first model is a hedonic equation which holds the prices of characteristics constant over time. This is called the "simple hedonic" by Case, Pollakowski, and Wachter (CPW, 1991):

$$LnY_{it} = \alpha + X_{it}\beta + \sum_{j=2}^{T} D_{jt}\gamma_j + \epsilon_{it} \qquad i = 1, \ldots, N \quad t = t_{i_1}, \ldots, t_{i_T}, \qquad (1)$$

where Y_{it} is the price (or value) of house i at time t, α is a constant, X_{it} is a vector of property (and possibly owner) characteristics, β is the vector of corresponding prices, the D_{jt}s are dummies corresponding to the T time periods, and the γ_js measure the changes in the house price index.[6] Also, $t_{i_1}, \ldots, t_{i_T}$ are the time periods in which house i is surveyed. Since not all houses are included in all T surveys, the number of observations per house will differ. This model can be extended by including neighborhood characteristics as well, and will be called the "expanded simple hedonic."

Both simple hedonic models can incorporate changes in the prices of housing characteristics by interacting the D_{jt}s with the X_{it}s. CPW call this a "complex hedonic" and it is specified as:

$$LnY_{it} = \alpha + \sum_{j=1}^{T} D_{jt}X_{ij}\beta_j + \sum_{j=2}^{T} D_{jt}\gamma_j + \epsilon_{it}, \qquad (2)$$

where the vector of prices of the house characteristics, β_j, is allowed to vary across time. This model also can include neighborhood characteristics and will then be called the "expanded complex hedonic." We can choose between the simple and the complex hedonic by testing the hypothesis that the coefficients (other than the intercept) are constant across time. We use the standard F-test as well as the Ohta–Griliches (1975) procedure. The latter is a less restrictive version of the F-test that has been used in the literature (for example, Palmquist, 1982). Ohta and Griliches suggest that the pooled model (constant coefficients) be used if the difference between the standard errors for the restricted and unrestricted models is less than 10%.

Hedonic-based indices will be unbiased estimates of true house price changes only if the functional form is correctly specified and if all relevant variables are included in the regression. Utilizing the supplemented AHS data allows us to overcome the latter problem, although the former remains. In addition, hedonic regressions ignore information contained in repeat sales models if housing attributes have not changed over time. Finally, sample selection bias can be problematic if houses that sell are different from those that do not. Employing value-based data eliminates this difficulty.

The traditional repeat sales model is estimated using only those houses whose characteristics have not changed over the sample period, yet have sold more than once. This is called the "restrictive repeat sales model." If estimated with owner-stated values, then all houses without changes in characteristics can be included, and the model is called the "restricted repeat valuation model.":

$$\Delta LnY_{it} = \sum_{j=2}^{T} \Delta D_{jt}\gamma_j + \Delta\varepsilon_{it} \qquad i = 1,\ldots,M \quad t = t_{i_2},\ldots,t_{i_\tau}, \tag{3}$$

where, in general,

$$\Delta W_{it} = W_{it} - W_{i(t-1)}.$$

The number of houses included in the repeat valuation model, M, is less than the number in the hedonic models, N, since houses that are only surveyed once are not included in (3). The repeat valuation model can be expanded to include changes in characteristics; it then becomes a "hybrid model." The hybrid model is obtained by taking first differences using (1):

$$\Delta LnY_{it} = \Delta X_{it}\beta + \sum_{j=2}^{T} \Delta D_{jt}\gamma_j + \Delta\epsilon_{it}. \tag{4}$$

Changes can occur in housing characteristics and in neighborhood characteristics.

Repeat sales-based indices can be biased if prices of attributes are not allowed to change. They can also suffer from sample selection bias, if houses that sell more than once are different from other houses, or if houses without changes in attributes are different from those with changes. Hybrid models alleviate the latter problem, while a complex hedonic addresses the former. Repeat sales-based indices are also inefficient due to the strict data requirements, but using the AHS to estimate the repeat valuation model reduces this problem, as houses only need to be in sequential surveys. Finally, the repeat sales approach does not allow the impact of time to be separated from the impact of the aging of the housing units. Again, with hedonics (and the hybrid model), one can include the age of the house to capture the aging effect.

5. Empirical Results

In this section, we address the data-suppression issues of top-coding and bracketing, then estimate and compare house prices indices based on the models in section 4. The names and definitions of the variables used in the regressions are given in Table 1. These include the housing and occupant's characteristics and neighborhood quality proxies. Because income numbers are in nominal terms, they have been deflated using the MSA-specific Consumer Price Index, all items less shelter. The base year is 1990. The results given in this section are for the percent changes in the house prices indices, or appreciation rates, between interviews which are given every three or four years. Appreciation rate are easier to compare with other reported estimates than indices, since the latter are often normalized around different base years.

Table 2. Appreciation rates for top-coded and bracketed data.

	Chicago 1987–1991		Denver 1986–1990		Philadelphia 1985–1989	
% top-coded	6.3%		1.8%		2.8%	
Index: full data / # obs	17.10	2117	−13.34	2039	33.97	3555
Index: not top-coded / # obs	16.62	1984	−11.71	2002	32.87	3454
Index: top-coded / # obs	8.74	133	−42.91	37	−3.12	101
Index: bracketed / # obs	16.87	2117	−13.59	2039	34.51	3555

5.1. Data Suppression Issues

With access to the raw AHS data, we can determine whether the top-coding of house values has a significant effect on house price indices. Indices based on hedonic regressions are calculated using the full data and the subsets that are and are not top-coded for the last two interviews for each city.[7] The appreciation rates for these indices are presented in Table 2. The percent of houses that are top-coded is 6.3%, 1.8%, and 2.8% for Chicago, Denver, and Philadelphia, respectively; thus, only a small percent of houses are top-coded. While there are substantial differences between the appreciation rates for the indices based on the subsamples that are and are not top-coded, the appreciation rate for the index using the subsample that is not top-coded and the one based on the full sample are quite similar.

Another issue raised in section 3 is that the owner's valuation is bracketed in the public-use survey. To test if this has an impact on house price indices, we use the continuous owner's valuation variable for the full sample to create a variable that is the midpoint of the interval in which the actual value falls (using the brackets given in the manual for the public-use version of the AHS). Since we have access to the actual value for observations more than $250,000, we create additional brackets so that these observations can be included.[8] The appreciation rate for the index based on this bracketed variable is very similar to the rate for the index based on the continuous owner's valuation variable using the full sample (see Table 2). Thus, it does not appear that bracketing or top-coding has much of an impact on indices estimated using the AHS.

5.2. Empirical Results from Estimating House Price Indices

We create a series of house price indices using the models discussed in section 4. The estimates of the appreciation rates based on these indices for each of the three cities are given in Table 3. These indices will be referred to according to the model from which they derive: (1) simple hedonic; (2) expanded simple hedonic, (3) expanded complex hedonic, (4) restrictive repeat valuation, and (5) hybrid. We also calculate an expanded simple index (6) based on the neighborhood quality variables that are included in the AHS.

Indices are also created using sales data: the simple hedonic (7) and the expanded simple hedonic (8). For comparison, indices based on owners' valuations from a data set restricted

Table 3. House price appreciation rates.

Model	Chicago				Denver				Philadelphia			
	1979–83	1983–87	1987–91	Number of observations	1979–83	1983–86	1986–90	Number of observations	1978–82	1982–85	1985–89	Number of observations
(1)Simple Hedonic	13.26	22.79	23.76	9433	23.40	3.36	−4.62	4670	27.10	16.70	62.91	12319
(2)Expanded Hedonic	3.18	8.82	16.53	9433	15.97	−1.51	−10.26	4670	18.36	2.00	40.58	12319
(3)Expanded Complex	2.53	13.12	13.53	9433	16.74	−3.55	−13.38	4670	20.49	3.17	37.00	12319
(4)Repeat Value	11.55	21.32	21.81	2101	21.76	0.91	−3.89	940	28.89	13.95	58.28	1712
(5)Hybrid	14.18	22.14	25.82	3469	25.38	3.64	−2.67	1949	20.56	1.75	43.09	3938
(6)AHS Expanded	13.02	22.48	24.79	9433	23.57	3.91	−4.79	4670	27.49	14.91	63.10	12319
(7)Simple Hedonic–Sales	17.97	14.51	39.21	376	24.73	−5.80	−5.75	297	20.38	26.16	55.86	437
(8)Expanded Hedonic–Sales	3.37	−0.02	23.86	376	11.46	−7.27	−12.24	297	15.70	3.75	28.90	437
(9)Simple Hedonic–Value	19.32	14.97	37.05	376	22.64	−5.27	−6.18	297	15.80	27.24	58.92	437
(10)Expanded Hedonic–Value	4.66	0.60	22.56	376	10.04	−6.63	−12.64	297	11.05	4.43	30.89	437
NAR	17.4	17.27	36.73		NA	9.84	0		NA	24.2	33.94	
Case and Schiller	NA	32.58	27.65		25.22	−0.21	−0.41		31.37	16.75	52.39	
HHK	NA	22.52	19.76		NA	1.85	1.82		NA	22.6	43.86	

to houses that sold are also estimated: the simple hedonic (9) and the expanded simple hedonic (10).[9] We have also included the appreciation rates for three other indices based on house prices developed by the National Association of Realtors (NAR); Case, Schiller, and Weiss (CSW), 1995); and Haurin, Hendershott, and Kim (HHK, 1991), for comparison.

The appreciation rates for the first two indices make clear the importance of including neighborhood characteristics in the hedonic regressions. In all nine cases, the appreciation rate for the simple hedonic index is substantially higher than that for the expanded simple hedonic index. For example, index (1) estimates that prices have increased in Philadelphia by 27.10%, 16.70%, and 62.91% during the 1978–1982, 1982–1985, and 1985–1989 periods, respectively. The comparable changes using index (2) are 18.36%, 2.00%, and 40.58%. Hypothesis tests for the equality of the appreciation rates for indices (1) and (2) are carried out and are rejected at the 1% significance level in all cases. It appears that the simple hedonic index is confounding increases in neighborhood quality with actual increases in the price index (for a constant quality house).

The third index is based on the hedonic regression where all coefficients are allowed to vary across time. This amounts to running separate regressions for each time period. While the F-test rejects the hypothesis that the coefficients, other than the intercept, are constant (all F-statistics have p-values less than 0.001), the percent change in the standard errors is only 2.09%, 3.13%, and 3.63% for Chicago, Denver, and Philadelphia, respectively. Thus, according to the Ohta–Griliches procedure, the expanded simple hedonic index (constant coefficients) is preferred to the expanded complex hedonic index. This is consistent with the (relatively) small differences in the appreciation rates for indices (2) and (3). We find that house prices increased by approximately 30% between 1979 and 1991 in Chicago and showed very little, if any, increase in Denver during the 1979–1990 period.

The appreciation rate for the restrictive repeat valuation index (4) is similar to the one for the simple hedonic index (1) for all three cities. This is not surprising, since neither index accounts for changes in neighborhood characteristics. But for Chicago and Denver, including changes in house, household, and neighborhood characteristics leads to estimates of price changes (index (5)) that are even farther from the appreciation rates for the expanded simple hedonic (index (2)) than those for the restrictive repeat valuation index. On the other hand, the appreciation rates for the hybrid index (5) for Philadelphia are very similar to the rates of change for the other two indices that account for changes in neighborhood characteristics (indices (2) and (3)). This divergence in results is related to the fact that the changes in neighborhood characteristics are significant in the hybrid model for Philadelphia but not for the other two cities.

While the AHS does provide information on neighborhood quality, it is self-reported and hence is likely to be endogenous. We use the variable which indicates whether the respondent believes that the neighborhood is in excellent, good, fair, or poor condition.[10] The percent of households that claimed their neighborhoods were in excellent or good condition is 89.1%, 88.2%, and 83.8% for Chicago, Denver, and Philadelphia, respectively. The subjective nature of the AHS variable is reinforced by the fact that the neighborhood quality variables from the AHS and STF are not highly correlated. The rate of change of the expanded simple hedonic index (6) based on the AHS neighborhood quality information is quite similar to the appreciation rate for the simple hedonic index (1) but is different from the one based on the expanded simple hedonic (2) that includes the neighborhood quality information from the STF. Thus, it is not enough to include the AHS information to account for neighborhood quality; it is important to be able to include objective information such as that found in the STF.

The appreciation rates for the simple hedonic indices using sales prices and owners' valuations restricted to observations on houses that sell, (7) and (9), are very similar and the differences between them are not statistically significant at the 5% level for all three cities. The appreciation rates for the comparable indices based on the expanded simple hedonics, (8) and (10), are also very similar. This is further evidence that owners' valuations are comparable to sales prices when creating house price indices. The differences between the rates of change of indices (7) and (8) and indices (9) and (10) are statistically significant at the 1% level: again, this highlights the importance of including neighborhood quality variables in the hedonic regressions whether using sales data or owner-stated values.

Another interesting comparison is between the expanded simple hedonic indices based on the owners' valuation for the full data set and for observations where houses sold, (2) and (10). The appreciation rates for these indices are quite different for all three cities, which brings into question whether the subsample of houses that sold is representative of the population of houses.[11]

5.3. Comparison with Other Indices

In Table 3, we also present appreciation rates calculated using other sources of data, as well as other estimation techniques, to see how the AHS-based indices compare with them. The NAR index is prepared by the National Association of Realtors, and is based on median sales prices of existing single-family homes. Thus, this index does not control for quality changes over time. The index should be similar to the hedonic index based only on houses that sold, not including neighborhood characteristics (7). The NAR index is fairly close to the AHS index, but it clearly overstates appreciation when compared to the index that controls for neighborhood effects (8).

The Case, Schiller, and Weiss (CSW) index is based on repeat sales of houses that have no changes in any observed characteristics; neighborhood quality is not observed. It is most comparable to the AHS repeat value index (4) and the simple hedonic based on houses that sold (7). The appreciation rate for the CSW index is higher than the rate of change of the repeat value index in Chicago and Philadelphia, indicating that houses that sell are different from the population of houses in general. Kiel (1994) found that houses which transact have higher than average appreciation rates, which biases repeat sales indices upwards. The appreciation rate for the CSW index is higher than the one for the simple hedonic in Denver. This suggests, again, that neighborhood effects should be controlled for. Unfortunately, most sales data do not include this type of measure, so it must be added by the researcher.

The index reported by Haurin, Hendershott, and Kim (HHK) is based on the NAR index discussed above, which they adjust for changes in quality over time; the Coldwell Banker series, which is based on the price of a house with specified characteristics drawn from three observations; and American Chamber of Commerce data on the price of a specified house based on at least five observations. HHK then estimate a LISREL (Linear Structural Relationship) model, which assumes that there is a "true" price series, "rather than differing price trends for different qualities of housing" (p. 455). This index is most comparable to the simple hedonic (1) and the simple hedonic based only on transaction data (7). The results are mixed, although the appreciation rate for HHK is always higher than the rate of change of the indices that control for neighborhood quality.

6. Conclusions

In this article, we have evaluated the usefulness of the AHS for creating house price indices. We have shown that top-coding and bracketing have little impact on the appreciation rates of house price indices and that appreciation rates for indices based on owners' valuation are comparable to those based on sales prices. However, we found substantial differences in the appreciation rates for indices based on the full sample and the subsample of houses that sold. This is evidence that the subsample of houses that sold is not a random sample from the population of all houses, raising questions about indices based on sales prices and particularly those based on repeat sales.

One major finding from our analysis is the importance of neighborhood characteristics in estimating house price indices. We found significant differences in the appreciation rates for indices that were based on models that did and did not include neighborhood characteristics, bringing into question house price indices that do not take these into account. The AHS does provide self-reported information on neighborhood quality, but it was shown that this data had no impact on the estimated appreciation rates. Thus, it seems that one important drawback of the AHS for creating house price indices is its lack of objective information on neighborhood characteristics. This is also likely to be a drawback of many other data sets used to construct house price indices. For example, the three other indices which we considered—NAR; Case, Schiller, and Weiss; and Haurin, Hendershott, and Kim—not only exhibit significant differences among themselves, but also overstate the increases in house prices when compared to the simple and complex hedonic indices that control for neighborhood characteristics.

Acknowledgments

The data set used in this article was developed while Zabel was an ASA Research Fellow at the U.S. Census Bureau. The views here do not necessarily reflect those of either the U.S. Census Bureau or the Department of Commerce. We would like to thank the journal editor and anonymous referees for helpful comments.

Notes

1. Starting in 1978, the sales price for houses which sold in the 12 months prior to the interview is reported. Beginning in 1984, the most recent sales price is available.

2. Kendall and Grundy Counties were added to the Chicago MSA in 1987, and Douglas County was added to the Denver MSA in 1986. Houses from these counties that are part of the AHS data from Chicago in 1987 and 1991 and Denver in 1990 are included in our samples for those years. Since the populations of these counties are small relative to the rest of the MSA, few houses from these counties are included in our samples; hence, their presence will have little impact on the results.
3. The STF data correspond to 1980 and 1990 census tracts, while the AHS is based on 1970 and 1980 census tracts. There have been a number of changes in census tract designations for each decennial census, particularly the splitting of census tracts in the peripheral areas. Census tract conversions between 1970 and 1980 and 1980 and 1990 are given in the 1980 and 1990 Census of Population and Housing Reports for MSAs by census tracts (PHC80 series for 1980 and CP3 series for 1990). This information is used to convert the census tracts in the AHS into 1980 and 1990 census tracts so that the two data sets can be merged.
4. Kiel and Carson also test the AHS and report similar results.
5. Details of the creation of the bracketed variable are given in section 5.1.
6. To get the percent change in the house price index, it is necessary to make the transformation $(e^{\gamma - \gamma_{t-1}} - 1) * 100$ for $t = 3, \ldots, T$ and $e^{\gamma_1} * 100$ for $t = 2$.
7. We only use the last two interviews, because we do not have access to the top-coded values for the two earlier interviews.
8. The brackets that we create are [300,000, 350,000), [350,000, 400,000), [400,000, 450,000), [450,000, 500,000), [500,000, 600,000), [600,000, 700,000), [700,000, 800,000), [800,000, 900,000), and 900,000 and above. We assigned the value 950,000 for houses with values in this last interval.
9. Owners' characteristics are not included in the regressions used to create indices (7)–(10), because these variables are not traditionally included in sales price hedonics due to lack of data.
10. For later surveys, respondents were asked to rate their neighborhoods on a scale from one (lowest) to ten (highest). We converted this scale so that a nine or ten is excellent, a seven or eight is good, a five or six is fair, and a one through four is poor. The percent of owners in these groups coincides with the percent in the excellent, good, fair, and poor categories from earlier interviews.
11. Note that the hedonic regressions that give rise to these indices do not include the same independent variables, since the occupant characteristics are not included as regressors for index (10). But when these variables are added, the resulting index is still very different from index (2).

References

Case, B., H.O. Pollakowski, and S.M. Wachter. "On Choosing Among House Price Index Methodologies," *American Real Estate and Urban Economics Association Journal* 19 (1991), 286–307.
Case, Schiller, and Weiss. Private correspondence (January 1995).
Clapp, J.M., and C. Giaccotto. "Estimating Prices Indices for Residential Property: A Comparison of Repeat Sales and Assessed Value Methods," *Journal of the American Statistical Association* 87 (1992), 300–306.
Follain, J.R., and S. Malpezzi. "Are Occupants Accurate Appraisers?" *Review of Public Data Use* 9 (1981), 47–55.
Goodman, J.L., and J.B. Ittner. "The Accuracy of Home Owners' Estimates of House Value," *Journal of Housing Economics* 2 (1992), 339–357.
Haurin, D.R., P.H. Hendershott, and D. Kim. "Local House Price Indexes: 1982–1991," *American Real Estate and Urban Economics Association Journal* 19 (1991), 451–472.
Heckman, J.J. "Dummy Endogenous Variables in a Simultaneous Equation System," *Econometrica* 46 (1978), 931–959.
Ihlanfeldt, K.R., and J. Martinez-Vazquez. "Alternative Value Estimate of Owner-Occupied Housing: Evidence on Sample Selection Bias and Systematic Errors," *Journal of Urban Economics* 20 (1986), 356–369.
Jud, G.D., and T.G. Seaks. "Sample Selection Bias in Estimating Housing Sales Prices," *Journal of Real Estate Research* 9 (1994), 289–298.
Kain, J.F., and J.M. Quigley. "Note on Owner's Estimate of Housing Value," *Journal of the American Statistical Association* 67 (1972), 803–806.
Kiel, K.A. "The Impact of House Price Appreciation on Household Mobility," *Journal of Housing Economics* 3 (1994), 92–108.

Kiel, K.A., and R.T. Carson. "An Examination of Systematic Differences in the Appreciation of Individual Housing Units," *Journal of Real Estate Research* 5 (1990), 301–318.

Kiel, K.A., and J.E. Zabel. "The Accuracy of Owner Provided House Values: The 1978–1991 American Housing Survey," Tufts University Working Paper 95-07, 1995a.

Kiel, K.A., and J.E. Zabel. "House Price Differentials in U.S. Cities: Household and Neighborhood Racial Effects," *Journal of Housing Economics* 5 (1995b), 143–165.

Kish, L., and J.B. Lansing. "Response Errors in Estimating the Value of Homes," *Journal of the American Statistical Association* 49 (1954), 520–538.

National Association of Realtors. *Existing Home Sales*, various issues.

Ohta, M., and Z. Griliches. "Automobile Prices Revisited: Extensions of the Hedonic Hypothesis." in Nestor E. Terleckyj (ed.), *Household Production and Consumption*. New York: National Bureau of Economic Research, 1975.

Palmquist, R.B. "Measuring Environmental Effects on Property Values Without Hedonic Regressions," *Journal of Urban Economics* 11 (1982), 333–347.

Robins, P.K., and R.W. West. "Measurement Errors in the Estimation of Home Value," *Journal of the American Statistical Association* 72 (1977), 290–294.

Thibodeau, T.G. "Housing Price Indexes from the 1974–83 SMSA Annual Housing Surveys," *Journal of the American Real Estate and Urban Economics Association* 17 (1989), 100–117.

Thibodeau, T.G. *Residential Real Estate Prices from the 1974–1983 Standard Metropolitan Statistical Area American Housing Survey*. Blackstone Books: Studies in Urban and Resource Economic, 1992.

Journal of Real Estate Finance and Economics, 14: 203–222 (1997)
©1997 Kluwer Academic Publishers

Spatial Dependence and House Price Index Construction

AYŞE CAN
Fannie Mae

ISAAC MEGBOLUGBE
Fannie Mae

Abstract

Accurate estimation of prevailing metropolitan housing prices is important for both business and research investigations of housing and mortgage markets. This is typically done by constructing quality-adjusted house price
indices from hedonic price regressions for given metropolitan areas. A major limitation of currently available
indices is their insensitivity to the geographic location of dwellings within the metropolitan area. Indices are constructed based on models that do not incorporate the underlying spatial structure in housing data sets. In this article,
we argue that spatial structure, especially spatial dependence latent in housing data sets, will affect the precision
and accuracy of resulting price estimates. We illustrate the importance of spatial dependence in both the specification and estimation of hedonic price models. Assessments are made on the importance of spatial dependence both
on parameter estimates and on the accuracy of resulting indices.

Key Words: spatial dependence, house price index, hedonic house price model, locational effects, GIS

1. Introduction

House price indices are a major input in the investigation of housing and mortgage markets
for both research and business reasons. They constitute a critical input for the measurement
of housing demand; comparative analysis of price trends locally, regionally, and nationally;
the evaluation of residential real estate investment decisions; assessment of new mortgage
products as well as risk/default assessment of existing ones; and formulation and design of
housing/mortgage policies, programs, and products. Therefore, accurate and precise indices
are highly sought after for their utility in research and business applications.

There is consensus in the literature that an econometric approach based on the hedonic
price regression is the most suitable one for constructing cross-sectional quality-adjusted
house price indices. This involves first the specification of a house price function which
relates observed housing expenditures to selected structural and/or neighborhood characteristics that are considered to influence house prices. The second stage applies the estimated
coefficients to a standard housing bundle to construct indices.

The accuracy and the precision of the indices will be affected by a number of factors,
including the selection of characteristics, the functional form of the hedonic function, behavioral assumptions both on the parameter vectors and on the random error terms, and
the econometric procedures used to estimate parameters. In this investigation, we focus on
spatial dependence in constructing house price indices. Building on earlier works by Can
(1990, 1992), we offer a new strategy to incorporate functional interdependence into spatial hedonic models. This strategy explicitly acknowledges the presence of spatial spillover

effects in the house price determination process and is an extension of the well-known "comparable-sales" method in the residential real estate appraisal industry. Upon the estimation of selected hedonic price models, we empirically validate the models. This is done by cross-validation of the predictive performance of each model. Indices constructed via the spatial hedonic models which we develop are shown to be more precise and accurate, based on our assessment of their out-of-sample predictive performance. An additional benefit of our models is their suitability for constructing reliable house price indices with a limited number of structural attributes, a commonly encountered limitation in very large commercially available transactions-based databases.

The data set used in the estimation of the hedonic models consists of single-family housing transactions for Dade County (FL) during 1990. Data processing and model estimation is facilitated by the use of Arc/Info, a vector-based Geographic Information Systems (GIS) software. As such, this investigation demonstrates the benefits associated with the use of GIS technology in housing research.

In section 2, we present the relevance of spatial dependence in house price index construction both from a substantive and methodological stance. We explore the relationship between locational effects, economic value of a property, and spatial dependence. Section 3 presents the alternative models employed, based on three major specifications of the hedonic price function, namely, a traditional hedonic and two spatial hedonic specifications. Section 4 presents the sample and the functional forms used in estimation. Section 5 presents the parameter estimates and provides a comparative assessment of the prediction performance and accuracy of the resulting indices. We conclude in section 6 with implications for future directions.

2. Spatial Dependence and Hedonic House Price Index Construction

The first step in the construction of house price indices involves the estimation of a hedonic price function that functionally relates a selected measure of housing value, e.g., transaction price or owner's estimate, to a set of attributes that are considered to have influenced the observed housing value. The general form of a hedonic house price function can be represented as:

$$P = f(S\beta, N\gamma) + \epsilon, \tag{1}$$

where P is a vector of observed housing values; S is a matrix of structural attributes containing variables such as the age and size of the house; N is a matrix of neighborhood characteristics including measures of socioeconomic conditions for area residents, environmental amenities, and public service provisions; β and γ are the parameter vectors corresponding to S and N, respectively; and ϵ is a vector of random-error terms. Upon the selection of an empirical functional form and its estimation, the second stage involves the application of the estimated coefficients to a standard housing bundle to construct indices.

As with any other econometric approach, the accuracy and the precision of the indices constructed will therefore be affected by the selection of characteristics vectors (S and N), the functional form (f), and the behavioral assumptions both on the parameter vectors (β

and γ) and on the random-error terms (ϵ). For example, most studies assume linearity in the functional form and assume that parameter vectors, β and γ, are stable ("fixed") in space and/or time. The vector of error terms are commonly assumed to be independent with covariance $\sigma(\epsilon_i, \epsilon_j) = 0$ and homoskedastic ($\sigma^2(\epsilon_i) = \sigma^2$).[1]

Given the geographic nature of the data sets used in estimating house price models, it is not unusual to anticipate that the error covariance, $\sigma(\epsilon_i, \epsilon_j)$, is not equal to zero but may be a function of spatial proximity among houses. This phenomenon is referred to as spatial dependence or spatial autocorrelation.[2] Although, in theory, under a purely competitive market system, one could assume that the error terms are randomly distributed representing random market imperfections (e.g., limited information or random shocks in interest rates), in empirical investigations, this assumption may be difficult to satisfy in light of conspicuous similarity in house prices in geographic space. In an empirical context, the assumption of uncorrelated random-error terms can only be made if the hedonic price function (1) is properly specified in terms of incorporating complex dynamics in the operation of local housing markets.

In this investigation, we focus on the role which spatial dependence plays in the specification and estimation of the hedonic price function within index construction. We are motivated by two concerns. The first one is substantive in nature and directly corresponds with the notion of spatial externalities or locational effects in the operation of urban housing markets. The second motivation is methodological and captures spatial dependence that may arise in the estimation of econometric models resulting from model misspecification. As houses that are close in geographic space will also have similar attributes, omitted and/or incorrectly measured variables will lead to error dependence (or autocorrelation).[3]

Both forms of spatial dependence will affect the statistical validity of results, since their presence will lead to biased estimates of the residual variance and inefficient estimates of the regression coefficients when OLS is used. Spatial dependence in residuals will therefore make standard inferential tests, such as the t- and F-tests, invalid and lead to unreliable estimates of the dependent variable, due to inflated variances in the regression coefficients. All of these will affect the precision and accuracy of house price indices constructed using models that suffer from spatial dependence. Thus, it is very important to test for the presence of spatial autocorrelation in geographic modeling and to take appropriate measures in both model specification and estimation.

2.1. Locational Effects and Property Value

The economic value of housing will be very much affected by its geographic location because of two attributes: durability and fixed position in space. Because the housing structure is fixed in its geographic location and alterations are costly, locational effects or spatial externalities are an integral component of the way in which housing markets function, both at the individual and aggregate level. In addition to the structural attributes of housing units, locational characteristics enter into individual housing demand/supply decisions and the resulting market-level behavior from these interactions.

Locational effects can be defined as all attributes that are associated with the geographic location of a house, both its absolute location and the neighborhood in which it is located.

Can (1992) distinguished between two levels of locational effects: (1) *adjacency effects,* which are externalities associated with the absolute location of the structure and (2) *neighborhood effects,* which are the array of locational characteristics (neighbors, accessibility, public service provision) that will lead to differential household housing demand for certain locations. Neighborhood effects can be capitalized into housing prices directly as a "premium" or can lead to varying marginal attribute prices, depending on neighborhood context. Can (1990) formally represented the latter using a spatially varying parameter specification of the hedonic price function via Casetti's (1972) "expansion method."

Although neighborhood effects are well-recognized and incorporated into the hedonic price models, adjacency effects are largely ignored in the traditional hedonic house price literature. Our present investigation extends the spatial hedonic models advanced in Can (1990 and 1992) and focuses specifically on the specifications of adjacency effects in hedonic house price models. Adjacency effects are spatial spillover effects that capitalize into house prices, such as maintenance/repair decisions of neighbors affecting the market value of a given house or the fact that premium households are willing to pay just for the "snob" value of a particular location, i.e., price differentials that cannot be justified only on the basis of housing services. Adjacency effects, therefore, refer to functional interdependence or spatial dependence in the house price determination process and need to be formally represented in hedonic house price models.

The strategy which we develop to incorporate spatial dependence closely resembles the practice of the "comparable-sales" approach employed in residential real estate appraisals. The comparable-sales approach is widely used by realtors, assessors, appraisers, and even sellers and buyers in estimating property value and is based on the notion that the price history in the immediate neighborhood of a given property will have spillover effects on its market value. Typically, the prices of between three to six most recently sold "comparable" properties are considered in estimating the market value of a property, controlling for differences in their structural attributes and neighborhood characteristics. Although the comparable-sales approach is a widely employed practice, it has not yet been incorporated into hedonic price models used in index construction.

3. Alternative Hedonic House Price Models

Based on considerations presented in the previous section, we employ three alternative specifications of the hedonic price function (1) which are subsequently used in index construction.

(1) Traditional hedonic specification.   This is the most typical specification employed in house price index construction. Variations in house prices are explained in terms of differences in their structural characteristics (S) for $k = 1, \ldots, K$ and/or neighborhood characteristics (N) for $1 = 1, \ldots, L$.

$$P = \alpha + \Sigma_k \beta_k S_k + \epsilon \tag{2}$$

$$P = \alpha + \Sigma_k \beta_k S_k + \Sigma_l \gamma_1 N_1 + \epsilon. \tag{3}$$

The error term, ϵ, in (2) and (3) has two components: The first component is error resulting from misspecification of the functional relationship or from measurement errors such as missing variables, an incorrect functional form, and inadequate sampling. The second component is "transaction error" which represents the difference between transaction price and the "expected" market price relative to other houses in the market. Thus, a negative error, from the perspective of the buyer, is a "good deal" (a bargain), whereas a positive error is a "bad deal" (a loss) (Linneman, 1986).

In an empirical context, these two components of the random-error term cannot be distinguished and will be present in model estimation. Interest in the correct identification of transaction errors in local markets emphasizes the need for a correct specification of the hedonic price function. As argued in Can (1990 and 1992), there is a need to explicitly incorporate adjacency or spatial spillover effects into hedonic price models to more accurately represent the local housing market dynamics. This is adopted in Model 2.

(2) Spatial hedonic specification. The transaction price of a house at any given point in time t will be determined not only by its structural attributes and the desirability of the neighborhood but also will be subject to absolute price effects from prior sales within its vicinity. Thus, there will be a functional interdependence between the transaction price of a given house at time t and the prior sales prices within its immediate neighborhood. These price effects are indeed recognized and injected by the participants in the residential real estate industry via a practice known as "comparable-sales" to more accurately estimate property market value.

We formally introduce this functional interdependence, using a spatially autoregressive term into (3), as follows:

$$P_{it} = \alpha + \rho \Sigma_j w_{ij} P_{j,t-m} + \Sigma_k \beta_k S_{ik} + \Sigma_l \gamma_l N_{ilt} + \epsilon_{it}, \quad m = 1, 2, \ldots; j \neq i, \quad (4)$$

where P_{it} is the transaction price for a given house i at time t and w_{ij} is a measure (or weight) that specifies the extent of influence which a prior sale P_j (that occurred between $t - m$ and t) has on P_{it}; and ρ is a measure of overall level of spatial dependence among $\{P_i P_{j,t-m}\}$ pairs for which $w_{ij} > 0$. Thus, once (4) is estimated, the coefficient of ρ will give us a measure of absolute price effects on present sales of prior transactions.

The spatial hedonic model which we introduced in (4) formally incorporates both temporal and spatial functional dependencies between the present transaction price, P_{it}, and the prior sales. The most critical element in this specification is the definition of w_{ij}, as its value will determine which j's are considered "neighbors" in time and space, as well as the extent of their influence on the transaction price for i. In accordance with general spatial interaction theories, we hypothesize that the extent of influence on a given sale of prior sales will be an inverse function of distance (d_{ij}), in that the closer sales will have a larger influence. Based on this definition of w_{ij} and substantive concerns expressed in section 2, we use two specifications for the spatially lagged price variable, $\Sigma_j w_{ij} P_{j,t-m}$, which are two variations of the comparable sales approach. In both of these, we limit the time period to the past six months and set t to 1 month. In the first specification, we include all prior sales that occurred within a 3km (about 1.8 mile) radius of a current transaction within the prior six months. The distance cutoff is based on exploratory work of the spatial structure of Miami, MSA, which illustrated that localized spatial dependencies are concentrated within a two-mile radius. The first spatially lagged price variable, LAG_D_3, is constructed as follows:

$$\text{LAG\_D\_3} = \Sigma_j[(1/d_{ij})/\Sigma_j 1/d_{ij}]P_{j,t-m},$$
$$m = 1, \dots, 6; j = 1, 2, 3, \dots, N; d_{ij} \leq 3\text{km} \tag{5}$$

Our second specification includes only the three closest prior sales for any transaction. The resulting spatially lagged price variable, LAG_NGH, is as follows:[4]

$$\text{LAG\_NGH} = \Sigma_j[(1/d_{ij})/\Sigma_j 1/d_{ij}]P_{j,t-m}, \quad m = 1, \dots, 6; j = 1, 2, 3 \tag{6}$$

As depicted in Figure 1, these spatially lagged price variables, LAG_D_3 and LAG_NGH, can be interpreted as spatially weighted averages of the prior transactions prices. For example, the construction of LAG_D_3 for a selected transaction (shown as triangle) would be based on a spatial search within a 3km radius of all prior transactions (Figure 1A). Computationally, the construction of LAG_NGH involves a less time-consuming spatial search, as it only uses three prior sales. The comparison of transaction prices against the values of these spatially lagged variables can also aid in error checking and data cleaning. As can be seen in Figure 1B, a transaction with over a million dollars is surrounded by neighbors with the price range $19K to $31K, as computed by LAG_NGH and LAG_D_3. Although it is not unlikely to find a transaction price of this type for the study area, it is quite unlikely to find it located within close spatial proximity to low-priced housing. This indicates an error in data collection and/or recording. Therefore, the construction of these lagged sales values is very helpful in examining these cases. In our data preparation stage, we have identified

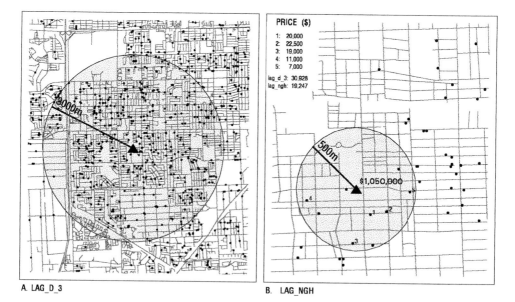

A. LAG_D_3   B. LAG_NGH

Figure 1.

spatial outliers, using a 500m radius in our geoprocessing for purposes of error checking and data cleaning.

In addition to capturing spatial and temporal dependencies in the house price determination process, the inclusion of these spatially lagged price variables brings another advantage in the estimation stage. One frequently mentioned source of bias in estimation is the potential systematic variation in the estimated standard deviation of the random-error term, ϵ, on the basis of frequency of transactions in different market periods (e.g., Gatzlaff and Ling, 1994). As the amount of information on the functioning of the market will increase with the volume of transactions, it is expected that the transaction prices will be closer to their expected levels on the basis of their differentiated attributes. Since the weights which we use in the construction of LAG_D_3 in our spatial hedonic model are the distances between a given transaction and its comparables, we explicitly incorporate fluctuations in transaction frequencies into our model specification and thus expect more reliable coefficient estimates.

(3) Spatial expansion hedonic specification. This specification differs from the spatial hedonic specification introduced in terms of its conceptualization of how neighborhood effects are capitalized into house prices. In contrast to (4) (and (3)), which hypothesize that neighborhood characteristics enter as direct determinants of house prices, we can also consider the case in which neighborhood effects might lead to spatially varying marginal attribute prices. This conceptualization built upon the modeling strategy advanced by Casetti (1972, 1986) can be formally represented as follows:

$$P_{it} = \alpha + \rho\Sigma_j w_{ij} P_{j,t-m} + \Sigma_k\Sigma_1(\beta_{0k1} + \beta_{lk}N_{ilt})S_{ik} \quad (7)$$
$$+ \Sigma_1\gamma_1 N_{ilt} + \epsilon_{it}, m = 1, 2, \ldots; j \neq i$$

This specification postulates that the coefficient vector, β, associated with the structural attributes contained in S may not be "fixed" across geographic space but may vary ("drift"), depending on neighborhood context (for a detailed discussion, see Can, 1990).

4. Sample and Variables

The data set used in estimating the hedonic models consists of 944 housing transactions that occurred in Miami, MSA (Dade county, Florida) during the third quarter of 1990. This is a 25% random sample of 3,776 third-quarter, single-family housing transactions obtained from TRW. The price range of houses in the sample is confined between $30,000 and $300,000. Spatially lagged price variables, i.e., LAG_NGH and LAG_D_3, are constructed (prior to sampling) for each transaction in the third quarter, using the first- and second-quarter sales. Figure 2 depicts the spatial distribution of housing transactions both during the third quarter of 1990 for the study area (left) and those retained in the sample (right).[5] These maps also depict the 1990 Census block group boundaries for Dade county. The inset in Figure 2 shows the distribution of housing activity by month of sale. Out of 4,266 transactions originally contained in the TRW data set, we were able to retain 3,776 transactions with reliable information.

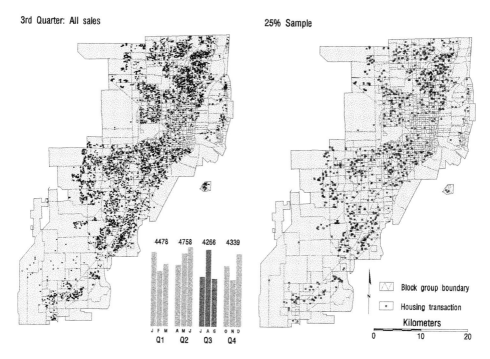

Figure 2.

The presence of very strong spatial dependence in transaction prices is clearly visible in Figure 3, which provides the scatterplots of transaction prices against LAG_D_3 and LAG_NHG, for all sales in the third quarter. These graphs reveal that LAG_D_3 better captures the spatial dependence in the system, as it is less sensitive to the frequency

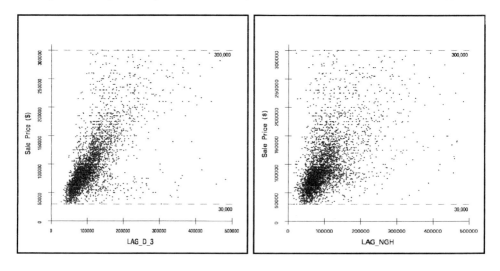

Figure 3.

of transactions, and it exhibits a more linear relationship. As indicated by the squared correlation between P and LAG_D_3, we can explain 42% of price variations for the third-
quarter sales by simply looking at the average sales prices within a 3km radius within the
last six months, without any information on the structural and neighborhood characteristics.
These graphs are very helpful in visually identifying spatial outliers, e.g., $(P_i, \text{LAG\_NGH}_i)$
or $(P_i, \text{LAG\_D\_3}_i)$ pairs that are further away from the linear trend. Figure 3 also shows that
LAG_D_3 retains the linear relationship at higher transaction price than LAG_NGH. These
observations lead us to consider that LAG_D_3 more closely mirrors the segregated housing
landscape in Miami.

Although the database is quite comprehensive in terms of the housing transactions (it
includes all sales obtained from local sales files as a part of closures), it is quite limited
in terms of the structural attributes of the houses. Only six structural attributes were reli-
ably available from the TRW data set, namely, the number of full bathrooms, the number
of bedrooms, the total living area, the building area, the land area, and the age of the structure. Based on extensive exploratory analyses, we have included three variables, namely,
total living area (LIVAREA), land area (LANDSQFT), and housing age (H_AGE), in the
estimation of our models as measures of structural attributes. Summary statistics on these
variables are included in Table 1A.

Each house is also assigned values of the selected neighborhood-level variables at the
block group level from the 1990 Census of Population and Housing (US Census, 1990).
Table 1B displays descriptive statistics for the neighborhood-level variables. Although
there is interest in singling out the individual contribution to house price variations from,
e.g., income or race variables, especially in light of the highly segregated spatial structure
of the Miami, MSA, we unfortunately found high multicollinearity among the selected
socioeconomic and demographic variables. These variables included owner-occupancy rate
(OWNRATE); median household income (INCOME); percentage of residents with college
education (EDU); percentage of households paying at least 30% of income on monthly housing costs (MORT30UP); median value of owner-occupied housing (VALUE); vacancy rate
(VACANT); median age of housing stock (AGE); percentage of detached single-family
units (DETACH); and percentage of white-headed (WHITE), black-headed (BLACK),
and hispanic-headed (HISPANIC) households. Therefore, we constructed a composite

Table 1a. Descriptive statistics on variables used in estimation.

PRICE:	transaction price
LIVAREA:	living area in square feet
LANDSQFT:	land area in square feet
H_AGE:	age of the structure
FACTOR1:	composite neighborhood quality score

Variable	Mean	St. Dev.	Min	Max	Range
PRICE	97023.51	48518.72	30000	280000	250000
LIVAREA	1678.314	576.006	806	4409	3603
LANDSQFT	12293.53	11060.47	2050	102090	100040
H_AGE	26.70127	16.07575	0	81	81
FACTOR1	0.4787129	0.6559713	-1.859944	3.100973	4.960917

Table 1b. Descriptive statistics on block group variables used in composite index construction.

	Ownrate	Income	Mort30up	Value
Mean	55.9279578	29367.5849	18.9606383	91847.4294
Std Dev	30.4533426	21187.2932	13.357686	77672.5804
	Vacant	Detach	White	Hispanic
Mean	9.93660983	54.2479147	67.7974919	41.4994444
Std Dev	17.90376	35.2317461	35.3863729	33.2009413
	Black	Edu	Age	
Mean	25.194636	27.5515072	72.7242366	
Std Dev	35.1071619	17.3407699	293.812452	

Correlations

	Ownrate	Income	Mort30up	Value	Vacant	Detach
Ownrate	1.00000	0.65364	0.36632	0.42075	-0.22724	0.85772
Income	0.65364	1.00000	0.14443	0.79025	-0.08991	0.55314
Mort30up	0.36632	0.14443	1.00000	0.15225	-0.25293	0.44801
Value	0.42075	0.79025	0.15225	1.00000	-0.04401	0.30670
Vacant	-0.22724	-0.08991	-0.25293	-0.04401	1.00000	-0.32062
Detach	0.85772	0.55314	0.44801	0.30670	-0.32062	1.00000
White	0.32925	0.41258	0.04147	0.44500	-0.04066	0.13668
Hispanic	-0.08733	-0.12949	0.06525	-0.04746	-0.17964	-0.09919
Black	-0.18654	-0.30052	0.05041	-0.35308	0.08660	-0.01441
Edu	0.45103	0.69667	0.02076	0.66085	0.06615	0.25433
Age	-0.27964	-0.21359	-0.21550	-0.18254	-0.08909	-0.22749

	White	Hispanic	Black	Edu	Age
Ownrate	0.32925	-0.08733	-0.18654	0.45103	-0.27964
Income	0.41258	-0.12949	-0.30052	0.69667	-0.21359
Mort30up	0.04147	0.06525	0.05041	0.02076	-0.21550
Value	0.44500	-0.04746	-0.35308	0.66085	-0.18254
Vacant	-0.04066	-0.17964	0.08660	0.06615	-0.08909
Detach	0.13668	-0.09919	-0.01441	0.25433	-0.22749
White	1.00000	0.56429	-0.90684	0.56553	-0.29582
Hispanic	0.56429	1.00000	-0.55713	-0.15273	-0.19183
Black	-0.90684	-0.55713	1.00000	-0.45411	-0.10678
Edu	0.56553	-0.15273	-0.45411	1.00000	-0.21399
Age	-0.29582	-0.19183	-0.10678	-0.21399	1.00000

neighborhood score (FACTOR1) using principle component analysis, which measures the socioeconomic composition of block groups.[6] Table 1B presents summary statistics on the locational variables used in the construction of FACTOR1.

We used a total of six equations corresponding to the three alternative hedonic price functions specified in section 3:

MODEL 1: traditional hedonic (1)

$$P = \alpha + \beta_1\text{LIVAREA} + \beta_2\text{LANDSQFT} - \beta_3\text{H\_AGE} + \beta_4\text{SQ\_AGE} + \epsilon \qquad (8)$$

MODEL 2: traditional hedonic (9)

$$P = \alpha + \beta_1 \text{LIVAREA} + \beta_2 \text{LANDSQFT} - \beta_3 \text{H\_AGE} + \beta_4 \text{SQ\_AGE} \\ + \beta_5 \text{FACTOR1} + \epsilon \tag{9}$$

MODEL 3: spatial hedonic with LAG_D_3

$$P = \alpha + \beta_1 \text{LAG\_D\_3} + \beta_2 \text{LIVAREA} + \beta_3 \text{LANDSQFT} - \beta_4 \text{H\_AGE} \\ + \beta_5 \text{SQ\_AGE} + \beta_6 \text{FACTOR1} + \epsilon \tag{10}$$

MODEL 4: spatial hedonic with LAG_NGH

$$P = \alpha + \beta_1 \text{LAG\_NGH} + \beta_2 \text{LIVAREA} + \beta_3 \text{LANDSQFT} - \beta_4 \text{H\_AGE} \\ + \beta_5 \text{SQ\_AGE} + \beta_6 \text{FACTOR1} + \epsilon \tag{11}$$

MODEL 5: spatial expansion with LAG_D_3

$$P = \alpha + \beta_1 \text{LAG\_D\_3} + \beta_2 \text{LANDSQFT} + \beta_3 \text{LIVAREA} + \beta_4 \text{LIV\_F} \\ + -\beta_5 \text{H\_AGE} + \beta_6 \text{SQ\_AGE} + \beta_7 \text{SQ\_AGE\_F} + \epsilon \tag{12}$$

MODEL 6: spatial expansion with LAG_NGH

$$P = \alpha + \beta_1 \text{LAG\_NGH} + \beta_2 \text{LANDSQFT} + \beta_3 \text{LIVAREA} + \beta_4 \text{LIV\_F} \\ + -\beta_5 \text{H\_AGE} + \beta_6 \text{SQ\_AGE} + \beta_7 \text{SQ\_AGE\_F} + \epsilon \tag{13}$$

Based on our preliminary findings, we included the square of housing age in these equations. This term will capture the nonlinearity generally assumed in housing depreciation (Goodman and Thibodeau, 1995). This term will diminish/increase the marginal price effects of older structures.

In the spatial expansion models, we expressed the coefficients for LIVAREA and SQ_AGE only as a function of the neighborhood composite score, FACTOR1, denoted as LIV_F ($=$LIVAREA*FACTOR1) and SQ_AGE_F ($=$SQ_AGE*FACTOR1). Unlike other economic goods, aging or housing size may increase or decrease its value depending on location. For example, an older house in a transitional neighborhood would be less valuable than an older house in a neighborhood that is undergoing gentrification. The effect of aging cannot be isolated from household maintenance/repair decisions, which are not solely determined by household income levels but by households' perceptions concerning the future value of their housing, which is primarily determined by "signals" that they receive from their immediate neighborhood. Similarly, price effects of housing size depend on the location of the house. The addition of extra living space in a low-income neighborhood will not affect the price as in a high-income area.

4. Results

4.1. Comparison of Parameter Estimates and Model Performance

Parameter estimates are presented in Table 2 for the traditional hedonic models; in Table 3, for the spatial hedonic models; and in Table 4, for the spatial hedonic expansion models. For each model, coefficient estimates and their standard errors based on OLS and adjusted-White covariance estimates are reported.[7] Adjusted-White covariance estimates are heteroskedasticity-robust, and therefore offer a more realistic significance assessment of parameter estimates under heteroskedasticity. The relatively higher adjusted-White standard errors are indicative of variance heterogeneity, which is anticipated in the context of hedonic price regression, given the segmented nature of housing markets.

It is observed that coefficient estimates are highly significant, except for the coefficient of LANDSQFT, based on adjusted-White p-levels. Models also achieve very reasonable estimates of marginal prices for selected attributes. For example, the coefficient estimates for living area range between $45 and $60 per square foot. An increase of 500 square feet

Table 2. Parameter estimates for traditional hedonic models.

Model 1:		OLS	Adjusted-White	
Variable	Coeff	S.D.	S.D.	Prob
CONSTANT	-13487	4487.49	4860.99	0.005528
LIVAREA	64.5256	1.87848	2.60455	0.0000000
LANDSQFT	0.0179172	0.0946392	0.0868791	0.836610
H_AGE	-531.292	185.62	206.889	0.010229
SQ_AGE	16.6588	3.30969	4.42963	0.000169

Adj. R^2 = 0.5715
$\sqrt{MSE}$ = 31776.9
[Robust LM(error)] = 8.5119
P-value = 0.00353

Model 2:		OLS	Adjusted-White	
Variable	Coeff	S.D.	S.D.	Prob
CONSTANT	1848.61	3840.21	4306.89	0.667762
LIVAREA	46.8232	1.80786	2.61938	0.000000
LANDSQFT	0.0685013	0.0793889	0.0642783	0.286560
H_AGE	-451.995	155.68	172.491	0.008783
SQ_AGE	13.6242	2.77911	3.4114	0.000065
FACTOR1	30463.6	1527.44	2252.33	0.000000

Adj. R^2 = 0.6988
$\sqrt{MSE}$ = 26642.7
[Robust LM(error)] = 9.154521
P-value = 0.00248

Table 3. Parameter estimates for spatial hedonic models.

Model 3:		OLS	Adjusted-White	
Variable	Coeff	S.D.	S.D.	Prob
CONSTANT	-9.222.5	3656.43	4837.71	0.056602
LAG_D_3	0.219438	0.0173271	0.0651029	0.000750
LIVAREA	41.8574	1.7168	2.93067	0.000000
LANDSQFT	0.0655937	0.0733978	0.0622124	0.291722
H_AGE	-297.17	144.449	170.868	0.082003
SQ_AGE	9.49218	2.59	3.49036	0.006537
FACTOR1	21145.1	1592.36	3191.64	0.000000

Adj. R^2 = 0.7425
$\sqrt{MSE}$ = 24632.0
[Robust LM(error)] = 6.8801
P-value = 0.0087

Model 4:		OLS	Adjusted-White	
Variable	Coeff	S.D.	S.D.	Prob
CONSTANT	-3400.74	3853.16	4456.22	0.445378
LAG_NGH	0.0739467	0.0116894	0.0207553	0.000367
LIVAREA	45.92	1.77714	2.63802	0.000000
LANDSQFT	0.0775668	0.0778007	0.0602518	0.197963
H_AGE	-393.554	152.819	174.171	0.023847
SQ_AGE	12.1855	2.73253	3.41992	0.000366
FACTOR1	27349.9	1575.5	2240.56	0.000000

Adj. R^2 = 0.7108
$\sqrt{MSE}$ = 26105.3
[Robust LM(error)] = 3.8961
P-value = 0.0484

would lead to an increase in house price of between $20,000 and $32,500, which is very reasonable.

These findings reveal that spatial dependence plays an important role in the house price determination process. The coefficients of LAG_D_3 and LAG_NGH are very stable across the spatial models. In addition, the standard error estimates of the coefficients estimates are relatively smaller in the spatial models, especially those that use LAG_D_3 as the spatially lagged variable. The coefficient estimate of LAG_D_3 is moderately strong, with 0.219 for Model 3 and 0.202 for Model 5. The coefficient of LAG_NGH, as anticipated, is not as strong, with 0.074 for Model 4 and 0.068 for Model 6. These values translate into about a $200 increase in the transaction price of a house from a $1,000 increase in the weighted-average price of its comparable sales (for LAG_D_3).

The most significant outcome on comparative performance is the marginal increase in percent of variance accounted when the spatially lagged variables are incorporated into the traditional hedonic model. As seen by increases in R^2, the contribution to Model 1 is 17.1%

Table 4. Parameter estimates for spatial expansion hedonic models.

Model 5:		OLS	Adjusted-White	
Variable	Coeff	S.D.	S.D.	Prob
CONSTANT	2718.55	3989.76	5548.83	0.624183
LAG_D_3	0.201667	0.017671	0.0633907	0.001466
LANDSQFT	0.0334981	0.0728869	0.0624477	0.591670
LIVAREA	36.5515	1.99421	3.2283	0.000000
LIV_F	9.58859	1.02733	2.20297	0.000013
H_AGE	-221.205	145.139	171.7	0.197634
SQ_AGE	5.7815	2.74177	3.09766	0.061984
SQ_AGE_F	3.416	0.928882	1.6694	0.040732

Adj. R^2 = 0.762
$\sqrt{MSE}$ = 24453.9
[Robust LM(error)] = 3.4302
P-value = 0.0640

Model 6:		OLS	Adjusted-White	
Variable	Coeff	S.D.	S.D.	Prob
CONSTANT	11225	4097.4	4562.63	0.013886
LAG_NGH	0.0682881	0.0115342	0.0200002	0.000639
LANDSQFT	0.0371137	0.0764051	0.0575947	0.519320
LIVAREA	38.6113	2.08289	3.18668	0.000000
LIV_F	12.057	1.04459	1.92576	0.000000
H_AGE	-276.074	152.019	179.062	0.123126
SQ_AGE	6.76179	2.8729	3.18717	0.033874
SQ_AGE_F	4.66876	0.965455	1.73131	0.007004

Adj. R^2 = 0.7214
$\sqrt{MSE}$ = 25624.5
[Robust LM(error)] = 0.8479
P-value = 0.3571

by Model 3, 13.93% by Model 4, 17.47% by Model 5, and 14.99% by Model 6. As with any econometric specification, Models 1 and 2 may suffer from misspecification due to the limited number of structural housing attributes.[8] The major focus of this investigation is not to search for a comprehensive explanatory model of house price determination, but rather to demonstrate the contribution of spatially referenced variables. Since both traditional and spatial hedonic models use the same set of structural attributes, we can attribute the improvements in model performance to the presence of spatially lagged prices in Models 3–6. It should also be noted that, since the omitted structural variables will be likely to be auto-correlated in space, their price effect will be partially captured through the spatially lagged price variables in the spatial models. This is definitely an added advantage to using spatially referenced price variables.

Even with a spatially autoregressive structure, in hedonic price models, there is still the possibility of an incomplete specification of the hedonic price models which may be reflected as residual autocorrelation. Our visual examination of the geographic distribution of standardized residuals revealed that there is less concentration of residuals with very high positive and negative values for the spatial models. In addition, we observed that the distribution of residuals is much less clustered for the spatial models. These visual observations are quantified by conducting a formal diagnostic test, LM (error), for residual autocorrelation. This test is robust to local misspecification of spatial dependence (Anselin et al., 1995). As indicated by the results of this statistic in Tables 2–4, the extent of remaining spatial dependence in the form of residual autocorrelation is relatively insignificant.

4.2. Predictive Performance of Alternative Hedonic Models

Using the estimated coefficients for the structural attributes, we computed the expected market value for a house with "typical" characteristics (living area 1,678.314 square feet, land area 12,293.53 square feet, and housing age 26.7 years). Table 5 provides the resulting predicted prices, using the beginning and ending quartile values of FACTOR1 (the composite neighborhood index). For models that use the spatially lagged dependent variable,

Table 5. Predicted house prices by location.

	Quartile 1		Quartile 2	
FACTOR1	-1.8599	0.0795	0.0795	0.4275
Model 1	92717	92717	92717	92717
Model 2	22258	81339	81339	91941
Model 3	37785	78793	83052	90411
Model 4	27262	80305	81970	91489
Model 5	43345	79278	83191	89640
Model 6	35029	80728	82266	90467
	Quartile 3		Quartile 4	
FACTOR1	0.4275	0.8991	0.8991	3.1010
Model 1	92717	92717	92717	92717
Model 2	91941	106308	106308	173385
Model 3	93278	103250	114052	160611
Model 4	92849	105747	108616	168837
Model 5	92275	101013	110940	151736
Model 6	91723	102836	105485	157370
	LAG_D_3	LAG_NGH		
Quartile 1	74953.43	72107.28		
Quartile 2	94359.38	94630.22		
Quartile 3	107425.7	113025.6		
Quartile 4	156650.1	151817.3		

the indices are constructed using its average value by quartile of FACTOR1. These values are listed in the bottom of Table 5.

In Figure 4, we graphically illustrate the resulting indices for Models 1, 2, 3, and 5. In this figure, the predicted prices are expressed as the ratio of predicted price by each model to the predicted price on the basis of the traditional hedonic model, which gives the average market value of $92,717. The value of the house price index for Model 1 is therefore $100(=\$92,717)$ and remains the same regardless of geographic location, as it does not contain FACTOR1 in its estimation. It is striking to see how the predicted price varies across neighborhood context. Model 3 and Model 5 exhibit larger price differentials by geographic location than the others.

It is desirable to test the predictive power of alternative hedonic price models using a different sample than that used for estimation. The predictive performance within the sample is not the same as out-of-sample performance. Although a high level of model performance

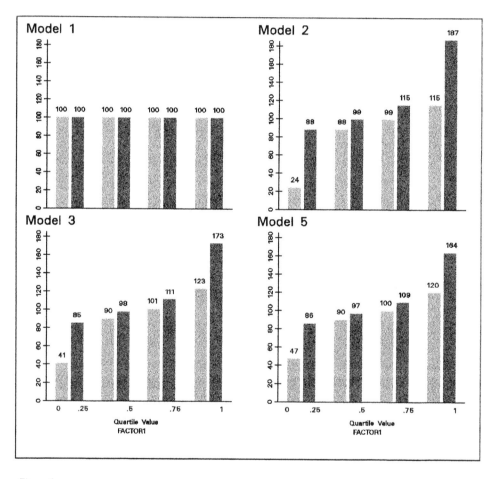

Figure 4.

Table 6. Predictive performance of alternative models.

	Mean	Std Dev	Minimum	Maximum	R^2_{pp}	$\sqrt{MSE}$
Price	98708	50373	30000	300000		
Predict1	99864	39779	37346	383057	0.5646	33311.461
Predict2	99076	41198	1261	385682	0.6489	29851.535
Predict3	99105	42318	13204	413247	0.6830	28367.408
Predict4	98875	43642	5498	517112	0.6128	31622.868
Predict5	98805	42600	24018	516977	0.6855	28261.929
Predict6	98481	43778	20196	515167	0.6279	28497.315

can be achieved as measured by R^2, this is not necessarily a good indicator of the model performance for forecasting purposes as R^2 measures in-sample error. Although we could use the remaining observations in the third quarter, we preferred to use the fourth-quarter sales in 1990 for cross-validation, in order to minimize the potential correlation between the error terms in the estimation and prediction equations.

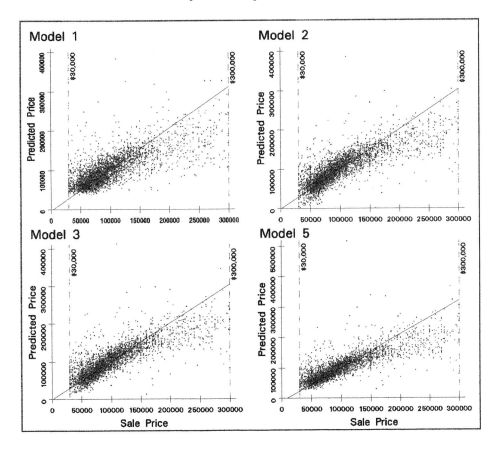

Figure 5.

As a quantitative measure of comparative predictive performance, we computed the average of the squared deviation between the predicted transaction price and the actual transaction price for the fourth quarter. Table 6 reports these, as well as the squared correlation between predicted and observed transaction prices. Although the differences across models are small, the best predictive power is achieved by Model 3 and Model 5, the spatial hedonic and spatial hedonic expansion models. These results are visually manifested in Figure 5, which displays the plots of predicted prices against the fourth-quarter sales prices.[9]

5. Conclusion

The reliability of house price indices is a direct function of the specification of the hedonic price model. In this article, we presented the importance of spatial dependence on the specification of a house price function due to the presence of spatial spillover effects in the operation of local housing markets. Spatial dependence is a local issue, and its extent will vary across metropolitan areas as well as over time. With the spatial models which we constructed, it would be possible to adjust the confidence intervals of the metropolitan-level indices to reflect the localized dependencies in the house price determination process. This can be done easily by taking periodic samples from commercial transactions databases, which are becoming increasingly accessible. With GIS technology and developments in digital communication, it would even be possible to interactively input the address for a property and get an accurate estimated market value.

This study represents an attempt to derive useful house price indices from large data sets containing only a limited number of variables. We have shown that it is possible to construct reasonable price indices on the basis of measurements on housing age, living space, and land area, by taking into account locational effects—both adjacency and neighborhood effects. Using the techniques outlined in this article, researchers can construct accurate predictive models, not by having meticulously detailed data sets, but by using the inherent power of GIS tools to analyze spatial dependence in large, readily available transactions data sets.

This study also offers a strategy for periodically updating appraised values in mortgage portfolios or local tax rolls. Current lending or taxation practices do not lend themselves to easy updating of property values and therefore place too much emphasis on the appraised value at the time of sale or refinancing. The strategy which we offer here can be used very easily to automate appraisal and will lead to more accurate estimates than the current practices offer.

Acknowledgments

We would like to acknowledge the valuable GIS research assistance provided by Song Wang of OHR. This research uses Arc/Info® and SpaceStat©. An earlier version of this article was presented at the 1995 Midyear AREUEA meetings in Washington, D.C. We would like to thank the anonymous referees and the editor for their constructive suggestions.

Notes

1. It should be noted that these assumptions are indirectly challenged by studies on market segmentation (e.g., Schnare and Struyk, 1975; Bajic, 1985; Michaels and Smith, 1990) that explore the appropriateness of a single hedonic price function. To the extent that error variance is correlated with this partitioning, the homoskedasticity assumption is challenged. A few recent studies have also addressed the extent to which the age of housing might lead to heteroskedastic error terms (e.g., Goodman and Thibodeau, 1995).
2. See Cliff and Ord (1973) for a seminal treatment of spatial autocorrelation in geographic research.
3. The issue of spatial error autocorrelation in the context of house price indices is addressed explicitly in Dubin (1988, 1992). For example, Dubin (1992) uses kriging, a method from geostatistics, in order to model error spatial dependence.
4. Although no initial distance threshold was placed on this specification, it was found that every sale in the sample had all its three prior sales within a 3km radius.
5. The geographic position of each transaction is obtained through the process known as geocoding, which assigns geographic coordinates to each address in the transactions database.
6. The selection of these variables is based on extensive preliminary analysis, using a larger pool of variables. FACTOR1 accounts for about 40% of total variation. FACTOR1 was singled out as the most significant contributor in our preliminary regression analyses, in which we employed all principal components with an eigenvalue greater than 1 (which altogether accounted for 81% of variation). We also found out that FACTOR1 gave better results than using various combinations of income, race, and education variables in our estimations.
7. As opposed to OLS-variance estimates, which are computed as $\text{var}(\beta) = (X'X)^{-1}.s^2$, adjusted-White covariance matrix is estimated as $\text{var}(\beta) = (X'X)^{-1}.X'E.X(X'X)^{-1}$, where E is a diagonal matrix of squared residuals (see Anselin, 1988).
8. We would like to thank an anonymous reviewer for bringing this issue to our attention.
9. The plots of transaction prices against predicted prices in Figure 5 suggest the possibility of nonlinearity. In addition to the linear functional form, we used the semi-log form and found no significant differences in results. For simplicity, we retain the results of the linear models.

References

Anselin, L. *Spatial Econometrics: Methods and Models*. Dordrecht: Kluwer Academic, 1988.

Anselin, L., A. Bera, R. Florax, and M. Yoon. "Simple Diagnostic Tests for Spatial Dependence." West Virginia University, Regional Research Institute, Research Paper 9503.

Bajic, V. "Housing-market Segmentation and Demand for Housing Attributes: Some Empirical Findings," *AREUEA Journal* 13(1) (1985), 58–71.

Can, A. "The Measurement of Neighborhood Dynamics in Urban House Prices," *Economic Geography* 66(3) (1990), 254–272.

Can, A. "Specification and Estimation of Hedonic Housing Price Models" *Regional Science and Urban Economics* 22 (1992), 453–474.

Casetti, E. "The Dual Expansions Method: An Application to Evaluating the Effects of Population Growth on Development" *IEEE Transactions on Systems, Man, Cybernetics* 16 (1986), 29–39.

Casetti, E. "Generating Models by the Expansion Method: Applications to Geographical Research," *Geographical Analysis* 4 (1972), 81–91.

Cliff, A., and J. Ord. *Spatial Autocorrelation*. London: Pion, 1973.

Dubin, R. "Estimation of Regression Coefficients in the Presence of Spatially Autocorrelated Error Terms," *Review of Economics and Statistics* 70 (1988), 466–474.

Dubin, R. "Spatial Autocorrelation and Neighborhood Quality" *Regional Science and Urban Economics* 22 (1992), 433–452.

Gatzlaff, D.H., and D.C. Ling. "Measuring Changes in Local House Prices: An Empirical Investigation of Alternative Methodologies" *Journal of Urban Economics* 35 (1994), 221–244.

Goodman, A.C., and T.G. Thibodeau. "Age-related heteroskedasticity in Hedonic House Price Equations," *Journal of Housing Research* 6 (1995), 25–42.

Linneman, P. "An Empirical Test of the Efficiency of the Housing Market," *Journal of Urban Economics* 20 (1986), 140–154.

Michaels, R.G., and V.K. Smith. "Market segmentation and Valuing Amenities with Hedonic Price Models: The case of Hazardous Waste Sites, *Journal of Urban Economics* 28 (1990), 223–242.

Schnare, A.B., and R.J. Struyk. "Segmentation in Urban Housing Markets," *Journal of Urban Economics* 3 (1976), 146–166.

U.S. Census. "Census of Population and Housing, 1990: Summary Tape File 3 Technical Documentation." Washington, DC: U.S. Census Bureau, 1990.

Journal of Real Estate Finance and Economics, 14: 223-233 (1997)

The Co-op Discount

ALLEN C. GOODMAN
Department of Economics, Wayne State University, Detroit, MI 48202

JOHN L. GOODMAN, JR.
National Multi Housing Council, Washington, D.C. 20036

Abstract

Cooperative and condominium housing differ in several ways that might be expected to influence their pricing. Most but not all of these differences argue for a higher valuation for condominiums. Hedonic equations estimated on a national sample indicate that the price differential on the average condo/co-op unit in 1987 was 12%. Condos maintain a price premium under a variety of specifications, although its magnitude depends on the bundle of attributes being priced.

Key Words: cooperative housing, condominium, house prices

Most owner-occupied housing in multiunit structures takes on one of two legal forms. One is condominium ownership, in which the occupant has title to a specific apartment and a part interest in common areas and facilities. The second form, cooperative, is a corporation that issues stock representing an ownership stake in the project and entitling occupancy of a specific dwelling. Initial share allocations are proportional to the size and amenities offered by the different units in the co-op project.[1]

Debt financing in condo projects occurs via mortgages on individual units. Co-ops use a "blanket" mortgage (also known as a master mortgage, a project mortgage, or an underlying loan) on the entire project, with the co-op corporation as the borrower. In addition, if the project has appreciated over time, resales of individual shares are often financed by "share loans" to the individual owners. These share loans are collateralized by the shares.

Some co-ops have limited equity status, a vehicle for promoting preservation of affordable housing. In a limited equity cooperative, the cooperative corporation, through its bylaws, places a limit on the return allowed when shares are sold, with the intent of keeping the unit in the affordable housing stock, regardless of current market values.

Condos and co-ops thus differ in ways that might result in different market valuations for physically and locationally comparable units. This article discusses those differences and estimates their market importance.

1. Evolution of the Markets for Condos and Co-ops

Cooperative housing in the U.S. dates back to the 1870s. Prior to the early 1960s, real estate laws were such that the cooperative form of ownership was the only practical way of allowing occupant-ownership of units in multifamily structures. Many co-ops went bankrupt during the depression of the 1930s, tarnishing the image of this type of housing. However, following World War II, the FHA introduced an insurance program for the "blanket" mortgages on cooperatives. This insurance program renewed lender confidence in co-ops, and it is estimated that half of all co-ops in 1970 had FHA insurance coverage of their mortgage.

Although there does not appear to have been any outright prohibition of condominium housing in 20th century U.S. markets, there was little development of this ownership form until the 1960s, when states began to enact enabling legislation. By 1967, all but one state had enacted condominium legislation. Condominium development expanded rapidly thereafter, especially during the 1970s, when the interaction of inflation and the tax code drove down the real cost of home ownership. Co-op growth lagged that of condos during this period, but accelerated during the 1980s, supported by new loan programs in the secondary mortgage market. Nonetheless, by 1991, condos outnumbered co-ops about six to one, with co-ops concentrated in the Northeast. Together, condos and co-ops account for about 5% of the nation's housing stock.

We argue later that several aspects of co-op ownership impose economic externalities on owner-occupants. By limiting these externalities, condominiums may offer advantages over cooperatives, and these advantages may cause condo demand to exceed co-op demand. In many jurisdictions, however, the regulations faced by developers seeking to convert an existing rental project were less onerous for co-op conversion than for condo conversion (HUD, 1980), and this supply cost advantage benefited the expansion of cooperatives.

Nowhere was this supply cost advantage of cooperatives more apparent than in New York. New York City and its surroundings have always had a disproportionate share of the nation's cooperative housing and today account for about one-third of the U.S. total. The expansion from World War II to 1970 seems driven largely by landlords' desires to avoid the city's rent-control constraints (Sahling and Stein, 1980). Even though New York State legislation in 1964 authorized condominiums, the tax-driven boom to owner occupancy in the 1970s in New York City was channeled mostly into cooperatives. Part of the reason for New York's continued emphasis on co-ops was the relative ease of conversion to cooperatives, combined with the absence of much developable residential land in the city. In addition, both consumers and lenders in New York were already familiar with the cooperative form, and the information costs and illiquidity encountered elsewhere were less a factor in New York.

Another factor favoring co-ops in New York was the state usury law that, until the early 1980s, permitted interest rates on co-op blanket loans to exceed those on condos by one percentage point. Finally, perhaps in New York more than elsewhere, there was demand for the exclusivity more readily available through cooperatives than condos. We expand on this point later.

2. Sources of Different Market Valuations for Co-ops and Condos

Co-ops and condos differ in several ways that would be expected to lead to different market valuations of physically and locationally comparable units. The first four of these characteristics tend to lower the value of co-ops relative to condos, although the fifth could add to the value of co-ops.

1. Risk sharing.   A co-op involves more financial risk sharing among owners than does a condo building. In a condo project, if an owner defaults on his/her mortgage, the lender forecloses on, and disposes of, that unit, with no direct financial consequences for owners of other units, although there may be indirect "neighborhood" consequences of having empty units nearby. A co-op share owner is subject to the same neighborhood consequences of a default, but also bears a direct financial risk. If a co-op share owner fails to make his/her scheduled payments on the project's blanket mortgage, the other shareholders must make up the shortfall, or risk throwing the loan, and the co-op corporation, into default.[2] This financial externality of co-ops gives condos, which minimize the common property elements, an advantage in "organizational efficiency" over co-ops (Hansman, 1991).

2. Financing.   Financing costs differ for owners of condos and co-ops. Blanket loans have recourse only to the co-op corporation, whereas condo mortgages, at least in theory, have recourse back to the individual borrower. Also, because co-ops are less common than condos in most local markets, the substantial economies of scale in mortgage lending suggest that co-op financing would be more expensive—as measured by either interest rate or fees— than condo loans. In addition, if only one or two lenders serve co-ops in some markets, the resulting market power could lead to higher rates. Some mortgage lenders offer only blanket loans, others only share loans, and some lenders provide both. And the secondary market for co-op loans is not nearly as fully developed as that for condo mortgages, which in many respects are treated by the market as single-family loans.

Co-ops may have their own set of scale economies, however. One large blanket loan on a co-op is less expensive to originate and to service than the sum of *n* smaller condo loans. This could result in some cost savings for co-ops.

While direct comparisons of interest rates and nonrate terms are difficult, it seems unlikely that co-op financing is less expensive than condo mortgages, and co-op financing may well be more expensive. If this is so, the differences in financing should be capitalized into the market value of the units. In addition, blanket mortgages on co-op projects, typically made in a prior year, may carry interest rates either above or below market. In a period of stable or declining interest rates, above-market interest rates are probably more common on co-op blanket loans than on condominium purchase loans, because blanket loans occasionally involve prepayment "lockout" periods in which refinancing is contractually prohibited. These interest rates would be expected to be capitalized in buyers' bid prices (Kelly, 1995).

3. Information, search, and liquidity.   The greater externalities involved with co-ops imply that prospective buyers must incur greater search costs (time and money) learning about each co-op than for a comparable condo unit. If buyers' bidding strategies are set to minimize the total costs—purchase price plus search costs—of securing a bundle of housing attributes, in equilibrium, buyers will bid less for co-ops than for otherwise comparable condos.

Similarly, on the sell side, the idiosyncratic nature of co-ops is such that co-op units can expect to have a longer marketing period than condos (Haurin, 1988). This longer marketing period involves costs for the seller, which should be capitalized into the initial bid price at the time of purchase.

4. Tax considerations.   The federal tax treatment of owner-occupied co-ops and condos is similar. Condo owners can deduct both property taxes and interest on their mortgage. Co-op owners can deduct their pro rata share of property taxes on the project and interest on the blanket mortgage. Co-op owners can also typically deduct interest on their share loan.

But on the supply side, in conversions of rental properties, co-ops have a tax advantage over condos. If a rental project is converted to a co-op, any gain on the sale from the landlord to the co-op corporation is taxed at the capital gains rate, because it is treated as a transfer between corporations (as are sales of rental projects). In most instances, profits from subdividing a rental project into condominium units are considered regular income and taxed at a higher rate (Marcus, 1985). This unfavorable tax treatment can be avoided only at the cost of bringing in a middleman by selling the project to a real estate firm that then undertakes the conversion (HUD, 1980). The supply cost of co-ops brought to the market by conversion therefore is lower than that of condos, and all else equal, this cost advantage should result in greater prevalence and lower market value for co-ops relative to condos. The preferential regulatory treatment of co-op conversions in New York and some other jurisdictions has similar effects on the supply of co-ops relative to condos.

5. Demand restrictions.   Co-op boards review every prospective purchaser and have the power to restrict entry for any reason that does not violate the applicant's civil rights. Condo associations do not have this right, and condos' bylaws and restrictive covenants, which are generally related to use of the property rather than individual owner characteristics, are less effective instruments for influencing ownership and residency. Co-ops' greater ability to restrict entry has an ambiguous effect on their relative market valuation, with even the direction of effect depending on how this power is exercised by the co-op board.[3]

While the risk sharing inherent in co-ops causes a reduction in demand (or at least an adverse selection problem) relative to condos, co-op boards also often deliberately restrict demand. Part of the justification is to protect the financial interest of the other co-op owners because of the financial interdependence mentioned above. Requirements can, however, be severe, such as requiring that the unit be bought with cash rather than with a share loan. This requirement can be a major constraint if the project has appreciated considerably since it was formed as a cooperative. More generally, the financial standards applied by co-op boards can be more restrictive than those typically applied by mortgage lenders. But applicants are rejected for nonfinancial reasons as well. Rock stars, former U.S. presidents, and other public figures are occasionally denied ownership because of the anticipated loss of peace and quiet. As one consumer guide to co-ops describes it: "The cooperative looks not only at the financial stability of a prospective member but also considers the likelihood that other members would want to have this person as a new neighbor and business partner."[4]

Not only do these entry restrictions reduce demand directly, but they also have indirect impacts since potential buyers may feel that their resale options are limited. The tradeoff, of course, is that other prospective buyers may be attracted to the project by these restrictions, if the restrictions are viewed as reducing the financial and life-style risk of owner-occupancy in the project. Following Cannaday (1994), consider a co-op in which each resident has the following utility function:

$$U_i = f(Z_i, Z_{-i}), \qquad i = 1, \ldots, n, \tag{1}$$

where U_i = utility of the ith resident. Z_i (scaled positively) is the ith resident's unit-specific ease of marketing one's shares to whomever he or he pleases. Z_{-i} (also scaled positively) is the ease of marketing shares for residents other than the ith resident, and:

$$\partial U_i/\partial Z_i \geq 0; \qquad \partial U_i/\partial Z_{-i} < 0; \qquad \text{and} \quad \partial^2 U_i/\partial Z_i^2 < 0. \tag{2}$$

$\partial U_i/\partial Z_i \geq 0$ implies that residents value freedom to sell to whomever they want, but the marginal utility of this freedom is diminishing and approaches zero. Complete freedom for each resident, ignoring the externality, allows him or her to set Z_i such that (at the limit) $\partial U_i/\partial Z_i = 0$, which would be the equilibrium solution if residents acted autonomously.

However, increased Z_i is equivalent to increased Z_{-i} for everyone else. Since one person's freedom may impinge on someone else's utility, $\partial U_i/\partial Z_{-i} < 0$. Hence, individual i's freedom may decrease the utility of others, if it increases the difficulty in marketing co-ops for all other residents.

A governing board of a multiunit structure may wish to recognize the interdependence of the residents in maximizing the *sum* of the residents' utilities. Maximizing $F = \sum_{i=i}^{n} U_i$ with respect to Z_i yields the first-order condition:

$$\partial F/\partial Z_i = 0 \qquad \text{for each } i = 1, \ldots, n. \tag{3}$$

From (3), it can be shown that

$$\partial U_i/\partial Z_i = -\sum_{\substack{j=1 \\ j \neq i}}^{n} \partial U_j/\partial Z_j. \tag{4}$$

Since each term on the right-hand side of (4) must be negative, the negative of the sum must be positive. Hence, the optimizing governing board would set optimum Z_i to be less than the equilibrium Z_i in the absence of governance. Cannaday (1994) derives this result in discussing the tradeoff between a condo/co-op owner's desire to have a pet and that same owner's desire not to live in a building with a lot of pets.

The utility functions of co-op owners may well differ depending on their own moving plans. Owners with no plans to move presumably have little immediate concern over resale value and may therefore tend to be more restrictive in admission criteria. (They will place a small weight on Z_i and a big weight on Z_{-i}.) Owners planning to sell in the near future may be more concerned about broadening the market for their shares and less concerned about the possible externalities from accepting an undesirable applicant. The restrictiveness of entry for these mixed buildings will depend on who controls the co-op board.

Thus co-ops are able to restrict entry relative to condos, with the net impact on asset values depending on the restrictiveness applied by the co-op board, and on local market conditions. Co-ops in markets with exclusivity at a premium may be able to command higher purchase prices with restrictive entry policies than would be possible with open admission. New York might be an example. But if admissions exclusions are exercised inconsistently, some high bidders are prevented from buying, while residents do not gain the advantages which they attached to exclusivity. If co-op boards wanted to tune the exclusivity so as to maximize value, the lowest possible value outcome would be that co-ops equal condos in value, because co-ops' boards have this adjustment tool and condo associations do not. But it is not necessarily the case that co-op boards attempt to maximize value.

To summarize, if the cost of producing the two types of housing is the same, then, given an upward-sloping, long-run supply curve, the consumer demand arguments listed under characteristics 1 through 3 above would lead to the expectation that prices would be less for co-ops than for condominiums with the same physical characteristics and location. The effect of demand restrictions (5) on valuation is ambiguous. On the supply side (4), the lighter regulatory and tax burden on co-op conversions means that the supply function for these units probably lies below that for condos, and this too should cause the price of co-ops to be less than the price of condos. All told, there are more reasons for expecting co-op values to be less than condos' than the opposite.

3. Data

Data for the study come from the national and New York metropolitan samples of 1987 American Housing Survey. The national sample consists of 1,095 owner-occupied units,

Table 1. National sample characteristics.

	Condo	Co-op	Pooled
Age of unit (years)	13	29	17
20+ units in structure (%)	25	47	29
Elevator building (%)	16	44	22
2–3 story building (%)	26	10	23
7+ story building (%)	8	37	13
Garage included with unit (%)	60	37	54
Rooms	4.9	4.7	4.9
Bathrooms	1.9	1.5	1.8
Balcony (%)	85	62	81
Central air-conditioning (%)	76	38	68
Central heat is warm air (%)	65	46	61
Fireplace (%)	33	15	29
Structural problems (%)	2	30	8
Gas cooking fuel (%)	24	64	32
Property tax rate (%)	1.3	2.0	1.5
New York metro (%)	5	41	12
Other Northeast (%)	13	12	13
Midwest (%)	20	14	18
South (%)	34	24	33
West (%)	28	9	23
Expensive, non-NY metro area (%) (Boston, Wash., D.C., Chicago, Los Angeles, San Francisco, Seattle, Honolulu)	27	9	23
Sample size	860	235	1095

Source: 1987 American Housing Survey

21% of which are in cooperative projects and the remainder are in condominium developments.[5] As shown in Table 1, a disproportionate share of all cooperative units are found in the New York metropolitan area, for the reasons mentioned above. Because of this concentration, we replicated the national analysis on the separate New York MSA sample. We present the full results from the national survey and summarize the results from New York.

Two key variables in the analysis are the owner's estimate of the market value of the unit and the identification of a unit as either a co-op or condo. Recent research has concluded that owners' estimates of value are biased upward, but that the extent of bias is generally uncorrelated with characteristics of the respondent or the unit (Goodman and Ittner, 1992). Consequently, our estimates of the difference in values of co-ops and condos are not likely to be affected by this bias.[6] Respondents are also relied upon for the designation of their unit as either a condo or a co-op. Analysis by the Census Bureau indicates that some units, especially cooperatives, are misidentified. Presumably, many of these misreportings are by renters (who occupy about one-third of all co-op/condo units). In our sample of owner occupants, response errors to this question should be moderate.

Co-ops tend to be older than condos, to have fewer rooms, and to be located in larger buildings (Table 1). They are less likely to be centrally air- conditioned, and they generally carry higher property tax rates than do condos.

4. Specification and Results

Our empirical approach is to consider hedonic price equations for both condominiums and co-ops, and to calculate the differences in bundle prices. Goodman (1978) established that the stratification of samples, as well as the specification of the underlying hedonic regressions, may have major impacts on the magnitudes of the effects measured.

Consider attribute bundle $A = \{a_1, a_2, \ldots a_s, \ldots\}$. The hedonic price function for vector A is:

$$V = g(A) \tag{5}$$

with the hedonic price of characteristic a_s calculated as $\partial g/\partial a_s$. One application of the hedonic price method is to respecify the model as:

$$V = g(A, k), \tag{6}$$

in which k represents the type of ownership (condominium or co-op). In this formulation, the coefficient on k represents the differential effect of ownership type.

The formulation in (6) is problematic for two reasons. First, it assumes that the impact of ownership regime is unrelated to the characteristics of the unit itself. Hence, k represents a shift variable. Second, the formulation restricts the underlying equations, and hence hedonic price coefficients, to be constant across both ownership types.

An alternative specification releases these constraints, by setting:

$$V_{condo} = A_{condo}\alpha, \text{ and:}$$

$$V_{co\text{-}op} = A_{co\text{-}op}\beta. \tag{7}$$

where α and β are vectors of attribute prices.

It is also appropriate to consider the functional form of the underlying hedonic. The Box–Cox transformation in some instances can provide a specification preferable to conventional linear and semi-log transformations.[7] Here, for the condominium model (and similarly for the co-op model):

$$V(\lambda) = (V^\lambda - 1)/\lambda = \alpha_0 + \Sigma\alpha_S a_S + \epsilon.$$

Searching on increments of 0.1, the likelihood function for (6) and (7) maximize at a value of $\lambda = 0.4$. Using this λ, the pooled estimation, (6), has an adjusted R^2 of 0.38 (column 1 of Table 2). All of the structural characteristics that are statistically significant have the expected signs, as do the property tax rate and the set of locational identifiers. Co-ops are significantly discounted; the shift term indicates that an otherwise similar condo unit is valued 21% higher.

Not surprisingly, the data reject the specification of (6), that is, the null hypothesis that $\alpha = \beta$. Accordingly, the explanatory power of the model is improved when the parameters are not constrained to be the same for co-ops and condos. Comparing the disaggregated regressions (columns 2 and 3 of Table 2), most of the independent variables maintain the same signs in the two subsample estimations, although fewer of the variables are significant in the smaller co-op sample.

Condos have a greater market value than co-ops for a variety of attribute bundles. That is, F-tests indicate that

$$A_{condo}\alpha > A_{condo}\beta,$$

$$A_{co\text{-}op}\alpha > A_{co\text{-}op}\beta, \text{ and}$$

$$A_{pooled}\alpha > A_{pooled}\beta,$$

where A_{pooled} is a weighted average of A_{condo} and $A_{co\text{-}op}$. Results from the bundle comparisons are given in Table 3. This functional specification results in the estimate that condo valuations exceed those of co-ops by 8 to 30%, depending on the bundle being priced. On the pooled sample, perhaps the single most representative choice, condos are valued 12%, or $9,100, higher than co-ops, on average.[8]

Finally, limited equity co-ops (LECs) might be expected to have lower market valuations than other co-ops because of the restrictions on resale prices in LECs. Whether a unit is in an LEC is not recorded in the American Housing Survey. But tests using proxies for LEC status indicated that the effect on value is statistically insignificant; that is, LECs and other co-ops appear to be valued similarly, conditional on their structural and locational characteristics.

Table 2. Hedonic regression coefficients.

	Pooled	Condo	Co-op
Intercept	154.57*	145.05*	137.31*
Age of unit (years)	-0.39	-0.42	0.28
Age squared	0.01*	0.01	0.00
20+ units in structure	1.35	-1.35	24.03
Elevator building	12.93*	11.49*	2.95
2–3 story building	3.67	2.99	13.99
7+ story building	4.16	10.31	-16.76
Garage parking	15.41*	22.39*	3.63
Rooms (#)	5.04*	6.09*	2.39
Bathrooms (#)	22.43*	19.71*	35.16*
Balcony	1.79	4.12	3.53
Central air-conditioning	4.85	1.18	8.91
Warm air heating	-5.55	0.47	-18.03
Fireplace	17.03*	12.92*	40.84*
Structural problems	9.18	11.79	3.35
Gas cooking fuel	-9.91*	-11.78*	4.55
Property tax rate (%)	-194.86*	-170.04*	-174.36*
New York metro	59.01*	58.26*	37.17
Other expensive metro	31.81*	32.80*	43.35*
Other Northeast	20.67*	35.97*	-33.99
Midwest	-32.94*	-31.44*	-43.45*
South	-21.03*	-13.85*	-43.61*
Co-op (1=yes; 0=no)	-17.56*	—	—
Adj. *R*-squared	.38	.42	.34
sample size	1095	860	235

Note: dependent variable: $(V^{.4} - 1)/.4$, where V = owner's estimate of the market value of the housing unit; unless otherwise indicated, independent variables are dummies that take the value 1 if the unit possesses the characteristic.
* significant at 5% level.

Table 3. Predicted bundle prices.

	Bundle		
	Condo	Co-op	Pooled
Prices ($)			
Condo	89,072	83,012	87,362
Co-op	82,599	63,784	78,262
Condo Premium			
$	6,474	19,228	9,100
%	7.8	30.2	11.6

The national analysis was repeated on the New York MSA sample, deleting the inapplicable locational variables from the right-hand side and but adding a city-suburb dummy variable. On the pooled (6) model, the condo premium was 14% although the t-statistic for the co-op dummy was only 0.95 (most likely due to the relatively small sample size). Hence, we cannot reject the null hypothesis of no discounting in New York. The premium in the corresponding national model was 21%. It appears, then, that co-op discounting is less in New York than elsewhere, a finding which would follow from some of the institutional and market advantages that New York co-ops enjoy.

5. Summary and Conclusions

Cooperative and condominium housing differ in several ways that might be expected to influence their pricing. Most but not all of these differences argue or a higher valuation for condominiums. Hedonic equations estimated on a national sample indicate that the price differential on the average condo/co-op unit in 1987 was 12%.[9] Condos maintain a price premium under a variety of specifications, although its magnitude depends on the bundle of attributes being priced.

Looking forward, it is difficult to project a resurgence for cooperative housing. Its market disadvantages relative to condominium housing appear to exceed its advantages. The relatively low valuations of co-ops, and their declining market share, despite some supply cost advantages, suggest that demand for this form of housing falls considerably short of condo demand. Absent a significant change in consumer preferences or the regulatory/tax treatment of co-ops or condos, cooperative housing seems likely to diminish further in importance.

Acknowledgments

This research was conducted while the second author was on the staff of the Board of Governors of the Federal Reserve System. Views expressed are not necessarily those of the Board of Governors or the staff of the Federal Reserve System. The authors are grateful to Joseph Nichols for his assistance on this project, to the U.S. Bureau of the Census for providing access to unpublished data from the American Housing Survey, and to Peter Colwell, Michael Grupe, Austin Kelly, Leonard Norry, Tom Thibodeau, Daniel Weinberg, and a referee for their comments on an earlier draft.

Notes

1. The third form of owner-occupancy in multiunit structures occurs when the owners of the building occupy one of its apartments.
2. Co-op owners typically will differ in their balances on both their blanket loans and share loans. Thus, the default option will not be in the money simultaneously for all owners. Furthermore, co-op owners are vulnerable to "nonrational" defaults by their fellow owners.

3. Limited equity co-ops also restrict demand. Because price caps are put on co-op shares in these projects, depending on market conditions, prices may be held below market-clearing levels. In these instances, some form of nonprice rationing of the units likely occurs.
4. Washington Mortgage Group, Inc., undated.
5. For confidentiality, the variable distinguishing condos from co-ops is suppressed on the public-use tape of basic records. We are grateful to the Census Bureau for providing controlled access to this variable.
6. The question in the AHS is: "How much do you think the apartment would sell for on today's market?"
7. This transformation nests the linear ($\lambda = 1$) and semi-log ($\lambda = 0$) regressions into a form that is easily tested. Although in principle both the left- and right-hand side could be transformed with a different parameter λ_s for each a_s, in practice, it is extraordinarily difficult to undertake such estimation. Hence, almost all applications transform the left-hand side only. Also, as noted by Thibodeau (1992, chapter 5), the estimator of house price obtained by transforming the dependent variable may be a biased estimator of average housing price. This bias is unimportant, however, since we are estimating the price difference, and the bias affects condos and co-ops similarly.
8. The t-statistic of the difference, calculated on untransformed values of the estimated equation (with $\lambda = 0.4$) is 2.40.
9. Our finding is broadly consistent with Kelly (1995), who found an 8% co-op discount, in a comparison of matched co-op and condo projects in Washington, D.C.

References

Cannaday, R.E. "Condominium Covenants: Cats, Yes: Dogs, No." *Journal of Urban Economics* 35 (1994), 71–82.
Goodman, A.C. "Hedonic Prices, Price Indices and Housing Markets," *Journal of Urban Economics* 5 (1978), 471–484.
Goodman, J.L., Jr., and J.B. Ittner. "The Accuracy of Home Owners' Estimates of House Value," *Journal of Housing Economics* 2 (1992), 339–357.
Hansmann, H. "Condominium and Co-operative Housing: Transactional Efficiency, Tax Subsidies, and Tenure Choice," *Journal of Legal Studies* 20 (1991), 25–71.
Haurin, D. "The Duration of Marketing Time of Residential Housing," *AREUEA Journal* 16 (1988), 396–410.
Kelly, A. "Capitalization of Above Market Financing: Or a Tale of Two Condos." Paper presented at the annual meeting of the American Real Estate and Urban Economics Association, 1995.
Marcus, H. "Yours, Mine and Ours," *Mortgage Banking* (July 1985), 15–32.
Sahling, L.G., and R.B. Stein. "Co-op Fever in New York City," *Federal Reserve Bank of New York Quarterly Review* (Spring 1980), 12–19.
Thibodeau, T.G. *Residential Real Estate Prices: 1974–1983.* Mt. Pleasant, MI: The Blackstone Company, 1992.
U.S. Department of Housing and Urban Development. *HUD Condominium Cooperative Study*, 1975.
U.S. Department of Housing and Urban Development. *The Conversion of Rental Housing to Condominiums and Co-operatives*, 1980.
Washington Mortgage Group, Inc. "A Consumer's Guide to Financing a Cooperative Unit Using Share Loan Financing," undated.

Journal of Real Estate Finance and Economincs, 14: 235-255 (1997)
© 1997 Kluwer Academic Publishers

Constructing Indices of the Price of Multifamily Properties Using the 1991 Residential Finance Survey

JAMES R. FOLLAIN
Center for Policy Research, Syracuse University

CHARLES A. CALHOUN
Office of Federal Housing Enterprise Oversight

Abstract

Indices of the price of constant-quality, owner-occupied single-family housing are widely available and have been instrumental in learning about the operations of the market for owner-occupied housing. Such is not the case for multifamily rental housing. The purpose of this article is to provide information about movements in the price of multifamily properties during the 1980s and early 1990s using the 1991 Residential Finance Survey (RFS). Several conclusions are drawn from the development and analysis of indices of the price of multifamily housing for the nation and four large states (California, Florida, New York, and Texas). First, indices for the period 1983–1991 generate similar patterns among the various methods employed; furthermore, movements in the index during the period 1983–1991 seem reasonable. Second, much regional variation exists. Prices in Texas were particularly hard hit, falling by over 25% in nominal terms between 1983 and 1991. Third, the impact of the Tax Reform Act of 1986 does not appear to have been as dramatic as some have suggested. Indeed, price declines do not show up in either the 1986 or 1987 indices for the nation, California, or New York.

Key Words: multifamily housing; price indices; repeat-sales indices; Tax Reform Act of 1986; Residential Finance Survey

1. Introduction

Indices of the price of constant-quality, owner-occupied single-family housing are widely available and have been instrumental in learning about the operations of the market for owner-occupied housing. They have been particularly important in the study of the demand for housing and the determinants of mortgage default. Such is not the case for multifamily rental housing, where multifamily is defined to be a rental property with five or more separate housing units. No widely available index of the price of multifamily rental housing properties exists. The available indices are recent, usually proprietary, and based upon specialized types of property. For example, the National Real Estate Index (1994) and the Russell–NCREIF index (1993) are available only since the mid- to late 1980s; both are proprietary and focus on high-quality apartment structures, likely to be attractive to institutional investors. The Commerce Department developed an index of the cost of multifamily structures, but this is experimental and based upon newly constructed units (deLeeuw, 1993). Individual investors can usually obtain information about price trends within particular markets from local appraisers, but such information is usually proprietary and focused on recent transactions.

Despite its limited supply, the demand for a broad index of the price of multifamily properties is likely to be substantial. Two ways in which such an index can be useful are discussed in order to support this point. First, and most importantly, price indices are valuable in the study of multifamily mortgage default. Unfortunately, little is known about the sensitivity of multifamily default with respect to its price, because the indices needed to conduct such studies are unavailable. Holders of multifamily mortgages, especially those who have experienced losses in their multifamily mortgage portfolio, e.g., Freddie Mac, are surely interested in learning more about the default process and the role of price. Abraham (1994) discusses some of these issues in his recent look at multifamily default.

A multifamily price index would also be useful to standard market analysis. Appraisers are very good at computing the value of a particular real estate property during stable times. What neither appraisers nor economists do very well is predict the responsiveness of the general level of commercial real estate prices to major shocks in the economy. For example, our understanding of the impact of the Tax Reform Act of 1986 (TRA) upon the asset price of real estate is primarily based upon anecdotes. A definitive study of its impact is unavailable, because we lack an index of multifamily housing prices before and after the passage of TRA. Blackley and Follain (1996) discuss this issue and some of the controversy, literature, and evidence surrounding it.

The purpose of this article is to provide information about movements in the price of multifamily properties during the 1980s and early 1990s. The key ingredient is the 1991 Residential Finance Survey (RFS). The RFS provides two estimates of the market value of a broad sample of multifamily properties. One is the price at which the current owner acquired the property and the second is the owner's estimate of market value at the time of the survey, early in 1991. This information allows the computation of what we label as a "quasi-repeat sales" index. Although the data permit the construction of an index with a rather long time series, attention is focused on the period 1983–1991, which was particularly tumultuous for commercial real estate. Ample data are available during this period to construct a national index and indices for four large states: California, Florida, New York, and Texas.

The remainder of the article is divided into four sections. The next section discusses the approaches used to generate the indices and some of the literature relevant to the topic. The following section presents some basic information about the 1991 Residential Finance Survey and the sample employed in this analysis. The results of the analysis are presented in the fourth section; they are compared to some alternative indices in the fifth section. The final section summarizes the main conclusions of the research and provides suggestions for further research.

2. Methodology

The object of a price index is to measure movements in the market price of a particular commodity or service. It is essential that the index measure the price of a commodity or service whose quality remains constant over time or among markets; otherwise, the index will be a composite of price and quality change. The fundamental problem associated with the estimation of price indices for real estate is its heterogeneity: the greater the heterogeneity, the more difficult it is to measure price change due to changes in quality. As a result, the estimation of an index of the market price of real estate must employ a method that controls for the variations in the quality of the properties over time and among markets.

Two methods have been used to estimate price indices for housing. The first is the hedonic approach. Regressions are estimated for different markets or time periods that explain the price of a housing unit as a function of the property characteristics; an index is computed by evaluating the estimation regression for a particular bundle of characteristics, e.g., three-bedroom units. The hedonic approach is commonly employed in the market for owner-occupied housing. Blackley and Follain (1986) and Thibodeau (1989) explain the approach and use the American Housing Survey to estimate a set of metropolitan indices of the price of owner-occupied housing and the rent on tenant-occupied housing.

Unfortunately, the hedonic approach is generally not feasible for commercial and rental properties because of the lack of comprehensive databases about these properties and their characteristics. In addition, the heterogeneity of this type of real estate probably surpasses that for owner-occupied housing, especially the portion of the owner-occupied market comprised of relatively standard single-family housing units. A recent exception is Guttery and Sirmans (1995). They estimate hedonic equations and develop price indices for the period 1983–1988 for two samples of smaller rental properties in Baton Rouge, Louisiana and a portion of eastern Connecticut. Among their findings is the stark contrast in the behavior of prices between the two cities. Eastern Connecticut experienced a 70% increase in prices, while prices in Baton Rouge declined by 65%.

The alternative approach and the one used in this article is the repeat-sales (RS) approach. The RS approach controls for variation by tracking movements in the selling prices of the same property at different points in time. Differences in the average appreciation rates between properties bought and sold in the same year produce an estimate of the cumulative inflation rate between those two years. Estimating appreciation rates among a large sample of properties bought and sold in various years produces an index of the movements in the price of housing over time. A large literature has emerged in recent years that applies this approach. Abraham and Schauman (1991) use this approach with Freddie Mac data. A recent and comprehensive application of this approach is provided by Stephens et al. (1995). They survey the literature regarding the RS approach and develop the Agency Repeat Transactions Index of the price of owner-occupied housing, using over 1.5 million observations on repeat transactions obtained in the Fannie Mae and Freddie Mac database. Although this approach has its limitations, it is surely a major improvement over an index based upon movements in the average prices of all sold properties with no correction for quality or size.

Data available from the 1991 RFS allow the RS approach to be applied to multifamily properties. Two estimates of market value are provided by the RFS. One is the original purchase price of the property, and the other is the owner's estimate of the market value of the property at the time of the survey in early 1991. Since the date of purchase is also known, and these dates vary widely among the properties in the sample, it is possible to construct RS price indices of multifamily properties using the 1991 RFS.

The nature of the RFS data require two potentially important differences between our approach and the standard RS application, which lead us to label the approach as quasi-RS. First, the second or final estimate of market value for each property is the estimate of the market value of the property provided by the owner or landlord. Normally, the RS approach uses actual sales prices, although applications such as the recent Agency Repeat Transactions Index (ARTI) do employ appraised values. Although we know of no studies to use owner estimates of value for multifamily properties or to assess their accuracy, the estimates of value provided by owner-occupants are commonly used in the hedonic literature. Indeed, several studies have found that owner estimates are reasonably accurate, e.g., Goodman and Ittner (1992). Furthermore, it seems reasonable to assume that professional investors and landlords have a strong incentive to stay abreast of market developments and have the potential to provide reasonable and unbiased estimates of market value in a survey of this type.

A second difference between this approach and the standard RS approach is that all of the second estimates of value refer to value on the same point in time, early 1991. The standard RS approach usually has more than one observation per property, and the last estimate of value need not be the final quarter of the data set. This difference actually simplifies the application of the RS approach to the RFS data, because it is only necessary to keep track of the purchase date. All appreciation rates pertain to the number of years between acquisition and 1991.

These differences and our application of the RS approach can be seen more clearly by introducing some notation. The price of the property in 1991 can be written as:

$$P_{91} = P_t e^{\alpha_0 + \alpha_t}, \tag{1}$$

where P_t is the purchase price of the property in year t and P_{91} is the owner estimate of market value in 1991. α_0 and α_t are parameters that indicate the cumulative percentage change in the value of this property between 1991 and t years prior to 1991. Indices reported below set the index in 1991 equal to 100. The ratio of the prices in any two adjacent years gives rise to an expression for the appreciation rate between these two years:

$$\ln P_{t-1} - \ln P_t = \ln \frac{e^{\alpha_0 + \alpha_{t-1}}}{e^{\alpha_0 + \alpha_t}} = \alpha_{t-1} - \alpha_t. \tag{2}$$

Thus, the annualized appreciation rate between two adjacent years is the difference between the $\alpha_t s$ for the two years.

There are two equivalent ways of estimating the parameters of this model. The standard method for estimating these parameters is to estimate a regression that explains the appreciation in the property between the dates of purchase as a function of a set of dummy variables that indicate the years in which the property is bought and sold. This approach forces α_0 to be zero for all properties. Another equivalent method is to simply calculate mean appreciation rates for each year of purchase. The equivalence of these methods arises only because the second estimates of market value all pertain to the same point in time, early 1991. Another variant of this approach focuses on median price changes, which reduces the influence of outliers.

An alternative approach computes a regression of the following type:

$$\ln P_{91} - \ln P_t = \alpha_0 + \sum_{i=1}^{T} \alpha_i TIME_i + \sum_{i=1}^{K} \beta_i X_i, \tag{3}$$

where the TIME variables represent a series of zero-one dummy variables that equal 1 if the property was purchased in year t and zero otherwise. The X_is are another set of zero-one dummy variables that indicate a variety of property characteristics. These include location, ownership type, whether the property receives some type of assistance, e.g., below-market loans, property size, and several other features of the property or its mortgage. The coefficients of these variables indicate whether the property appreciates above or below the path associated with the left-out categories. They also provide insights about the performance of particular segments of the multifamily market.

There are advantages and disadvantages of each approach. If the sample size is large enough, then sample means can be computed for many different years, property types, and locations. This effectively eliminates the need for the exogenous variables (the X's) in the regression model. Unfortunately, the sample size is limited; as a consequence, the degrees of freedom can be increased by pooling groups of properties thought to have experienced similar appreciation patterns. This is the logic underlying the regression approach, which increases the degrees of freedom in the estimation by, effectively, forcing the annual appreciation rates to be constant among all property types and locations used to estimate the regression.

3. 1991 Residential Finance Survey (RFS)

The Residential Finance Survey is conducted by the Bureau of the Census and is designed to provide data about the financing of nonfarm, privately-owned residential properties in the United States. The survey has been conducted as part of the 1950, 1960, 1970, 1980, and 1990 Censuses of Housing. The potential universe in the 1991 RFS is about 66,000,000 properties securing about 38,000,000 mortgages. About 70,000 properties were in the sample; 26,038 were in the rental and vacancy survey and the remainder in the owner-occupied survey.

Although the RFS is available on a public-use file, we encountered a number of problems in using this file. Most of these difficulties stemmed from the Census Bureau's need to preserve the confidentiality of individual respondents and properties. The public-use file employs several methods to preserve the confidentiality of respondent data: use of ranges in place of exact values for such variables as interest rates, top-coding of responses, introduction of random noise for some responses, and the "mean value in interval" approach for reporting a number of financial characteristics. In order to eliminate the confidentiality problems and to access geographic identifiers not available on the public-use file, we have benefited from the opportunity to conduct this research at the Census Bureau. The data set used for the analysis was constructed from an internal Census Bureau file; this file includes no top-coding or masking of responses.

Bogdon and Follain (1995) describe the RFS in more detail and present a variety of statistics from it. Here attention is focused on the subsample actually used to estimate the price indices. Four sets of restrictions were employed. First, only multifamily properties (properties with five or more units) are included; mobile homes and condominiums are excluded. This produces 19,216 multifamily properties. Second, several criteria are employed to eliminate properties that may have experienced major changes in usage or renovation and properties for which the market-value estimate might not be arm's-length. Specifically, properties were eliminated if the land and building were acquired at a different time or if the property was recently converted from nonresidential use. Properties were also deleted if they were acquired other than by purchase. These restrictions reduced the sample to 12,455 observations. Third, properties in nonmetropolitan areas were eliminated; this reduced the sample to 11,875 properties. The final set of restrictions was imposed in order to eliminate observations with highly suspicious or incomplete information about price change. Properties were eliminated if the property was acquired in 1991 and if information about the purchase price, current market-value estimate, or the number of units in the property was missing. A few very large properties with the number of units in excess of 1,000 were eliminated, as were properties with rent-to-value ratios in excess of unity, with annual appreciation rates in excess of 25% or with an average current value per unit or purchase price per unit in excess of $500,000. Properties with a value per unit less than $5,000 and with a ratio of current mortgage debt to current market value of the property in excess of two were also eliminated. This last group of restrictions reduced the sample to 9,020 properties.

Table 1 provides information about the nature of the sample used to construct the multifamily price indices. The reported statistics are unweighted in order to make clear the data actually used in the price index estimation. Bogdon and Follain (1995) report and emphasize weighted statistics in their analysis.

A few comments about the sample are in order before moving to the indices. First, more than half of the properties were acquired at least once since 1983 and almost 25% since 1986. This suggests that turnover among multifamily properties is substantial and capable of providing valuable information about movements in the market price of housing. Second, most properties in the sample are in the West; the smallest fraction is in the Midwest. California contains the most multifamily properties and samples for Florida and Texas are substantial. Third, most (62%) of the properties in the sample are located inside the central cities of metropolitan areas. The percentages of the properties inside central cities are particularly high in the Northeast and West; about one-third of all multifamily properties in the sample are located in the central cities of the Northeast and West. Fourth, among properties in the sample with a first mortgage, 11.8% are insured by the Federal Housing Administration (FHA). Most multifamily properties have no mortgage insurance. Fifth, the unweighted statistics highlight the dominance of large properties within the sample, because they are over-sampled in the RFS relative to smaller properties. This also produces a relatively large number of properties owned by partnerships (limited and general), equal to about 38% of the sample. Sixth, the RFS reports limited information about the various types of assistance offered to tenants of multifamily properties and their owners; for example, 1.1% of the

Table 1. Selected statistics from the 1991 residential finance survey.

						Other property characteristics			
Year Acquired	%	Location	%	Property in Central City in:	%	Insurance on First Mortgage*	%	Assistance to Property Owner or Tenants	%
1990	5.6	Northeast	24.8	Northeast	16.7	FHA Insured	11.8	Any assistance	24.7
1989	6.8	South	28.6	South	17.4	No Mortgage Insurance	54.1	Below market loan	10.3
1988	6.7	Midwest	17.5	Midwest	10.6	Number of Units		Section 8	17.7
1987	5.4	West	29.9	West	17.2	50 or more	76.4	Grant	0.5
1986	6.9	New York	14.3	New York	12.1	10 to 49	15.6	Tax relief	3.9
1985	7.6	Florida	5.7	California	10.4	10 or fewer	8.0	Low income housing tax credit	1.1
1984	6.8	Texas	9.6	Texas	7.5	Ownership		Tax exempt mortgage	4.8
1983	6.0	California	18.7	Florida	2.1	Partnership	37.9		
1980–1982	11.9			Inside Any Central City of an MSA	62.0	Nonprofit	3.6		
1976–1979	12.1					Individual Investor	27.6		
1971–1975	10.5					REIT	1.1		
1966–1970	5.8								
1961–1965	2.9								
1950–1959	1.6								
Before 1950	3.7								

Note: N = 9020 for most variables; those with some missing variables have less.
*Computed as a percent of properties with an outstanding first mortgage (*N* = 5960). Percentages refer to the number of properties in the sample. All statistics are unweighted.

Table 2. Financial information about multifamily properties from the 1991 residential finance survey.

Variable	Mean	Standard Deviation	Minimum	Maximum
Property value	$6,735,313	$10,107,153	$30,000	$231,765,000
Purchase price	$4,844,440	$7,383,643	$3,500	$207,500,000
Purchase price/unit	$30,467	$30,596	$48	$451,389
Number of units	153	137	5	1,000
Current LTV (percent)	45.0	40.0	0.0	200.0
Initial LTV (percent)	72.0	1.17	0.0	53.0
Mortgage payment	$299,475	$792,445	0	$47,940,000
Rent to value (percent)	16.0	8.7	0.0	98.0
Annual appreciation rate	4.0	7.2	-66.0	25.0
Original mortgage	$2,994,862	$5,258,101	0.0	$210,000,000
Current mortgage	$2,792,591	$4,731,692	0.0	$123,326,880

property owners report using the low-income housing tax credit enacted by TRA, and 17.7% of property owners indicate that they or some of their tenants benefit from the federal Section 8 housing program.

Information about the financial characteristics of the properties is provided in Table 2. Average property value is about $6.7 million, and the average property has 153 units. The average ratio of the outstanding mortgage debt to current market value of the property is 45%, although the initial loan-to-value ratio at the time of acquisition averages 72%. These statistics further amplify the dominance of the sample by large properties.

The distribution of value per unit for the entire sample and the four states is contained in Table 3. The mean for the United States is about $44,000, which is $11,000 above the median. Property values are more highly skewed in New York, but the other states are similar or a little less skewed than the national sample. Average value per unit varies considerably among regions. The most expensive units are in New York and California, with mean prices of $70,646 and $60,351, respectively. The lowest values are found in Texas. The value per housing unit with multifamily housing properties is uniformly below the average sales price of existing single-family housing. The United States average sales price according to the National Association Realtors Existing Home Survey in 1991 was $100,300. Values for the four census regions were $141,900 (Northeast), $88,900 (South), $77,800 (Midwest), and $147,200 (West).

Table 3. Distribution of value per unit value at various percentiles.

	N	Mean	75%	50%	25%	99%	1%
Nation	9020	$44,344	$51,841	$32,852	$21,518	$242,424	$7,143
New York	1290	$70,646	$84,831	$43,333	$25,974	$400,000	$7,407
Florida	514	$34,184	$40,625	$29,490	$22,135	$112,721	$8,947
Texas	863	$23,660	$28,761	$20,089	$14,000	$85,396	$5,667
California	1683	$60,351	$71,429	$55,072	$41,304	$180,180	$15,278

4. Price Indices

The analysis and presentation of the price indices focus on three aspects of the results. First, how do multifamily property prices vary over time? One particular issue is whether the indices responded similarly to the passage of the Tax Reform Act of 1986. Second, do price patterns differ widely among regions, and do the patterns bear a rough resemblance to the economic characteristics of those regions? For example, did prices drop severely in Texas during the early and mid-1980s when Texas experienced substantial problems because of the end of the oil boom. Third, how sensitive are the indices to the method of estimation? Indices based upon four different approaches are reported in order to address this question. The first two rely upon mean and median changes in cumulative price appreciation rates. The third and fourth are based upon regression analysis. One of these excludes the intercept and includes only the time dummies; the other adds an intercept and selected exogenous variables.

4.1. Distribution of Cumulative Price Appreciation Rates

Information regarding the distribution of cumulative price changes by year of acquisition is presented in Table 4. This is an extensive table that displays several points of the price change distribution for the nation and the four states. The statistics include the number of observations per state, the mean and median price changes, and the price change associated with the first, 25th, 75th, and 99th percentiles. Indices based upon these cumulative prices are reported below in Table 7. Here attention is focused on the sample sizes used to compute the price changes and the variation in the cumulative appreciation rates over time and among states.

The number of observations per region and year of acquisition seem sufficient in most cases to provide reasonable estimates. In only one case, New York in 1990, is the sample less than 30 observations. The smallest samples occur for certain years in both Texas and Florida. Sample sizes in California typically exceed 100.

Consider the pattern of price changes revealed by mean price changes since 1983. Prices in the United States were higher in 1991 than in previous years, but appreciation rates during the 1980s were modest. On average, properties acquired in 1983 appreciated by 18.5%. Cumulative appreciation rates for each year between 1983 and 1991 are also positive and generally decline. The median price changes tend to be smaller, which suggests the presence of some skewness. Note, also, the wide distribution of these cumulative price changes; for example, 25% of properties acquired in 1983 actually declined in nominal value by at least 8.6%.

Substantial variation in price changes exists among the four states. Prices in Texas were 15 to 23% lower in 1991 than they were during the 1983–1985 period; indeed, 25% of the properties acquired in 1987 report price declines of more than 12% since 1987. A substantial number of properties in Florida also experienced price declines in the early and mid-1980s, but prices seem to have risen among the majority of properties since then by modest amounts. California and New York properties were more likely to experience appreciation. Most New York properties purchased in the early 1980s doubled in value by 1991; properties purchased in the late 1980s actually experienced declines, on average.

Table 4. Multifamily price changes by region and years since property acquisition.

	Year	N	Mean	75%	50%	25%	99%	1%
Nation	1990	506	1.7	8.5	0.0	0.0	22.3	−48.6
	1989	609	3.9	16.9	5.7	0.0	41.9	−78.5
	1988	601	8.3	23.8	7.4	−1.4	58.8	−63.5
	1987	486	10.4	29.4	9.7	−2.2	84.1	−72.3
	1986	625	14.7	37.3	14.3	−4.1	102.5	−73.7
	1985	682	14.1	39.2	12.7	−4.3	117.7	−120.7
	1984	609	15.0	40.5	14.3	−8.7	142.9	−91.6
	1983	538	18.5	47.5	14.1	−8.6	168.6	−91.6
New York	1990	27	−3.0	9.0	0.0	−11.0	17.0	−49.0
	1989	41	−7.0	16.0	0.0	−18.0	41.0	−161.0
	1988	57	3.0	19.0	0.0	−5.0	63.0	−85.0
	1987	65	14.0	32.0	12.0	0.0	84.0	−72.0
	1986	92	24.0	50.0	22.0	−3.0	110.0	−69.0
	1985	82	41.0	82.0	41.0	7.0	130.0	−136.0
	1984	85	52.0	75.0	43.0	16.0	156.0	−67.0
	1983	76	46.0	89.0	37.0	9.0	177.0	−170.0
Florida	1990	37	4.0	12.0	0.0	0.0	18.0	−34.0
	1989	38	4.0	12.0	2.0	−2.0	38.0	−64.0
	1988	41	10.0	21.0	8.0	−5.0	62.0	−59.0
	1987	32	11.0	35.0	0.0	−7.0	84.0	−49.0
	1986	30	7.0	33.0	4.0	−13.0	59.0	−73.0
	1985	44	−8.0	10.0	0.0	−20.0	76.0	−251.0
	1984	45	5.0	18.0	0.0	−7.0	107.0	−67.0
	1983	30	9.0	28.0	11.0	−28.0	114.0	−63.0
Texas	1990	118	3.0	9.0	0.0	0.0	22.0	−34.0
	1989	105	6.0	22.0	10.0	0.0	42.0	−86.0
	1988	80	9.0	29.0	11.0	0.0	59.0	−71.0
	1987	70	5.0	29.0	3.0	−12.0	89.0	−115.0
	1986	55	−7.0	16.0	0.0	−34.0	76.0	−94.0
	1985	38	−23.0	11.0	−13.0	−48.0	100.0	−253.0
	1984	45	−15.0	7.0	−13.0	−52.0	114.0	−93.0
	1983	67	−19.0	1.0	−18.0	−51.0	169.0	−269.0
California	1990	101	2.0	8.0	1.0	0.0	22.0	−38.0
	1989	152	7.0	15.0	7.0	0.0	43.0	−44.0
	1988	162	12.0	22.0	9.0	0.0	54.0	−35.0
	1987	100	16.0	29.0	14.0	4.0	69.0	−59.0
	1986	130	26.0	40.0	22.0	10.0	102.0	−31.0
	1985	124	21.0	39.0	19.0	4.0	101.0	−69.0
	1984	87	29.0	45.0	30.0	10.0	129.0	−65.0
	1983	58	44.0	61.0	38.0	27.0	132.0	−24.0

4.2. No Intercept Regression Results

An alternative method of computing price indices relies upon the coefficients of an ordinary least-squares regression. The dependent variable is the natural log of the owner's estimate of the market value of the property in 1991 minus the natural log of the purchase price at its acquisition. The independent variables include a set of dummy variables indicating the year in which the property last sold. Differences in the coefficients of these time variables are used to produce the estimates of annual appreciation rates. This particular approach omits the intercept and is designed to estimate the parameters in (2). The regression is estimated for the United States and for the four states. These results are presented in Table 5.

Dummy variables are included for each year of origination back to 1983 (TIME1 to TIME8); beyond this year the time dummies represent particular groups of years, e.g., TIME9T11 represents properties acquired nine to 11 years prior to 1991. The left-out category includes properties acquired more than 40 years ago. Annual dummy variables are only included for the last eight years for a couple of reasons. First, estimates of the appreciation rate are likely to diminish over time because of potential sample-selection problems; in particular, it is increasingly likely that properties that have not sold in many years are different in some important ways from those that have sold more recently. Second, the sample size of properties sold in a particular year are often zero for some regions, especially urban areas in the Northeast. For these reasons, attention is focused on the construction of indices during the period 1983–1991.

The first thing to note about these regression results is their similarity to the mean cumulative changes in Table 4. In fact, the coefficients of the time dummies are identical to the mean cumulate appreciation rates in Table 4. For example, the coefficient of TIME1 is .0174 for the national regression, and the mean cumulative appreciation rate for national properties acquired in 1990 is 1.74%. Second, the only modest advantage of the regression approach is the familiar representation of the t-statistics computed by the regression. These reveal the same pattern in all five regressions; the coefficient estimates are more likely to be significantly different than zero the longer the number of years since acquisition. In fact, several of the dummy variables are not significantly different than zero, which simply means that price changes during the latter 1980s were often not statistically different than zero. As one would expect, this same picture emerges from a review of the mean cumulative changes in Table 4.

4.3. Regressions with Intercept and Exogenous Variables (Fixed Effects)

The final approach is also based upon a regression approach, except that this regression includes both an intercept and a set of exogenous variables. This regression is intended to estimate the parameters in (3). The exogenous variables indicate certain characteristics of the property: its mortgage, its location, and its ownership. The coefficients of these exogenous variables indicate the differential cumulative appreciation (or depreciation) rate of property values for these characteristics relative to the base case. The confusing aspect of the exogenous variables is that they do not have a specific time dimension to them; they simply indicate that a particular property experienced a higher cumulative appreciation rate

Table 5. No intercept regressions.

	National		New York		Florida		Texas		California	
	Estimate	T-Ratio	Estimate	T-Ratio	Estimate	T-Ratio	Estimate	T-Ratio	Estimate	T-Ratio
TIME1	0.017	0.668	−0.032	−0.200	0.042	0.638	0.033	0.854	0.021	0.472
TIME2	0.039	1.659	−0.073	−0.569	0.041	0.630	0.060	1.471	0.066	1.818
TIME3	0.083	3.450	0.027	0.242	0.103	1.639	0.088	1.881	0.115	3.256
TIME4	0.104	3.917	0.135	1.317	0.109	1.521	0.051	1.016	0.159	3.522
TIME5	0.147	6.259	0.240	2.783	0.069	0.935	−0.074	−1.301	0.259	6.552
TIME6	0.141	6.284	0.409	4.476	−0.085	−1.391	−0.227	−3.328	0.209	5.151
TIME7	0.150	6.318	0.522	5.812	0.053	0.877	−0.152	−2.431	0.285	5.904
TIME8	0.185	7.294	0.462	4.867	0.093	1.260	−0.194	−3.790	0.441	7.443
TIME9T11	0.370	20.672	0.763	12.536	0.241	4.471	−0.059	−1.278	0.479	12.868
TIME1215	0.667	37.537	1.191	17.220	0.502	8.339	0.111	2.035	0.919	32.175
TIME1620	0.863	45.167	1.000	13.990	0.636	10.806	0.340	5.561	1.266	40.009
TIME2125	1.084	42.114	1.259	14.516	0.704	11.164	0.452	5.384	1.636	32.461
TIME2630	1.358	37.221	1.703	17.824	0.966	7.573	1.126	5.997	1.642	23.599
TIME3140	1.770	35.785	1.732	18.127	1.100	3.853	1.722	7.104	2.231	19.790
Root MSE	0.587		0.827		0.404		0.420		0.451	
R-square	0.486		0.555		0.453		0.185		0.749	
Dep Mean	0.422		0.833		0.231		0.037		0.568	
Adj R-sq	0.485		0.551		0.438		0.172		0.747	

than another type, all else equal. For this reason, they are often not reported in some papers that apply the repeat-sales approach. Nonetheless, we do report them as the fixed-effects results and develop indices based upon them in order to determine the sensitivity of the indices to the method and to identify any broad patterns that may exist among property types. The results for this regression approach are included in Table 6. The adjusted R^2 for the national equation is .40, and the standard error of the regression is .54. The R^2s for the other equations range between .18 and .61. The standard errors are between .40 and .70.

The most important coefficient estimates are those of the time dummies, because these are the basis of the price indices. These are all highly significant for the national regression and New York. This is not the case for the other three states; some coefficients are significantly different than zero, and some are not. The dummies for the regional, state, and central-city variables in the national regression do indicate the presence of significant differences among locations, but these differences are more obvious and consistently measured using the regression results for specific regions.

A number of interesting patterns emerge from an examination of the coefficients of the exogenous variables. First, large properties (NUM50M) tend to appreciate less than the smaller properties (NUMLT10). For example, large properties appreciated 4.4% less than the left-out category (properties with 10 to 49 units), and small properties appreciated 8.7% more. Second, partnerships appreciate less rapidly than the left-out category, which is a collection of a variety of relatively less important ownership types. Properties owned by individual investors tend to appreciate a little faster at the national level, but this is not a strong result among the state regressions. Third, properties that have their first mortgages insured by FHA appreciate at lower rates than uninsured properties for the national sample and in California, but this pattern does not emerge for the other states. Fourth, properties that receive some type of assistance for the project appreciate less rapidly than properties that do not receive assistance, for all but Florida. Assistance includes Section 8, below-market rate loans, and several other types of project-based assistance. Fifth, there is evidence of above-average appreciation rates in the central cities of New York, California, and Florida.

4.4 Summary of Price Indices

Indices based upon the results in Tables 4, 5, and 6 are summarized in Table 7 for the nation and for the four states, for the period 1983–1991. The indices all equal 100 in 1991; annual inflation rates based upon these indices are also reported. The top panel reports indices using the median price changes from Table 4. The middle panel can be viewed as using either the mean changes from Table 4 or the regression results of Table 5; they are equivalent. The bottom panel reports those based upon the fixed-effects regression of Table 6.

First, compare the three national indices obtained using three different methods. The median-based indices reveal little or no appreciation during 1983 and 1985, and cumulative inflation of 10% or so since. A similar pattern emerges using the mean-based indices, although differences in the estimates of annual inflation rates are sometimes more than a full percentage point, e.g., 1983. The indices based upon the fixed-effects regressions show a different pattern; they show faster appreciation before 1986 and slower appreciation since then.

Table 6. Regressions with intercept and other fixed effects and price indices.

	National		New York		Florida		Texas		California	
	Estimate	T-Ratio	Estimate	T-Ratio	Estimate	T-Ratio	Estimate	T-Ratio	Estimate	T-Ratio
Intercept	0.531	11.610	1.918	15.782	0.039	0.430	-0.137	-1.181	0.282	3.294
TIME1	-0.511	-13.314	-1.920	-11.945	-0.023	-0.350	0.178	1.478	-0.244	-2.757
TIME2	-0.515	-13.868	-1.995	-14.113	0.018	0.268	0.176	1.470	-0.174	-2.053
TIME3	-0.488	-13.099	-1.871	-14.508	0.036	0.508	0.237	1.991	-0.122	-1.488
TIME4	-0.462	-11.935	-1.746	-14.072	0.016	0.215	0.264	2.143	-0.084	-0.948
TIME5	-0.446	-12.043	-1.673	-14.536	-0.122	-1.573	0.220	1.751	0.031	0.364
TIME6	-0.420	-11.490	-1.488	-12.621	-0.267	-3.084	0.074	0.623	-0.017	-0.196
TIME7	-0.385	-10.329	-1.353	-11.533	-0.202	-2.426	0.230	1.938	0.090	0.997
TIME8	-0.336	-8.834	-1.403	-11.624	-0.206	-2.716	0.272	2.174	0.225	2.337
TIME9T11	-0.192	-5.605	-1.102	-10.670	-0.110	-1.557	0.381	3.322	0.275	3.227
TIME1215	0.087	2.528	-0.632	-5.881	0.054	0.703	0.634	5.422	0.690	8.394
TIME1620	0.290	8.263	-0.794	-7.257	0.272	3.323	0.780	6.594	1.097	13.145
TIME2125	0.496	12.874	-0.575	-4.987	0.337	3.336	0.842	6.801	1.451	15.866
TIME2630	0.693	15.319	-0.142	-1.178	0.978	4.928	1.108	6.633	1.380	13.453
TIME3140	1.011	18.379	-0.160	-1.327	1.512	5.889	1.261	4.120	1.896	14.112
NUM50M	-0.044	-2.479	-0.173	-2.844	0.047	0.677	-0.005	-0.097	-0.033	-1.169
NUMLT10	0.087	3.468	0.062	0.620	0.270	2.249	0.132	1.683	0.115	2.984
OWNP	-0.049	-3.217	-0.113	-1.857	-0.060	-1.803	-0.059	-1.184	-0.012	-0.389
OWNNP	-0.002	-0.056	0.035	0.323	0.310	2.012	0.181	1.944	-0.085	-1.326
OWNIINV	0.057	3.362	0.092	1.714	-0.020	-0.411	-0.009	-0.150	0.044	1.494
OWNREIT	0.021	0.372	0.519	1.042	-0.168	-1.301	-0.127	-0.686	0.079	0.555
ASSIST	-0.085	-5.262	-0.105	-2.161	0.065	1.300	-0.104	-1.923	-0.051	-1.626
FHA1	-0.056	-2.598	0.023	0.312	0.035	0.474	-0.050	-0.659	-0.296	-6.076
UNINSUR1	0.004	0.344	0.139	3.265	0.020	0.661	0.019	0.479	-0.049	-2.030
TAXEXPT1	-0.116	-4.013	-0.433	-4.125	-0.204	-1.982	0.012	0.108	-0.080	-1.049

	National		New York		Florida		Texas		California	
	Estimate	T-Ratio	Estimate	T-Ratio	Estimate	T-Ratio	Estimate	T-Ratio	Estimate	T-Ratio
NE	0.144	3.714								
SO	0.030	0.772								
MW	0.002	0.062								
NEWYORK	0.144	3.207								
CALIF	0.224	6.170								
TEXAS	-0.125	-2.689								
FLA	-0.098	-2.533								
NECITY	0.033	0.938								
SOCITY	-0.067	-2.099								
MWCITY	0.056	2.010								
WECITY	-0.095	-2.538								
NYCITY	0.088	1.599	0.064	1.152						
CALCITY	0.109	2.385							0.002	1.000
TEXCITY	0.007	0.120					0.056	1.479		
FLACITY	0.109	1.846			-0.027	-0.782				
Root MSE	0.542		0.696		0.417		0.399		0.434	
Dep Mean	0.422		0.833		0.037		0.231		0.568	
Adj R-sq	0.403		0.416		0.179		0.327		0.609	
R-square	0.405		0.427		0.203		0.360		0.615	

Table 7. Summary of various indices (in percent).

	National		New York		Florida		Texas		California	
	Index	Inflation Rate	Index	Inflation Rate	Index	Inflation Rate	Index	Inflation Rate	Index	Inflation Rate
Median based indices (Table 4)										
1991	100.0		100.0		100.0		100.0		100.0	
1990	100.0	0.0	100.0	0.0	100.0	0.0	100.0	0.0	99.0	1.0
1989	94.4	5.7	100.0	0.0	98.0	2.0	91.3	9.1	93.1	6.1
1988	92.8	1.7	100.0	0.0	92.5	5.9	90.2	1.2	91.8	1.4
1987	90.8	2.3	88.8	11.9	100.0	−7.8	97.2	−7.5	87.9	4.4
1986	86.7	4.6	79.9	10.5	96.4	3.7	100.0	−2.8	82.1	6.8
1985	88.0	−1.6	66.4	18.5	100.0	−3.7	115.4	−14.3	83.8	−2.2
1984	86.7	1.6	65.0	2.1	100.0	0.0	114.5	0.8	77.1	8.3
1983	86.9	−0.2	68.7	−5.6	90.0	10.5	122.3	−6.6	72.5	6.3
No intercept based indices (Table 5)										
1991	100.0		100.0		100.0		100.0		100.0	
1990	98.3	1.7	103.2	−3.2	95.9	4.2	96.8	3.3	97.9	2.1
1989	96.1	2.2	107.6	−4.2	96.0	−0.1	94.2	2.7	93.6	4.5
1988	92.1	4.3	97.4	10.0	90.2	6.2	91.6	2.8	89.1	4.9
1987	90.1	2.2	87.4	10.9	89.7	0.5	95.0	−3.7	85.3	4.3
1986	86.3	4.3	78.7	10.5	93.3	−4.0	107.6	−12.5	77.2	10.0
1985	86.8	−0.6	66.4	16.9	108.8	−15.3	125.4	−15.3	81.2	−5.1
1984	86.0	0.9	59.4	11.3	94.9	13.7	116.4	7.5	75.2	7.7
1983	83.1	3.4	63.0	−6.0	91.1	4.0	121.5	−4.2	64.4	15.5
Fixed effects based indices (Table 6)										
1991	100.0		100.0		100.0		100.0		100.0	
1990	98.1	2.0	96.3	3.8	96.0	4.1	98.4	1.6	96.3	3.8
1989	98.4	−0.3	89.7	7.1	96.2	−0.2	94.4	4.1	89.7	7.1
1988	95.8	2.7	85.2	5.2	90.5	6.0	92.7	1.8	85.2	5.2
1987	93.3	2.6	82.0	3.8	88.1	2.8	94.7	−2.0	82.0	3.8
1986	91.8	1.6	73.1	11.5	92.0	−4.4	108.7	−13.8	73.1	11.5
1985	89.5	2.5	76.7	−4.8	106.6	−14.7	125.6	−14.5	76.7	−4.8
1984	86.4	3.5	68.9	10.7	91.1	15.7	117.7	6.6	68.9	10.7
1983	82.3	4.9	60.2	13.5	87.4	4.2	118.2	−0.5	60.2	13.5

Second, substantial variation exists among the four states. The indices for Texas reveal the largest drops in multifamily property prices. Prices appear to have declined by over 22%. Most of this happened between 1983 and 1987, with 1985 being the year of the largest declines—prices dropped by 14 to 15%, on average. 1985 also appears to have been a bad year for Florida multifamily properties. The indices show more variation for Florida on a year-to-year basis, but they do seem to tell a similar story for the entire period and similar ones for groups of two or three years. New York and California registered the largest appreciation rates. During this period, the price indices rose from a base of 60 to 70% to 100. The median-based indices show the smallest increase, and the fixed-effects indices show the largest increase.

The third and perhaps most interesting result pertains to the 1986–1987 period. This is the period in which one would expect to observe the most direct effect of the Tax Reform Act of 1986. All three national indices show modest, but positive, appreciation rates for both years. So do the results for New York and California. 1986 appears to have been a bad year for Florida, but declines during the two-year period are less than 4% among the three indices. The largest declines in these two years are reported for Texas. The indices in the lower two panels show double-digit declines in 1986 and declines for both years. Perhaps this is a tax-driven decline, but a more plausible explanation surely includes some of the other changes taking place in Texas during that period. These other factors include the decline in the price of oil and the problems stemming from the savings and loan debacle. In sum, it is hard to identify a strongly negative impact of TRA upon multifamily housing prices during this two-year period for any place but Texas.

5. Comparison to Other Sources

Although widely available indices of multifamily property prices do not exist for long-time series, several indices do exist. These include:

1. **Department of Commerce Index.** This is an experimental index developed to measure movements in the cost of multifamily rental housing. deLeeuw (1993) develops these indices using information based upon surveys of newly constructed multifamily rental housing. It uses a hedonic approach, much as the Census's constant-quality price index for new single-family housing does.
2. **Russell–NCREIF Apartment Index.** Russell–NCREIF was among the first to develop indices of the returns to investment in commercial real estate. Their indices report a total return as well as the return due to appreciation and net operating income. In 1987 Russell–NCREIF began tracking a separate index for apartments. The data upon which the index is based come from large institutional investors who purchase high-quality real estate with all equity. We chose results from their first quarter report for 1993, i.e. National Council of Real Estate Fiduciaries and Frank Russell Company (1993).
3. **National Real Estate Index (NREI).** This is probably the most comprehensive information available about movements in the prices of apartments and other types of commercial real estate. The index is based upon actual transactions of apartments in a large number of metropolitan areas; a national index is also produced. The starting dates of the indices differ by metropolitan area, but most began in the late 1980s. The indices are printed in an NREI publication (1994), which can be purchased from the producers of the data.
4. **Freddie Mac Repeat Sales.** An official repeat-sales index of multifamily properties has not been produced by either Freddie Mac or Fannie Mae. However, Abraham (1994) does produce a short-time series, based on his recent analysis of multifamily mortgage

default. Details about the calculations underlying this index are not provided in the article.

In this section, these indices are reviewed and compared to the RFS indices presented above.

Table 8 contains all of these indices, along with the RFS mean-based indices in the middle panel of Table 7. The indices set 1989 equal to one in order to simplify the comparison to the Commerce data, which is only available through 1989. Although the NREI data are available for about 20 metropolitan areas, only five are presented in Table 8: Boston, Dallas, Houston, Miami, and Los Angeles.

Focus first on the national indices. The Commerce index shows steady appreciation through the period 1983–1989. The cumulative change in the Commerce index is about 8% more than that for the RFS national index and reveals less year-to-year variation than the RFS index. The Russell–NCREIF index is quite short, since it only began reporting separate indices for apartments in 1987. It shows a very small increase in 1988 and a small decline between 1989 and 1991. The NREI for the United States shows a modest and relatively steady rise between 1985 and 1990; the NREI index declines by about 2% in 1991. Freddie's index shows much more volatility. The net increase during this period is a modest 3%, but the index rose substantially between 1987 and 1989, only to fall by over 25% after 1989.

The only index for which metropolitan information is available is provided by NREI. The areas selected are meant to be the basis of a comparison with the results obtained for the four states. Boston is the closest major urban area to New York City, which is not available in their survey. These indices show substantial variation among time and metropolitan areas. Dallas declined by over 36% since 1985 and another 18% in 1986. Since that time, prices in Dallas actually improved until a 7% decline in the 1990–1991 period. Two of the areas, Boston and Dallas, show actual declines in multifamily price levels since the origination of the index; Dallas drops by over 35%. Houston, on the other hand, shows a modest 11% nominal growth over the same period. Miami and Los Angeles generally depict small but steady increases in their indices.

A comparison of the NREI metropolitan indices to the RFS indices presented above suggests several tentative conclusions. First, the NREI indices for Dallas are relatively close to the RFS index for Texas; both show substantial nominal declines since 1985, the bulk of which took place in the mid-1980s. The RFS index for Florida shows about the same rate of inflation for the period 1986–1991, but the NREI index shows relatively higher rates before 1989 and relatively lower rates between 1989 and 1991. The NREI index for Los Angeles tends to move similarly to the RFS index for California. The Boston NREI index paints quite a different picture than the RFS index for New York; New York shows substantially more appreciation between 1985 and 1991 than the NREI index for Boston.

Lastly, it is interesting to compare movements in the multifamily price indices to those in the United States GDP price deflator, which is a measure of inflation in overall prices. The national GDP deflator grew by nearly 30 percentage points between 1983 and 1991; the national RFS index of multifamily housing prices moved by less than 20%. In real terms, this translates into a 10% or so decline in the real price of multifamily housing between 1983 and 1991. The real decline in Texas was closer to 50% in real terms. Only California and New York experienced real price increases between 1983 and 1991.

Table 8. Comparisons of various multifamily price indices (1989 = 100) (in percent).

	Commerce	Russell–NCR EIF	National Real Estate Index						Freddie Mac MF WRS	US GDP Deflator
			National	Boston	Dallas	Houston	Miami	Los Angeles		
1991		97.1	100.7	94.6	99.7	100.7	100.7	100.7	75.5	108.6
1990		98.4	102.3	97.2	106.5	102.3	102.3	102.3	81.0	104.3
1989	100.0	100.0	100.0	100.0	100.0	100.0	100.0	100.0	100.0	100.0
1988	98.9	99.6	97.0	103.0	101.5	97.0	97.0	97.0	94.7	95.8
1987	92.5		94.2	106.1	90.1	94.2	94.2	94.2	83.9	92.2
1986	89.0		91.6	108.6	108.0	91.6	93.1	91.6	78.5	89.3
1985	84.3		89.1	106.8	135.8	89.1		89.1	72.4	87.0
1984	81.2									83.9
1983	79.0									80.4

	Fannie Mae and Freddie Mac WRS SF Indexes				1991 RFS Mean Based MF Price Indexes (Table 5)				
	Nation	Mid-Atlantic	South Atlantic	West	Nation	New York	Florida	Texas	California
1991	104.5	99.8	104.1	105.0	104.0	92.9	104.2	106.2	106.9
1990	101.2	98.0	100.4	103.0	102.2	95.9	99.9	102.8	104.6
1989	100.0	100.0	100.0	100.0	100.0	100.0	100.0	100.0	100.0
1988	93.7	93.8	92.1	83.9	95.8	90.5	94.0	97.2	95.2
1987	87.6	79.3	84.9	75.5	93.7	81.2	93.5	100.9	91.2
1986	81.1	66.6	78.7	69.6	89.8	73.1	97.3	114.3	82.5
1985	76.0	57.1	73.9	64.9	90.3	61.7	113.4	133.2	86.8
1984	72.7	49.7	69.6	62.6	89.5	55.2	98.9	123.7	80.3
1983	70.3	44.8	66.9	62.0	86.5	58.5	95.0	129.0	68.8

6. Conclusions

Several conclusions emerge from the research. Some pertain to movements in the price indices and some to the ways in which future research ought to proceed. First, the analysis
suggests that the repeat-sales methodology and the 1991 RFS generate indices of the price of
multifamily housing that are largely consistent among index methodologies and not exces-
sively volatile. This conclusion is different from the one drawn by Abraham in his analysis
of Freddie Mac data on multifamily prices.

Second, much regional variation underlies the national average. Indices are computed for
four states: New York, Florida, Texas, and California. Prices in Texas were particularly hard
hit, falling by over 25% in nominal terms since 1983 and in excess of 50% in real terms.
New York experienced the most substantial appreciation, most of which occurred between
1985 and 1989.

Third, the impact of TRA upon multifamily housing prices does not appear to be dramatic. Prices did decline substantially in Texas, according to the indices, but prices had
been declining for two or three years prior to TRA and also declined in 1987. These declines may have been caused by TRA but were almost surely affected by the decline in the
price of oil and the savings and loan debacle. Price declines in 1986 and 1987 do not show
up in the national indices or the indices for New York and California. Although this effect
is smaller than some others have attributed to TRA, it is consistent with the story told by
Follain, Hendershott, and Ling (1987) in their simulation analysis of TRA. They argued that
the net impact of TRA upon the price of rental housing was likely to be quite small and less
than 10% in all but the slowest growing areas. The fact that Texas experienced the largest
decline within our sample is also consistent with their distinction between slow-growing
and fast-growing areas.

There are many ways in which this research can be improved, foremost being the examination of smaller groups of properties. For example, distinctions by property size, ownership
type, and quality of the real estate ought to be examined. Also, the possibility of selectivity
bias ought to be investigated carefully to determine whether a potential bias is generated by
using a sample of properties that differ widely in the time since acquisition. This issue has
been raised in the study of single-family house price indices by a number of authors including Stephens et al. (1994) and Jud and Seaks (1994). Another potential source of bias stems
from the usage of owner estimates of market value. Much has been done on this topic for
owner-occupied housing; we know of nothing for multifamily housing. Lastly, efforts ought
to be made to explain the variations in price movements among regions, property types, and
neighborhoods. This is a subject on which substantial progress has been made regarding
single-family housing; this line of research has only just begun for multifamily housing.

Acknowledgments

This is the first in a series of four articles to be written about multifamily housing using the
1991 Residential Finance Survey. Other members of the research team who will contribute
to future reports include Amy Bogdon and George Galster. The research is supported by the

Office of Policy Development and Research of the U.S. Department of Housing and Urban Development. The research has benefited from the comments of numerous people, including Jesse Abraham, Frank Nothaft, John Goodman, Ed Szymanoski, and Tom Thibodeau. Robert Dunsky, Cathy Smith, Matthew VanderGoot, and Nelson Wong provided valuable research assistance. Amy Bogdon, Peter Tatian, and several members of the Bureau of the Census staff—Dan Weinberg, Peter Fronczek, Ellen Wilson, and Howard Savage—have been particularly helpful in this study. We are grateful to all of these people for their assistance and comments.

References

Abraham, J. M. *Credit Risk in Commercial Real Estate Lending.* Washington, DC: Freddie Mac, 1994.

Abraham, J. M., and W. S. Schauman. "New Evidence on Home Prices from Freddie Mac Repeat Sales," *AREUEA Journal* 19 (1991), 333–352

Blackley, D. M., J. R. Follain, and H. Lee. "An Evaluation of Hedonic Price Indices for Thirty-Four Large SMSAs," *AREUEA Journal* 14 (1986), 179–205.

Blackley, D. M. and J. R. Follain. "In Search of Empirical Evidence that Links Rent and User Cost," *Regional Science and Urban Economics,* 26(1996), 409–33.

Bogdon, A. and J. R. Follain. "Multifamily Housing: An Exploratory Analysis Using the 1991 Residential Finance Survey." Unpublished manuscript, 1995.

deLeeuw, F. "A Price Index for New Multifamily Housing," *Survey of Current Business* (February 1993), 33–41.

Follain, J. R. "Some Possible Directions for Research on Multifamily Research," *Housing Policy Debate* 5 (1995), 533–568.

Follain, J. R., P. Hendershott, and D. Ling. "Understanding the Real Estate Provisions of Tax Reform: Motivation and Impact," *National Tax Journal* 40 (September 1987), 363–372.

Goodman, J. L., and M. R. Grupe. "Top Ten Surprises about Ownership and Financing of Rental Housing," *Real Estate Finance* (Winter 1995), 1–7.

Goodman, J. L., and J. B. Ittner. "The Accuracy of Home Owners' Estimates of House Value," *Journal of Housing Economics* 2 (December 1992), 339–357.

Guttery, R. S., and C. F. Sirmans. "Creating a Constant-Quality Index for Small Multifamily Residential Housing." Working paper, University of Connecticut Center for Real Estate and Urban Economic Studies, 1995.

Jud, G. D., and T. G. Seaks. "Sample Selection Bias in Estimating Housing Sales Prices," *Journal of Real Estate Research* 9 (Summer 1994), 289–298.

National Real Estate Index. *Market History Reports: 1985–1993.* Emeryville, CA: Liquidity Financial Group, July 1994.

National Council of Real Estate Investment Fiduciaries and Frank Russell Company. *The Russell–NCREIF Real Estate Performance Report.* Tacoma, Washington, first quarter, 1993.

Stephens, W., Ying Li, V. Lekkas, J. Abraham, C. Calhoun, and T. Kimner. "Conventional Mortgage Home Price Index," *Journal of Housing Research,* 6 (1995), 389–418.

Thibodeau, T. G. "Housing Price Indexes from the 1974–1983 SMSA Annual Housing Surveys," *AREUEA Journal* 17 (1989), 100–117.

U.S. Bureau of the Census. *1991 Residential Finance Survey* (machine readable data file). Washington, D.C., 1994.